Mexico

Mexico

*The Struggle
for Democratic Development*

SECOND EDITION

Daniel C. Levy
and Kathleen Bruhn

With Emilio Zebadúa

UNIVERSITY OF CALIFORNIA PRESS
Berkeley · Los Angeles · London

University of California Press, one of the most
distinguished university presses in the United States,
enriches lives around the world by advancing scholarship in the humanities, social sciences, and natural
sciences. Its activities are supported by the UC Press
Foundation and by philanthropic contributions from
individuals and institutions. For more information,
visit www.ucpress.edu.

University of California Press
Berkeley and Los Angeles, California

University of California Press, Ltd.
London, England

Library of Congress Cataloging-in-Publication Data

Levy, Daniel C.
    Mexico : the struggle for democratic development /
Daniel C. Levy and Kathleen Bruhn ; with Emilio
Zebadúa. — 2nd ed.
        p.   cm.
Includes bibliographical references and index.
ISBN 0-520-24694-2 (pbk. : alk. paper)
    1. Democracy — Mexico. 2. Mexico — Politics
and government — 1988– I. Bruhn, Kathleen, 1963–
II. Zebadúa, Emilio. III. Title.
    JL1281.L49   2006
    320.972 — dc22   2005016501

Manufactured in the United States of America

14   13   12   11   10   09   08   07   06
10   9   8   7   6   5   4   3   2   1

Printed on Ecobook 50 containing a minimum 50%
post-consumer waste, processed chlorine free. The
balance contains virgin pulp, including 25% Forest
Stewardship Council Certified for no old growth
tree cutting, processed either TCF or ECF. The sheet
is acid-free and meets the minimum requirements
of ANSI/NISO Z39.48-1992 (R 1997) (Permanence
of Paper). ∞

To Our Parents

Contents

Acronyms and Abbreviations

AFL-CIO	American Federation of Labor and Congress of Industrial Organizations
ANIT	Asociación Nacional de Industrias de la Transformación/National Association of Transformation Industries
CANACINTRA	Cámara Nacional de Industrias de la Transformación/National Chamber of Manufacturing Industries
CCE	Consejo Coordinador Empresarial/Coordinating Business Council
CIA	Central Intelligence Agency
CNC	Confederación Nacional Campesina/National Peasant Confederation
CONCAMIN	Confederación de Cámaras Industriales/Confederation of Industrial Chambers
CONCANACO	Confederación de Cámaras Nacionales de Comercio/Confederation of National Chambers of Commerce
CTM	Confederación de Trabajadores de México/Confederation of Mexican Workers

EZLN	Ejército Zapatista de Liberación Nacional/Zapatista Army for National Liberation
GATT	General Agreement on Trade and Tariffs
IDB	Inter-American Development Bank
IFE	Instituto Federal Electoral/Federal Electoral Institute
IMF	International Monetary Fund
INEGI	Instituto Nacional de Estádistica, Geografía e Informática/National Institute for Statistical and Geographic Information
INS	Immigration and Naturalization Service
ISI	Import substitution industrialization
NAFTA	North American Free Trade Agreement
NATO	North Atlantic Treaty Organization
NGO	Nongovernmental organization
OAS	Organization of American States
OECD	Organization for Economic Cooperation and Development
OPEC	Organization of Petroleum Exporting Countries
PAN	Partido Acción Nacional/National Action Party
PEMEX	Petróleos Mexicanos/Mexican Petroleum Company
PMS	Partido Mexicano Socialista/Mexican Socialist Party
PRD	Partido de la Revolución Democrática/Party of the Democratic Revolution
PRI	Partido Revolucionario Institucional/Institutional Revolutionary Party
TELMEX	Teléfonos de México/Mexican Telephone Company
UNT	Unión Nacional de Trabajadores/National Workers' Union
WTO	World Trade Organization

Acknowledgments

Authors tend to assume that invitations to undertake a second edition reflect their wondrous efforts in the original edition and consequent great success. More likely, the University of California Press invitation regarding our book reflects the continued great importance of Mexico and its struggle for democracy. In any event, we are grateful for the opportunity to update our views. Our fundamental argument remains unchanged: that struggles for democracy and development constitute the main parameters that define Mexican political conflicts, and that these struggles are connected in important ways, both positively and negatively. Moreover, we continue to affirm that Mexico has made important strides in both dimensions, albeit still incomplete and with limitations. In this second edition, however, we make use of new information from the administration of Mexico's first non-PRI president to analyze the implications of alternation in power for political and economic reform, matters that were largely speculative at the time of the first edition. Some expectations played out as anticipated — alas, including the pessimistic ones. Other developments, like the speed of the PRI's political recovery, have come as more of a surprise.

Even in the first edition, the development of the book changed course as Mexico itself changed course to reinvent itself and enter new territory in its struggle for democracy. Originally, the joint authors were Daniel Levy and Emilio Zebadúa. Zebadúa's appointment to Mexico's Federal Election Institute, a key agency in the pursuit of fair elections and democracy, made it impossible for him to continue as anticipated. Kathleen

Bruhn then became co-author. Zebadúa continued to play a role in shaping the treatment of Mexico's struggle for democratic development in an increasingly internationalized setting. For two of the chapters in the first edition, his initial drafts provided some of the material and perspectives. For all the chapters, he continually provided facts, insight, and suggestions, with particular attention to changing trends and Mexican perceptions of them. Levy is the main author of Chapters 1, 2, 4, 6, and most of 7. Bruhn is the main author of Chapters 3, 5, 8, and the section on trade in 7. But Levy, Bruhn, and Zebadúa worked together on all chapters. Revisions for the second edition have involved just Levy and Bruhn, with Bruhn taking the lead.

We are grateful to many for help in the preparation of this book. John Bailey, Roderic Camp, Andrés Rózental, Gabriel Székely, and Keith Yanner are among those who provided astute comments. Morris Levy keenly read the entire manuscript. For varied assistance, the authors also thank Jorge Arenas Basurto, Jozef Bastiaens, Aaron Levy, April Levy, and Armando Martínez. It has been a pleasure to work with Reed Malcolm, editor at the University of California Press and, for this second edition, with Mari Coates. Levy is grateful to the CIDE (Center for Economic Research and Teaching) for a visiting professorship that helped during the book's formative stages and to his colleagues at the State University of New York, Albany. Bruhn likewise thanks her colleagues in Mexico and at the University of California, Santa Barbara. Above all, we acknowledge with admiration the Mexicans who are authors of the riveting and unfolding reality we endeavor to understand.

Daniel C. Levy,
Albany, NY

Kathleen Bruhn,
Santa Barbara, CA

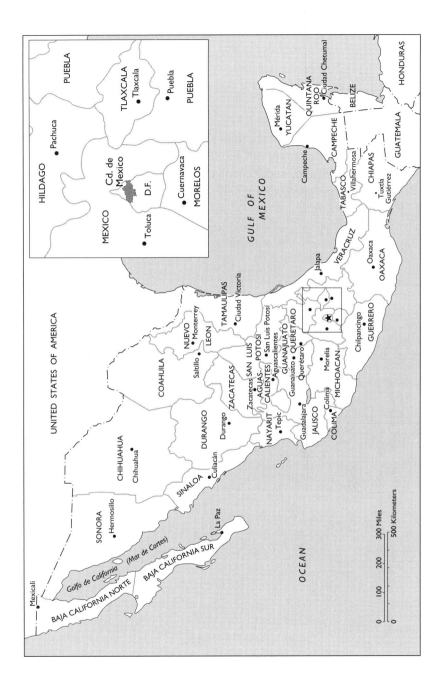

UNITED STATES OF AMERICA

BAJA CALIFORNIA NORTE
Mexicali
Golfo de California (Mar de Cortes)
BAJA CALIFORNIA SUR
La Paz

SONORA
Hermosillo

CHIHUAHUA
Chihuahua

SINALOA
Culiacán

COAHUILA
Saltillo

DURANGO
Durango

NUEVO LEON
Monterrey

TAMAULIPAS
Ciudad Victoria

ZACATECAS
Zacatecas

SAN LUIS POTOSI
San Luis Potosí

AGUAS-CALIENTES
Aguascalientes

NAYARIT
Tepic

JALISCO
Guadalajara

COLIMA
Colima

GUANAJUATO
Guanajuato
Querétaro

QUERETARO

MICHOACAN
Morelia

GUERRERO
Chilpancingo

GULF OF MEXICO

VERACRUZ
Jalapa

OAXACA
Oaxaca

TABASCO
Villahermosa

CHIAPAS
Tuxtla Gutiérrez

CAMPECHE
Campeche

YUCATAN
Mérida

QUINTANA ROO
Ciudad Chetumal

BELIZE

GUATEMALA

HONDURAS

OCEAN

0   100   200   300 Miles
0   500 Kilometers

HILDAGO
Pachuca

PUEBLA

TLAXCALA
Tlaxcala

MEXICO
Toluca

Cd. de Mexico
D.F.

Puebla
PUEBLA

Cuernavaca
MORELOS

Foreword to the
First Edition

In general, the accounts of Mexican reality written by outside observers — the perspective of the "other" — have been neither better nor worse than those written by Mexicans themselves. They are simply different, and their importance lies precisely in that difference. When the view from the outside has been the combined result of good writing, intelligence, and scholarship, the result has been outstanding, as shown in *The Discovery and Conquest of Mexico* (1632) by the Spanish soldier Bernal Díaz del Castillo, the *Political Essay on the Kingdom of New Spain* (1807–1811) by the Berlin scientist Alexander von Humboldt, *Insurgent Mexico* (1914) by the North American revolutionary John Reed, or *The Politics of Mexican Development* (1971) by the Harvard political scientist Roger D. Hansen, to cite only a handful of classics. We now welcome a fresh systematic overview of Mexican reality coming from Daniel C. Levy and Kathleen Bruhn, with the participation of Emilio Zebadúa (who helps highlight Mexican perspectives). Together these three capture a picture of the political process in Mexico at a time when both the country and the regime have been changing dramatically. As a result of the elections of July 2, 2000, Mexican society has peacefully brought an end to the regime born in 1916 out of the Mexican Revolution, and which led to seventy-one uninterrupted years of guaranteed stability through the monopoly of a single party.

This latest change in Mexico is without historical precedent. Ever since the dramatic encounter between the Europeans and the native

Mexicans at the beginning of the sixteenth century, all changes of regime have occurred through violence: the establishment of Spanish control, independence, the restoration of the republic during the second half of the nineteenth century, and the Mexican Revolution of 1910.

This book by Levy, Bruhn, and Zebadúa concentrates on the transformation of contemporary Mexico. Starting from an analysis of the present, the book attempts to look into the immediate future — the only goal within reach of the social sciences. The authors begin with the proposition elaborated thirty-five years ago by Pablo González Casanova in *Democracy in Mexico* (1965) and which continues to be as valid today as it was then: in order for Mexico to achieve true modernization, it is necessary to establish a political democracy.

For the authors of *Mexico: The Struggle for Democratic Development*, the appropriate definition of the Mexican political system that existed up to July 2, 2000, is not the one employed by a majority of analysts — that of authoritarian — but a more generous variation — that of "semidemocracy." This term takes into account the encouraging results of the federal election of mid-1997 when, for the first time since 1929, the opposition managed to wrest control of the Congress from the state party, the Institutional Revolutionary Party (PRI). The country was then on the threshold of democracy; with a little luck, it could leave behind the old authoritarianism and begin to build a real democracy. And when fortune did, in fact, smile upon Mexico on July 2, 2000, it brought to an end, without bloodshed, eighty-three years of uninterrupted control by the revolutionary elite and their successors of the powerful presidency, Mexico's fundamental political institution, the one on which all the others depend.

With the presidential election of 2000 — a competitive election that took place under more favorable conditions than ever before — Mexico won its democratic spurs, though not the "democracy without adjectives" that Enrique Krauze demanded in 1986 after the electoral fraud in Chihuahua. The authors of this work have turned to Mario Vargas Llosa, the famous Peruvian writer — another foreigner who has observed and judged our country with precision — to baptize the newly born Mexican political democracy with his term: "difficult democracy." This difficulty is due to the many obstacles it will have to overcome before it can be consolidated.

No one can refute the authors' affirmation that even though the first constitution of independent Mexico, that of 1824, was a democratic constitution, as were also those of 1857 and 1917, the reality of democracy is fundamentally new in Mexico. The country does not have any political history of the effective exercise of democracy. As opposed to the United States, the Mexican experience of the prehispanic and colonial eras, the nineteenth century, and the century that has just ended and that ran its course in the shadow of the Revolution of 1910 offered few opportunities to prepare for democracy. In practice, that broad span of several hundred years served more as a constant reaffirmation of Mexico's antidemocratic characteristics. As a result, Mexico opens today a new and decisive chapter in its political life, without having developed the institutions and practices necessary for the exercise of democracy. Nonetheless, in order to become a successful society in the twenty-first century, Mexico has no alternative but to throw itself into the ocean of democracy and learn to swim. There is no question that Mexican democracy promises to be difficult!

Levy, Bruhn, and Zebadúa argue, and argue well, that the political competition that gave rise to the results of July 2 — the death certificate of the old regime — is causally linked to the opening of the country to market competition over the last fifteen years. In effect, the 1970s showed that Mexico's semi-statist and protectionist models were no longer viable; in 1982, these models fell apart altogether. Because of the importance that the management of the economy then acquired for the survival of the political system based on the state party — in particular, the management of an enormous and growing external debt — the technocrats and neoliberal politicians displaced the traditional and neopopulist politicians though they continued — also to no avail — to try to save authoritarianism until the very end.

Over the past three presidential terms, and without much ceremony, a small technocratic elite took over the leadership of the PRI. Using the PRI as a lever it moved Mexico out from behind its old nationalistic and protectionist walls and placed it fully in the field of tough competition within the global market through a subordinated and dependent association with the United States as framed by the North American Free Trade Agreement (NAFTA). This shift meant undermining in necessary and irreversible ways the corporatist and nationalist underpinnings of the authoritarianism inherited by the technocrats. It was the beginning of the end for the old regime. From this perspective, the regime born in the Mexican Revolution became an unviable arrangement at the end of the twentieth century — the free market was incompatible with a statist and presidential economy whose goal was to preserve the corporatist social bases of the state party — though the exact moment of its demise was not pre-determined.

For the authors, the three fundamental dimensions of modern democracy are liberty, accountability by public officials, and political equality. Clearly Mexico has problems, and serious problems at that, in all three areas and will continue to have them in the foreseeable future.

It is in the arena of formal liberty where this book shows the greatest and the most well-founded optimism. In effect Mexican mass media have made great strides, and civil society is very much alive and already a systematic producer of independent organizations. Nevertheless accountability of government officials to the public is an arena where, without denying progress, there is much less optimism. If on the one hand, Mexican citizens who make demands on and ask questions of authorities are replacing the old vassals, the technocracy's style of governing that dominated Mexico in the last two decades of the twentieth century — isolated from the social bases of the system — was a step backward in terms of accountability. The defeat of the PRI and the arrival of a new political group, on the Right though committed to democracy, give room for some hope by citizens for progress in the art of making demands and insisting on accountability. Unfortunately, the terrible legacy of corruption that the new regime inherits will make the implementation of an effective and law-abiding state very problematic; the battle for legality is yet to be fought in Mexico.

It is in the field of political equality where the authors quite aptly find the biggest obstacle, the Achilles' heel of the new Mexican democracy. In every capitalist system, true political equality is detoured and deformed by existing economic inequality; in Mexico, the lack of social equity is especially brutal. The most worrisome aspect is that the economic policy implemented within the framework of neoliberalism leads us to believe that rather than basic inequality diminishing, it will increase. Official figures in 1998 confirm that social inequality continues to deepen; today the richest 10 percent of homes receive 40 percent of available income, while the poorest 10 percent must be content with barely 1 percent. In this context, the recently won Mexican democracy will have to operate in a very difficult environment: social contradictions will grow sharper without the new system being able to offer any equivalent to the traditional authoritarian controls that could moderate the contradictory demands of social groups. The old dikes of authoritarianism are broken, and demands for improved standards of life made by the vast majority of the population may flood a political system that enjoys very limited means to either manipulate internationalized economic variables or come to the assistance of the many losers of this economic competition.

The space this book dedicates to the bilateral relationship between Mexico and the United States is so realistic as to be brutal. More than half a century ago, in 1947, just as the recently deceased authoritarian system was entering the years of its greatest glory, one of its first and most notable critics, Daniel Cosío Villegas, wrote an essay entitled "The Crisis in Mexico" published in *Cuadernos Americanos*. In it, Cosío claimed that the heirs of the Mexican Revolution, having abandoned their commitments to democracy and legal and social justice, would sooner or later bring the regime down a dead-end street. At that juncture, the ruling elite would be tempted to ask for North American help; the country to the north could give it, but the cost would be that Mexico should stop being Mexico. The prediction came true; as a result of the great crisis of 1982, the Mexican technocracy, with no other way out, ended up asking the United States for the North American Free Trade Agreement (signed in 1993) thereby internationalizing the Mexican economy by integrating it into the formidable productive apparatus of the world's greatest power. The economy was revitalized, but Mexican nationalism, so laboriously constructed over the course of two centuries, disappeared. Mexico, as the authors affirm, is destined to become more and more a "normal" country, that is, like any other at the same stage of development. The consequences of the disappearance of Mexican independence and nationalism remain to be studied.

Political stability was the central characteristic of the old authoritarian Mexican regime. The price of more than seven decades of the stability that Mexican elites and the outside world valued so much — especially the United States, since, among other things, it allowed for great security along its southern border during the Cold War — was paid by the majority of Mexican society with a lack of liberty, the perpetuation of an anti-democratic civil society, the institutionalization of corruption in all levels of government, the uncontrolled growth of organizations linked to drug trafficking, and, finally, the consolidation of great social inequality. It is with this heavy weight on its back that Mexican society must quickly construct new democratic institutions, now the only kind that are compatible with the internationalization of its economy.

The authors of this book are fully conscious of the formidable task that the Mexicans are facing. Nevertheless, in the end, they are cautiously optimistic. Those of us most directly affected, the Mexicans themselves, are obliged to do nothing less than adopt a similar attitude, quite simply because any other alternative is so terrible as to be unacceptable. We must move toward the future — the possible democracy — with our eyes wide open. This book — thanks to the measure of anxiety it instills in the reader — will help to keep us in a state of alert.

Lorenzo Meyer
Professor of Political History,
El Colegio de México

CHAPTER I

The Changing Course of Development

DEMOCRATIC DEVELOPMENT

Democracy is central to an understanding of Mexico's present and future. It is the main theme in the discourse over where Mexico is headed and where it ought to be headed. Deficiencies in democracy are often blamed for much of Mexico's past and persisting problems, and democratization is commonly taken as key to the accomplishment of other development goals: with a robust democracy, economic and social gains are possible and the future will be brighter; without such democracy, the future is bleak.

The Democratic Imperative

The perception that democracy is imperative has become so strong that those wishing to influence Mexico's course of development have tied all their major goals to it. *Because this democratic imperative is thematic to Mexican development and discourse, it is thematic to this book.* Accordingly, the book couples its analysis of wide-ranging development concerns — historical, political, social, economic, and international — with a focus on how these issues both affect and depend on democratization.

By viewing democracy as the heart of development, Mexico has signed on to a major worldwide tendency. This does not mean that Mexico will achieve the democracy it needs, however; alternatives are possible.[1] Political rivals in Mexico often portray each other as undemocratic, sometimes with good reason. Authoritarian practices persist both inside and outside government, and not all proclaimed commitments to democracy are sincere. Nonetheless, most Mexicans realize that democracy is now the mandatory battleground in the ongoing struggle for power. Additionally, a consensus that democracy is central to development does not mean a consensus over what democracy is. Rather, definitions of democracy vary widely in Mexico. Some definitions go beyond the common emphasis on freedom and elections to include socioeconomic benefits or equality. Similarly, Mexicans are divided over what is part of the definition of democracy as opposed to the probable or desired outcome of democracy (e.g., expanded citizen interest in politics, expanded educational opportunity). Mexicans are also divided over what brings about meaningful democracy, over the role different actors should play, and over what degree of power each player should have to facilitate democratization. These divisions shape Mexico's struggle for democratic development.

Although this book identifies the different views of democracy (and development) at hand in Mexico, we do not suggest that all perspectives are equally valid. Rather, we adopt a definition of democracy close to the mainstream definitions of political science, which stress honest political competition that is open to the citizenry. These definitions usually include three overlapping components:

·   Open competition among alternative public policies that are meaningfully different and organized, so that choices largely reflect citizens' preferences;

·   Similarly open participation in selecting leadership, especially through fair elections;

·   Freedom broad and secure enough to guarantee citizens' basic rights and the integrity of the competition and participation just mentioned.[2]

Judgments about when Mexico might have become democratic turn largely on how high one sets the threshold for compliance — how competitive must competitive be, how fair must fair be, and so on. There is little debate about the past: Mexico has historically fallen far short on all three criteria (let alone the socioeconomic criteria some demand). But with political liberalization since the 1970s, intensified in the 1990s,

Mexico moved much closer on each measure. Some argued that Mexico in the 1990s finally met the basic democratic criteria. Others maintained that Mexico still basically lacks one or more of the three criteria. These critics continued to apply the common label for Mexico's classic political system: authoritarian, although usually with a qualifying adjective (such as benign, moderate, or inclusionary) to indicate differences from harsher varieties of authoritarianism. Our preferred label for Mexican reality for most of the last two decades of the twentieth century is more generous: *semidemocracy*. This term captures the sense of a system between authoritarian and democratic but at least as democratic as authoritarian, with prospects of a proximate democratic future.[3]

Indeed, Mexico stepped dramatically into that democratic future with the 2000 presidential elections. Through an open, free, and competitive process, Mexicans voted an opposition party into the presidency and a coalition it headed into a congressional plurality, while overwhelmingly reinstalling another opposition party into control of Mexico City. In retrospect, the 1997 congressional elections appear as a watershed. They established the precedent that a cleaner and more open electoral process could lead to an opposition majority in the legislature and victory in the first-ever local election in Mexico City, without resulting in constitutional breakdown or chaos. When then President Ernesto Zedillo declared that the 1997 elections demonstrated that Mexico had reached "democratic normality," his statement rang much truer than when his predecessor, Carlos Salinas, had spoken of "perfecting democracy." The peaceful transition of power from President Zedillo to President Vicente Fox in December 2000 left even *semidemocracy* as too stingy a term.

Mexico's entry into the democratic club is an epic event, but it marks the continuation of a complex process of change. It is important to understand authoritarian Mexico and semidemocratic Mexico, including the persistent elements and legacies of each, because many features of Mexican politics today remain better described as authoritarian or semidemocratic than democratic. Just as Mexico made significant democratic progress in the decades before 2000, so further progress is needed. For one thing, a challenge for any new democracy is consolidation. For another, although a summary evaluation of the Mexican political system overall is that advances meet reasonable thresholds on the three criteria of democracy, incompleteness, doubt, and fragility remain on all three. A set of free elections is thus necessary but insufficient evidence of clear, vibrant democracy.

The club of democratic nations encompasses a great variety of political realities. Many Latin American democracies, including those dating from the 1980s and further back, suffer from limitations on fair competition, open and inclusive participation, free expression, secure rights, and accountability to the citizenry. Mexican scholar Enrique Krauze's call in 1986 for a Mexican "democracy without adjectives" resonates throughout the region and remains relevant today for Mexico.[4] In fact, real-world democracy nearly always comes with adjectives, and even advanced democracies struggle to make democracy more robust and less qualified. For countries such as Mexico the challenge is more fundamental: the character and strength of democracy are yet to be determined. So although the general and quite inexact one-word label "democratic" is now appropriate for the Mexican political system, the struggle for less qualified democracy remains at the heart of the struggle for development.

Mexico's struggle ties into more than a regional dynamic. For one thing democratization has become a central issue in much of the developing world as well as in the formerly communist countries. The debate over democracy — its meaning and its centrality to development — is now a common one. Beyond that, political change in Mexico has become inextricably intertwined with internationalization. For Mexico "internationalization" primarily means entry to a U.S.-led political-economic world. Not all external influences on Mexico or all steps to link Mexico to other nations have democratic effects.[5] Rather, the point is that Mexican development now depends intimately on both democratization and internationalization, simultaneously and in vigorous relationship with one another. Fusing these two imperatives successfully is Mexico's great challenge. Linked to the overarching theme of democratic development, this challenge receives considerable attention in this book.

The U.S. public tends to see democracy as a matter of will, as something that honest and well-intentioned people can rather easily agree upon and achieve; once democratic elections occur, many believe, a country has arrived. Scholarship on democracy tells a different story, however. Democracy has been much more the exception than the rule in developing countries: it is difficult to agree on what it is and how to pursue it, and it is difficult to bring it about — and then difficult to expand, consolidate, and maintain it. No simple blueprint exists. The struggle for democracy requires that advocates and scholars alike take a broad look at development and the mix of elements (socioeconomic, etc.) that may support democracy. If, for example, a higher gross domestic product (GDP) correlates with robust democracy, would an economic policy that increases GDP encourage democracy even if it favors business groups and foreign interests over most workers? Mexico's struggle for democracy cannot be isolated from its general struggle for development.

From Stability without Democracy to Crisis and Opportunity

Any consideration of Mexican development — what it has been and how it is changing — must come to grips with political stability. This book examines how stability dating back to the 1930s has been crucial to undemocratic development and how its transformation is crucial to the struggle for democratic development. Many of the building blocks of Mexico's stability (such as the regular, peaceful turnover of civilian leadership) have routinely been considered integral to stable democracy elsewhere, but in Mexico they supported stability *without* democracy. In fact, stability facilitated economic growth, and this success had antidemocratic consequences, strengthening the system's ability to ward off democratic demands. The best that could honestly be said for the impact of stability on democracy was that its effect was indirect or limited: stability might build the demand and underpinnings for democracy in the long run by supporting economic growth and social change; meanwhile, by reducing the rulers' perceived need for repression, it softened the nondemocratic system. Today political stability remains essential to Mexican development, but perceptions of its prerequisites have changed. Stability increasingly depends on successful democratization.[6] Some have even identified democratization as a key "national security" issue, necessary for Mexico's internal peace and stability.

For most of the twentieth century the linchpin of Mexico's vaunted political stability was a unique set of political institutions that limited competition and choice, yet incorporated broad social groups and permitted some pluralism of opinion within a diverse ruling elite. Stability was the achievement on which Mexican development was unmatched in Latin America. Defying repeated cries that instability would ensue if Mexico did not solve this or that development problem or meet the justified demands of this or that dissident group, Mexico maintained its political regime throughout most of the century. The party intertwined with the regime outlasted the Communist Party of the Soviet Union as the longest-ruling party in the world, right up to 2000.[7] Thanks to the regime's skill and flexibility, as well as the rewards it helped bring to many, Mexico is the only major Latin American nation to have avoided both a military coup and a serious communist rebellion in the post–

World War II period. Every president selected since 1934 has survived his six-year term and then relinquished office peacefully to his successor. This experience contrasts with the rise and fall of democratic and authoritarian regimes throughout Latin America, making Mexico the Latin American country most often cited by governments, international banks, and political scientists as a model of development through political stability.

The price, in the view of many critics, has been a model of development that subordinates democracy and socioeconomic justice to a sterile stability. The obsession with stability has even been portrayed as a curse, allowing government to impose unpopular and ineffective policies without democratic accountability. Peruvian novelist Mario Vargas Llosa coined the ironic phrase "the perfect dictatorship" to convey how skillfully the Mexican system functioned until recently to limit popular influence by creating a pretense of democracy.[8]

The contemporary struggle for democracy has also implied a struggle over the terms of political stability, particularly the relationship between stability and the institutions that used to guarantee it. Mexican stability used to mean regime hegemony. The regime had a considerable capacity to control and contain political conflict, to determine development policy, to shape events and outcomes, to mold social organization, and to establish dominant social values. Yet perpetuation of such a regime became an unlikely basis for long-term political stability, and its restoration is now an equally unlikely basis. The regime largely lost the magic by which it could present itself as nearly synonymous with the political system, sometimes even with the nation or its course of development. In fact, the regime turned into a tottering spectacle.[9] Conflicts between regime and society and within the regime itself became common, and as the regime struggled to reconstruct itself on new ground, the old sense of security gave way to surprises. Uncertainty overtook certainty. Whereas a rumor of a military coup once could be laughed off, in the 1990s such a rumor could unnerve financial markets. Whereas the metaphor of the "revolutionary family" used to suggest a tightly knit establishment, that family image began to look more like negative portraits of the modern U.S. family: besieged, insecure, dysfunctional, and unstable. Even if the long-reigning party returns to rule under competitive elections, it can never again rule on its own terms as a government party. Nor can any other party in power. The major question about stability, and thus a primary theme running throughout this book, becomes, How can stability be reconstructed on a more democratic and competitive basis?

Just as the democratic imperative transforms the meaning and underpinnings of political stability, so too it transforms the role of economic change. Mexico's stable development depended on a mutually reinforcing relationship between political stability and economic growth. Stability made investment worthwhile and, in turn, growth provided rewards that the regime could distribute to gain further support. This was particularly true as long as the government maintained ownership of certain critical parts of the economy and provided key incentives for other sectors. In the 1990s, however, Mexico enthusiastically joined an international "neoliberal" trend that stressed reduction of the government role in the economy. Chapter 5 in this book contrasts the old and new economic models, but the point here is that Mexico's long-standing political-economic relationship is in flux. Both the political and economic systems must change fundamentally to remain viable, and they are changing, but fundamental change in one area brings challenges to the other. For example, economic changes inflict at least short-term losses on many citizens just when the political system has lost its prior ability to control opposition. Some doubt whether the changing political system retains the resilience to survive the sorts of economic crises the authoritarian system weathered in the past. Mexico's regime transition and its continued democratization carry risks of volatility, uncertainty, and performance failures that could jeopardize the political stability necessary for economic growth.

To be sure, Mexico's stable development has long allowed flexibility rather than stubborn resistance to change; Mexico has earned the characterization "adaptive authoritarianism." Yet recent change has come to be less adaptive than reflexive — less the result of adroit manipulation than an increasingly ad hoc reaction to crises. The old political system could no longer dictate the pace or direction of change. Crises came with increased frequency and severity to both the political and economic systems.[10] No new political system will reestablish the prior system's control over change. We must assess the challenges as well as the democratic opportunity in how contemporary Mexico has coped with and will foster change.

In the 1990s signs of the deterioration of political management in Mexico were staggering, sometimes melodramatic and downright embarrassing. Violence reached into the upper levels and inner sanctums of power, exposing ruptures at the heart of the establishment. Assassinations, which had riddled Mexico in the early decades of the twentieth century and then disappeared during the decades of strong stability, returned with chilling frequency: most prominently, in 1993, the cardinal of Guadalajara; in 1994, the official party's presidential nominee, almost surely the next president; and also in 1994, the party's number-two official. None of these cases has been satisfactorily resolved and a torrent of mutual accusation and conspiracy theories persists.[11] In the case of the slain presidential candidate, a barrage of charges and countercharges plagued the investigation. Although the assassin was captured on videotape and caught in the act, questions about his motives and possible accomplices immediately arose, paralleling theories about the second gunman and the real motives behind the assassination of U.S. President John F. Kennedy. However, in the Mexican case President Carlos Salinas himself was widely accused of planning the assassination of the candidate he had just handpicked; Salinas in turn accused a former president. After leaving office, Salinas fled Mexico and went into hiding, first to Cuba, then to Ireland. Before leaving, the once mighty ruler staged a pathetic hunger strike at his home to protest denunciations of his role in the sudden economic debacle immediately following his term. Such incidents illustrated not only the corruption and lack of cohesion at the top but also the lack of the system's credibility to explain and resolve such scandals.

In addition to this wrenching soap opera at the summit, equally startling instability erupted from below. On January 1, 1994, the day the North American Free Trade Agreement (NAFTA) went into effect, armed rebels in Mexico's poorest state, Chiapas, declared war against NAFTA and the corrupt political system in favor of a long-overdue social justice and democracy. This *zapatista* insurrection — pointedly identifying with the legendary Emiliano Zapata's revolutionary struggle for land and liberty — was the first guerrilla uprising in a quarter century and was soon followed by others. Militarily, the rebels posed little threat to the state; when the initial Chiapas fighting ended after ten days, the two thousand to twenty-five hundred zapatistas held little or no territory. But the rebellion exposed the regime's fragility, a consequence of the widening gap between its performance and the public's demand for more broadly distributed socioeconomic development.[12] It is precisely the perception of such gaps, more than abject deprivation alone, which often leads to rebellion. Also striking was the way this guerrilla movement gained public support by framing its case as part of the wider struggle for Mexican democracy.

Mexico is by no means the only Latin American nation at the dawn of the century to face a simultaneous struggle to escape economic crisis and define its new political identity, an identity whose viability depends on

The zapatista rebellion of 1994 in the poverty-stricken state of Chiapas called national and international attention to the people and causes left behind in Mexican development.

consolidating and invigorating democracy. But no other Latin American nation has engaged in this struggle against a historical backdrop of such exceptionally strong economic performance and such firm political footing. For Mexico, far more than for the other nations, this struggle is unprecedented. Nostalgia for the more predictable, undemocratic past may be correspondingly strong. As Mexico's economic and political performance slipped, East Asian countries increasingly took Mexico's place as international exemplars of development through political stability with economic growth, especially as they generally had turned in superior performances to Mexico on social development and equality.[13] Mexico's significant and peaceful democratization in the past few years buoys hope that Mexico may once again become a sustained model of political-economic development, but this time a democratic one.

The historical association between Mexico's development and a stable but undemocratic political system naturally raises questions about the effect of the demise of that system on both economic development and political stability. Economic and political crisis that does not spell collapse can create opportunity for democratic transformation. "Stability" no longer means the preservation of an undemocratic regime but the establishment of new conditions for political order. This transition is not completed with the 2000 elections. We must now study how much transition represents both risks and democratic opportunity.[14]

In this book we depict the movement from stability with adept regime control and success on its own terms to a period of fragility, uncertain change, and democratic opportunity and progress as part of a broad decline of Mexican "exceptionalism." Especially through a peak "stable development" period of about three decades starting with the 1940s, successes allowed Mexicans to emphasize how their country was different, even unique, in certain important ways. However brief this peak period appears in retrospect, it was then that Mexico's success in matters so coveted and rarely achieved in the Third World (chiefly, political stability and economic growth) gained great attention for a "Mexican model."[15] Exceptionalism has also had a cultural component and rationale. Culturally as well as economically and politically, a key challenge has been preserving identity and autonomy in the shadow of the United States. Declining exceptionalism involves a kind of "normalization" that is itself part of the internationalization of Mexican development. That is, as the distinctive old regime has disintegrated, the struggle for democratized development represents movement toward norms, policies, and structures rather like those in many other nations. Each country has its distinctive features, but we must increasingly understand Mexico through its growing similarities with other nations, including its efforts to insert itself into a largely U.S.-led world.

SOCIAL DEVELOPMENT AND CALAMITY

A sense of things falling apart applies powerfully to Mexico's social affairs, but Mexico has not been lauded as a model of social development as it has been for political stability and economic growth. What links all these elements is that Mexicans increasingly believe that socioeconomic problems must be addressed in a framework of democratic development. This challenge is not easy. The achievement and even the perpetuation of electoral democracy does not automatically bring socioeconomic progress on all major fronts. But one of the few consistent findings about the evolution of democracy, and certainly robust democracy, is that it is far more common in countries with higher levels of socioeconomic development.[16] Our analysis repeatedly highlights the reality that not all good things go together in democratic development. The purpose of the brief discussion here is to introduce social concerns, including the severe problems of everyday life, into our consideration of the struggle for development.

Mexico's Overall Socioeconomic Standing

Even many who have praised Mexico for its economic growth — and for its political record in stability, institution building, and at least formal inclusion of the citizenry — have conceded that the social realm is Mexico's Achilles' heel. Defenders have claimed that Mexico's economic growth provides the most reliable long-term route to social improvement. But for critics, Mexico has epitomized the hoax of trickle-down development in the Third World. Mexico has thus loomed as a key case in the wide-ranging debate over the relationships between economic, political, and social development.

Mexico holds an average position among Latin American countries on many measures of human development, which puts it far above Latin America's low end, let alone that of the Third World. On most indicators Mexico ranks well ahead of most of Central America, Brazil, Bolivia, and certainly Haiti. Mexico manages to get as high as first place on GDP per capita among Latin American nations and a few rungs lower on such measures as life expectancy at birth (seventy-four years), child malnutrition, and energy consumption. Numerical rank should not deceive readers into regarding Mexico's performance as decent, however. First, the rankings steer attention away from the glaring socioeconomic inequalities within the country; while part of Mexico boasts a statistical profile that puts it near the top with Chile, another part of the country comes out near Bolivia. Second, Latin America overall has done poorly in social development. Third, Mexico should be judged with reference to the capabilities that come from its comparative economic prowess. Although Mexico falls far short of its northern neighbor in economic strength, it has one of the world's ten largest economies and accounts for over one-third of the total GDP of Latin America and the Caribbean. Yet on social dimensions Mexico usually trails far behind the region's leading nations, both large and small. Thus Mexico's infant mortality rate exceeds Costa Rica's (twenty-four versus nine per thousand live births), and its illiteracy rate of about 10 percent more than doubles that of Argentina, Uruguay, Chile, Cuba (and the United States). Finally, Mexico ranks fifty-third in the world on the United Nations Human Development index and seventeenth in the world in inequality as measured by the Gini index.

The gap between Mexico's economic size and productivity on the one hand and its social conditions on the other hand reflects not only a colonial legacy of inequality, but also the failure of Mexico's economic policies to address social concerns. Even the government acknowledges the terribly inadequate results of traditional policy. Critics on the Left argue that public policy (with no change linked to the democratic alteration of conservative parties) deliberately has made economic growth and political control the priority over social justice. Indeed, they charge that the shift toward neoliberal economic policy is responsible for further social deterioration and lacks a design for social improvement. Promoters of the policy shift, however, see it as a break from populist approaches that provided only piecemeal attention to social problems, a break that promises progress through sustainable economic growth, expanded opportunity, and targeted distribution programs.[17]

Under President Salinas (1988–94) and successor Zedillo (1994–2000), and into Fox's administration, Mexico regained its stature as the darling of the international financial community. It adopted the neoliberal reform package urged by the United States and leading international financial interests on all countries, especially developing ones: slash government spending, privatize, deregulate, and open economies to international trade and investment. Salinas privatized telephones, banks, and communal lands, while deregulating business and liberalizing investment, opening even the oil industry (the proudest nationalization in Mexican history) to foreign investment, and pushing Mexico into NAFTA. Zedillo continued the neoliberal thrust, carrying privatization into such areas as social security. Fox pledged basic continuity with invigorating initiatives.

The early macroeconomic results of neoliberalism encouraged proponents. Standard economic indicators (like growth and inflation) were positive. However, the benefits of this growth were distributed unequally. A few Mexicans got very rich, but most people failed to improve their lot substantially. A shocking reversal came in the mid-1990s, with an economic crisis, unemployment, plummeting wages, and inflation. Similar maladies have emerged in Venezuela and other nations implementing neoliberal policies, but again the Mexican example stands out because of the contrast to its history of economic success. Whereas Salinas had become an international spokesperson for what to do in economic policy, Zedillo was called on in his first year to lecture Latin American colleagues on what *not* to do. The Right attributed the economic collapse to political pressures and miscalculations. The Left viewed the crisis as the natural result of neoliberal policy, noting that it had exacted a high social cost even when the standard economic indicators were positive. A political system that in the past could usually invoke evidence of social improvement, however slow and inadequate, faced spreading complaints: even positive economic indicators failed to alter the trend of deteriorating social welfare.

As the economy improved markedly toward the close of the century, defenders of neoliberal policy saw their hand strengthened. Only time will tell whether Mexico's new economic policy will ultimately aggravate, alleviate, or have little effect on the country's long-standing social development problems. But painfully clear — however one perceives its causes, solutions, and prospects — is the basic socioeconomic profile in place throughout decades of Mexican economic growth and political stability without democracy. Painfully clear is that even recent bursts of economic growth that bring some social development have so far left Mexico with appalling problems of inequality. Democratic development should pressure governments to address citizens' needs, but how and how much remains unclear. Persistent failure to address the backlog of social demands would undermine the legitimacy of democracy.

Socioeconomic Inequality

Poverty and inequality are deeply rooted in Mexico. The government's own figures indicate that almost half of the population lives in poverty, unable to meet the Food and Agriculture Organization's minimal food intake standards, and about seventeen million are in what is classified as extreme poverty. That Mexico is not listed among the world's poorest countries, because much of the rest of the population is relatively well off, is little solace for these millions of people. The juxtaposition of these "two Mexicos" gives the country one of the world's most unequal income distribution profiles. A tenth of Mexicans account for over 40 percent of income, compared with just over 10 percent captured by Mexico's poorest two-fifths, with less change over the years than either defenders or critics of the regime often imply. Peasants account for about one-third of the population and less than 10 percent of the GDP. Indians are the worst off. They concentrate in states with the lowest GDP per capita, under U.S.$1,000 annually, compared to more than $5,000 in Mexico City, followed by northern states such as Nuevo León. Indians on average earn only about 36 percent of what other Mexicans earn. Despite these figures, *Forbes* magazine reported that by 1993 Mexico had jumped to fourth in the world in the number of billionaires, and in 1998 ten capitalists reportedly controlled 15 percent of Mexico's GDP and accounted for one-fourth of net sales on the Mexican stock exchange.[18]

Middle- and upper-class Mexico often enjoys First World socioeconomic status, even as the poorer parts of Mexico often approach Africa. Prosperous urban and suburban neighborhoods have entered the era of cellular phones, answering machines, cable television, satellite dishes, and electronic mail, yet as recently as 1990 Telmex was an attractive stock to foreign investors because at that time Mexico still had just one telephone line for every seventeen people. As elsewhere in the world, the telecommunications and computer revolution has made some impacts that increase inequalities between rich and poor. Privileged Mexico flocks onto e-mail listings, often internationally based ones. Telecommunications is another example where Mexico ranks in the middle of Latin American nations. In fact, in many cases the more a particular social indicator deals with items that are available to just a small minority, the higher Mexico ranks.[19]

Consider health and education. One Mexico receives modern health facilities, while the other depends on folk cures and herbs and bears the brunt of underweight births (comparable to rates in El Salvador and Nicaragua) and thousands of deaths annually from such medically curable diseases as cholera. New diseases hit poorer Mexico with greater frequency and severity because of inferior health care; as of the mid-1990s Mexico was tenth in the world in AIDS cases. Only 66 percent of Indians are literate, compared to national rates of 90 percent. Nearly 20 percent of the adult population has not finished primary school. Though rates of attendance have improved, nearly a million children aged six to twelve are not in school. Yet 11 percent of the adult population now has completed a college degree — much higher than the 1 percent figure of 1960 and not far behind parts of Europe — and the elite increasingly attends power-enhancing U.S. graduate schools.

Transportation offers yet another example of increasing contrasts. In urban settings those living in developed Mexico use private automobiles and taxis; those in less-developed Mexico must rely on crowded buses or (in Mexico City) subways. Between cities, those in developed Mexico travel by plane, car, or luxury-class bus equipped with air-conditioning, movies, toilets, assigned seats, and complimentary soft drinks. Second-class buses are rarely equipped with these features, as passengers must pack themselves in the overcrowded buses along with live animals, fruit, and other market wares.

Development policy has contributed to grave inequalities that leave the rural population behind. Mexico has favored big industry over agriculture, especially subsistence agriculture. Rural modernization (e.g., new production techniques) did not lead to "rural development" defined as improvement in living standards. In fact, rural modernization was aimed not so much at rural but at urban development, accepting rural misery in the hope of inexpensively feeding the growing urban population. Despite its own suffering, however, rural Mexico long succeeded in feeding urban Mexico, but rural productivity deteriorated from neglect. Yet to improve rural productivity, neoliberalism has taken Mexico even further from food policies aimed at equity in ownership, production, and consumption. It trusts unequal ownership to enhance economies of scale, total productivity, and international trade, in the hope that the indirect impact on overall living standards will be positive.

Whatever the contrasting views on how best to address Mexico's egregious inequalities, there may be not only a moral but also a democratic imperative for improvement. Without improvement, inequality may undermine the participation and support necessary to sustain democracy. If the poor attempt to use democratic procedures to improve their position, and elites react by limiting democracy or otherwise failing to fulfill rising aspirations, the poor may well perceive a failure of democracy — and reject democracy as a system. But, and obviously easier said than done, a successfully responsive system would become both stronger and more democratic.

Social Deterioration: Crime and Pollution

Social deterioration also poses significant challenges to government performance in other areas. Crime and pollution are major examples. Both, particularly crime, affect popular evaluations of government. And democracy relies largely on the rule of law — with citizens' trusting that their rights and persons will be respected; corruption is a form of crime that is often especially corrosive of trust in government. Furthermore, while poverty and inequality are long-standing social problems that obviously plague some of the population much more than others, crime and environmental problems plague most of the population significantly, although they often affect the poor more severely.

Mexico has come to resemble the United States in its crime rates, surpassing it in some ways. Although Mexico still lags behind Colombia or Brazil in urban street crime, robberies have skyrocketed and, worse, so has violent crime, which is now about 40 percent of Mexico City's crime. Gone are the days when crime largely meant theft when residents were not at home. Per capita, Mexico ranks sixth in the world today in murders, sixth in robberies, and second in kidnappings.[20] The acceleration of crime is startling in Mexico City: up about 40 percent from 1963 to 1980, up more than that in the 1980s, and more than that again in the first half of the 1990s.[21] Many other cities, such as Guadalajara and

Tijuana, also suffer from surging crime. Passengers on first-class buses traveling between cities are subjected to searches for weapons before boarding, and truck hijackings have soared.

Some national public opinion polls show that seven in ten Mexicans consider crime the number-one issue (even in 1995, amid a devastating recession). Wealthier Mexicans often hire private security to protect their homes and children; Mexico has become a leading world market for bullet-proof cars and other elements of the security industry, including private bodyguards. As "pirate" taxis increase insecurity, a market grows for special taxi services that serve well-to-do customers. For all their advantages and precautions, however, even the wealthy are not safe. Indeed, they are often special targets. Mexico suffers a wave of high-visibility crimes, such as abductions of businessmen or their family members and assassinations of political and media personalities. All of this contributes to the sense of a system breaking down. Yet crime's salience makes Mexico look increasingly like much of Latin America. In this case "normalization" is about joining an unfortunate regional tendency.

The new insecurity in society relates to a new weakness in the Mexican government. Some of the government weakness refers to decay in the old rulership, while even relatively clean and democratic rulers lack the control the Mexican government once had to forestall crime and to punish it. Government itself is certainly part of the problem rather than the solution, when it is rife with corruption and uses its repressive power illegally against citizens. These problems, which will not disappear overnight, make for an unflattering contrast, although of course not a total one, between Mexico and its northern neighbor. Not only do police fail to provide adequate protection, but they are often the active organizers of "professional crime," taking advantage of their special information, contacts, and skills. No wonder some 70 percent of Mexicans view the police as corrupt and feel unprotected. Private citizens increasingly take enforcement into their own hands, sometimes providing security but sometimes a mob justice incompatible with the rule of law.

The government has issued startling admissions about crime. For example, in 1998 the national government announced that 94 percent of all violent crime in Mexico City was not prosecuted or resolved. In 1997, Mexico's attorney general announced that the police were responsible for a mass slaying of peasants in Chiapas. Such statements reflect at least two crucial points. The obvious and painful social one is that crime is horribly out of control. The less obvious point is more political: crime is a salient issue for an aroused citizenry that demands accountability from its government. In June 2004, 250,000 Mexicans gathered to march through the streets of Mexico City to protest rising crime and delinquency and to demand energetic government action. One of the largest marches ever recorded in the city, it was notable also for the extraordinarily diverse backgrounds of its participants: union leaders marched with business organization leaders, top politicians from all of the major political parties marched with housewives from Mexico City's poorest neighborhoods, priests marched with punks. What they shared was a concern about how crime had undermined their living conditions.

Parallels with the United States develop in the way crime plays out as a political issue within the increasingly competitive and polarized Mexican context. Crime is a natural issue for the Right. As in the United States, the Right in Mexico views crime as part of a general breakdown in morality and control. Consistent with its position, survey data show a decline in deference to authority and in religiosity, although church attendance remains high. Prosperous yet troubled Mexicans are increasingly likely to seek professional psychological help (while the poor tend to rely on religious figures or do not define their problems as psychological). For the Right the familiar culprits contributing to the crime wave include liberal public policy and schools, which they believe should return to teaching traditional ethical values and respect for authority.[22]

Also as in the United States, the Left suffers if it downplays crime or confines itself to blaming an inequitable economy. Still, the Left has laid much of the blame at the government's doorstep (at least until leftist mayors took over Mexico City and its police). The Left opposes the application of excess public force to repress what it sees as largely socioeconomic problems. The force of the state must come through democracy and development, not coercion.[23] To the Left, it is not the breakdown of families that leads to the breakdown of society so much as the other way around. Seen through a liberal lens, the general decline of authority, obedience, self-sacrifice, and religion may be a painful part of a healthy long-term march toward a less hierarchical and fatalistic society, opening the door to democracy and individual choice.

The clash of conflicting explanations regarding the rising social disorder — combined with a breakdown of authoritarian policy making based on limited citizen participation — spills over into contentious debate over public policy and sometimes into heightened hostility among citizens.[24] The Left accuses business of being antiwoman in its use of pregnancy tests, which it can then use to deny women access to the workplace. Similarly, the question of abortion — once the subject of little public discussion — heats up with fiercely divisive debate over the conditions, if any, under which abortions should be legal.[25]

More than crime and other interpersonal conflicts, the social problem of the environment is brought on by development itself. Urbanization, industrialization, and the automobile are major contributors. The government reports that 95 percent of factories release toxic waste. It also reports that 80 percent of forests suffer degradation, 30 percent severely; the importance of deforestation is underscored by the fact that Mexico ranks tenth in the world in forest area.[26] Mexico's Secretary of Environment and Natural Resources reports that 64 percent of Mexico's soil suffers from some degree of degradation; over half of that can be directly attributed to the clearing of land for farming and ranching.[27] Put another way, environmental problems result in part from the mismanagement of development. These problems, with ramifications for Latin America (indeed the Third World and the world at large), have reached drastic levels in Mexico. Mexico City's air pollution has been among the world's worst. In 1984 the U.S. State Department labeled Mexico City an unhealthy post for its employees and awarded them extra benefits for working there. The number of truly horrible days has diminished since the early 1990s after intense efforts to reduce pollution. Where in 1991, 62 percent of days had air quality in zones classified as dangerous by the World Health Organization, only 4 percent got there in 2001. Nevertheless, 84 percent of days still had air quality below satisfactory.[28] The problem has spread to secondary cities, as in the industrial state of Chihuahua, and to the border, where it becomes a United States–Mexico issue. National statistics also report that Mexico now produces eighty-eight thousand tons of garbage daily, about half of which is not biodegradable. Nearly 40 percent of municipal solid waste is not collected in managed dumps but is rather tossed into streets, rivers, and other sites, where it contributes to air and water pollution. About 15 percent of the population lacks running water at home, and many others worry that what they drink is unhealthy; 25 percent of the population lacks sewage treatment service, and the human waste filtering into the groundwater system enters the main city supply through breaks in older or seismically sensitive pipes.[29] Here again the problems extend to secondary cities and rural areas. Some activists speak of "ecocide" and an environmental crisis integrally related to political decay.[30]

Most Mexicans and independent observers agree that the government's environmental policies have been too little, too late. Even when laws have been put on the books, with the first general law in 1988, enforcement has lagged, in part because of corrupt or poor administration and in part because of economic cost. It is also true that part of the problem is an unhappy by-product of nature: Mexico City's high altitude means that automobile engines produce more pollution, and since the city lies in a valley, pollution gets trapped like an ugly cloud. Significant efforts have been made in response to environmental calamities, partly in response to international pressure from environmental groups and trading partners. And several achievements are noteworthy. The introduction of unleaded gas is an example. Although levels of some dangerous materials have surpassed what the World Health Organization defines as acceptable, overall pollution levels in the city have diminished, perhaps markedly. Further results could help counter the feeling that government cannot accomplish much.

When government acts resolutely, it risks losing economic growth and political support — two critical and problematic commodities. For example, school closings and postponed daily openings during the year's worst pollution months have inconvenienced many parents (students have not been heard to voice similar complaints). The environmental restrictions that most upset citizens concern private cars, the main contributors to Mexico City's pollution. Although the government has also retired some old buses and taxis and forced trucks to use unleaded gas, motorists have been forced to pay for cleaner fuels, emission screening, and better cars, and they face having their polluting cars impounded. In the 1990s Mexico City and the surrounding areas began a "no-circulation" policy, prohibiting each car from driving one day a week; when air quality falls below a certain level, a second weekday and one weekend day are added. Motorists learned to their chagrin that this is one public policy that is toughly enforced. Some complained bitterly that government has picked on ordinary people rather than going after industry, so as not to risk growth and profits for the wealthy, though government successes can lead to greater support.

Increasingly, environmental policy has tried to mix market-pricing incentives with government regulation. For example, in 1996 the nation's capital tried to address its water problem by removing government subsidies, privatizing, and charging prices that reflect real cost. As water bills soared, however, so did citizen complaints — especially because the quality of service did not increase with the price. Another example is the incentive used to exempt about one-third of cars from the no-circulation policy if they had integrated electrical systems (from 1994 on) or catalytic converters (from 1991 through 1993), or if they had been judged in excellent mechanical condition. Although this sounds logical, such

For all its problems Mexico City remains the country's center of development.
(Mexican National Tourist Council)

"merit" criteria clash with "equity" criteria for the treatment of different
social classes. Wealthier Mexicans are more likely to own a car that
meets the standards and can afford a second and even a third car, so that
they are not forced to use public transportation even when one car is idle.

Pollution and crime are worst in Mexico City. Traffic jams, for example, have become unbearable. Some thirty million city trips are made
daily.[31] Whether using cars or public transportation, residents may spend
up to four hours daily in transit. Calculations of work and leisure hours
lost are staggering. Citizens cannot move closer to their jobs in part
because the city suffers from a shortage of inexpensive housing. City
traffic, crowded especially on a few main streets, is worse than in any
U.S. city, and its rush hours are longer. Yet public transportation is not as
good an alternative to private cars as it should be. Despite increased
routes and technical efficiency, the Metro suffers from such a heavy pas-
senger load that for a few hours each morning and again each evening it
becomes a congested battleground. During crunch hours, for example,
women and children are separated from men for their own protection
and funneled toward different cars.

Understandably, then, the city's many problems are a major theme for young Mexican writers. The seeming intractability of problems — a widespread belief is that the best way to help the city is to shift population and economic activity elsewhere — contributes to the sense that government is incapable of molding development. But citizens must balance their yearning to escape the city's social deterioration against their opportunities in employment, education, culture, and other realms in which the city is truly the capital of a still highly centralized country. There is always a danger of focusing on problems and deterioration to the point of overlooking what continues to function well or even improve. Some studies have found that the great majority of Mexico City residents have their basic needs met.[32] For many, then, life in Mexico City remains attractive, despite the problems.

THE PEOPLE AND THEIR LAND

Demography, ethnicity, culture, regionalism, geography, and natural resources may not determine prospects for either economic development or democracy, but they often have an effect. They shape the raw material for development — a nation's people and its resources — and help define some of the key social divisions with which any political system must come to terms.

The Mexican People

Spectacular population growth is a reflection of development, especially as improved public health means disease prevention and cure, lower infant mortality, and extended life expectancy. At the same time, however, most observers believe that population growth has aggravated chronic problems (such as poverty) and created others (such as environmental pollution). Just to stay even, a soaring population requires more food, jobs, education, health care, and land. Mexico City's special problems with pollution and crime, as discussed earlier, come partly from being the world's largest city, with the highest population density. The Mexico City area already has about twenty million people.[33] (Sadly, the rat population is higher.)

Population growth in Mexico is relatively recent. As late as 1872, Mexico probably did not have many more people than at the time of the Spanish Conquest. Population grew at about 1 percent a year early in the twentieth century and, as political stability replaced revolution and widespread violence, the rate increased to 1.7 percent a year in the 1930s. It then jumped to 3.4 percent a year in the 1960s, making Mexico one of the world's fastest-growing countries. By 2000, Mexico had nearly one hundred million people, making Mexico one of the world's eleven most populous nations. It is easily more than twice the size of any other Latin American country except Brazil and is the largest Spanish-speaking country in the world.

The government began taking action on population issues in the 1970s. After having boasted of his opposition to population control as a candidate, President Luis Echeverría initiated a family planning program in the mid-1970s. Since then the birthrate has decreased considerably, helped by a proportional decline in rural population (where large families are common) and the spread of middle-class norms. The percentage of married women using contraceptives more than doubled (to 63 percent) between 1976 and 1992. From a peak of roughly 3.7 percent a year in 1977, population growth fell below 2.5 percent by the early 1980s and to 1.8 percent in the 1990s, although still substantially above the goal of 1 percent.[34] This still means dynamic population growth, including projections for Mexico to increase its population by more than half from 1990 to 2025, while the United States and Canada would increase by one-fifth. Only by the end of that period will Mexico fall to simple population replacement, with an average of two children per woman. But this figure must be compared with the seven-children-per-woman figures of 1965. The new trend means that Mexico will no longer have such a high percentage of its population under twenty-five years old (53 percent in 2000). It also enhances Mexico's prospects for economic development because the ratio of dependents to workers falls.

Dynamic shifts within the population have accompanied growth. Urbanization is the main example that can be identified with both development and its problems. The shift from rural to urban areas is historically associated with industrialization, growth, opportunity, the rise of a large middle class, "modern" cultures and attitudes, and so forth. Although Mexican cities have lacked the industrial bases to provide sufficient employment, cities continue to grow even faster than population, as frustrated villagers leave in search of opportunity. Migration often brings special problems for the migrants themselves as well as for the increasingly overcrowded cities. Urban centers account for roughly 75 percent of the population. At the end of the twentieth century, 25 percent of Mexico's people lived in cities of more than a half-million people, most of these in cities of more than a million. Furthermore, most Mexicans living outside of major cities live in villages, not in rural isolation.

The urban-rural contrast is but one aspect of Mexico's diversity. Most Mexicans are mestizos, products of the mixture of two ethnic groups, native Indian and Spanish. Because few Spanish women came to the New World, relations between Spanish males and Indian females were inevitable. Mestizos vary from mostly Indian to mostly Spanish, but the balance leans more toward the Indian side than in most other large Latin American countries, where immigration from Europe was greater. Within Mexico the balance differs regionally, as seen in physical characteristics (skin color, facial features, height, and so on) and in social and cultural characteristics. Estimates vary on how many Indians live in Mexico, as definitions of "Indian" vary. Some anthropologists rely more on physical traits, others more on cultural habits or whether people have greater ties to their villages than to the nation. Still others rely on self-perceptions. The Left tends to make high estimates, in the 10 to 15 percent range, as it emphasizes the extent of development's failures. Others caution that such estimates understate the degree of integration into Mexican society. According to the 2000 census, about 7 percent of Mexicans over five speak some indigenous language; however, over 80 percent also speak Spanish.[35] Indians have a substantial presence in such large central states as Michoacán and Puebla and form a majority in poor states such as Oaxaca and the Yucatán.

Within the Indian population itself, there is great diversity, with more than fifty ethnic groups. Different Indian groups are concentrated in different regions. Descendants of the Mayas are found in the south and the Yucatán, for example, and have more in common with much of Central America than with the rest of Mexico; Zapotecs and Mixtecs are concentrated in Oaxaca, Tarascans in Michoacán, Yaquis in the northwestern state of Sonora, and Aztec descendants in central Mexico. Different groups have their own languages, customs, dances, music, and clothing. Maya and Nahuatl are the most common languages. Some groups may also have their own economic systems, based on corn and home industries (such as pottery and textiles) or on collective labor, concentrating on one key product to trade with other villages. In short, Mexico is fragmented not just by the divisions between Indians and others, but by the differences among Indians themselves. This fragmentation is reduced, however, by the Indian influence on social norms, cultural relations, and political habits in the larger Mexican society. One cannot describe mestizos without also referring to Indian culture. *Compadrazgo* (a godparent relationship), for example, is an Indian custom but also a Mexican custom, which may help bind a community together through reciprocal obligations. Most Mexicans, not just Indians, eat corn and beans and tortillas, even if many Mexicans also rely increasingly on packaged, canned, and processed products.

Religion is an especially important example of Indian penetration of the general population's life. Its importance stems largely from its major role in Mexicans' lives, from how they go about daily activities and special life-cycle events, and from how they see themselves and others. This also holds for the millions who do not engage in formal or orthodox observance. But many millions do regularly attend church and otherwise carry out formal obligations. Plainly clothed Mexicans in every tiny village and large city stream solemnly throughout the day into simple churches. Their devotion reflects a large meaning and commitment that can easily be lost in an analytical account of Mexican political development. Indian religious practice fuses with Spanish Catholicism to produce Mexico's special hybrids. While Catholics in much of the world observe All Souls' Day, Mexicans, especially in rural areas, observe the Day of the Dead. Although the Day of the Dead borrows some customs from All Souls' Day, it incorporates Indian aspects as well. Similarly, while the Virgin Mary is a central symbol for many Catholics around the world, the dark-skinned Virgin of Guadalupe — a culturally blended image produced by the believed appearance of the Virgin Mary in Mexico during early colonial times — is the central symbol for Mexicans. Furthermore, analyses of Mexican culture frequently trace attitudes to an ancient Indian past. Many of these attitudes have political consequences, including deference to authority and hierarchy, which may support authoritarianism, and a characteristic fatalism (involving acceptance that life is not fair), which may help explain Mexicans' extraordinary patience — at least until recently — toward shortcomings in government performance.[36]

Since the 1980s important religious change has occurred in Mexico. Although Christianity remains dominant (alongside small Jewish and Muslim communities), tensions have risen among Christians. A strong evangelical movement reflects social upheaval and brings political conflict, including vigorous denunciations by the Catholic Church. Protestants are now more than 5 percent of the population and growing.[37] In some states, especially in southern Mexico, evangelical Protestants make up as much as 14 percent of the population.

Ethnic diversity in Mexico often means something quite different from a melting pot, notwithstanding Mexico's success in building national

Evangelical church in southern Mexico, where the Protestant movement has made strong inroads.

identity.[38] Various European and Middle Eastern communities in the country socialize largely within their own educational, religious, and recreational institutions; their relationships to mestizos and others are often employer to employee or master to servant. At the other socio-economic extreme, Blacks were brought to Mexico as slaves in early colonial times. Just as Indians tend to be clustered in certain regions, so Blacks — or more commonly, Mexicans of mixed Black-mestizo origin — are clustered along the coasts. Veracruz, for example, resembles in many ways a Caribbean city more than an inland Mexican city. Ethnic region-alism naturally accompanies cultural regionalism. In music, for example, the typical sound ranges from mariachi bands in the west to *zapateados* (rapid step dancing characteristic of Veracruz and the north) to Carib-bean salsa. Cultural identity helps explain why Mexicans often retain great pride in their hometown and state, even if they have migrated to a large city or to the United States.

For all its diversity, however, Mexico is one nation and the degree of homogeneity is increasing. Although the different groups have made their mark on the national culture, as seen with Indian religion or African music, these distinctive groups are now receding into smaller enclaves. Spanish is increasingly pervasive, as Indian monolinguism has declined since 1930. The zapatista rebellion perhaps demonstrates a countertrend with its demand for indigenous autonomy, echoing the rising self-identity of many ethnic groups within countries worldwide. But the rebellion also demonstrates shared aspirations, such as the demand for democracy.

Modern transportation and communication continue to play a unifying role, and expanding education has similar effects through socialization. Urbanization also diminishes the intensity of regional differences. Likewise crucial to our study is the centralization of political life in Mexico City. Although scholars have appropriately emphasized how regionalism retains a political as well as cultural meaning, and chapter 3 discusses trends toward political decentralization, political centralization has historically been a great source of national integration. Regional, topographical, ethnic, and cultural cleavages notwithstanding, political power is concentrated in Mexico City. Most political roads lead to — and from — the capital. This political centralization is remarkable when one considers the centrifugal forces — geographical and cultural — with which Mexican politics has to cope.

Finally, gender also fits a picture of large yet declining differences within the population. Within all ethnic and economic groups, the roles and treatment of women and men have been distinct. Usually this has meant marked inequalities in power, status, and opportunity, although the influence and fulfillment that women have often enjoyed in managing their families should not be underestimated. The international women's movement has reached Mexico with considerable effect. The government routinely refers to the special and unequal plight of women, and it conspicuously launches such campaigns as its National Program of the Woman (1995–2000), although these usually amount to declarations of goals (e.g., reducing female poverty or increasing female leadership) more than concrete actions.

Evidence of prominent change includes the fact that nearly one-third of Mexico's workforce is female, and more than 20 percent of Mexican households are headed by women. For some these are signs of social development and decreasing inequality. For others, however, they are mostly signs of social deterioration. Those who would prefer to maintain earlier gender role distinctions certainly see their deterioration, but many feminists also see a deterioration in women's positions, resulting from social and economic calamities like soaring teenage pregnancy and the declining ability of working men to earn a living wage. These developments have pushed women into low-paying jobs in unfavorable conditions, with little reduction in their traditional household duties. Although some women have felt liberated, others have mostly felt depressed. Discrimination remains deeply embedded in the culture and economy.[39] A perverse sort of equalization often occurs where men fall into women's tragic roles: alongside the ubiquitous young mother holding a child with one hand and begging with the other is a young father doing the same.

The Land

Mexico is as large and varied in geography as it is in its people. Its 760,000 square miles (1,968,000 square kilometers) make it the third-largest nation in Latin America, after Brazil and Argentina, and one of the ten largest in the world. A profound geopolitical aspect is the 2,000-mile (3,200-kilometer) northern border with the United States. On the southern side lies a 600-mile (960-kilometer) border with Guatemala and a 160-mile (260 kilometer) border with Belize. Beyond these southern borders lies the rest of Central America. Apart from Mexico's sheer size and proximity to the world's superpower, two geographical factors deserving mention in a political context are natural resources and regional diversity. With the exception of oil, Mexico is neither unusually unfortunate nor unusually fortunate in its natural resources. There is, however, a centuries-old myth of special richness. To secure greater support from Spain, Spanish conquerors succumbed to a combination of enthusiastic miscalculation and calculated exaggeration.[40] Subsequently, both Mexicans and foreigners have perpetuated the myth, sometimes to blame those in power for Mexico's failures, sometimes to stereotype Mexicans as lazy or ignorant or to justify some sort of foreign intervention.

On the positive side, however, Mexico is rich in minerals. Attractive for its gold and silver since colonial times, Mexico has remained a leading producer of silver. Other important minerals have included lead, zinc, copper, and sulfur. Mexico also has some good ranching and timberlands, as well as fishing waters. Along parts of its five thousand miles of coastline, oil has become the foremost natural resource. But realists must also appreciate the harsher economic side of Mexican geography. Much of its best agricultural land was lost in nineteenth-century warfare with the United States. Today, aside from its coastal areas, Mexico's land is mostly mediocre agriculturally. Only about 12 percent of the land is arable. The climate tends to be hot and unfavorable from sea level to 2,000 feet (600 meters) before becoming more temperate at 8,000 feet

(2,400 meters) and cooler above. Rainfall is also a problem, insufficient in some regions, excessive in others. More than half of Mexico is dry; about one-fourth, mostly mountainous, is rainy and temperate; and the rest is tropically rainy. Earthquakes, volcanoes, and hurricanes buffet the tropical areas, which house many of the country's valuable resources.

Mexico also suffers from rugged topography. Its mountains hinder large-scale agriculture as well as transportation and communication, and they have impeded national homogeneity by dividing Mexico into regions. The Mexican government has usually classified Mexico into five regions. The North Pacific, with the states of Baja California, Sonora, and Sinaloa, is the second largest. But because much of the land is desert, the region has a relatively small population. A second region, the North, stretches from the Western Sierra Madre (the mountains connected with the Sierra Nevada in the United States) to the Gulf of Mexico. Comprising the states of San Luis Potosí, Zacatecas, Chihuahua, and Coahuila, it covers two-fifths of Mexico's land, including the eastern Sierra Madre (connected to the Rocky Mountains in the United States), but has only one-fifth of Mexico's population. So the main geographical features of the northern half of Mexico are the two Sierra Madre ranges, with a plateau in between. Central Mexico, surrounding the Federal District, is the third-largest region in area but holds roughly half of the country's population. This valley region lies in high volcanic terrain, which accounts for its earthquakes. The Gulf Coast, including Veracruz, Tabasco, and the Yucatán, is a level lowland region, limited in size and population alike. Finally, the South Pacific is the most rural region, including Oaxaca and Chiapas. Mexico's topography and regions present greater challenges to achieving political or cultural homogeneity than size alone would indicate. They have much to do with Mexico's ethnic, cultural, social, economic, and political divisions.

THE U.S. INTEREST

In addition to Mexico's size and its importance for the study of development are the various special reasons for U.S. readers to take an interest in Mexico. With no other country does the United States have such extensive and intensive relationships, on cultural, geographical, economic, and political levels. Historically powerful, these relationships have increased in intensity and will continue to do so in the future. Analysis of the political and economic relationships appears in all chapters, especially Chapters 6 and 7, which both explore the heightened U.S. interest in

Mexico as the countries are increasingly intertwined. Mexico's relationship with the United States has important and complex effects on the struggle for democratized development. As Mexico becomes more democratic, the democratic practices and beliefs of its northern neighbor increasingly influence it. U.S. groups play a growing role in Mexico's domestic politics. To be sure, relations with the United States have long been compatible with undemocratic Mexican politics, and many in the United States remain more concerned with Mexico's political stability and predictable economic reform than democracy. But there appears to be increasing awareness that continued democratization is imperative for other political and economic goals. U.S. understanding of Mexico's struggle for democracy has become more important.

From Ignorance to Knowledge?

U.S. interest in Mexico has been surprisingly limited. Neither educational curriculum nor mass media have given Mexico nearly the attention it deserves. Even leading news outlets have repeatedly managed not to make lead stories out of events crucial for Mexico's democratic and other development prospects. Worse, U.S. images of Mexico, seen from Hollywood and in school textbooks, are often stereotypic and negative.[41] Contrary to liberal faith, proximity and interaction do not necessarily breed understanding. Nor does understanding necessarily reduce resentment or tension. But mutual knowledge increases the prospects that Mexican-U.S. interactions would be handled more intelligently.

It is therefore heartening to note some positive trends. Although remaining well below what is merited, U.S. attention to Mexico has grown over the years. The 1976 announcement of Mexico's great oil resources provided one spark. More generally, bilateral interactions have become just too much to ignore. The launching of NAFTA in 1994 is one such landmark. Furthermore, the profound political changes within Mexico have an obvious impact on the United States. At times, they are such that the United States no longer takes the stability of its neighbor for granted. At other times, epitomized by Mexico's 2000 elections, democratization leaps into the news. The political-economic combination of democratization and neoliberalism perhaps makes Mexico look increasingly relevant, familiar, and attractive to many U.S. interests. Meanwhile, the political and economic changes have brought wider acceptance within Mexico of the U.S. role that is crucial to Mexican development.

There is also an upsurge of pertinent news coverage and scholarly attention in both countries; the volume of academic work in each nation, about the other nation, continues to soar.[42] Public and private bilateral commissions deliberate.[43] The largest U.S. diplomatic mission in the world is in Mexico. Meetings between the two nations' presidents, once rare, are frequent. Signaling their realization of Mexico's importance to the United States, George H. W. Bush, Bill Clinton, and George W. Bush all sought meetings with their Mexican presidential counterparts while still presidents-elect. Mexican presidents are also often the first official foreign visitors for incoming U.S. presidents.

Moreover, beyond this increased interest lies evidence that attitudes may have become more informed and positive than many scholars suggest. Many citizens on both sides of the border have developed views based on their own interactions with citizens on the other side. The explosion of public opinion polling in Mexico shows remarkably positive attitudes about U.S. society and politics as well as about official Mexican policies to link the country even more closely to its neighbor. One wonders whether the survey results reflect changing attitudes or whether attitudes have long been more positive than believed. One also wonders whether knowledge of how Mexicans really view their neighbor might in turn contribute to more positive U.S. views of Mexico. Progress notwithstanding, there is a long way to go. The NAFTA debate and subsequent debates over U.S. assistance to Mexico highlight the enduring force of bad information. Those urging the United States to stand back have often painted a scandalously negative picture of Mexico, while those urging increased cooperation have often resorted to painting a rosy future of democratic prosperity that belies the seriousness of Mexico's problems and the difficulties of development.

Two Nations Culturally Intertwined

U.S. influence on Mexico is pervasive, having soared in the past few years above an already high level. "Americanization" — reaching to political norms, structures, and practice, including democratization — forms a central theme in this book. In trade, suffice it to note that Mexico has vied with Japan to rank behind only Canada as a U.S. partner. Even if the United States had no self-interest in learning about Mexico, it would have a moral responsibility to do so to be able to consider reasonably its own impact on so many millions of lives. No one can understand contemporary Mexico without appreciating the enormous extent of U.S.

penetration. This includes the cultural and social penetration manifest in everyday Mexican life.

Many Mexicans live by a range of behavioral norms imported from the United States.[44] Convenience foods reshape the diet, and McDonald's, Domino's, and Kentucky Fried Chicken franchises appear throughout Mexico (Taco Bell has yet to make real inroads). English words have become part of Mexican speech, especially as the majority of films and television programs come from the United States. Reruns of shows like *The Simpsons* air every weekday night. Cable television and satellite dishes accelerate the penetration. The Left may decry cable television as a foreign invasion that undermines Mexican culture, but it does so at its own peril: Mexicans who have it like it, and others covet it. On a 1999 visit, Fidel Castro complained that Mexican children seem to know less about their country's historical champions than about Mickey Mouse. Television news comes increasingly in U.S. formats, emulating *Sixty Minutes*, *20/20*, man-woman dual anchors, and the like. Mexico's most widely read magazines are adaptations of *Reader's Digest* and *TV Guide*. U.S. pop music has also gained a huge following, and Mexicans often copy U.S. musical styles, including rap. Mexico City boasts a huge U.S.-style amusement park, owned by Six Flags. Wal-Mart has plans to build a major outlet within sight of Mexico's oldest monument: the pyramids just outside Mexico City known as Teotihuacán. Soccer remains easily the number-one sport, but U.S.-style football is more popular in Mexico than in any other Latin American country, baseball is more popular than in all but a few, and basketball has also gained a significant following. *Monday Night Football*, the *Super Bowl*, and the *World Series* have become Mexican television sports institutions. In addition, Mexico's rapid privatization and openings to the international economy greatly affect cultural institutions; for example, universities, museums, and arts facilities increasingly seek advice from the United States on fund-raising, nonprofit tax law, and ties with business.

At the same time cultural penetration is very much a two-way phenomenon. Latinos are now surpassing African-Americans as the largest minority group in the United States. The United States is perhaps the fifth-largest Spanish-speaking nation in the world, and Mexican-Americans, or Chicanos, account for about three-fifths of the Latino total. Roughly one-third of the population of the largest U.S. state, California, is of Mexican heritage, up from roughly one-tenth as recently as 1970.[45] Migrants constitute an ongoing major source of the Chicano population; descendants of the population inhabiting the land taken by the United States from Mexico in the nineteenth century constitute another. Thus there are wry jokes about a Mexican reconquest by way of population growth. Many Mexicans have relatives in the United States or have visited the United States.

Catering to the Mexican-American and Latino population, hundreds of Spanish-language newspapers, magazines, and radio and television stations flourish in the United States. Mexican television via cable reaches millions in cities such as Los Angeles, New York, and Washington, D.C. Food, music, and language are further manifestations of Mexican culture in the United States. Although the customs flourish mostly in the Chicano community, they go beyond it as well. Even the U.S. "national pastime" has felt a Mexican presence: Fernando Valenzuela was one of baseball's top attractions in the 1980s and other Mexican players have followed. Mexico hosted the first-ever official big league game outside the United States or Canada and the 1999 season opener in Monterrey.

Education provides another good example of an important Mexican influence on the United States, notwithstanding great U.S. influence on Mexico. At the higher education level bilateral institutional exchanges blossom. Meanwhile, the Chicano percentage of U.S. enrollment rises at elementary through university levels. Half of the kindergarten pupils in Los Angeles have Spanish surnames. Bilingual education and Chicano-relevant curricula are prominent, and school districts far from the traditional geographical centers receive a Chicano influx. Culturally related political muscle also grows. "Chicano consciousness" is naturally strongest in the American Southwest, where most Chicanos live, but it is significant in major urban centers such as Chicago. Recognition of this power has been evident in U.S. presidential elections since 1980.

Mexico also voices concern for persons of Mexican descent living in the United States. Although the interests of Chicanos and Mexican citizens (let alone the Mexican government) often do not coincide, the Mexican government became active in the 1990s in building ties, especially with the Mexican-American business community. Political committees formed in U.S. cities and links developed with Mexican "sister" cities. Zedillo intensified overtures to win support from Chicanos, probably hoping to imitate patterns in which U.S. domestic ethnic groups lobby for their country of origin. Most ties have developed outside official channels, however, reflecting the government's declining power to control social organization. Also reflecting the growth of competitive politics in Mexico, parties now appeal for support from Mexican citizens in the United States. A 1996 law allows these citizens to vote in Mexican presidential elections (if they return home) and allows Mexicans abroad to retain Mexican citizenship even if they become citizens of a foreign country. Mexico's 2000 elections thus included competition for support among approximately seven million potential voters within the United States. Like his main opponent, recent presidential victor Fox went north for help, even passing out three-minute prepaid phone cards and asking recipients to "phone home" and tell their friends and relatives to vote for him. In many ways the Chicano political presence becomes more visible.

The intertwined fates of the two countries is on vivid display on the border, an increasingly porous international zone rather than a rigid dividing line between separate nations. Millions live within a short distance of the border, and the population is growing rapidly. The politics, economies, and cultures on each side shape those on the other side. Mutual influences involve political parties, nongovernmental organizations, labor-capital interchanges, and family ties. This is the world's busiest border.[46] Despite interaction and homogenizing influences, however, the border still marks a division. Rarely, in fact, are adjacent nations so ethnically, culturally, socially, economically, and politically different. Moreover, the differences between Mexico and the United States reflect a critical division between the less developed world and the more developed world. Nowhere else do a developed and a developing nation share such a long border.[47]

In sum, two broad realities must be appreciated. One reality is the enormous, multifaceted, and underlying contrast between the two nations. Mexican politics and development are very different from those of the United States. But the other reality is that extensive and rapidly growing bilateral penetration increasingly makes the countries more alike. Mexican politics and development increasingly incorporate and emulate U.S. orientations. The challenge is simultaneously to understand Mexico on its own terms and in its U.S.-oriented international context.

BOOK STRUCTURE

Chapter 2 provides a historical overview of Mexican development, emphasizing how stability was finally attained in the first half of the twentieth century but without democracy. By analyzing how certain political, economic, and social goals fared in previous periods, the chapter offers a historical context from which to evaluate contemporary Mexico. Chapter 3 identifies the main political actors and structures, including the electoral process. It concentrates on the rise of competitive politics. Chapter 4 then provides a broader view of Mexico's democratic evolution and difficult democracy. It considers how freedoms could precede and continue to outstrip both organized political action and accountability of rulers to citizens.

Subsequent chapters shift the focus from domestic political matters to their mix with other aspects of development. Chapter 5 identifies the key features associated with Mexico's enduring and widely heralded economic development model. It then analyzes the shift to neoliberal policies and the social legacy Mexico is left to grapple with. Chapter 6 turns to a complementary change in the role of the state: whereas the Mexican government long prided itself on controlling its own affairs, Mexico has now opened itself to a variety of economic and political forces from the outside. By far the strongest of these forces, crucial to the course of Mexican development, comes from the United States. Chapter 7 considers four major bilateral policy issues: drugs, migration, tourism, and trade, including NAFTA. Chapter 8 draws together the book's findings on Mexico's struggle for democratic and internationalized development and poses critical questions about the country's future.

Although each chapter has a different focus, certain themes are central. The most overarching is the struggle to achieve democratic development. The chapters repeatedly consider the relationship between democracy, or the lack thereof, and other aspects of development. The struggle for democracy is part of a broad decline of Mexican exceptionalism in favor of a "normalization" of development pursuits and patterns. Mexico largely abandons claims to its own distinctive course of development as it internationalizes under invigorated U.S. influence. This book is about Mexico's struggle to reinvent itself politically and restructure its overall development. The struggle lies at the heart of evolving relationships between state and society, between government and the market, between Mexican citizens and their organizations, between Mexico and the world, and between the past and the future.

CHAPTER 2

Legacies of Undemocratic Development

HISTORICAL THEMES

The political history of Mexico is not one of democratic development. Most Latin American countries have spotty histories of democratic rule, but Mexico ranks low even within this group. Its contemporary struggle for democracy has been an effort to achieve something that is fundamentally new. Lack of democratic precedent, however, is hardly a good reason to ignore the past. To understand the present challenges of democratization in Mexico, one must understand why democracy has been so rare there. Although today democracy appears crucial to all other major aspects of development, this has not historically been so. Mexico's past is full of monumental struggles whose outcomes were consequential for the Mexican people even though they did not produce democracy. For our purposes most of the country's nearly two centuries of independence can loosely be divided into two sets of circumstances: political instability accompanied by economic weakness and political stability accompanied by economic growth.

Stability and economic growth rank as the most enduring goals of Mexican governments. To these we add three other goals that have been more controversial: increased socioeconomic equality, national independence, and political democracy. Governments have only sporadically pursued these three goals and, in fact, have often opposed them in practice; in any event these goals represent the historical aspirations of many citizens. Even when overwhelming support has existed for one goal or another, Mexicans have usually quarreled over the meaning and priority of each goal and its relationships to the other goals, including forced trade-offs. Mexico has never decisively resolved these divisions. Victories for a particular principle have often proved ephemeral. This is also reflected in the fact that Mexicans remain divided about their past: They celebrate different as well as similar victories and defeats. As the understanding of any country requires an understanding of its past, in Mexico we must explore the diverse perceptions of historical reality.[1]

Because the five goals we track represent recurrent themes in Mexican history and still command wide support today, exploration of their fate in different historical eras helps provide conceptual coherence for our chronological overview. This overview (leaving the role of the United States in Mexican history for Chapter 6) emphasizes two realities above all others: the belated but epic achievement of political stability in Mexico (including its impact on other historical goals) and the absence of democracy.

UNDEMOCRATIC CENTURIES

Before Nationhood

The roots of Mexican national identity go back long before Mexico became a nation, indeed long before Mexico became a colony of Spain. Indigenous people inhabited the land and built civilizations. When the Spaniards arrived in 1519, they conquered the Indians but did not drive them into oblivion; instead, the civilizations mixed. Continuity in the population therefore runs from ancient Mexico to modern Mexico. Indians were likely attracted to the region by such factors as water and warm climate. The urban civilizations of Olmecs, Mayas, Toltecs, and Teotihuacanos came with the shift from hunting to agriculture and more permanent settlement. Aztecs abandoned the arid north for the fertile central valley in the twelfth century, built Tenochtitlán (later Mexico City), conquered their enemies, and established an empire with governors of provinces, tax collectors, courts, and ruling military-religious castes. Aztec rule is often compared with Mexico's modern regime: both forged a centralized, authoritarian, hierarchical, stable system. Yet Aztec rule is also a symbol of Mexican independence that was never fully vanquished by the foreign conquerors who would establish "new Spain." The Aztecs were defeated by a few hundred Spaniards under Hernán Cortés. Mexico

Mayan ruins at Palenque.

then had perhaps twenty-five million inhabitants, about three times the total population of Spain itself. But superior weaponry, personal daring, and fortuitous (for the Spaniards) native religious beliefs that white gods would one day appear all aided the conquerors. Most significant, Mexico's Indians were divided. The vulnerability of a disunited Mexico would become a theme in Mexican history. The Aztecs ruled other tribes, some of whom saw the Spanish arrival as an attractive opportunity to rebel against the Aztecs. Images of a simple, harmonious, peaceful society succumbing to the warlike invaders are misleading. Pre-Columbian Mexican society was politically complex and conflictual. Some Indians defied Cortés, while others were uncertain, submissive, or even support-ive. Leading the defiant ones was not the Aztec emperor Moctezuma but his nephew, Cuauhtémoc, who was eventually captured and tortured to death by the Spanish. Cuauhtémoc is memorialized in Mexican books, landmarks, and street names as the earliest symbol of independence.

Some contemporary Mexicans, particularly conservatives, emphasize what they consider to be positive features of Spain's three-century colo-nial rule. The conquerors introduced Christianity, converting most of the population. For believers in Christianity as the route to salvation, this event cannot be overemphasized. Some care was taken by the Spanish to protect the Indians, however, while hoping to convert and assimilate them — quite different from the English settlers' efforts to push aside or kill the natives in what would become the United States. Under the Spanish, Mexico also achieved a degree of political integration and stability. Mexico City became one of the two centers of development (Lima was the other) for Spanish America.

Most Mexicans, however, hold a less sanguine view of the colonial era. Spaniards sought assimilation to impose their religion, values, and privileges on the indigenous peoples. Spain's mercantile economic system exploited even the Spaniards who settled in Mexico. It robbed Mexico of minerals while prohibiting free trade, greatly restricting commercial ties beyond the mother country. Spain's appointed viceroy had powers unchecked by accountability to his subjects. Socially, Mexicans endured a rigid hierarchy. Spaniards, or *peninsulares*, were at the top, followed by *criollos*, those of Spanish descent born in Mexico, followed far behind by mestizos, and still further by the Indian masses. The Indians' plight probably worsened, in fact, as settlers carved out large estates at the expense of traditional communal landholdings. Crown and church together guaranteed that Spanish rule was elitist and authoritarian, which ensured political stability in the colonial era. But Spanish colonialism did not encourage equality or democracy, much less national independence.

Contrasts between Mexican and U.S. colonial experiences provide insight into contemporary differences. The contrasts start with the mother countries themselves. Spain had an absolute monarchy, strong church-state ties, and a largely feudal economic system. England had a more limited monarchy, a vibrant parliament, self-government, church-state separation, and an incipient capitalist economy that would lead the Industrial Revolution. Spain's corporatist, conservative tendencies contrasted with England's more individualist, pluralist, liberal ones. Another key contrast involved the native populations. Whereas the English confronted nomadic tribes who could be largely pushed aside, the Spanish confronted urbanized and politically complex empires. Thus the English transplanted their relatively liberal politics and culture largely intact, while the Spanish mixed their conservative culture with a similarly hierarchical native society. Within Spanish America itself an interesting contrast emerged. Those countries with the biggest and most settled and developed native civilizations (e.g., Mexico and Peru) naturally attracted the colonizers' interest; these countries became very inegalitarian in their political, economic, and social affairs. Those countries with smaller and more nomadic native civilizations (e.g., Argentina and Uruguay) attracted less colonial interest; thus nineteenth-century European immigrants found fresh terrain on which to establish themselves and import some European or U.S. liberal tendencies. In a sense countries with the strongest native and Spanish colonial influence were handicapped in pursuing many of the goals associated with democratic development.

Independence

Political independence, established in 1821, was the product of both weakened colonial rule (in the wake of Napoleon's conquest of Spain) and accumulated Mexican grievances that were exacerbated by setbacks and frustrated expectations. Democracy was among the goals sometimes pursued but not achieved. Central power did not collapse suddenly, but its legitimacy and authority eroded — a possible parallel to contemporary Mexico. Criollos and privileged mestizos confronted the peninsulares and the Spanish establishment. They did not fight for equality for the masses, however. Mexico differed from Spain's other rebel colonies in its involvement (albeit aborted) of many Indians. Their leader was Miguel Hidalgo, priest, champion of the oppressed, nationalist (whose cry for independence is still recalled in an annual ritual by Mexico's president on September 15) — and failure. Criollos deserted the cause and generally feared the aspiring masses more than Spanish rule.

Like the Mexican Revolution a century later, the War for Independence (1810–21) was complicated, protracted, decentralized, and ultimately unfulfilling for the masses. Independence came only when the Mexican upper class finally turned against Spain, partly because Spain itself adopted a liberal constitution, including democratic voting rights. The struggle for national independence was not a revolution for broad socioeconomic equity and, unlike the American Revolution, would not lead to democracy, despite the efforts of figures such as José María Morelos. Freedoms would increase for the few but not for most Mexicans.[2] Mexico's War for Independence failed to achieve independence in the sense of creating a stable government able to defend national territory. Instead, the new republic sank into a vicious cycle of political instability and economic failure which left Mexico vulnerable to foreign attacks on its sovereignty. These decades contrast with the positive political-economic cycle that Mexico would achieve for much of the twentieth century.

Independent Mexico inherited an economy in dreadful shape, with debt, a bankrupt treasury, and weak commercial ties to European markets. The crippled economy desperately needed a great deal of capital.

Both "liberals" and "conservatives" (to use political labels that would crystallize later) shared this view. Liberals did not subordinate economic growth to concerns for equity, and conservatives did not simply hark back to a bygone age. Both favored powerful banking institutions and foreign investment. Yet Mexico could not attract capital without first establishing political stability — and this seemed impossible. Only two presidents completed their four-year terms during the thirty-five-year span from 1821 to 1856. Part of the problem was fundamental disagreement about the design of political institutions. A major example is the church's relationship to politics and the economy. Conservatives wanted to uphold the strong church-state partnership established under colonial rule, whereas liberals wanted to separate the church from the state and reduce its power. Another example is the state's role in the economy. Conservatives defended a strong state role in the economy, whereas liberals trusted more to the market.[3] Overlapping the liberal-conservative split was a divide between federalists (favoring power to the provinces) and centralists (interested in building power in Mexico City).

Serious as such differences were, the inability of elites to cope with them contrasts with the skills of compromise elites attained a century later and helps explain the cycle of failure. Successive nineteenth-century governments could not garner the resources to make themselves legitimate, to distribute benefits, and to make it worthwhile to the masses not to revolt. This resource problem related to the regional struggle. Central governments could not extract more resources from society without engendering provincial challenges. Yet without those resources they could not even pay the army, thus provoking military coups. So just as Mexico could not get needed capital without stability, it could not establish stability without capital. Understanding the negative relationship between political instability and economic stagnation during much of the nineteenth century will help us to appreciate, by contrast, Mexico's positive stability-growth relationship in much of the twentieth century.

This backdrop of deep political and economic problems helps explain the spectacular personal successes that notoriously irresponsible or incompetent leaders gained over the more responsible ones. Soon after Mexico freed itself from Spain, Agustín de Iturbide appointed himself emperor. The first ironic result of independence was royalty; the second ironic consequence was vulnerability to military "heroes" like Antonio López de Santa Anna throughout the decades of short-lived governments. This victor of the Alamo eventually became Mexico's most despised and traitorous native son when he presided over the loss of roughly half of Mexico's territory during the 1846–48 war with the United States (the Mexican-American War).[4] During this period almost no one could establish a viable government and economic base.

Mexico's problems were greatly aggravated by foreign intervention.[5] The Mexican-American War had had disastrous consequences, especially given the harsh terms of surrender. Soon thereafter, France, Great Britain, and Spain all demanded reparations for losses suffered during Mexico's turmoil. Mexico suspended payment on its foreign debt, and in 1864, France's Napoleon III named Austrian Archduke Maximilian to rule Mexico. Mexican independence suffered whenever domestic strife and instability weakened the nation's ability to defend itself — a fairly constant condition during the first half of the nineteenth century. However, Mexico eventually defeated the French, who lost interest in Mexico as resistance continued to increase the costs of occupation. This victory remains a singular and still much celebrated triumph for national independence.

Although they could not build much political stability, liberals held the upper hand for much of the third quarter of the century, known as *La Reforma* (the Reform era). Warfare limited their opportunity for effective rule until 1867 through 1876, but their accomplishments were numerous. These included establishing a greater degree of political liberty and democracy than Mexico had ever experienced or would experience for a long time to come, although with limited suffrage. Other pillars of the reform, integrally tied to the liberals' vision of democratic development, set the stage for future reform efforts. For example, the liberals attacked the church's enormous privileges, permanently reducing its large tracts of (nontaxable) lands, its immunity before the law, and its control over social affairs such as education and marriage. They also expanded public educational facilities. Mestizos captured some privileges previously reserved for a small elite. The Reform's great leader, Benito Juárez, was himself an Indian from the poor state of Oaxaca. According to historian Daniel Cosío Villegas, the liberals were "without equal in our history, men with the virile optimism of those who feel a nation being born from their own hands, and for whom liberalism was a new religious faith."[6] A less flattering evaluation is that the liberals opposed traditionalism and communitarianism, whether oriented toward the church or the Indian. They worshiped classic nineteenth-century democracy, not socio-economic or political equality.

However one evaluates the liberals' ideology, their Reform's reach exceeded its grasp. Reform limited church privileges more than it established a new liberal order. Regional oligarchs took advantage of formal democratic structures to thwart progressive change, so that both Juárez and his liberal successors had to rule largely through special executive authority. Democracy's maiden voyage in Mexico ended badly. Not even limited, oligarchic democracy was established. This did not make Mexico exceptional, for Peru, the Dominican Republic, and other Latin American countries also suffered failure. But the failure left twentieth-century Mexico behind the region's nineteenth-century leaders and left the country without a successful, guiding, democratic precedent. When the liberals lost power in 1876, the traditional conservatives could not regain control. Instead, Porfirio Díaz, a general in Mexico's successful fight against the French, became Mexico's supreme leader. Under his administration a new political philosophy reigned. "Positivism" stressed that science and order lead to progress and development. Like liberalism, positivism was imported from "progressive" Europe by most Latin American nations, but few felt its impact as strongly as Mexico. Also like liberalism, positivism was generally indifferent or hostile to both tradition and egalitarianism. But unlike liberalism, it did not embrace individual liberty.

The achievements of the Díaz regime, the *porfiriato* (1876–1910), were nonetheless substantial. Political stability and economic growth were foremost. Stability must be appreciated against the nation's background of frightful instability. Governments had come and gone so often that the military had become a desirable career for mobile mestizos, offering access to power and corruption. Mexico could not compete with Argentina or the United States in attracting the European settlers that were thought to spur development. And of course political instability had doomed efforts to attract foreign capital and technology. Under Díaz, Mexico finally had an extended political stability, which contributed to substantial economic growth and modernization. Thus the porfiriato reversed the vicious cycle of economic weakness and political instability that had characterized the early postindependence period. Foreigners gave Mexico high credit ratings and made secure, profitable investments. Railroads, oil, electricity, steel mills, and sugar mills led the way. The porfiriato also extracted increased tax revenues from the population. National income soared, along with exports and imports.

Order and growth were achieved, however, at the expense of democracy. Power sharing between the national and state governments and separation of powers within the national government lost out as Díaz centralized authority into his own dictatorial hands. The Reform period's free elections and political liberties (such as freedom of speech and freedom of the press) were lost. The government co-opted peasants and bandits by offering good salaries, uniforms, and power; it then unleashed these *rurales* to repress dissent in the countryside. Considerable repression was necessary to implement dictatorial policies that were economically hard on the masses. Porfirian development required cheap peasant and urban labor and no strikes. Equality therefore fared no better than democracy.

Positivism provided the handy rationale that the intellectually fittest of society must lead the rest. Neither ignorance nor shortsighted humanitarianism should impede that progress. Thus the government did not worry about terrible education in rural areas. Economic growth was expected to help the rich, the small middle class, and — through trickle-down economics — the poor. Only these first two groups were aided, however. Large landholders increasingly pushed peasants off their land into laborer status, often culminating in debtor status. World depression at the turn of the century hit the masses hardest. After decades of "order and progress," wages and living standards deteriorated for many Mexicans, and probably more than four in five remained illiterate.[7] While most Mexicans suffered, foreigners prospered. The porfiriato encouraged foreign penetration of major sectors of Mexico's economy. Independence took a step backward, though Díaz exercised some autonomy by playing U.S. against European interests.

Parallels to the institutional Mexican rule begun around 1940 are striking.[8] In both cases leadership emerged from the ruins of progressive movements (the Reform, the revolution). Yet the masses did not benefit, at least not nearly in proportion to the economic growth of the period. Repression limited dissent, but the regimes offered co-optation, and expanding economies and bureaucracies produced jobs and opportunities for corrupt gain. Both regimes also promoted scientific and professional pursuits, whether for positivism or modernization. Both used the trappings of democratic liberalism to obscure authoritarian behavior. Both boasted a positive cycle of political stability and economic growth, encouraging foreign investment. And both could reasonably claim that, whatever their shortcomings, the real alternative to authoritarianism in Mexican history has not been democracy and widely shared prosperity but destructive political instability, a crippled economy, and consequent vulnerability to foreign intervention.[9]

A key challenge for modern Mexico is to avoid paralleling the porfiriato in death as it did in life. The porfirian decline culminated in the Mexican Revolution and then in the construction of a nondemocratic regime. The postrevolutionary regime's decline has so far lifted hopes for democratic development without a catastrophic explosion, and a reeling political elite may draw lessons from the consequences of denying democratic aspirations.[10] A reborn liberal movement established the intellectual foundations for rebellion against the porfiriato. It demanded, at a minimum, free elections, a free press, and a return to the Reform's 1857 constitution. Where Díaz might have seen a democratic imperative, he instead repressed and fumbled. Suggestions in 1908 that he would retire were followed by a typically rigged reelection. This about-face was the match that ignited a flammable accumulation of grievances. So began, nearly a century after the start of the War for Independence, an equally protracted and far bloodier revolution.

Revolution

Like many revolutions Mexico's started with a moderate stage. So brittle had Díaz's dictatorship become that it collapsed without a massive revolutionary push. Mexico's new president, Francisco Madero, was a young, foreign-educated idealist from a wealthy landowning family. He was no fiery revolutionary, and his socioeconomic agenda was limited. But Madero and his movement had a democratic political agenda. His slogan — "effective suffrage, no re-election" — would be enshrined in law and lore, though only the second stipulation became reality for most of the twentieth century. Madero restored the Reform's key tenets of a free press, individual property rights, and — for a shining moment — free elections. To be sure, suffrage was limited to only part of the population; a form of political liberty, not political equality, was Madero's abiding principle.

Seen in the sweep of Mexico's historical reality and present yearnings, however, even formal democracy was an achievement. It serves as a very rare precedent for the country's contemporary democratization. Sadly, the precedent was short-lived and weak. Mexico furnishes its own proof that achievements in elections and democracy do not necessarily lead to democratic consolidation. Before it was over, the revolution would bring the death of roughly a tenth of the population and many others would flee the country. Courageous as he was, Madero ultimately failed because he neither smashed the old regime (its politicians, civil service, army, and entrenched economic interests) nor controlled the revolutionaries bent on so doing. The first — and perhaps until 1994 the last — competitively elected president of Mexico in the twentieth century was murdered in a 1913 coup, covertly aided by the United States. The coup installed dictator

Victoriano Huerta, who destroyed political freedom but, like the democrat Madero, did not overhaul the porfiriato's governing elite or consolidate power.[11] Mexico sank into the revolution's most violent period.

The three major armies that fought the new dictatorship were not a united front. Emiliano Zapata led peasant forces whose chief demand was clear: land. When Madero called for moderation, Zapata withdrew his support, effected land reform in his home state of Morelos, and pressed to spread the revolution. Zapata's forces (*zapatistas*) had a coherent revolutionary program but perhaps also a conservative social hue. Even their cry for land was an attempt to preserve their communal, insulated traditions while gaining restoration of land that had been expropriated during the liberal and porfirian periods. The second army, Pancho Villa's forces (*villistas*), lacked a similarly coherent program but had a certain ideological populism and displayed the violent revolutionary zeal commonly attributed to them.[12] The third army was the least revolutionary. Headed by Venustiano Carranza, the "constitutionalists" drew largely on ranchers and self-made men. If they did not represent society's established elite, neither did they represent the masses. Perhaps the key factor was that the group included many who had been excluded from the insufficiently flexible and open porfirian ruling elite. By 1915, allied with the powerful "Northwest Group," the constitutionalists defeated the zapatistas and villistas after these groups had abandoned Mexico City for their regional strongholds.[13]

More revolutionary turmoil than revolutionary change came in the next few years. Carranza himself had been a landlord, a senator during the Díaz regime, a governor during the Madero era, and a *cacique* (regional strongman with his own army). Reform was limited by Carranza's nonrevolutionary values and his keen political sense. To secure a degree of reform necessary to consolidate the new regime, he had to support the 1917 Constitutional Convention. The convention probably went well beyond Carranza's wishes and resulted in a truly revolutionary and strongly nationalistic constitution. This new constitution asserted Mexican state control over all natural resources. Its pledge of land reform and labor rights made it, in some ways, the first modern socialist constitution, preceding the Soviet Union's.[14] The Constitution, like Mexico's earlier Reform efforts, also replicated many U.S. concepts of democracy, including federalism, separation of powers, a bicameral congress, and an elaborate Bill of Rights. The framers of Mexico's Constitution attempted to include what they saw as the best of both socioeconomic and democratic rights.

Implementation was another story. Carranza's attempt to circumvent free elections by installing a puppet successor led to his own murder and a coup by the Northwest Group. The group's leader, Alvaro Obregón, became president. From 1920 to 1924, Obregón pushed beyond Carranza's restrained reform, particularly in labor and educational policies. He built schools and launched a literacy campaign. Whereas Carranza, the politician, did what he thought the circumstances dictated, Obregón, the statesman, pressed for a new society. If Díaz had represented repression of popular demands for socioeconomic change and Madero a gentlemanly indifference, Carranza represented political acquiescence and Obregón active partnership.

Plutarco Elías Calles, another leader of the Northwest Group, peacefully assumed the presidency in 1924, but his plot to circumvent the no-reelection rule by reinstalling Obregón in 1928 was foiled by Obregón's murder. Calles nonetheless remained the supreme power behind the throne. Though a revolutionary in his attacks on the church, he failed to push many promised social reforms. His major accomplishment was to establish the basis for Mexico's uniquely successful one-party system. Calles pointed Mexican politics toward political stability, with substantial limits on democratic freedoms, and economic modernization (centralized banking, improved tax collection, financial stability, agricultural credits, and infrastructure development), without effective redistribution of the newly generated wealth.

If Calles thought he had appointed yet another subservient successor in Lázaro Cárdenas (1934–1940), he soon learned otherwise. Cárdenas's strength derived from a strong bond with Mexico's masses. Never before (or since) had the revolution produced such a revered politician. Contemporary reverence for Cárdenas reflects longing for the revolution's major absent-but-not-forgotten goal: greater socioeconomic equality. If the porfiriato provides a historical parallel to Mexico's development model for decades starting around 1940, Cárdenas's administration provides a symbolic alternative. As president Cárdenas distributed more land than all his revolutionary predecessors combined.[15] Ironically, this distribution did not directly reduce income inequality or improve real wages for the masses. Peasants got land in small plots, without the adequate capital, irrigation, or skills to develop them. Yet Cárdenas cut through the usual cynicism of Mexican politics. He reined in official luxury, provoked the wrath of business leaders, nationalized the oil industry (1938), and established warm, supportive relations with Mexico's masses who revered Cárdenas as their president.

Cárdenas's concept of an activist state at the people's service had little in common with liberal democracy, however. Reforms were initiated more from the top down ("for the people") than from the bottom up ("by the people"). Benefits to the poor would not come by allowing the poor their own autonomous and representative organizations. Rather, they would come by paternalistic presidential grace and by the president's cooperation with caciques supporting some equalization. Most of all, peasant and worker demands were carefully handled through the official party. Labor should restrain itself, Cárdenas argued (as, years later, would Fidel Castro in communist Cuba and socialist Salvador Allende in Chile), because labor was properly integrated into a progressive state, which was one of its major employers. Educational policy makers tried to bolster the regime's legitimacy through socialist education in a way that offended many leading conservative intellectuals who felt that this endangered freedom of thought and expression. Finally, like his less economically radical predecessors and heirs, Cárdenas directly pursued political stability much more than political democracy or "bourgeois freedoms."

Cárdenas contributed to the regime's stability by buttressing its claims to the popular goals of greater equality and national independence. He also strengthened the presidency.[16] And by leaving the presidency peacefully, without constant efforts to interfere in the administrations of subsequent presidents, Cárdenas set a valuable precedent of obedience to Mexico's cardinal political principle of no reelection, thus avoiding a repeat of porfirian scenarios.

TO THE PRESENT

A Revolutionary Legacy?

Some question the degree to which a revolution occurred. They point out that Mexico switched one elite for another, the plight of the masses did not substantially improve, and revolutionary nationalist fervor notwithstanding, foreign interests maintained their economic involvement. A pertinent cartoon shows one peasant asking another, "Who finally won the revolution, the zapatistas or the villistas?" Answer: "Neither one; the Revolutionary Family governs us."[17] Upheavals need not change everything to be revolutions, however, and certainly revolutions need not be democratic. Whether Mexico truly had a revolution, then, depends on interpretation. If violence is among the criteria of revolution, Mexico's more than qualifies. Lasting changes occurred in the composition of political actors. A much broader ruling elite replaced a fossilized oligarchy. Peasant participation guaranteed policy consequences, such as land distribution. Labor became a major institutionalized political factor. A formidable civilian party structure emerged.

Mexico also experienced a cultural revolution — one with a strong political flavor. This revolution largely postdated the actual fighting. A defining element was a new nationalism, which helps explain the persisting attachment Mexicans feel to their revolutionary icons even amid today's cynicism about government. If economic and political independence did not go nearly as far as revolutionary pretense might have it, cultural nationalism flourished. Although foreign influences remained strong in education and some related fields, the revolution dissociated itself from the explicitly European orientation of the Díaz regime. The distinctly Mexican alternative that arose based itself largely on the country's indigenous heritage.[18] The Indian emerged in literature not as an exotic savage but as a mature person to be integrated into Mexican life — even sometimes as the source of all that was good in Mexico.[19] Composers Carlos Chávez and Silvestre Revueltas worked with folk themes. Writers Samuel Ramos, Jesús Silva Herzog, Octavio Paz, and Leopoldo Zea explored the essence of Mexican identity. Painters celebrated the culture of the masses rather than the culture of the elites. Murals depicted indigenous and revolutionary themes. Among the famous muralists were Diego Rivera, David Alfaro Siqueiros, José Clemente Orozco, and Rufino Tamayo. For once foreigners would be less the source of inspiration, the pioneers, and the teachers and more the admirers, emulators, and consumers. Popular nationalistic culture also thrived in film. Cultural independence advanced greatly during this period, and the cultural impact persists today. Folk music and dance remain proud features at official government gatherings. Mexico's most renowned museum is the Anthropological Museum in Mexico City, which acknowledges Mexico's Indian heritage. As Carlos Fuentes notes: "Never again can we hide our Indian, mestizo, European faces: they are all ours."[20]

The Evolving Postrevolution

The political-economic consequences of the revolution for the post-1940 system is analyzed in the following chapters. However, a brief chronology here illustrates two themes of this book: the centrality of stability as a goal and the pragmatic flexibility shown by Mexico's political leaders in the pursuit of this goal. Rather than rigidly adhere to "revolutionary principles," the Mexican elite adapted to changing circumstances, alternating between more conservative and more revolutionary styles in order to hold together the broad postrevolutionary coalition. These would be the decades of peak strength and performance for the regime, the period during which Mexico was enshrined as a model of development.

The successor to leftist president Cárdenas, President Manuel Avila Camacho (1940–46), concentrated on softening revolutionary rhetoric, whether directed against the church, against business, or against the United States, to repair the damage done to state relationships with these groups. National unity was a major achievement. Another accomplishment was the creation of a social security system, though Mexico still lags behind the region's leaders in coverage. Next, President Miguel Alemán (1946–52) became the antihero of leftist historical interpretations, the symbolic antithesis to Cárdenas. Alemán favored industrialization, business, and the trickle-down approach to distributing wealth, explicitly pursuing economic growth while hoping that all might eventually benefit from the bigger pie. Agriculture, notably communal agriculture, plunged to extended low-priority status. Nevertheless — and crucial to the Mexican regime's institutionalization and stability — Alemán did not undo all of Cárdenas's reforms or declare them illegitimate.[21]

President Adolfo Ruiz Cortines (1952–58) then proclaimed a "balanced revolution," that is, one balanced between the *alemanista* and *cardenista* approaches. His moderation, integrity, popularity, and relative restraint made him something of a Mexican Eisenhower. Although President Adolfo López Mateos (1958–64) next declared himself a leftist "within the revolution," nearly all administrations since 1940 have really inclined more to the alemanista line. By the mid-1950s the state's role in the economy had diminished, leaving more leeway to the private sector, and still greater emphasis was given to industry over agriculture. López Mateos repressed labor, particularly the rebellious railroad workers, to protect the growth-stability model. President Gustavo Díaz Ordaz's (1964–70) inclination toward the alemanista approach was unquestioned. A tragic example of how the regime could interpret the imperative for stability came when the president perceived a possible challenge to the regime from university students. The ensuing slaughter of hundreds of students during a demonstration in October 1968 would remain an indelible blight on the regime. It was also an early sign that regime control was vulnerable after all.

Although he was probably involved in the 1968 events, President Luis Echeverría (1970–76) tried to restore regime legitimacy. He did not attempt this through significant democratization; though he granted increased freedom, he clamped down on governors, the press, and peasants. Instead, he undertook a loudly leftist and nationalist stance in foreign policy and tried to deviate from alemanista socioeconomic policy. Results were mixed at best. Echeverría raised food and housing subsidies and increased state control over economic activities, including communications, commerce, industry, and foreign investment. He failed dismally in other efforts, such as tax reform. His efforts to fortify the public sector, limit foreign competition, and redistribute wealth ultimately earned the enmity of foreign economic interests and of Mexico's middle and upper classes. The stagnation of Mexico's economy deepened.[22] That a successful reinforcement of the economic model could not be achieved was another warning sign.

Until near the end of his own term, President José López Portillo (1976–82) restored the confidence of those sympathetic to Mexico's basic development model. The country's oil boom helped. The political system seemed restabilized, aided by a mild reform; the economy once again grew at enviable rates; and the middle and upper classes as well as foreign and domestic investors were pleased. Mexico maintained a progressive tone in foreign policy but with moderation of strident rhetoric. During most of López Portillo's administration, political liberty probably flourished more than it had in preceding administrations. Corruption expanded well beyond its usual proportions, however, and the presidency itself was widely implicated. Moreover, government austerity replaced Echeverría's banner of fundamental socioeconomic reform. Wages increased far less than inflation, and the government decided that no further grants of land to peasants were possible. Populist policy yielded to more technocratic policy. But the return to a priority on economic growth over increased socioeconomic equality did not prevent López Portillo's administration from ending in economic crisis. It felt compelled to cut spending, subsidies of basic consumer goods, and public works projects. Then, in a desperate effort to stem capital flight, the government dramatically took over domestic private banks. Mexico was forced to count on foreign interests for a multibillion-dollar rescue package, largely on foreign terms. The return to the tenets of Mexico's vaunted stability-growth model seemed either less complete or less desirable than many had previously thought.

President Miguel de la Madrid (1982–88) tried to restore confidence. In contrast to his two erratic, populist, and even demagogic predecessors, de la Madrid used prudence and pragmatism which went so far that he was criticized as being boring. He launched a "moral renovation" campaign against corruption and allowed expanded political liberties and dissent. However, de la Madrid's major policy focus was economic. He opened the economy to more foreign investment and competition, decreased public subsidies, sold off many unprofitable government enterprises, and dismissed thousands of bureaucrats. The economy initially rebounded, but unemployment, plummeting wages, and austerity took a severe toll on many, while inflation and debt undermined domestic and international business confidence and capital fled Mexico. Social reform slipped off the agenda, elections were tainted, and even stability came into doubt.

In contrast to past patterns, protest from the Left was not met under de la Madrid's successors by progressive reforms. Instead, President Carlos Salinas (1988–94) decided that the only way out was to break through to a new development model based on neoliberal principles: markets, privatization, deregulation, and free trade. His successor, President Ernesto Zedillo (1994–2000), continued this approach. Both presidents effectively abandoned even rhetorical commitment to many cherished "revolutionary" principles, including land reform. Salinas amended the 1917 Constitution to eliminate the state's commitment to land redistribution and communal forms of ownership. Chapter 5 discusses in more detail these radical reforms, which President Vicente Fox (2000–2006) is committed to uphold. Both Salinas and Zedillo coupled radical change in economic policy with pragmatic adaptations. Salinas adopted a social welfare program to win political support and soften the blow of economic restructuring, while Zedillo oversaw or at least accepted political reforms to counter the regime's eroding legitimacy and, more broadly, to preserve political stability with internationalizing economic reform. Yet even the more democratic Zedillo tolerated selective repression to minimize dissent — points of continuity with the period of more stable regime rule. Future chapters examine the mix between continuity and change.

INSTITUTIONALIZATION

Official Mexico maintained that the revolution did not end when stability was established, but a claimed "institutionalized revolution" seems to be an oxymoron. Most observers believe the revolution died around 1940.[23] Institutionalization of the revolution then meant cementing certain changes — and shielding the system from further change. Such institutionalization lies at the heart of the development model that operated so well in Mexico on its own terms for decades and until recently. The common claim that Mexican politics is different or even unique often finds its roots in the institutionalized aftermath of the revolution. Institutionalization is highlighted here with reference to the official party, the military, the church, and the university. Subsequent chapters deal with the contemporary status of the party, labor, business, and other institutions.

The Party

The linchpin of institutionalization was the development of Mexico's official political party. Calles was the principal architect. As Obregón's murder in 1928 continued the pattern of violence around elections, a preoccupied Calles sought a mechanism to resolve successions peacefully.[24] He ably persuaded most regional and labor caciques that a centralization of political power was in their interest. He further proposed that this centralization take place by merging the dozens of regional and cacique-led parties into in a central party that would control the succession process and distribute power among the various cacique factions, on the grounds that everyone would lose if the existing disorder continued. Recent events dramatized Calles's case: Madero, Zapata, Carranza, Villa, and Obregón had all met unnatural deaths.[25] Unlike Colombian and Venezuelan leaders decades later, however, Calles's recipe for replacing violence with elite pacts did not include democracy.

Calles was remarkably successful — either by the persuasiveness of his arguments or the alternative for some rival powerholders to be bought out of politics with lucrative business opportunities. From the nineteenth century on the party "system" had been fragmented, with many weak parties often rising and falling with their leaders. But from fifty-one registered parties in 1929, Mexico was down to four by 1933.[26] And the more Calles and his successors ruled through the party and dispensed favors to it, the stronger that party became. Popular leaders who failed to join soon found themselves powerless as influence and benefits increasingly came through the party. Thus the regime overcame the regional dispersion of political power that had often contributed to instability. The party was a mechanism to centralize political power in Mexico City.

The possibility that the party would serve to perpetuate Calles's own power at the expense of institutionalization ended when Cárdenas, as president, cut Calles loose from the party.[27] Cárdenas then used his own popularity to strengthen the party. He reorganized it from a regional basis, important initially to bring in the local caciques, to a functional basis in order to incorporate the masses. The hero of land distribution organized local peasant leagues into an official agrarian sector. He similarly backed the organization of a giant central labor union. The incorporation of labor in the face of more radical activity and options is generally viewed as crucial to the regime's institutionalization. It would be many decades before the state-labor alliance began to disintegrate.[28] The peasant and working masses whose rising expectations might otherwise have created further revolutionary pressures instead became pillars supporting the political regime.

Given the plight of peasants and workers in recent decades, their incorporation into the official party arguably produced greater gains for political stability than for equality or democracy. By including peasants and workers in the formal political structure, the regime blocked their independent development. Serious attempts to pressure the regime for fundamental socioeconomic reform have often faced damaging opposition from official peasant and worker representatives. The party's non-revolutionary nature was reinforced by the 1942 addition of a "popular sector" composed of diverse groups (e.g., small industrialists, professionals, youth, women's groups), mostly of middle-class background and with little revolutionary heritage or outlook. In 1946 the party, originally the National Revolutionary Party then the Party of the Mexican Revolution, assumed its current poignant name: the Institutional Revolutionary Party, or Partido Revolucionario Institucional (PRI). Right up until its stunning defeat in the 2000 elections, it would be in many ways Latin America's strongest sustained party, but unlike most of the region's major parties, it would be essentially undemocratic, tailored to functioning in a nondemocratic system.

The Military

The rise of a strong political party contributed greatly to the taming of Mexico's military. Cárdenas actually brought the military into the party structure. He reasoned that the military was involved de facto in politics already — why not integrate it into an institution controlled by civilians? The significance of taming the military can be grasped by looking at nineteenth-century Mexico, when it had one of the worst records of military intervention in politics of any Latin American nation.[29] Local armies loyal to caciques were decisive political forces. Military might usually determined who ruled Mexico. The armed forces served as the prime vehicle of social mobility. Soldiers might rise through the ranks, but power-seekers could also realize their dreams by toppling existing governments. Although Benito Juárez and especially Porfirio Díaz had made progress in curbing the military, it remained a decisive element in the first decades of the new century.

Obregón and his successors took matters in hand with a carrot-and-stick approach. They put all generals on the federal payroll, eventually provided social security for soldiers, and allowed ample opportunities for corruption. They purged disloyal generals, shifted others away from their power bases, and contained military expenditures. Although the military's loss of power was not sudden, it was major and definitive. No longer would the military play a dominant and direct role in politics. It was now removed from the formal party structure.[30] Whereas no president prior to Alemán in 1946 had been a civilian, all have been civilians since then. Eight military officers held cabinet positions unrelated to defense between 1929 and 1946; only one has done so since 1946. Officers held fifteen governorships in 1940, but after that the practice nearly ceased. There have been military challenges, such as a general's electoral campaign in 1940, but the ease with which the civilian regime turned them back showed its strength rather than its vulnerability. Even such limited challenges have been less frequent since 1940.

The taming of the military is startling by comparison not only with Mexican history but also with that of almost all of modern Latin America, where it has been common for the military to topple governments and even to rule directly for extended periods. In countries where civilians ostensibly rule, they often must share considerable power with the military. Not in Mexico. The Mexican government has been in the hands of a professional civilian elite, not soldiers in uniform or soldiers newly turned civilian. The historic democratic transition in 2000 did not involve passage of power from generals to civilians but from civilians to civilians. Compared with its regional counterparts, Mexico's military has had much less power to veto or influence civilian policy or to demand big payoffs for nonintervention. Power over the country's internal political and security matters drained early on from the Ministry of War to the civilian Ministry of Gobernación (Government). Mexico has spent much less of its budget on the military than most Latin American countries, and this remains the case despite an increase in the 1990s (after decreases in the 1970s and 1980s).

Mexico's military has functions, but these mostly have served rather than threatened the civilian system. The military has watched for potential threats to the established order. It has been an arm of repression against those who have challenged the regime. It also has engaged in development projects to build Mexico's infrastructure and has helped fight the nation's war against drug trafficking. The military's allegiance to civilian rulers, promoted by heavy socialization, is a source of legitimacy for both groups. The civilian regime has been careful to pay the military leadership off with opportunities for corruption, job opportunities, control over its internal budget, and loud praise for its role in preserving orderly constitutional rule. Civilian groups opposing the political system have found no support within the military; on the contrary, they have faced the military's loyalty to the system. A major challenge for the consolidation of Mexican democracy is that military loyalty to a civilian democracy be as strong as military loyalty was to a civilian system that was not democratic.

If Mexico's military appears unique, it is fundamentally the civilian political system that has been unique. The civilian system has determined the military role. Unlike much of Latin America, conservative interests have been able to count on Mexico's civilian structure to maintain political order and economic privilege. If this structure fails in the future, the military role could well change. In any event a more typical civilian system might mean a more typical military. In fact, the military's role has already grown, as we examine in Chapter 3. For decades, however, Mexico's military has been uniquely institutionalized within the civilian-dominated political structure. The subordination of the military has been an outstanding feature of Mexican exceptionalism.

The Church

The importance of peaceful church-regime relations likewise must be seen against a turbulent historical background. In pre-Columbian and colonial Mexico dominant religious and political institutions were tightly bound, but church influence sometimes was a counterweight to the newly independent government. Church ownership of perhaps one-third of Mexico's land gave it extraordinary resources. Together with other large landholders, the church significantly shaped Mexican politics. Political liberals and many capitalists challenged the church in their quest for a more open economic system and more revenue for government from otherwise untaxed land. The Reform's 1857 Constitution seriously eroded church power.

Revolutionaries launched a fresh attack on church privileges after the church partly recuperated in the porfiriato. The church was therefore tamed before the military. Compared with the separation of church and state in the United States, Mexico would display much more hostility and build a higher, thicker wall. The Mexican system was less concerned with protecting the church from the state than with protecting the state (and the nation) from the church. The 1917 Constitution prohibited property ownership by religious institutions or personnel, forbade church participation in politics, denied voting rights to the clergy, and limited participation in education. After only sporadic enforcement, church-state tensions peaked when Calles launched a virulent antichurch crusade and many Catholics (*cristeros*) engaged in armed rebellion. Calles's crusade was part of his unyielding attempt to centralize political power.[31]

The regime accepted the church only after the regime itself became more secure and the church in turn retreated from political affairs. Cárdenas relaxed the crusade, although his brand of progressivism guaranteed anticlerical politics. His successor displayed no such negative posture toward the church. "I am a believer," Avila Camacho declared. The period in which revolution had preempted Catholicism as Mexico's only sanctioned religion was over. From that time forward, reality would mock harsh constitutional restrictions. The normalization of church-state relations took a further giant step in the 1990s with the lifting of certain constitutional bans (for reasons analyzed in Chapter 4). But from much earlier on, many provisions have been honored in the breach. Seminaries, church-run schools, and religiously inspired universities have flourished, priests have walked about in clerical garb, and government employees have received "spring vacations," which could be called vacations for Holy Week (between Palm Sunday and Easter).[32] As the regime eased its restrictions, the church became more functional. Church activities offer living proof of a degree of political liberty. Also, in Karl Marx's words, religion may be a flower on the chains of repression, deflecting the masses' attention from their material plight. The church has sometimes been a useful counterweight against those pushing for greater equality, though the church itself is now split on that issue.

The church-state accommodation should not imply the absence of tensions, however. Many Catholics have resented the government's antichurch posturing. The government, for its part, has often worked to limit the church's influence. Strong mass allegiance to the church, contrasted to manifest apathy or cynicism about the government, is downright embarrassing. The outpouring of enthusiasm by perhaps twenty million Mexicans for Pope John Paul's 1979 visit was uncomfortably similar to the preference shown by the Poles for the pope over their communist premier; a 1990 papal visit to Mexico attracted some thirty million or more. The regime was also wary of the prominent role reform-minded priests have played in much of Latin America, opposing authoritarian regimes in the 1960s, 1970s, and 1980s in Brazil, Chile, and Central America. The era of inevitable church allegiance to Latin America's conservative forces is over.

Tensions between church and state have not sent Mexico back toward an era of blatant government repression. Instead, even the curbs characterizing the period of stable development have diminished. Moreover, as the church's political voice is reinvigorated, it turns out to be many voices. Even critics of the political status quo have been divided on Left-Right and other dimensions. More sympathetic voices have not necessarily been manipulated or heavily restricted by the government. The national government victories in 2000 of a party whose historical roots are largely religious further reverse the postrevolutionary Mexican exceptionalism of political restrictions on the church.

The University

The university is an institution rather prone to dissent and even disorder. It has a potential democratizing as well as destabilizing effect on national politics. Universities in less developed nations often lead the way in using available room for free expression within authoritarian systems and in initiating protests that contribute to the demise of weak regimes. Mexico's national university had a nineteenth- and twentieth-century history of turmoil rivaling that of the military or the church. It was part and parcel of the country's recurrent political and economic instability. But when the country entered its period of stable development, the university became part and parcel of the new system. It would often engage in democratic dissent, but mostly it would buttress the system.

Until 1867 the university had been a pawn in the liberal-conservative struggles that wracked independent Mexico, especially over church-state issues. It was repeatedly closed and reopened before it was finally shut down in 1867, leaving only individual professional schools in operation. A new national university opened in 1910, dedicated to the porfiriato's goals of progress and order, but was almost immediately ripped apart by the revolution. The university was indicted for challenging the revolutionary regime's authority and serving elite and esoteric ends rather than practical problem solving or serving the masses. After Calles was espe-

cially harsh, as he was against the church,[33] Cárdenas promoted a socialist constitutional reform that challenged pluralist academic freedom, and
he withheld government subsidies until the university joined in the
"social program of the revolution." Many professors resigned. For
regime supporters the issue was socioeconomic equalization; for detractors it was antidemocratic action.

University-government relations remained tense, and the university
remained internally divided. Between 1933 and 1944 not one of its rec-
tors (presidents) lasted more than two years. Nor was the revolutionary
fight restricted to higher education; teachers were assassinated in the
countryside. Yet while both Calles and Cárdenas wanted revolutionary
control, they also wanted order, as their party-building efforts suggest.[34]
The government offered carrots as well as sticks, and the university,
which could not survive without public funds, pledged its loyalty to the
revolution. A new 1944 statute limited student and faculty power, establishing instead a strong rectorship and a U.S.-style governing board. Such
a board, along with its appointed rector, was unlikely to engage in disorder or to challenge the regime.

The university itself became much more stable, and rarely since 1944
has disorder there seriously threatened the regime. When it might have,
in 1968, the government resorted to brutal repression. The situation
varies in the public universities in each state, but rare threats to state governments have not endangered the national political system. On the contrary, the university has generally been functional for that system. It has
provided a steady stream of professionals and the government's own
bureaucrats and highest leaders, as well as technical and political advice;
through the access offered to an increasing portion of the citizenry, it has
built the regime's social and political standing. At the same time the university has offered a semisanctuary for dissent that may have steered
opposition away from more dangerous outlets; it has allowed the government to maintain some beneficial ties with opponents.

To get something, the government has had to give something. Indeed,
it has given a lot. It resumed its subsidies to and greatly reduced its ideological assaults on the university. It has invited faculty, alumni, and
administrators into government positions. Most of all, the government
has allowed the university considerable autonomy, as the university
makes many of its own policies even though these, or their inefficient
implementation, often displease the government. Autonomy has rarely
promoted revolutionary ends. But then the regime no longer pressed for
a revolutionary university once the regime itself was no longer revolu-

tionary. Early in 1946 the regime changed the socialist amendment on education, replacing the doctrine of class struggle with the doctrine of national unity. As with the church, the state-university accommodation would not hold forever in its established form. But also as with the church, the breakdown would not bring a return to historical patterns. Universities would instead become inevitably though unevenly transformed by political-economic trends involving privatization, decentralization, and internationalization.

From Institutionalization to Disintegration?

With its unusually inclusive official party, civilian control over the military, and accommodation with the church and university, the Mexican regime protected itself from threats often faced by other Latin American regimes. The feat is all the more remarkable because all four arenas had earlier represented a threat to the regime.[35] The regime earned fame for transforming a weak political system in which social forces competed to control feeble political institutions into a system subordinating these social forces to strong political institutions. Institutionalization lay at the heart of Mexican exceptionalism. And the genius of institutionalization lay in how the regime attained such extensive control without more blatant and brutal repression. For each of these four institutions, the regime worked out what it could afford to give in return for almost incontestable control over matters it deemed crucial to its success.

What the regime gave was sometimes ample. To all but the church, it provided resources. Thoroughly in contradiction to democratic practice, the official party was given key advantages over opposition parties — money, use of national symbols, and media coverage. The military also enjoyed special access to corrupt money. Like the military but more so, the university benefited from ongoing subsidies and autonomy regarding their internal distribution. In these areas the regime awarded subsidies according to a political calculus that contradicted its own notions of economic rationality: money was used to buy legitimacy and ward off greater opposition even if that meant supporting overexpansion, lax academic norms, and public financing of activities better handled through a mix of public and private funding. Along with the university the church was allowed ample autonomy to run its own affairs; the regime would not control the fundamentals of either religious or higher educational practice.

But through this giving, the regime controlled public policy making.

Some institutions were left out while others were included under its powerful direction. Both approaches limit competitive and democratic participation. This marginalization of others from public policy making
marks a huge achievement for the regime, particularly regarding the military. The regime's control gave it a strong hand to determine the priority
of the five development goals considered in this chapter. It put political
stability above all, or in equal conjunction with economic growth, subordinating both democracy and equality as well as defining national
independence to fit its stability and growth priorities. Most evaluations
of the consequences for Mexican development based on ideals — or on
the revolution's proclaimed goals — are rather harsh. More lenient evaluations result where the criterion is comparison with prior performance.
Where postrevolutionary Mexico has failed to fulfill historical aspirations, it has hardly been unique in Mexican history; where it has had
more success, the historical precedent is limited.

Consider first the two great weaknesses in postrevolutionary Mexico:
democracy and equality. Democratic freedom has rarely been achieved in
Mexico; the principal precedents are the Reform period and the brief
Madero presidency. Also rare has been any sustained effort to decrease
economic inequality. The key symbolic precedent would be the Cárdenas
years or perhaps the early years of revolutionary struggle. Regarding
national independence, neither the war against Spanish colonial rule nor
the Revolution prevented significant dependence on foreign powers.
Finally, the postrevolutionary regime's clearest successes lie in its own top
priorities: political stability and economic growth. Although the porfiriato provides historical precedent, the frequent political turbulence and
poor economic results in Mexican history make the postrevolutionary
regime's achievements look impressive.

But the regime's performance had eroded substantially by the 1980s.
Old institutions suffered considerable disintegration. Because this carries
us into contemporary affairs (and therefore into other chapters), just a few
observations suffice to close this section on institutionalization. First, erosion of governmental control has occurred in the handling of all four
institutions — the party, the church, the university, and the military —
notwithstanding important continuities in each case. Some tenets have
been fundamentally undone, such as proscriptions on the church's direct
involvement in politics. Some have been partly undone, such as proscriptions on the military's role in political affairs. Other tenets and practices
remain but no longer function smoothly to buttress the government's
legitimacy or its ability to set priorities. An example is favoritism for what

has usually been the official party; this has come to clash with demands for democracy, and unresponsiveness endangers stability and growth. Thus the regime had to deal more than before with opposition parties. As old formulas have no longer yielded desired results, they have changed.

Second, in the case of the party, the church, and the university, a key change involves pluralism. Historically, institutionalization established itself between the regime and leading organizations: the official party, the military, the national Catholic Church, and (though to a lesser extent) the national university. These favored organizations had anything from a monopoly to clear preeminence over other organizations in their field. Hierarchy within each of these organizations helped ensure compliance with the regime's rules.[36] Today the institutional context is much more plural and competitive. To control the one party is no longer to control the electoral system or to be almost fully protected from the demands of labor. To subsidize the national university is no longer to subsidize the institution that has a near monopoly on feeding graduates into elite political and economic positions. So the political game becomes less one that revolves around one-to-one relationships and more one that involves true bargaining and competition.

The new game presents certain opportunities for the government. As the church divides into many political factions, government can obtain open support from sympathetic factions or from the burgeoning evangelical movement. When his party squirms for some distance from unpopular policies, the president can gain support from members of another party. In the university realm the rise of private institutions provides a fresh source of disciplined, elite talent often regarded by the government as superior to what its own public university provides. In turn, success of private institutions helps the government to cut back on what it long regarded as economically inefficient subsidies and to pressure a stubbornly autonomous public university. Government officials can also try to turn the disintegration of prior institutionalization into a virtue by seeking credit for a process of pluralist democratization. Entrenched government and party elites who once enjoyed institutionalization that gave them political control are now left to fight for influence on a playing field that is much more level than before.

CONCLUSION

This chapter ends with a schematic summary of how Mexico has historically approached the interrelationships among political stability, democracy, economic growth, inequality, and national independence. The Spanish Crown stressed political stability combined with economic gain for the mother country. It would not grant more than the modicum of democratic liberty it granted to its own citizens in Spain, and it of course opposed independence for the colonies. It delegated the inequality issue to the church, ensuring that it would be approached far more as a spiritual than an economic issue.

The criollos of the early nineteenth century pursued national independence as their prime goal, hoping that independence would subsequently underpin their own political and economic control. As those Indians who joined in the independence struggle soon discovered, the criollos staunchly opposed redistributing economic resources. Nor did the criollo movement help establish a democracy, as did the privileged classes in the United States. Democracy did, however, emerge as a chief preoccupation of many of Mexico's nineteenth-century liberals, whose crowning success came with the Reform and the 1857 Constitution. Democracy was deemed compatible with both political stability and economic growth.

The new order would naturally benefit the masses, it was argued, but opinions differed on how much direct effort should be made on their behalf. The liberals proved their commitment to independence by opposing perpetuation of colonial customs and by fighting to oust French occupation forces. Conservatives were more sympathetic to Mexico's inherited colonial culture and less sympathetic to democracy. Nonetheless, they generally shared the liberals' frustrated concern for political stability and economic growth and were even less likely to raise the banner of economic equality. As the Reform yielded to the porfiriato, it gave way to a ruling creed that displayed unusually clear priorities. Political stability and economic growth were the twin idols. As strong national independence would be incompatible with economic growth, foreign investment was encouraged. And as neither stability nor growth could be rationally guided if the system betrayed itself by pandering to principles of political democracy or economic equality, progress was entrusted to "survival of the fittest," not to the popular will.

The porfiriato's vaunted political stability exploded early in the twentieth century. Madero broke sharply with the positivists' political beliefs, although not as sharply from their economic beliefs. Zapatistas and villistas struggled to decrease inequality and to promote independence while remaining relatively indifferent to Madero's brand of liberal democracy. If much of Mexican history has been about the pursuit of goals not including democracy, Madero's efforts were directed toward

In 1994, Subcommander Marcos launched the zapatista uprising in Chiapas that adroitly evoked the revolutionary struggle for land and liberty led by the legendary Emiliano Zapata during the Revolution.

democracy without sufficient attention to other development imperatives. Carranza's constitutionalists began to point Mexico away from both Madero's emphasis on political democracy and the zapatista and villista emphasis on economic redistribution, moving instead toward firm priorities of stability and growth. Calles intensified these tendencies.

Cárdenas recalled the Mexican Revolution to its goals of national independence and egalitarianism but maintained the emphasis on political stability rather than liberal democracy. In Cárdenas's view greater national independence and more equal distribution of wealth were not just compatible with political stability but were necessary to it. Without them Mexico would be an unstable pawn of outside powers and a time bomb to be detonated from within by its own deprived masses. Alemán's followers, however, saw direct efforts to redistribute wealth as obstacles to economic growth; the two economic pursuits could be compatible only when growth expanded opportunities and the overall size of the economic pie. Alemanistas believed in foreign investment, credit, and trade to achieve growth and therefore stability.

Tellingly, no major and consistent split separated cardenistas and alemanistas regarding political democracy. Liberty could be accepted, even encouraged, but only insofar as it did not endanger political stability or economic growth. As the modern regime (since 1940) inclined decidedly toward the alemanista position, the objective of political stability was for decades consciously tied to the objective of economic growth. As the regime passed from a period of extraordinary success regarding its two primary targets of stability and growth into deepening economic troubles and then political weakness, it sought to modify the development model. Political stability and economic growth remained essential goals but the manner of pursuing them changed. Democratization is increasingly seen as essential though also dangerous to both goals. The porfiriato managed to achieve the twin goals with a closed political system, the modern regime with a much more flexible and adept authoritarian system. Salinas gambled that resurrected and restructured growth could postpone and limit the dangers of democratization. But even before 2000 it became difficult to deny the democratic imperative that growth and stability cannot be achieved without democracy.

Support has also grown, though less so, for the proposition that stability, growth, and democracy require a significant reduction of Mexico's horrendous inequalities. Although the moral imperative of diminished inequality has often been asserted, rarely outside the early revolution and the Cárdenas years has this goal been viewed (rhetoric aside) as pivotal to other goals. This leaves of course great disagreements about how to diminish inequality, particularly about whether the neoliberal approach constitutes a promising new alternative or a devastating step backward. Finally, Mexican policy makers have either lowered national independence as a priority or redefined it to fit new economic and international realities. To be sure, policy makers have long realized that a sovereign Mexico must attract foreign investment and trade — and pay special attention to the vital interests of its northern neighbor. But the degree to which Mexico is pressed to integrate itself economically, politically, and culturally to the values of a range of international forces is unprecedented.

Reflections of indigenous, colonial, liberal, conservative, positivist, and revolutionary pasts all exist today.[37] However, these pasts and the various principles they promote are not equally represented in modern Mexican politics. In general, the historical goals of political stability and economic growth have been the objects of greatest attention and success, trailed by national independence and especially democratization and economic equality. Mexico in the twentieth century moved to an extraordinary period of stability buttressed by institutionalization. The following chapters compare politics and development during that period to the present patterns of Mexican transformation. They examine the legacy of the classic regime, how it has broken down, and what is replacing it.

CHAPTER 3

The Rise of Political Competition

THE EROSION OF MEXICAN EXCEPTIONALISM

As the traditional pillars of governability eroded, Mexican politics became increasingly competitive. New actors joined the political scene, practically all framing their actions as contributions to a desired democratic transition. Even guerrilla movements claimed democracy as a goal and engaged in debates over how to define and construct Mexican democracy. Such appeals to democracy were not entirely new. The Mexican Revolution began partly in the name of democracy. Regular elections, even when they did not determine who would govern, incorporated democracy as a legitimating principle. On the Right, the conservative National Action Party (PAN) has stressed electoral legality since its foundation in 1939. On the Left, many groups have attempted to open up the electoral process and participate symbolically in elections even when Left parties were illegal.

What distinguished the 1990s, then, was not so much a preference for democracy, but a consensus shared even by most regime supporters that Mexico had so far failed to achieve it. Far more actors were willing to put democracy as a priority ahead of efficiency and order, equality and social justice. Perhaps most importantly, optimism about the achievability of democracy grew. As recently as 1987, most Mexicans saw the PRI's defeat as a long-term fantasy; by 2000, it had occurred.

What distinguishes Mexico's democratic transition from other cases is its unusually gradual nature. On the one hand, trends toward a more democratic system date back at least twenty years, if not longer, including the emergence of a more active and participatory society, stronger and more competitive parties, more aggressive demands by state and local governments for resources and autonomy, and an electoral administration that slowly became less dependent on the government. Even the long-submissive Congress started to show signs of life, contributing to debate about how to rein in an undemocratically powerful presidency. These changing relationships provided credible evidence of an impending political transition.

On the other hand, important elements of continuity persist, even after alternation in power. Many of the actors remain the same. Unlike transitions from military rule, the old authoritarian elite are still active in politics. For 71 years, the PRI and its associated unions were fundamental pillars in Mexico's extraordinary record of political stability; today, they face unprecedented challenges in adapting to competitive democracy, but their ability to adapt has always been remarkable. It is not out of the question that the PRI might return to national power in some future election. Similarly, most of the institutions and rules governing Mexico have not changed. Mexicans did not write a new constitution, in contrast to most examples of democratic transition. Instead, adaptation has been gradual. In part, for this reason, many remain dissatisfied with the quality of democracy in Mexico and continue to call for democratic reforms.

Chapter 4 will focus more closely on the quality of Mexican democracy. This chapter examines the rise of competitive politics. It focuses on the actors that first challenged the PRI, the efforts of the PRI (and its allies) to respond, and the reaction of state institutions to competitive pressures. It develops several related themes. First, the rise of competitive politics in one arena has often encouraged the rise of competition in other arenas and by other actors — a sort of "virtuous circle" where advances build on one another and it becomes harder to control the pace and direction of change.

Second, however, democratization also involves trade-offs and contradictions. Not only does the path from authoritarian stability to democratic stability lead through a period of increased instability, but also the rise of competition itself can have negative effects. Competition is neither neutral nor universally beneficial; in fact, it implies the existence of losers as well as winners. Those who feel they will lose in a democratic system may attempt to destabilize democracy. Formerly secure groups may use non-democratic tactics — such as violence — that they did not previously find necessary. And a competitive system that rewards organization for electoral purposes may leave unorganized Mexico even further behind.

Finally, the emergence of normal democratic politics makes Mexico more comparable to other political systems, reversing a long tradition of "Mexican exceptionalism." Again, this has contradictory implications. As politics normalizes, many barriers to democratic development implicit in Mexico's unique party system have disappeared. Yet at the same time, Mexico becomes subject to many of the ills that its political system protected against during the long period of stability and growth. Ultimately, the rise of competitive politics in Mexico demonstrates that there are costs as well as rewards in the struggle for democratic development.

SOCIAL ACTORS AND ORGANIZED GROUPS

Civil Society

Democratization in Mexico owes much to the push from below, from groups organized outside political parties and the state. Modern democratic theory refers collectively to these groups as civil society, meaning "the realm of organized social life that is voluntary, self-generating, (largely) self-supporting, autonomous from the state, and bound by a legal order or set of shared rules."[1] In Mexico, the composition of civil society has been clouded by the traditional incorporation of many special interest organizations, particularly labor and peasants, within the PRI. Through the party, the state had direct or indirect control over these groups, making them less clearly civil — or non-state — than in other countries. For this reason, we discuss the PRI-dominated labor and peasant sectors and the semi-incorporated business sector separately from "civil society."

These distinctions matter because it is relative autonomy from the state that gives civil society the potential to check state power and to provide a source of creativity and information outside of state plans. This explains why many people link a strong and healthy civil society with a strong and healthy democracy.[2] Conversely, the lack of a deeply rooted civil society is associated with authoritarian politics.

In Mexico, as in many developing countries, civil society has traditionally been weak, due in part to the lack of resources for participation as well as cultural attitudes that orient society more inward — toward families — than outward to larger political communities. In addition,

The devastating earthquake of 1985 led many citizens to depend less on the state and more on themselves and grassroots organizations.

those who tried to form independent organizations in Mexico ran into low official tolerance for association outside state control, a topic Chapter 4 explores further. Through its monopoly over public goods and services, the state managed to co-opt and contain most challenges; more intractable foes often found themselves targets of repression.

Since around the mid-1980s, however, civil society has blossomed in Mexico, ranging from human rights activists accusing the police of brutality to neighborhood associations demanding police protection, from middle-class feminists to squatters' associations, from environmentalists to church groups. According to data from the World Values Survey, civil society density in Mexico is higher than in Brazil, Chile, Uruguay, Argentina, and even some European countries (like France, Italy, and Spain).[3]

In part, the growth of civil society reflects social and demographic change. Rural Mexicans face higher costs of organization than urban Mexicans; even transportation and communication are more expensive across rural distances. As Mexico urbanized, barriers to organization diminished. Overall increases in education and income also increased the resources and capacity of Mexicans to participate.

Internationalization of the economy and cultural life encourage these trends and can promote civil society growth. The Catholic Church has played a more progressive role internationally since the 1960s, in promoting social organization and protecting organizers from repression.[4] More generally, many groups receive advice and resources from nongovernmental organizations (NGOs) based outside Mexico; some have become nearly dependent on international funding. Yet this type of dependence leaves them room to challenge the Mexican state. Successful international fundraisers, like the election-monitoring organization Civic Alliance, are among the most politically active groups.

Finally, civil society in Mexico has grown in part as a result of government mistakes. A key example is the response to the devastating earthquake that hit Mexico City in 1985. The ineffective official emergency response system angered citizens; worse still, the slow and corrupt distribution of disaster relief left victims unprotected. In contrast to government incompetence, Mexican civil society rapidly organized to carry out actions — until then, the exclusive domain of public agencies — such as organizing search teams, shelters, and food for the homeless. Later, many of these groups became advocates for victims, demanding state services and loans to rebuild lost homes. Perhaps in part reflecting this positive experience, Mexicans express more confidence in civil society organizations like churches (82 percent) or the environmental movement (54 percent) than in government (37 percent), or parties (25 percent).[5]

In the process of seeking state help, many groups lost their autonomy from the state. Ironically, economic crisis in the 1980s and 1990s helped preserve some groups' independence, by forcing state budget cuts and leaving the PRI without the resources it usually relied on to co-opt challengers. For example, the 1994 peso crash spurred the formation of a debtor's organization called El Barzón. El Barzón initially included small farmers unable to repay production loans after the government raised interest rates to meet international lenders' requirements for a bailout. El Barzón grew to include middle-class debtors and merchants with similar problems, whose credit card debt, business loans, and house payments skyrocketed by as much as 100 percent. Constrained by international commitments, the government could show little flexibility. Thus, Mexico's weak economy both increased levels of popular frustration with the government — the source of motives to organize — and decreased the government's ability to buy them off.

Mexican civil society has played a vital role in pushing for a more democratic political system and accountable government. Internally, some groups have adopted more democratic procedures than traditional unions, including regular assemblies to elect leaders. Smaller associations have often preferred direct participation, but as groups become larger and begin to form networks, participation mechanisms can decay and leaders can become entrenched.[6] Nevertheless, even non-democratic civil society can provide an independent check on government interference.

Some civil society organizations monitor the government directly. The group Civic Alliance first formed to conduct independent poll-watching of the 1994 presidential election and to verify the accuracy of official results. After the election, Civic Alliance began a program ironically titled "Adopt an Official," which watched elected officials to make sure they fulfilled campaign promises. Among other things, the efforts of Civic Alliance pushed the government to make public the salaries of top officials — including the president — and to eliminate the secret slush fund used by previous presidents to handle various kinds of political problems outside of congressional scrutiny.

Civil society also challenges parties to be more responsive to intense special interests. To win the support of popular associations, parties have to deliver benefits and access. Parties may offer space on candidate lists for civil society leaders, for example, or promise to put all major decisions to a vote. There is a trade-off here: access for civil society opens as democracy forces politicians to seek support from a larger base, but parties may become more divided as they try to include more diverse and conflicting interests. This can weaken the ability of parties to compete in elections or to govern effectively.[7]

Yet the relationship of civil society organizations with parties is tense. Such tensions are common in many countries and illustrate some of the trade-offs that democracy implies. The advantages of alliance include the opportunity to place one's leaders in city councils or Congress, gaining access to state resources. But influenced by the negative example of PRI unions, many groups fear that parties will try to control them. Others worry that fights among party factions will infect social movements with crippling divisions. Though electoral alliances have become more common since 1988, many organizations remain deeply divided about the wisdom of participating in elections.

Civil society's attitude toward parties contrasts in some ways with its relatively welcoming attitude toward the *zapatistas*. Although the EZLN is neither part of the state nor a political party, it is not technically a civil organization but a military one (albeit one that poses little military threat). The EZLN has used modern information technology, including a web site on the Internet, to seek support from civil society both inside Mexico and abroad.[8] The EZLN has also held rallies in the remote jun-

Even zapatistas engaged in armed rebellion speak of a democratic imperative, despite the fact that many political actors view their opposition as markedly undemocratic.

gles where it operates, attracting urban intellectuals, feminists, U.S. progressives, indigenous activists, even controversial filmmaker Oliver Stone. Most of its funding comes from external donations. At least twice, civil society protests averted the EZLN's impending military annihilation. The EZLN sponsored the creation of the Zapatista Front for National Liberation, which operates entirely in the civil arena. Organizations in this Front converge mostly around democracy, although they do not all mean the same thing by "democracy," and some of their ideas do not fit usual Western definitions. However, the debate within zapatista forums over what democracy means has influenced national institutional reform and parties as well.

The example of the EZLN also raises the critical point that not all of civil society supports stable democracy. Although the EZLN has contributed to a richer discussion of democracy, it has also taken up arms and disrupted several elections. Right-wing paramilitary groups have reacted to the zapatistas by stepping up their tactics of assassination and threats. Democratization makes room for the growth not only of prodemocracy groups, but also of anti-democracy ones. Every democratic society struggles with the problem of how much freedom to extend to organizations that would deny others' civil rights (like the Ku Klux Klan), or to separatist groups that reject state authority (like Basque groups in Spain). Mexico is not exempt from this problem.

Finally, civil society cannot yet supply alternatives to the traditional state-linked organizations of business, labor, and peasants. Civil society remains thin and uneven compared to advanced industrial democracies; it is especially weak in rural Mexico. Despite its weakness, civil society has helped push traditional organizations out of their political stupor, forcing them to work harder to maintain the loyalty of their members. Business representatives, labor bosses, and peasant organizers have adopted the rhetorical style of civil society. To understand societal actors, it is no longer sufficient to study groups associated with the PRI. But the weight of traditional groups remains substantial.

Labor

The incorporation of labor in the 1930s helped stabilize the Mexican state and consolidate the ruling party. Variations in how labor is organized can influence patterns of conflict or stability, levels of polarization, types of party system, and even prospects for democracy.[9] Where unions develop institutional ties with parties, as in Mexico, the governing coalition tends to stay in the political center and manage potential threats to the system. Where unions do not have such ties, they tend to challenge the state from outside, using strikes and demonstrations that may threaten the economic elite. In Mexico, elites were less tempted to call in the military because civilian institutions already incorporated labor in ways that helped prevent conflict from escalating and gave business some leverage against unions. In this system, known as state corporatism, special interest organizations do not compete openly with other organizations for support. Instead, they receive state subsidies and legal protection against rivals but face significant external limits on their autonomy.[10]

State corporatism in Mexico contributed to distinctly undemocratic outcomes for the political system. In many industrialized economies, labor unions play a critical role as one of the most easily mobilized mass groups. Labor's electoral support is very helpful to parties in democratic systems. But in Mexico, the extent of the PRI's control over unions gave the party public legitimacy and a solid electoral base without needing to bid for their electoral support. Opposition parties in Mexico had little chance to expand into this mass base, so they remained small and weak. Finally, corporatism gave the state leverage to limit labor demands and strikes — a useful aid in promoting economic growth. And growth in turn bolstered the position of the PRI despite its undemocratic record.

At the heart of organized labor in Mexico is the Confederation of Mexican Workers (CTM), created in 1936 and incorporated shortly afterwards into the PRI. Mexico's rulers never gave any union a monopoly over labor. Instead, they used competition among unions to limit any single union's power. Key unions, including the teachers' union and the union of state employees, were put into a separate sector within the PRI — the popular sector — again, in order to divide and conquer.[11] The largest umbrella organization (the Labor Congress) was too loosely organized to challenge the system and was dominated, in any case, by PRI unions. Still, the CTM has dwarfed most rivals in the labor sector since its foundation. It has been at the core of the state-labor deal in post-revolutionary Mexico.

The CTM's bargain with the PRI rested on a combination of "carrots" and "sticks." State controls over unions — the sticks — included provisions giving the state the power to declare strikes legal or illegal. Illegal strikes — the vast majority — were punishable by fines and the use of force if the union did not immediately drop them. Moreover, the state controlled union registration, required to negotiate a collective contract. The state also reserved the right to monitor and certify union elections; it could thus deny legal recognition to any union leader that refused to cooperate.

Yet the PRI regime recognized the simultaneous need to offer labor some incentives — the carrots — to bolster labor support for the regime and enhance its legitimacy. No government can rule entirely by force. Among other things, unions got representation on the board that sets minimum wages (to which most collective contracts in Mexico are pegged); representation on the Board of Conciliation and Arbitration (which hears disputes between labor and capital); the right to organize and strike; the right to a closed shop; generous financial subsidies of unions; and a share of congressional candidacies through the PRI. Unions in other nations have found these benefits both desirable and difficult to win.

However, benefits have been unequally distributed, with most going to the large unions in key sectors that could have caused the state trouble. The least threatening — the unorganized — benefited least. Most Mexican workers do not belong to a union, either because they work in the informal sector or in very small businesses. Estimates suggest that as of 2000, only about 43 percent of non-agricultural salaried workers belonged to unions.[12] About half the economically active population worked in the informal sector.[13] Non-unionized workers get lower wages, no formal representation, and little access to state social programs like subsidized housing and health insurance.

In addition, some benefits actually reinforced authoritarianism within the unions, encouraged widespread corruption, and undermined the incentives of union leaders to defend workers. By using the closed shop privilege, for example, a union leader could "fire" dissident workers by expelling them from the union.[14] As a result, union leaders tended to stay in power for long periods: the no re-election rule in party politics did not affect unions. Over time, long-term leaders became more responsive to the president than to their members, because the state, not workers, determined who could lead unions. The classic case is Fidel Velázquez. A founding leader of the CTM, Velázquez held unquestioned power from the 1950s until his death in 1997. He endorsed all state policies without hesitation, from the pro-labor policies of President Cárdenas to the pro-business policies of President Salinas, despite huge sacrifices for labor.

As long as the Mexican economy grew at an extraordinary rate, labor probably gained more than it lost in material terms. Real minimum wages rose from 1.5 pesos per day in 1938 to a peak of 3.4 pesos per day in 1976.[15] Nevertheless, independent unionism never died. In the 1940s and 1950s, railroad workers carried out memorable strikes. In the 1960s, medical workers staged an important strike. In the 1970s, electrical workers started a dissident, pro-democratic faction that spread to other professionally oriented industrial sectors. In all three decades, teachers and students were often a thorn in the side of the authoritarian state. Teachers held a nearly unique position of respect within local communities (together with priests, who could not legally participate in politics). Although this allowed teachers to play a vital role in the legitimation of the PRI and the state — and most teachers accepted the control of the official union — teachers also have perhaps the longest and most consistent record of mobilization against the state.[16] Dissident teachers shared with other dissident union movements a focus on the corrupt and undemocratic behavior of union leaders.

Thus, the economic crisis that began in 1981 did not initiate challenges to the PRI-labor relationship. But it did undermine one of the key terms in labor-PRI cooperation: the exchange of electoral support and legitimacy for benefits from the state. As state budgets were slashed, social benefits like housing and health care shrank. Many subsidies of basic products like tortillas and cooking oil — a state concession to make working class wages go farther — were cut. The state asked labor leaders to sell these cutbacks to their members.

At the same time, the state asked them to help stabilize inflation by accepting wage freezes. As a result, inflation significantly outpaced wage increases: real minimum wages fell 30 percent in the first three years of crisis and continued to drop throughout the 1980s.[17] While union leaders tried to convince their members that wage and benefit cuts were a good thing, civil society provided contrast, protesting government failures. Perhaps inevitably, the sales job fell short. Workers increasingly resisted when labor leaders called on them to vote for the PRI. And when unions could not deliver support, their electoral value fell further, making it easier to disregard labor in the next round of budget cuts.

The economic crisis coincided with a leadership crisis brought on by the aging and then death of the founding union leaders. The death of Velázquez in 1997 was a sign of this passing of the torch. Velázquez had fought in the Revolution, witnessed early post-Revolutionary instability, and participated in the creation of the PRI. He valued compromise and stability above the aggressive defense of labor rights. Younger labor leaders who do not share this experience have more immediate priorities.

Rising competition, leadership transition, and economic restructuring have produced diverse responses. Not all favored democracy. On the pro-democracy side, the number of independent unions has grown dramatically and democratic movements within official unions have gained strength. Several unions were emboldened by the death of Velázquez to exit the PRI's Labor Congress and form an independent federation, the National Workers' Union (UNT).[18] In 1986, only 67 unions were not affiliated to the PRI-dominated *Congreso del Trabajo* (CT); by 2000, 469 unions were not affiliated to the CT.[19] In December of 2003, another blow: the powerful Federation of State Employees (FSTSE) fell apart amid conflict over the re-election of the federation's PRI leader. As a result of the split, 17 of the FSTSE's 61 unions — including two of its largest affiliates and 80 percent of its membership base — vowed to leave the CT and join the UNT.[20] Like civil society, these unions have entered a new stage of dynamic politics. Where dissident union factions in the past often mobilized alone, today they can receive — and give — support to many other organizations. As elections became more competitive, the PRI has paid an ever higher electoral price for decisions that hurt labor. At the same time, opposition parties made strong if mostly unsuccessful efforts to persuade unions to switch sides. And competition for labor support increased.

Still, most unions have remained formally affiliated to the PRI even as the benefits of PRI affiliation eroded. The CTM alone had as many members in 2000 as all of the autonomous unions combined.[21] In part, the CTM's loyalty reflects the relatively small size of its member unions. These unions cling ever more tightly to the state, hoping that loyalty might give them an edge in the sharpened competition for state resources and assistance. Democratization involves choice. Some rational responses to competition do not reinforce democracy, but rather attempt to preserve islands of authoritarianism against the democratic wave.

The state also kept its historic methods of coercing labor, including legal control over union registry, union elections, and permission to strike, even as the rewards it used to offer disappeared. In some cases, PRI officials used these mechanisms to get rid of union bosses whose unpopularity damaged the PRI or who blocked economic reforms. The Salinas administration was particularly adept in adapting traditional methods to a modernizing discourse. While Salinas framed the firing of corrupt union leaders as a defense of morality, he was every bit as ruthless as his predecessors in limiting union democracy: corrupt leaders were replaced from above with leaders who helped him enforce policies resisted by union members.[22] President Zedillo was less active in managing internal union affairs but did not eliminate state controls. Thus, competition can motivate renewed use of state coercion.

The victory of a non-PRI candidate for the presidency put state-labor relations in a new light. Fox lacked the PRI's ties to unions, but controlled the state resources PRI presidents once used to keep unions loyal. Conversely, the PRI kept its traditional corporatist structure, but lost the capacity to use state resources and authority to back it up. This situation presents unions with a dilemma. Should they stick with the PRI and try to increase their influence within it? Join the growing independent union bloc to pressure the state from outside? Or try their luck with other parties? Without the backing of the state, loyalties, interests, and strategies are not so clear. Since 2000, PRI and non-PRI unions alike have often worked together to oppose Fox initiatives. They have managed, for instance, to block the PAN's efforts to reform labor law in a conservative direction, and have held joint marches to demand a reversal of the trend toward cutting benefits and wages for state employees.

However, unions continue to disagree over the wisdom of eliminating the legal tools long used to bolster PRI-supported union leaders: some leaders would like to change aspects of the law to enhance internal union democracy and autonomy but others feel their positions depend on controlling dissidents or hope for the return of the PRI to power. Still others simply think that at least some of these provisions (like the closed shop) could also help a more independent union sector.

Finally, any strategy chosen by unions must confront the constraints of globalization. Where the PRI regime could once promise to protect jobs and wages, Mexican governments under the neoliberal model face intense pressures to keep wages low and labor quiet in order to attract foreign investment. The incentives of labor leaders have long conflicted with the policy goals of neoliberal presidents, contributing to their increasing willingness to go it alone. This applies to the neoliberal PAN as well and would no doubt apply even to a potential Left/PRD presidency. The fracturing of the state-labor relationship implies increased conflict between labor and the president, between labor and the PRI, and within labor unions.

Labor thus demonstrates many of the themes in our discussion of civil society. On the one hand, the number and volume of voices increases. Old patterns of control are challenged, increasing competition for labor support. Dissident labor finds help in organizations outside the PRI; in turn, independent unions support the struggles of civil society — the virtuous circle. Like civil society, labor became increasingly alienated from the PRI as economic crises affected popular living standards and reduced government tools for co-opting labor. On the other hand, the mixed responses of labor also demonstrate resistance to reform. Nor does rising political competition automatically create access or influence for the historically marginalized, unorganized workers. And while economic crisis and internationalization alienated workers from the PRI, they have also weakened labor in important ways. Entering the global market means dealing with powerful transnational companies who can credibly threaten to move operations elsewhere if labor demands too much. Indeed, ever greater pluralism and competition may backfire. Organized labor will find it hard to replicate its former privileged position as more voices demand attention and no group can credibly claim that its support is sufficient for stability or electoral success.

Peasants

The incorporation of peasant organizations in the PRI also contributed decisively to the stability of the post-revolutionary regime. Along with the distribution of land and other benefits, incorporation eliminated a serious threat to the emerging Mexican state. Later, peasants provided the PRI's most reliable source of votes, compensating for declining support in urban areas.

Yet like labor, peasants have become increasingly independent of the PRI — and not just by peasant initiative. The PRI disengaged from peasants even more than from labor, due in part to the politically disruptive effect of agricultural reforms in the 1990s that seriously threatened the viability of many peasant communities. Peasant reactions likewise span a wider range, from loyal support to armed rebellion. Nevertheless, the problems of peasant organization remain formidable. As a result, political competition in the countryside has grown more unevenly and unpredictably than in urban Mexico.

As Chapter 2 notes, the incorporation of peasants into the ruling party took place under President Cárdenas. In the same way that the CTM became the backbone of the labor sector of the PRI, the National Peasant Confederation (CNC) became the backbone of the peasant sector.[23] As in the case of labor, peasants lost autonomy but gained benefits from close association with the state: positions in Congress, protection and subsidies for the CNC, and government help for agriculture. In order to apply for land through the redistribution program, peasants had to organize a "community" to petition for land rights. Communities were given land rights (in a form of collective property called the *ejido*) and incorporated in the CNC. The state could distribute subsidized inputs (like fertilizer or credit) in the same way, and portray price supports for agricultural products as favors from the PRI — to be paid back with loyal support.

Cárdenas' successors took this structure and turned it into an increasingly exploitative method of controlling rural communities. In fact, the terms deteriorated even more for peasants than for labor. The share of state credit and investment to agriculture declined steadily after the 1940s, shifting to the emerging industrial sector.[24] While minimum price supports to producers were maintained, price controls intended to keep food cheap for the growing urban population limited incentives to increase food production for the open market. Politically, the peasant sector lost resources and positions to other groups within the PRI. Nevertheless, peasants continued to supply the PRI with an electoral "green reserve." Maintaining the PRI's traditional 80–90 percent of the vote in rural areas required increasing coercion as incentives shrank, but as long as political competition remained low — and peasants had few alternatives — the cost in terms of declining legitimacy for PRI peasant organizations seemed tolerable.

In response to official neglect, some efforts were made to organize independent peasant movements. In the 1960s, former president Cárdenas sponsored the Independent Peasant Central (CCI) to stop the deterioration of state support for peasants. The CCI suffered a fate like that of many independent organizations at the time: the government fomented a division within its leadership, bought off one faction, recognized it as the official leadership, and jailed the independent leaders. Within a few years, the new leaders led the CCI into the PRI. This example demonstrates the blend of co-optation and soft repression with which the PRI managed social conflict at its peak.

But in the 1980s, economic crisis undermined the PRI's ability to co-opt peasant opposition, just as in the labor sector. The availability of credit and subsidies — never sufficient to help the majority of farmers — slipped even further. Peasants did have some advantages over labor in the economic crisis. Most notably, the prevalence of subsistence farming (for family consumption) insulated peasants to some extent from inflation and falling real wages. Nevertheless, their ability to produce depended on access to land and credit, and both were in short supply. Moreover, even subsistence farmers need money to buy things they cannot make. Poverty has long been deeper and more pervasive in the countryside than in urban areas, and the crisis made this worse.

Partly as a result, the 1980s brought increasing success to those who sought to organize peasant communities against the PRI. One such effort eventually led to the 1994 zapatista rebellion. Reforms in the 1990s further alienated peasants.[25] In addition to deep cuts in state subsidies, President Salinas introduced market incentives to discourage inefficient agricultural practices and reward productive ones. Trade liberalization (and NAFTA) lowered or eliminated price supports. Only in certain sectors did NAFTA permit more gradual reduction of import protection, delaying liberalization of corn — produced by more than 50 percent of Mexican farmers — for fifteen years, to give farmers time to switch to more productive crops or leave agriculture.

Salinas's most dramatic step changed Article 27 of the Mexican Constitution. One of the most important features of the post-revolutionary settlement, Article 27 committed the state to land reform and prohibited the sale or rental of ejido land. By reforming Article 27, Salinas declared an end to land redistribution. No new petitions could be filed. Limits on the amount of land any owner could hold were lifted. Ejido members gained the right to convert ejido land into individual plots. With private titles, small farmers could qualify for bank loans using their land as collateral; it would no longer be illegal for banks to seize land for default.

Rental contracts became fully enforceable, encouraging large buyers like Del Monte to provide credit in exchange for the crop at a fixed price. Farmers could even sell their land and get out of agriculture altogether. Commercial farmers and some peasants welcomed these reforms, seeing them as a way to stimulate investment and liberate them from paternalistic state interference.

However, the reforms to Article 27 ended any hope for the poorest peasants to gain land rights. These reforms also made it likely that land ownership would become increasingly concentrated in a few hands — as ejidos disbanded, banks confiscated land on defaulted loans, and wealthy landowners bought up the surplus. This was, in part, the goal: enabling productive agricultural producers to farm on a larger scale, at higher levels of efficiency. Expanding the exercise of choice by some in the agricultural sector may limit the choices available to others and increase inequality.

As with labor, peasant responses to these challenges have been mixed. Probably the most common response is individual rather than collective action — for example, migration by individual family members to U.S. or Mexican cities in order to supplement shrinking farm income. It is always hard to organize peasants, due to the high cost of communication and transport in rural areas, the lack of skills and resources, and the urgent demands of survival. Migration further lowers the chances of strong peasant organization, since it is often the most enterprising who migrate — the same types who could be peasant leaders.

Nevertheless, peasant organization is far from impossible. In some cases, organizations were built on the basis of strong communal bonds of trust associated with indigenous identities. In others, organizations originally built by the PRI became radicalized over time as their requests for help fell on increasingly deaf ears. Sometimes this contributed to the emergence of democratic competition and the growth of civil society in the countryside. In a number of cases, for instance, peasants created cooperatives to replace lost government services or banded together to increase their access to credit and inputs.[26] As their dependence on the distribution of rewards through the PRI decreased, peasants had less to lose by abandoning the PRI, and they became more available to opposition parties.

However, peasant activism also increased the risk of radical alternatives whose effects on democracy are far less positive. The zapatista army actually evolved from more moderate organizations that failed to win government assistance.[27] And the zapatistas are not alone: barely two years later, a second guerrilla group (the Popular Revolutionary Army) began operations. Thus, the formation of peasant organizations does not point unambiguously toward stable democracy. Even when they fall short of revolution, such rebellions make elections dangerous. Elections in rural zones are often accompanied by a kind of violence rare in urban areas. Far from the watchful eyes of television cameras and human rights groups, traditional economic elites threatened by competition have reacted by hiring private security forces to intimidate the opposition. In some cases, the growth of drug cartels has fed this volatile mix by flooding rural areas with sophisticated weapons. Democracy cannot take root in a culture of violence and illegality.

Somewhere in between lie the mostly peaceful demonstrations by coalitions of peasant organizations questioning the impact of NAFTA and neoliberal reform. These protests, quite remarkably, have brought together traditionally antagonistic groups. In 2003, the network of organizations known as the Countryside Can Bear No More sponsored some of the biggest peasant protests in Mexico City since the Revolution. The CNC and the PRI-affiliated Permanent Agrarian Council participated along with independent organizations like El Barzón and organizations close to the PRD. Serious divergences regarding tactics, goals, and political loyalties remain. Like the CTM, the CNC has reaffirmed its ties to the PRI even as other organizations move toward independence or affiliation with the PRD. Still, there has been widespread agreement among these diverse organizations on the central notion that the Mexican countryside is in crisis, and that it needs not only emergency state assistance and cancellation of debts but also a renegotiation of NAFTA to allow subsidies and protective tariffs for agriculture.

Our discussion of peasants has noted important parallels to the patterns and trends observable in labor and civil society. Economic crisis and structural reforms play a role in growing alienation from the PRI. Rising political competition encourages independent organization. The PAN victory in 2000 put the PRI-peasant relationship into question, as in the case of unions, but probably also made PRI membership more compatible with defending peasant interests; it is hard to imagine the CNC participating with independent groups in recent protests if the PRI regime had stayed in power

Despite these parallels, peasants face more obstacles to effective participation than either labor or middle-class organizations. Non-commercial farmers in Mexico benefit less from NAFTA over the long run. Labor at least anticipates an increase in jobs. But most peasants are corn producers, and most corn producers are not competitive under free trade. This means that many peasant demands (e.g., land, cheap credit, subsidies, and trade protection) are less compatible with the neoliberal package than labor's demands for economic growth and jobs. Moreover, peasants are less likely to organize, vote, or participate in politics just on practical grounds: they are more isolated, less educated, poorer, and less well informed. Where they do organize, peasant responses have frequently involved violence, in part because of these obstacles. But apathy is more common than organization of any kind.

In part, as a result, democratic competition has developed very slowly and unevenly in the countryside. Even in losing the 2000 election, the PRI continued to control a plurality of the peasant vote. Political parties have less to gain by wooing rural voters than by consolidating their hold on urban Mexico — more numerous and more likely to vote. The difficulty of organizing peasants may stabilize the political system, but leaves peasants with few alternatives, democratic or otherwise, for defending their interests.

Business

Compared to peasant and labor organizations, business organizations have traditionally enjoyed more freedom. They were never brought inside the PRI. Yet business has nonetheless exercised tremendous influence over policy. Relying mostly on informal channels, business leaders have blocked reforms that would adversely affect their interests. They have supported government initiatives believed to benefit business. As in other sectors, an increasingly diverse set of organizations has emerged, including some that oppose pro-business policies like NAFTA, and business has engaged in more openly political behavior. Political competition, in other words, has shown up in business-state relations as well.

Formal business organization dates to roughly the same time as peasant and labor organization. The oldest, founded in 1917, is the Confederation of Chambers of Commerce (CONCANACO). A year later, industrialists created the Confederation of Industrial Chambers (CONCAMIN); a rival group created the National Chamber of Manufacturing Industries (CANACINTRA) in 1941. Later, the state recognized other chambers in strategically important sectors, leaving CANACINTRA mostly to small and medium-sized industries. All of these organizations benefited from corporatist laws that required businesses to register with a state-approved chamber and pay dues.

But unlike labor and peasants, these business organizations never joined the PRI. Nor did business families run the state directly. Indeed, business and political families in Mexico have been remarkably separate in certain respects: educating their children in different schools, marrying into their own class, and pursuing the same kinds of careers as their parents.[28] The familiar U.S. pattern of drifting from business into politics and back again was traditionally uncommon in Mexico. Although politicians often went into business after retiring from politics, businessmen usually did not enter politics.[29] Under the PRI system of advancement through apprenticeship under experienced politicians, outsiders of any type — including business leaders — rarely succeeded in forcing their way into power.

Nevertheless, this formal separation did not mean a lack of cooperation with the state. Cooperation deepened during the peak period of PRI control. Domestic manufacturers benefited from state subsidies of key inputs, tax breaks, loans, and protective tariffs that limited foreign competition. The state also invested heavily in the infrastructure needed to industrialize, such as roads and electric power. Thus, domestic industrialists emerged as Mexico's dominant economic class without having to participate formally in politics and without losing as much organizational autonomy as labor and peasants. To influence government policy, business leaders relied less on organizational connections than on personal influence and economic clout.

Though usually effective, the method of informal pressure did not always work. In the early 1970s, for example, business leaders objected to the inflated budgets of populist President Echeverría. Many sent their money abroad, but they could not reverse the decision of the powerful president. This bitter experience led in 1975 to the creation of a new umbrella organization, the Coordinating Business Council (CCE), to fend off future challenges to free enterprise.[30] Only CANACINTRA, with the closest ties to the government, did not participate. The CCE gave business a more independent voice, and trained new business leaders. Nevertheless, business continued to accept a tacit partnership with the state, preferring political neutrality to activism and usually supporting the PRI.

In the 1980s, business became more independent, anti-PRI, and vocal, like peasants and labor, and for similar reasons — especially dismay at government mishandling of the economic crisis. But the turning point for business came earlier than for labor or peasants. The nationalization of

Mexico's private banks in 1982 by President López Portillo came as a profound shock, perhaps because López Portillo was initially seen as a pro-business president. If López Portillo could take such a radical step, no president could be trusted. While most business, and particularly big business, continued to support the PRI, bank nationalization finally pushed some businessmen to the end of their patience. These men chose to become politically active, mostly by supporting the conservative and pro-business PAN. Partisan competition, they thought, would rein in the PRI.[31] The number of business leaders who participated in and funded PAN campaigns grew substantially throughout the 1980s. After 1982, all but one of the PAN's presidential candidates and a growing number of candidates for mayor and governor have been former businessmen.[32] They often pointed to their business experience as proof that they had the skills to govern successfully. Today, the traditional separation between business and political leaders has been most thoroughly shattered within the ranks of the PAN, though the PRI has also felt compelled to compete for business support by offering a growing number of candidacies to successful regional businessmen.

Rising political competition lowers the costs of business defection, on several levels. In the first place, each successive defection lowers the risk for others, just as the spread of independent unions makes it harder for the state to clamp down on any individual union. In addition, the state's value to business has declined. When the state could securely control political mobilization, it was a valuable ally in holding popular classes (especially labor) in check. As the state-labor alliance deteriorated, the state's ability to guarantee labor peace declined. The move toward free trade also made the state less central to business success. Even when the state-business relationship was coziest, business was often torn between the benefits of a protective state and discomfort with its economic meddling. Under free trade, business profits depend less on state decisions. Entrepreneurs rely on the state mainly for macroeconomic stability and infrastructure, while markets have more influence on who profits and who loses money.

As business became more politically active, it has participated in democratization, in negative and positive ways. Business does not unconditionally support democratization. In many Latin American countries, the willingness of business elites to back military coups has been a significant problem. In Mexico, though military coups have not been a threat, business support for the PRI stabilized authoritarian rule. Democracy encourages governments to cater to popular demands, and those with money pay the bulk of the tax cost of state services. Moreover, workers outnumber business elites in the voting booth and therefore can pose a threat to business interests when votes are allowed to count. As in the United States, the growing cost of political campaigns always gives those with money extra leverage. In one notorious incident in 1994, President Salinas asked a dozen wealthy businessmen to contribute $25 million dollars each to the PRI campaign — and they readily agreed.[33] But as votes become more legitimate, special interests become less legitimate. Indeed, later publicity forced Salinas to return the money — another sign of the effect of newly competitive politics. Thus, the attitudes of business elites toward democracy may be ambivalent.

Nevertheless, business also has much to gain from a stable, consolidated democracy. For one thing, the largest companies and their associations can expect to enjoy the advantages of personal contact with the president, no matter what party he belongs to. For them, democratic stability means a secure political climate for investment.

In addition, business itself contains multiple interests who can take advantage of political opening to express and support multiple points of view. Markets encourage differentiation within the business sector. Conflicts of interest result from differences in size, markets, level of competitiveness, and economic sector. So as politics become more competitive, the voices rising from the business community increase in number and volume. Business leaders offer their views on major legislation, the state of the economy, and political events. Some even oppose neoliberal policies. Like labor and peasants, their political responses have been diverse. Some, like those organized in CANACINTRA, opted for clinging to remaining state privileges and protection. Others support the PAN. Still others (like the National Association of Transformation Industries — ANIT) back the PRD.

By contributing money and leadership to diverse political options, business has helped fund the emergence of democratic competition. As business dependence on the state shrinks, business leaders lose their fear of challenging the state, and the potential for such challenges tends to limit state power. In sum, though business has enjoyed more autonomy and influence than labor or peasants, it demonstrates similar trends toward diversity and independence, contributing to and benefiting from rising competition, but also sometimes attempting to block it and hold on to privileged access to power. The difference, as the next chapter will discuss, is that top business groups wield far more powerful weapons.

ELECTORAL POLITICS

The Emerging Electoral System

Though the rising participation of business, labor, peasants, and civil society organizations alone makes for increasingly competitive politics, participation must also find expression within an electoral system in order to meet the definition of political democracy. By the 2000 presidential election, the PRI faced significant electoral competition in all regions of Mexico, due in part to a reformed electoral system that does a better job of establishing more equal conditions for all parties and providing greater protection against fraud. Without this system, alternation in power might well have been postponed yet again.

In the past, Mexico's electoral system protected the PRI and guaranteed a monotonous succession of electoral victories. With few exceptions (at the municipal level), PRI candidates won every election well into the 1980s. Not until 1989 — sixty years after the foundation of the PRI — did an opposition candidate win an election for governor. Not until 1997 did the PRI win less than a majority of federal congressional seats. And not until 2000 did the PRI lose the presidency. During this period, Mexico could boast an enviable record of unbroken elections with participation by at least two parties, outlasting not only every other Latin American nation, but also France, Germany, Italy, and Japan. Elections could take place so regularly in part because they were so safe and predictable. By permitting opponents a limited voice, the regime lured them into staying inside legal channels, yet by guaranteeing PRI victories, it discouraged the polarizing competition that characterized Mexico during most of its first century of independence.

Regular elections were functional in other ways.[34] In the context of prohibitions against re-election, elections forced constant turnover despite the PRI's monopoly on power. An ambitious politician who lost one round could hope for better luck soon. Elections gave the PRI a way to renew its legitimacy as the heir of the Revolution. In fact, the PRI often cheated to increase its vote even when it won, in order to ratify its status as the party of all Mexicans. At the same time, the PRI was so concerned with maintaining at least a token opposition that it subsidized small parties and sponsored electoral reforms when discouraged opposition leaders threatened to quit. Such reforms were not intended to let opposition parties challenge the PRI, but to keep them in the game by offering incentives for participation and sanctions for non-participation.

Thus, the Mexican electoral system at the peak of PRI power rested on several key principles. First, it imposed restrictions on the number and kind of parties that got legal recognition, based on approval by institutions that the PRI controlled.[35] Second, electoral laws guaranteed overrepresentation of the largest party. This gave the PRI a bigger share of seats in the Congress than its share of the national vote, providing a cushion against electoral erosion. Third, the PRI was given — by law — more financial support and media access. Government subsidies for all parties went into effect in the 1970s, but the total subsidy was divided according to the share of each party in the previous election. If the PRI got 70 percent of the vote, it got 70 percent of government financing. The PRI thus kept its lopsided advantage with state help.

Finally, electoral laws guaranteed PRI control of the institutions that administered elections. This gave the PRI the ability, when needed, to cheat and get away with it. The Federal Election Commission was a division of the Ministry of Government (Gobernación), run by a presidential appointee with a governing board controlled by a majority of PRI-nominated representatives. Electoral results were evaluated not by an independent court, but by self-qualification: candidates who got victory certificates from the Commission voted to decide whether their own election was legal. Naturally, they usually decided that it was.

This system adapted constantly to opposition pressures. In the early 1960s, PAN threats to withdraw from elections led to the creation of minority seats in Congress. In 1977, the government took more significant steps: giving legal registration to the Communist Party and improving competitive conditions for the opposition, such as limited access to mass media.[36] In addition, the 1977 reform created 100 new seats in the Congress, saved for minority parties and allocated in proportion to each party's share of the vote. The 1977 law kept in place the existing system of three hundred winner-take-all districts, in order to give the PRI a secure base of at least 75 percent of seats, but proportional representation seats opened up access for the opposition. Later reforms expanded the areas subject to proportional representation. In 1986, the number of proportional representation seats in the Chamber of Deputies increased to 200.[37] Reforms in the 1990s doubled the size of the Senate, with additional seats allocated according to a complicated but more proportional formula.[38] And in 1996, access to media and government funding of parties was allocated more fairly; federal agencies monitored most media for compliance with equal time rules. [39]

However, perhaps the most critical change involved a gradual loosening of ties between the PRI and the institutions that administer elections. The 1988 presidential election appears in retrospect as a turning point. In 1988, Cuauhtémoc Cárdenas and several other prominent PRI leaders demanded compassion for victims of the economic crisis, changes in neoliberal policy, and more competitive selection of the next PRI presidential candidate.[40] When their demands were rejected, they left the PRI to support the presidential candidacy of Cárdenas. He was unexpectedly successful. Sunk in economic crisis for seven long years, many Mexican voters turned out to vote for the son of Mexico's most popular president. As early returns came in, it became clear that the PRI would lose badly to Cárdenas in the capital. Believing that the solid PRI rural vote would make up for Mexico City, top PRI officials ordered election workers to effect a crash of the computerized counting system to delay announcement of the results. But taking nothing for granted, they also worked feverishly to ensure that their candidate would win — inflating voting counts and burning thousands of ballots. Such evidence gave credence to Cárdenas's claim that he had won the election. Certainly, Salinas won less of the vote than he claimed.

Thus, Salinas took office amid vast skepticism about his right to govern. One of his first priorities was to make elections more credible. He created a new electoral registry, an electoral institute, and a system of electoral courts. Like other PRI reformers, Salinas did not intend to hurt the PRI. Taken one by one, his reforms seemed a small price to pay for credibility. Yet over time, they added up. Ironically, the PRI's need to cheat increased (due to volatile economic performance and a more independent civil society) precisely as reforms made cheating more difficult.

The PRI's grudging acceptance of reform reflected constant pressure from civil society and parties. Moreover, as markets opened, international actors began to pay more attention to Mexican elections. The PRI began to lose its ability to control the pace and content of political opening. The electoral registry was gradually upgraded to include a voter identification card with a picture, signature, and thumbprint, and subjected to outside audits. Electoral courts were given more power. And the Federal Electoral Institute (IFE) was finally made independent of the Ministry of Government as well as parties. Citizen councilors who cannot belong to any party constitute its governing board. These institutions deepened public trust that the vote is fairly counted, and discouraged sore losers from trying to cheat. This was a major achievement in the struggle for democracy.

The Major Political Parties

As confidence in electoral institutions grew, political parties had to adjust to the reality of electoral competition. At one time, it did not matter who parties chose as candidates or whether candidates campaigned at all. The outcome — PRI victory — was a foregone conclusion. Voters were bound by habit, and when needed, as Fidel Velázquez fondly promised, the PRI machine could deliver "110 percent support." No longer. Instead, an increasingly independent electorate votes for whichever party or candidate seems best in a given election. Elections have become increasingly centered on candidates rather than parties. Slick media campaigns overshadow traditional town rallies. Candidates adjust their platforms to attract new voters. In short, the behavior of Mexican parties has begun to demonstrate many features of normalization — both good and bad.

Partido Revolucionario Institucional (PRI)   On the morning after the historic 2000 presidential election, the front page headline said it all: "Adios to the PRI."[41] Many analysts argued gleefully that the PRI, cut off from state funding and discredited, would collapse and disappear.[42] In fact, this was never a convincing scenario. Unlike military governments that lose power, the PRI was already set up to participate in normal democratic politics. It had resources, infrastructure, loyal activists, and a recognizable identity among voters. Only the PRI had sturdy presence in all of Mexico's states. Even after losing the presidency, the PRI continued to control nearly two-thirds of state governments and the majority of municipal governments. It won more seats in the 2000–2003 legislature than any other single party. Its cooperation would be vital for Fox to secure the majorities he needed in order to pass legislation. And finally, the PRI had plenty of warning that its electoral support was fading. Since at least the mid-1980s, the PRI has been trying to reinvent itself to appeal more to voters in a world of increasingly competitive elections.

True, the PRI initially responded by trying to control the pace and direction of change. While agreeing to reforms, the PRI built in safeguards to protect its electoral position. Yet gradual erosion of the PRI's control over the electoral process made cheating more costly. Increasingly, cheaters got caught, and when caught, faced some kind of organized protest. Although resources for co-optation of challengers remained fundamental, the need to maintain a balanced budget drastically limited the size of the pot. Just as the number of demands raised by civil society began to grow dramatically, the state had less to bargain with. Finally, a freer media meant less success in keeping internal government problems from becoming public. Thus, the balance of power shifted. Normal for democratic politics, such patterns are decidedly novel for modern Mexico.

Part of the PRI's problem in adapting to competition is its original design: not to compete for power by seeking electoral support, but to distribute it among a circle of elites. Efforts to open the PRI up to new bases of support have sharpened internal conflict. For example, in the PRI, unions and peasant organizations were traditionally responsible for mobilizing voters at the polls and at campaign rallies. Rallies were not intended to win over uncommitted voters but to symbolically demonstrate PRI unity. Participants typically were coerced or bribed to attend. How could the PRI mobilize new voters when its traditional base began to erode? And what would this mean for the influence of union and peasant leaders? Modernizers argued that the PRI needed to develop district-based organizations to reach unorganized voters, especially in cities, and to rely more on modern media campaigns to communicate with voters. Union and peasant leaders resisted these shifts and argued in favor of strengthening popular organization to win back support.[43]

Still trickier is the question of how to select appealing candidates. One approach was to require that future presidential candidates have electoral experience; this 1996 rule resulted in a rush by technocrats to run for a safe congressional seat — and thus increased conflict between technocrats and traditional politicians fighting over candidacies.[44] Another approach involved adopting democratic conventions or primaries in order to select candidates with popular support. Such reforms broke the PRI tradition of selection from above, designed to limit conflict among the elite. The Mexican president historically acted as *de facto* head of the party, with the ability to appoint and fire the PRI's leadership and to nominate or veto candidates for office.

Whether or not democratic methods select better candidates, they surely increase conflict within the PRI. Primary campaigns involve public confrontations between party members, bringing conflicts out into the open and sometimes — as negative campaigning spreads — making them worse. Some disappointed candidates leave the PRI. Particularly for the PRD, these sore losers have provided a rich supply of candidates. Debates over primaries thus questioned the political risks. Do primaries improve the PRI's image and select better candidates or do they divide and weaken the party?

Nevertheless, pressures for democratic opening within the PRI grew as other parties moved toward such methods and denounced the PRI for failing to do so. During his 1994 campaign, Zedillo promised that he would not interfere in the selection of his successor — a promise he largely kept. The PRI's presidential candidate in 2000 was elected in a broad national primary. Although other internal candidates accused the president of favoring the winning candidate, the fact that the candidate had to endure an open competition marked a historic departure from the secretive selections of the past and enhanced the legitimacy of his candidacy. On the negative side, sly jibes at his credentials by fellow party members brought some of the PRI's dirty laundry into the open; opposition leaders capitalized on this. And the result of the national election demonstrated that PRI primaries do not guarantee the selection of successful candidates.

The PRI also worked to improve its image as a party responsive to voter concerns. Here too, there have been problems. Historically, the PRI often used material incentives — a bridge, an electrification project — to bolster electoral appeals. In the 1980s, state resources decreased just as declining party loyalties made it more necessary to use material incentives. After the PRI's close call in 1988, President Salinas tried to respond by reviving the old exchange of services for support. One of his first acts as president created the National Solidarity Program to take over most social spending, with distribution of benefits concentrated around election time.[45] Solidarity was accompanied by a massive publicity campaign. However, the PRI took heat from critics who charged that no party should use tax money to fund electoral appeals. The PRI's traditional style had become a burden as well as a blessing. Citizens accustomed to payoffs no longer got as many, creating a sense of disappointed expectations that reflected badly on the PRI. Narrowly targeted social programs encouraged views of the PRI's social spending as discretionary and probably unfair. And when the PRI did spend money, it was accused of buying votes.

Yet retooling the party to focus more on ideological appeals carried its own risks. The PRI was such a large party — including virtually the entire political elite — that it included a much wider range of ideological perspectives than most democratic parties. Focusing its ideological program meant alienating some of these groups, provoking internal discontent and even splits (like the 1988 Cárdenas campaign). With more competitive parties, the losers in ideological debates can seek opportunities in other parties where once they would have had to fume in silence.

Losing the presidency in some ways helped the PRI construct a new ideological identity that is potentially appealing to voters. Association with the state made the PRI publicly responsible for decisions over which party members had little control. Successive presidents expected the PRI to support unpopular legislation in Congress. Post-electoral analyses by PRI leaders blamed the party's defeat on President Zedillo's use of the party to approve unpopular policies. More generally, popular PRI themes like land reform, support for labor, and nationalism have been difficult to use electorally while PRI governments remained committed to neoliberal reform. The PRI's loss in 2000 freed it to re-focus popular attention on these themes. Its new slogan — the PRI is on your side — captures this intention.

As in the case of unions, not all *priistas* (PRI members) have responded to rising uncertainty in democratic ways. Some factions have turned to intimidation of opponents, violating the most basic expectations of democratic competition. Hundreds of local PRD activists were murdered between 1989 and 2000. Occasional episodes of electoral fraud persist, particularly in remote areas. In 2004, a PRI mayor shot and killed the PRD challenger for his office, who had promised to hold an audit of municipal finances. This is another example of a trade-off created by the rise of competition. Local PRI politicians paid the price for the national prestige gained by a law-abiding PRI. So local priistas often defied national party commands that they accept losses.

Moreover, the post-2000 PRI remains dominated by the old, win-at-all-cost culture. The president of the party after its 2000 defeat, Roberto Madrazo, had earlier faced a three-year insurrection within his home state of Tabasco over his violation of campaign spending limits in the governor's race as well as charges of electoral fraud and intimidation of voters. Madrazo stuck it out as governor, defying presidential orders to resign. The party's General Secretary, Elba Esther Gordillo, was the head of the powerful State Teacher's Union and a protégé of its corrupt former leader Carlos Jonguitud. The heads of the CTM, CNC, and other PRI unions remained in party leadership. Manuel Bartlett, who ran the Government Ministry during the fraudulent 1988 election, became a senator and a member of the committee on state reform. These leaders — with few if any democratic credentials — have been winning back some control of the party from the Salinas-era technocrats who once plotted to eliminate the union and peasant sectors. Unlike the technocrats, they know how to organize and they have the connections at the local level to win internal elections.

A return to the fusion of state and party probably cannot now occur, whatever Bartlett or Madrazo might like. Yet questions remain about what direction the PRI will take to remain competitive. Conservatives continue to stress the themes of order, economic nationalism, and contained political competition, associated with that past. Modernizers would like to see the PRI develop into a left-of-center social democratic party (like the Labour Party in Britain) more appealing to a professional, middle-class electorate, but without renouncing the PRI's historical identity. In any event, the PRI remains a formidable competitor. Voters know more about it than about any other party, and though much of it is not appealing, some of it is, like the PRI's record of stability with growth. The PRI has won 50 percent of the governors' races and 57 percent of the mayoral races held since its 2000 defeat. While a far cry from the dominance the PRI once had, it is only a little less than the 68 percent of mayoral races the PRI won from 1994–2000. And in the first major national test since 2000, the 2003 federal congressional elections, the PRI outpolled the PAN, ending up with 223 legislative seats to the PAN's 150. The PRI is down, but not out.

Partido Acción Nacional (PAN).   The PAN's adjustment to political competition has been almost as traumatic as the PRI's. However, where the PRI has struggled to cope with a shrinking base, the PAN has confronted a different problem: how to cope with success. Internally, the PAN has had to absorb a rapidly expanding membership; externally, its leaders have been diverted from political organization into government administration, leaving the party adrift. Perhaps most importantly, the PAN has its first presidential record to defend. Widespread dissatisfaction with this record has translated into weakening electoral support for the PAN.

Until the late 1970s, the PAN functioned within the Mexican political system as a small group of vocal critics. It was founded in 1939 by middle-class lawyers and businessmen with links to Catholic Action. They represented the reaction against populist strands in the post-revolutionary regime, particularly the mass-oriented reforms of President Cárdenas and the concentration of power in the state.[46] At its creation, the PAN assumed a primarily educational role. It did not expect to win elections, but used them as a forum to call for limits on presidential power, formal political democracy, and the rule of law. Socially, the PAN attacked secular reforms that tended to reduce the power of the Catholic Church, including limitations on parochial schools and the political rights of priests, and supported conservative family values. In the economic realm, the PAN opposed key elements of the post-revolutionary development model. The PAN defended private property, free trade, and a smaller role for the state in economic activity. It criticized land redistribution and state preferences for ejidos. The PAN would later argue with some justification that PRI neoliberal reforms stole the PAN's platform.

Yet despite its importance as a critical opposition, the PAN did not initially pose an electoral threat. Attractive mostly to a small sector of the middle class and business, it developed strength only in big cities and the wealthier northern states. It got more votes than other opposition parties because other parties were so weak, not because it had a solid mass base. Before 1979, the PAN won only a handful of congressional seats and scattered municipal victories.

In the 1980s, the PAN began to reverse both its historic marginality and its confrontational relationship with the PRI. These trends were connected to broader changes in Mexico, such as the leap into politics by disgruntled businessmen. As Mexicans became disconnected from the PRI, they were available to opposition parties, strengthening their electoral position. Moreover, the PAN and the PRI began to cooperate legislatively as the PRI moved decisively toward the free-market principles historically defended by the PAN. Cooperation became especially significant after the PRI lost its two-thirds majority in Congress in 1988; after 1997, the PRI lacked even a legislative majority. Ideological convergence also made it easier for the PRI to accept PAN victories in local elections, further strengthening PAN electoral growth. This tendency was encouraged by the Left's electoral rise after 1988, which both PRI and PAN viewed with alarm.

Yet ideological convergence carries costs as well. In the first place, its cozy relationship with the PRI sometimes hurt the PAN's public prestige. In the second place, the PAN had to distinguish itself electorally from a PRI that increasingly shared its traditional economic platform. This is one of the challenges produced by rising competition. If a strategy or theme works, other parties imitate it. Campaigning on social issues like support for the Church helps among conservatives, but the PAN has been burned by its association with moralistic policies to regulate the length of miniskirts or the exposure of women in advertising.[47] Campaigning on the issue of political reform got harder when the PRD began to claim that *it* better defended the goal of democratic transition. Another of the PAN's strongest planks — effective and honest administration — has not always been borne out by the performance of its mayors; as democratization brings non-PRI rule, it also brings records voters can judge. Thus, ideological adaptation has been a problem. In 2000, the primary strategy of the successful Fox campaign was to downplay ideology and concentrate on portraying Fox as the candidate capable of beating the PRI. In the end, 66 percent of those who voted for change cast their ballots for Vicente Fox. But it was not clear what change meant to them — other than *not* PRI.

As in the PRI, attempts to shift the PAN's ideological position to appeal to voters have contributed to internal conflict. So has the PAN's explosive membership growth. There is a circular relationship here between electoral success, membership growth, and internal conflict. The entry of charismatic leaders in the early 1980s contributed to electoral success — and electoral success inspired membership growth. But many new entrants lacked a clear understanding of PAN ideology. Some were motivated almost exclusively by the desire for power. As a non-electoral party, the PAN could afford the luxury of screening members for loyalty and ideological purity, but to win elections, better candidates had to beat pure but boring ones in internal battles. Thus, as the internal diversity of the party increased, so did its conflicts. This may be another sign of democratic normalization.[48]

Another challenge for the PAN in adapting to competition has been the development of a more effective party organization. A loose and unprofessional party structure worked well for a small party that did not expect to win elections, but was inadequate to organize electoral campaigns in hundreds of competitive districts. The PAN has had to build a permanent and professional infrastructure outside its historical strongholds. And it has had to shift from the mostly symbolic and educational campaigns of the past to increasingly sophisticated and complex media strategies.

The PAN's evolution illustrates two other themes of this chapter. First, rising competition in one arena leads to rising competition in others. Much as the PAN might like to, it cannot take full credit for its success. The PAN's rise has been fueled by the growth of competition on the Left and in civil society. The PAN has in turn contributed significantly to political opportunities for other actors. Its continued pressure for democratic reforms — albeit slower and more piecemeal than the Left would have liked — did play a key role in democratization. Its conservative ideology also eased the transition by reassuring elites that the first non-PRI government in seventy-some years would not dramatically change the course of the nation.

Second, democratization has imposed trade-offs on the PAN. Its willingness to accept some trade-offs — for example, to cooperate with the

PRI in matters ranging from electoral reform to economic policy — stabilized the transition considerably at the cost of some public prestige. More critically, the PAN's historic assumption of the presidency confronted the party with unprecedented challenges. By 2004, barely half of Mexicans approved of Fox's performance as president. His finest quality, according to 31 percent, was that he meant well. His problems, however, were serious: he "doesn't know how to govern" (40 percent), and he "doesn't keep his promises" (26 percent). Asked whether the PAN deserved another chance to govern the country, only 45 percent said yes — shockingly, less than the 47 percent who said the PRI did.[49] In 2003, the PAN as a party paid the price: it lost 58 seats in the Congress, nearly 30 percent of its legislative bench. The right to judge the PAN on its performance is a critical sign of democratic normalization. But some of the moral authority of the PAN has been lost forever.

Partido de la Revolución Democrática (PRD).   The main beneficiaries of the PAN's decline were the PRI, which picked up 14 seats, and the PRD, which picked up 45.[50] Mexico's youngest significant party, the PRD got registry only in 1989. The PRD's birth thus coincides roughly with the period of increased political competition; indeed, it contributed substantially to that trend. However, the PRD has struggled more than the PAN or the PRI with the challenges of competition. Where both the PAN and the PRI formed during non-competitive periods and adjusted gradually to rising competition, the evolution of the PRD was influenced by the threat of competitive elimination. The PRD also bore the brunt of PRI efforts to intimidate the opposition from 1988–1994.

Partly as a result, the PRD has a less developed ideological identity, a less stable social base, and more internal divisions. Only in 1997, nearly ten years after its emergence, did the PRD begin to approach the level of popular support of 1988 — and it proved short-lived, as the party lost nearly 40 percent of its 1997 voters in 2000. The PRD is on many levels a paradox: Mexico's first strong leftist party, which arose precisely as leftist and communist parties were declining around the world; Mexico's most openly democratic party, which was primarily constructed around the personality of a single leader; and Mexico's newest party, which gained strength largely by evoking the symbols, ideologies, and leaders of the past.

In contrast to the PAN, which began as an ideologically focused group of elites with few electoral expectations, the PRD began as a large and ideologically incoherent mass movement loosely tied to the electoral hopes of Cárdenas. Prior to 1987, the Mexican Left consisted of several small parties, with less than six percent of the total vote. The main Left party was the Mexican Socialist Party (PMS), the result of a series of mergers that included remnants of the Communist Party as well as other leftist groups. However, constant mergers and lack of a popular leader handicapped the Left in its search for electoral support.[51] Cárdenas offered a solution.[52] The Cárdenas campaign ignited the imagination of millions angry over the extended economic crisis and the PRI's authoritarian rule. For decades the PRI had largely neutralized leftist parties with a mix of nationalist-revolutionary claims and a crafty parceling out of material benefits. Its turn to the right in economic policy and its apparent indifference to widespread economic hardship created space for Cárdenas's appeal to nationalism and social justice. After the election, he called for a new political party to replace his loosely organized electoral coalition. The result was an enormously diverse party, with former communists, socialists, Trotskyists, priistas, Maoists, and social movement activists, many of them former rivals, who suddenly had to get along.

From this different starting point, the PRD shows similar effects of competitive pressure: ideological modification, organizational restructuring, and efforts to select more popular candidates. Perhaps because of its origins in calls for democratic reform within the PRI, the PRD's methods of candidate selection were determined more by ideological preferences for democracy than strategic calculations of what procedures would result in the most competitive candidates. More than any other Mexican party, the PRD has experimented with open internal elections for both candidates and party leaders. At the same time, it has implemented a series of internal quotas (for women, in particular), in order to ensure representativeness across candidate lists. Internal democracy gave the PRD an electoral identity and popular credibility, but has also imposed serious costs. The expense of holding internal elections eventually forced the party to hold fewer primaries and more conventions. More damning have been the repeated scandals caused by poorly organized elections and charges of fraud by competing PRD members. Too often, it seemed, the PRD recommended but could not practice democracy.

The PRD's ideological development has been remarkably slow. One of the reasons is unfortunate timing. The PRD emerged exactly as leftist parties around the world struggled to adapt ideologically to the fall of communism and the rise of globalization. Even established parties had trouble adjusting. The PRD, in addition, had no loyal voter base and no brand name recognition to call on. So it fell back on Cárdenas as a symbol of unity. Only Cárdenas stood above the bubbling stew of factions within the party. Only Cárdenas had proven his electoral appeal.[53] Without Cárdenas, the PRD might never have existed, or might have quickly fallen victim to external and internal pressures. However, the cost of relying on Cárdenas in this way was delayed institutional development and slow adaptation to the changing competitive environment. From its emergence until the 2000 election, the PRD's electoral fortunes rose and fell with the fortunes of its principal and perennial candidate.

Ironically, after 2000 the PRD next pinned its electoral future to yet another personalistic leader: Andrés Manuel López Obrador, the mayor of Mexico City. López Obrador has built support by a series of splashy public works initiatives (like the beautification of the historic district and the construction of a double-decker freeway) as well as by welfare programs like the pension for the elderly, which gives all older adults a small monthly income. López Obrador's aura has been tarnished by corruption scandals involving high officials in his administration and by tussles with the federal government over an alleged failure to obey a court order. As of May 2005, it remained unclear whether these charges — aggressively promoted by his political rivals in the PAN and the PRI — would eliminate him from the 2006 presidential race.[54] Yet regardless of López Obrador's personal fate, internal organizational disarray could encourage the party to once more fall back on the solution of a charismatic individual such as Cuauhtémoc Cárdenas, or his son Lázaro, elected governor of Michoacán in 2002.

As in the case of the PAN, the PRD's story demonstrates the reinforcing effects of rising competition. Electoral reform in 1996 depended on the strong position of the PAN in the Congress. In addition, as PAN candidates posed a more serious threat, PRD candidates became more acceptable to the PRI. The PRD has learned from and imitated the PAN's sophisticated media campaigns, supplementing its traditional grassroots campaigns.[55] On the other hand, democratization has imposed trade-offs. Internal elections in the PRD may help public legitimacy but also exacerbate internal divisions, increase ideological incoherence, and present opportunities for public scandal.

More than any other Mexican party, the PRD has been shaped by political competition. Adjustment problems continue to plague the party. Nevertheless, the PRD has survived longer than first expected and contributes to ideological choice, offering a modest alternative to the neo-liberal program. The complex strategic environment of the post-1997 Mexican Congresses, in which no party holds a majority of seats, offers new opportunities for influence to minority party benches. Such strategic incentives are more characteristic of party systems in democratic nations than of Mexico's one-party past, and thus are another indication of normalization.

Voting and the Party System

Normalization is reflected in the electorate in two specific ways. First, choice has become a normal part of elections in virtually every part of the country, affecting the PRI's traditional rural base as well as the modern sectors in Mexico's internationalizing economy. By 1997, the PRI got a 40 percent margin of victory in just 1 percent of electoral districts, compared to 89 percent of districts in 1967, and 70 percent after the 1977 electoral reform. Small parties declined in importance and the two major alternatives to the PRI gained strength. The PRI, PAN, and PRD controlled 97 percent of seats in the 1997–2000 Congress, 93 percent of the 2000–2003 Congress, and 94 percent of the 2003–2006 Congress. The existence of a viable right, center, and left brings the Mexican party system toward the common pattern of right-left divisions in many democracies.

A second point of convergence with advanced industrial democracies is the general decline in party identification. Where voters once identified almost exclusively with the ruling party, less than half of all Mexicans identified with any party at all by 2000.[56] The large number of uncommitted voters contributes to electoral volatility. The positive side of volatility is that it enhances responsiveness. Parties out of power will try to anticipate voter concerns in order to win over the uncommitted and parties in power will work harder to leave a good impression. All electoral campaigns will require more effort and more appealing candidates than in the past. The negative side of increased volatility is that it may lead to personality-based politics, and undermine party discipline.[57]

Yet differences with established democracies remain. Although the diminishing incidence of electoral fraud has made it possible for analysts to examine voting behavior in Mexico using techniques like statistical models and public opinion polls, a stable socioeconomic basis for the vote (using factors like education or gender to explain party choice) has yet to emerge across elections.[58] To the extent that patterns exist, PAN voters tend to be urban, young, educated, and well-to-do; PRI voters mostly rural and less educated. The vote of the Left has varied more, sometimes picking up the rural tone of the PRI vote, but also doing well

TABLE I. ELECTORAL SUPPORT AND
LEGISLATIVE REPRESENTATION, 1979–2003

	Percentage of Congressional Vote[a]				Percentage of Congressional Seats			
	PRI	PAN	Left[b]	Other	PRI	PAN	Left[b]	Other
1979	74.0	11.5	5.3[c]	9.1	74.0	10.8	4.5	10.8
1982	69.3	17.5	5.9[d]	7.3	74.5	12.8	4.3	8.3
1985	68.1	16.3	6.3[e]	9.2	72.3	10.3	6.0	11.5
1988	51.1	18.0	29.6[f]	1.3	52.0	20.2	27.8[f]	—
1991	61.5	17.7	8.9[g]	12.0	64.0	17.8	8.2	10.0
1994	50.3	25.8	16.7[h]	7.2	60.0	23.8	14.2	2.0
1997	39.1	26.6	25.7	8.5	47.8	24.2	25.0	3.0
2000	38.0	39.4[i]	19.2[j]	3.3	41.6	41.0	10.8	6.6
2003	36.8[k]	30.7	17.6[l]	11.4	44.6	30.0	19.4	6.0

SOURCES: Instituto Federal Electoral, 1991a; 1991b; 1994; 1997; 2000; Gómez Tagle, 1990; Cuellar and Martínez, 1994; www.ife.org.mx; www.cddhcu.gob.mx.

a. For comparability, congressional vote is used for all years, including presidential election years (1982, 1988, 1994, 2000). Figures reflect percentage of valid vote and may not add up to 100 percent because of rounding and omission of votes for nonregistered candidates.

b. "Left" refers to the independent left, not the "parastatal" parties allied to the PRI.

c. Vote of the Mexican Communist Party (PCM).

d. Votes of the Unified Mexican Socialist Party (PSUM), the Trotskyist Revolutionary Workers Party (1.3 percent), and the Social Democratic Party (0.2 percent).

e. Votes of the PSUM (3.4 percent), Revolutionary Workers Party (1.3 percent), and Mexican Workers Party (1.6 percent).

f. Votes/seats of the Cárdenas coalition plus the Revolutionary Workers Party (0.6 percent). Only the Mexican Socialist Party (4.5 percent) participated in the PRD.

g. Votes of the PRD (8.3 percent) plus the Revolutionary Workers Party (0.6 percent).

h. Vote of the PRD.

i. Votes/seats of the Alianza por el Cambio, including the PAN and the Green Ecological Party (PVEM)

j. Votes/seats of the Alianza por México, including the PRD, Worker's Party (PT), Social Alliance Party (PAS), Nationalistic Society, Convergence for Democracy.

k. The PRI vote (13.7 percent) came in districts where the PRI competed in coalition with the Green Ecological Party.

l. Vote of the PRD.

in urban areas like Mexico City.[59] Evaluations of government performance explain some voting behavior, but voters protesting poor PRI management have switched from the Right (PAN) to the Left (PRD) of the ideological spectrum and back again with little apparent concern for ideological differences.

Moreover, the weight of the past is evident. Most parties continue to be strongest in the same regions where they developed historically.[60] With the exception of central Mexico (around Mexico City), most Mexican regions have two-party competition pitting the PRI against the PAN or the PRI against the PRD. Where the PAN has historical support, the

PRD remains weak and vice versa, a pattern that enhances the PRI's prospects at the presidential level. By doing reasonably well in all areas of Mexico, the PRI might well pull out a plurality victory overall even when it loses to the PAN in some regions and to the PRD in others. Three-party systems often lead to the election of executives with less than a majority of the vote. In addition, the PRI's historical position in the ideological center has long split the anti-PRI vote on opposite sides of the political spectrum.[61] Indeed, the PRI's recovery in 2003 to become the largest legislative bench once more suggests that something of the sort might happen, provided that the PRI does not choose a presidential candidate who reminds voters of what they disliked about the old PRI: its lack of democracy, its corrupt tendencies, and its refusal to follow the rules. The question, in other words, is whether the PRI can overcome its internal tendencies to reward old-line PRI militants in order to select a fresher face more capable of appealing to today's voters.

This discussion suggests that tendencies toward normalization and Mexican exceptionalism are most likely to clash in presidential campaigns. In congressional elections, individual candidates are less important than party reputations, largely due to the significance of proportional representation, party list seats. In presidential campaigns, the weight of the uncommitted vote determines electoral victory or defeat, and the qualities of individual candidates matter more. Thus, in presidential elections the importance of candidates and modern media campaigns — signs of normalization — collide with the historical inheritance of party structures and the relevance of regional political traditions. Presidential election outcomes are hard to predict. This uncertainty, however, is perhaps a fundamental sign of democratization in Mexican politics.

STATE INSTITUTIONS

These changing patterns of competition have immediate implications for governance in Mexico. To what extent has electoral competition strengthened systems of democratic accountability within the Mexican state by empowering historically mute actors like the Congress, and to what extent does it encourage actors like the military to take undemocratic action against the increasingly chaotic clamor of voices from below? We contend that the growth in competition has had more positive effects than negative ones on state accountability, but that competition nevertheless falls far short of guaranteeing the development of predictable systems of rules — rule of law — on which stable democracies ultimately depend.

Developing Checks and Balances

One of the key changes in the governmental process is the development of effective checks and balances among the different branches of government. The Mexican Constitution has long imitated the U.S. model in its basic structure: federal, republican, with a bicameral Congress and a president. However, any resemblance remained mostly on the surface. As in much of Latin America, the legislative branch in Mexico has had little power. The Mexican Constitution assigns to the president broad patronage powers with little congressional oversight. The president can propose laws and use a line item veto (allowing him to return part of a law to the Congress).[62] Some of these provisions go beyond what the U.S. constitution — designed to prevent presidential authority from overwhelming the other branches — would allow.

Yet the Mexican legislature's conversion into a presidential puppet resulted less from constitutional prerogatives than from the informal characteristics of the party system. Balancing the Constitution's grants to presidents have been other provisions that limit his power.[63] Rather, it was the president's status as *de facto* head of the PRI — with veto power over candidate selection — that most ensured the submissiveness of PRI legislators. Since the PRI in turn controlled the Congress, Congress rubber-stamped presidential initiatives with minimal debate. Its opinion mattered so little that interest groups in Mexico rarely bothered to lobby congressmen, preferring to establish direct contact with federal agencies, or, if possible, the president. In part for these reasons, the PRI avoided introducing primaries at the congressional level, even as its presidential candidate endured a primary.[64]

The first step toward a more vigorous Congress thus began with a growing opposition presence in that body. The control exercised by PRI presidents over their own legislators became a less secure means of controlling the Congress as the PRI's hold on Congress diminished. Though the overwhelming majority of laws continued to come from the president's office, the rise of competitive politics brought Congress into policy-making, both as an agenda-setter and a catalyst of reform. In 1988, the PRI fell below the two-thirds majority of the Congress required to modify Mexico's detailed Constitution. In 1997, the PRI lost even a simple congressional majority. Emboldened opposition parties demanded a share of congressional committee chairs (previously held exclusively by the PRI), money to expand congressional staff, and a series of audits of executive commissions. The national legislature became an important arena for debate over central issues like the budget. The president needed help from other parties in order to pass laws. Fortunately for Zedillo, the PAN generally supported his economic initiatives — though at the cost of concessions. Rarely before had legislative pressure forced modification of presidential initiatives.

With the 2000 election, the situation became still more complex. Fox did not preside over a passive party bench, nor did he control a majority of the legislature. He could not simply assume, like PRI predecessors, that Congress would do whatever he wanted. Indeed, he could not even assume that fellow party members would follow his lead. On the other side of the aisle, freed of presidential interference in internal party matters, PRI legislators had incentives to take more independent stands, particularly when it came to potentially unpopular issues like taxes or the budget. PRI legislators may be reluctant to give up this discretion even if the party recaptures the presidency. In the post-2000 period, the Mexican president's authority may increasingly depend on his skills as a negotiator.

At the same time, Congress has yet to prove it possesses the ability to act as a check on presidential power. Congress is handicapped by numerous problems. It is, in the first place, divided among three large parties and a varying number of small ones. Since 1997, no single party has controlled a majority of seats, forcing the formation of legislative coalitions to pass all laws. Differences among (and within) parties inhibit cooperation to check presidential power. In the second place, Congress has pitifully few resources to do its own research on legislative initiatives. Where the U.S. House of Representatives employs well over 6,000 staff members, not counting the 3,000+ employees of the General Accounting Office, or the Congressional Budget Office, or the Library of Congress, Mexico's 500 *diputados* struggle along with only 60 paid researchers, most of whom leave at the end of each three-year term.[65] Finally, constitutional prohibitions against consecutive re-election make the accumulation of legislative experience difficult. Halfway through each president's six-year term, all 500 legislators are replaced by a new, fresh, but largely inexperienced batch of recruits. While the number of bills introduced by legislators is increasing, most important bills are still introduced by the executive and approved without significant amendment.

Greater checks on executive power also pose potential trade-offs, particularly if rising competition results in divided government, in which different parties control the executive and legislative branches. This has already occurred at the local level; the national level (from 1997–2004) features presidents lacking majorities but not facing a legislative majority of another party. In the United States, citizens tend to view divided government tolerantly, perhaps because they are confident of the stability of their institutions. In Mexico, democratic institutions are not as solid or as trusted. However, the few cases of divided government in Mexico have not produced serious conflicts. PAN support enabled the PRI to pass unpopular parts of Zedillo's economic program, including the budget, a tax increase (which the PAN argued against in electoral campaigns), and a controversial bank rescue plan. Cooperation on economic issues in particular made sense for the PAN and reduced the danger of executive-legislative deadlock. Party negotiations should become more prominent in future legislative battles.

Despite such risks, the consolidation of Congress as an autonomous institution is an integral part of the transition to democracy. Competition within the electoral system has contributed to the emergence of a livelier, more important, and more democratic Congress.

The judicial branch has developed more slowly, in part because it is more insulated from the direct effects of electoral competition. Judges are not elected by popular vote in Mexico. Judicial reform has also captured less attention than legislative reform. Nevertheless, judicial reform is a key part of democratic accountability. The judiciary upholds the rule of law and is therefore necessary for democratic consolidation. Democracies must replace the discretionary systems used by authoritarian regimes with predictable systems of rules. When public officials know that judges will not punish them, they feel free to engage in corrupt and repressive behavior. And when citizens know that courts will not punish crimes or abuses of human rights by the state, they lose faith in state institutions.

Despite its importance, judicial reform has proven difficult for many democratizing countries, including Mexico. The allocation of more resources to training and staff is one advance. Another is reforms to strengthen the legislative oversight of judges. While the president still nominates judges, nominees to the Supreme Court must now face hearings in the Senate and be approved by a two-thirds vote. President Zedillo also created a Judicial Council to monitor the conduct of judges and set their budgets.[66] This marked the first time the judicial branch had formal control of its own budget. Finally, the Mexican Supreme Court was given the right to rule on the unconstitutionality of laws. Following the U.S. precedent, judicial review gives Mexico's Supreme Court the potential to check presidential and legislative power.[67]

However, these reforms at the top did little to improve the day-to-day administration of justice by overburdened and often corruptible courts.

Long delays in the enforcement of contracts and the protection of patent rights tend to undermine business confidence and lower investment, ultimately reducing economic growth. According to World Bank ratings, Mexico's score on rule of law actually declined between 1996 and 2002. At the local level, fueled by rising rates of assault, robbery, and kidnapping, fed-up citizens have resorted to mob justice rather than trust courts — and especially, police — to do the job. Many crimes are not reported at all. The climate of fear and mistrust produced by this situation undermines trust in democratic institutions at large, especially the ability of democracy to provide ordinary security for its citizens.

New Federalism

In addition to checks and balances among the branches of government, many argue that Mexico needs more effective local checks against an overly powerful central government. Despite a formally federal system, the Mexican national government controls the lion's share of revenue and has oversight authority over state and local government. Alternation in power alone does not fix these problems.

However, the balance of power has shifted toward state and local governments. One reason is electoral competition. During the period of PRI dominance, central control was enhanced by party ties between the president and PRI governors, who owed their positions to presidential approval. Just as more non-PRI congressmen eroded presidential control over Congress, more opposition governors (and mayors) eroded presidential power over states. Leading up to the 2000 election, governors from parties other than the PRI had won election at least once in over one-third of Mexican states. More broadly, the trickle of mayorships lost by the PRI increased to a steady stream by the mid-1990s. While the PRI retained 78 percent of mayorships in 1996, PRI decline in the largest cities was remarkable.[68] In 1997, over half of the ten largest cities were opposition-controlled. The election of a PAN president immediately increased the share of local and state governments controlled by opposing parties (now, including the PRI). President Fox took office with two-thirds of Mexican states held by parties other than his own.

Decentralization has also resulted in part from the increased influence of the United States — a strong federal system, with powerful state and local governments — and the growing popularity of decentralization among international financial institutions like the World Bank. This pressure tends to reinforce the harmonization between patterns in Mexico and other nations, what we have called normalization. The "smaller state, more market" model favored by these institutions, and by the Fox, Zedillo, and Salinas administrations, tends to encourage less central planning and administration of funds.

Finally, pressures for decentralization have come from budgetary constraints. One way to cut the national budget is to give local governments responsibility — but not money — to provide services. The decentralizing effects of such reforms were more inadvertent than intended, but did enhance local responsibility.[69] They also spurred local efforts to develop new sources of funding.

However, municipalities and states remain dependent on the national government for most of their funding and are ultimately constrained by their financial limitations. Mexican *municipios* lag behind municipal governments in other Latin American countries in terms of resources and authority, and revenue falls far short of responsibilities. Limits on independent taxation continue.

Even where decentralization results in devolution of power, questions remain about its effects on the prospects for stable democracy. Two principal arguments persist.[70] The first perspective prefers decentralization on democratic grounds. If decisions are made locally, more people have the opportunity to participate, to know elected officials personally, and to communicate with them. In addition, some studies find that opposition local governments are more likely to challenge presidential power, creating effective checks and balances. Political opening in Mexico has led local politicians of all parties to demand more from the national government in terms of funding, services, and autonomy to modify laws.

The opposing argument suggests that, "during the present phase of the country's political evolution, the subnational political arena will be the principal source of inertia and resistance to democratization, rather than the prime breeding ground for democratic advances."[71] Decentralization may leave government in the hands of local elites who have no intention of governing democratically. The likelihood of this outcome is increased by the uneven quality of civil society in Mexico: while in some areas a vigorous civil society (and opposition parties) may force local elites to become more responsive, vast areas of Mexico lack strong parties or organizations outside the PRI — itself, now less capable of constraining local elites. A pattern of intimidation, murders, and disappearances by elite-controlled paramilitary forces continues to plague rural Mexico, as local elites accustomed to state protection attempt to protect their interests at the point of a gun. Even without violence, local elites often remain in control, since they have more of the resources (such as money and education) helpful in influencing government.

Finally, it is reasonable to question whether local democracy is meaningful in the absence of sufficient resources. Instead of giving people the power to solve their problems locally, national governments that keep a tight rein on funds may reinforce central control. And problems for which people might otherwise demand a national solution can be foisted off on helpless local governments — and thus avoided altogether. This could be a recipe for frustration.

One example of both the possibilities and the limits of local governance is Mexico City. When a Left candidate took over the mayorship of Mexico City in 1997, he faced the dismaying problems of deterioration noted in Chapter 1, including crime, police corruption, pollution, and serious service gaps (in water, sewage, transportation and housing). Other problems include underemployment, rape and domestic violence, and a growing number of street children addicted to cheap intoxicants. Finally, the first elected Mexico City mayors also faced a lack of cooperation from federal agencies controlled by political opponents, hostile media coverage, and the raised expectations brought by the victory of a candidate promising change. Small wonder that the first democratically elected government of Mexico City disappointed many voters.

At the same time, winning election as mayor of Mexico City has provided a national platform for aspiring politicians to position themselves for a run at the presidency. State governments too have become increasingly good springboards for national campaigns. Until 2000, PRI presidential candidates were drawn mostly from the cabinet of the retiring president. But in 2000, *all three* major party candidates had served at least one term as governor, and three of the four candidates in the PRI's internal primary were ex-governors.[72] This is not a conscious imitation of U.S. politics, but reflects similar imperatives. U.S. governors make good candidates for the presidency because such positions create a strong local base, an administrative record, and a chance to build a reputation apart from the flock of congressmen. While the balance of power still favors the center, the trend is moving toward state and local governments.

The Changing Military Role

Finally, we consider the role of the military in a competitive political system. Democracy is not simply about building up alternative sources of power to balance Mexico's strong president; indeed, building up military power could endanger democratic consolidation. As Mexican exceptionalism erodes in a pro-democratic sense, it may also erode in a more troubling way, with the rise of a politicized military bringing Mexico closer to the historical pattern of military involvement in other Latin American countries.

Unlike many Latin American militaries, the Mexican military did not get involved in politics, but rather demonstrated extraordinary loyalty to civilian rule. The military focused primarily on limited external goals (like protecting the southern border during the Central American wars of the 1980s) or carrying out humanitarian missions (like disaster relief). Particularly after its involvement in the repression of students in 1968, the army tried to avoid any role in public policing.

Since the early 1990s, however, it has become increasingly difficult for the army to stay out of domestic policing. Two trends have undermined the army's quiet neutrality: the emergence of guerrilla forces, and the rise of drug trafficking.[73] The army has become involved in meeting both threats. In large part as a result of these activities, the size and budget of the armed forces — once famously low compared to other Latin American nations — doubled in the 1990s over its level a decade earlier, though trends under Fox appear once again to have reduced the military's share of national budgets.[74]

The assumption of these tasks puts political pressure on the armed forces. Its anti-drug efforts expose the army to the corrupting influences long evident in branches of the Mexican police. Several top generals, including Mexico's former drug czar, have been arrested and charged with taking drug money. This is a potentially serious problem, which Chapter 7 will discuss in more depth.

The military's role in countering guerrilla activities may also prove dangerous. Fighting guerrillas requires the army to gather intelligence on the political activities of citizens in guerrilla zones, a task that in the rest of Latin America has often preceded army decisions to eliminate threats through a campaign of terror, arbitrary arrests, and torture. It means that the army most often fires on Mexicans rather than on foreign enemies. Public demonstrations in favor of withdrawal from guerilla zones subject the army to popular censure. Finally, since permanent solution of guerrilla threats means addressing underlying political problems, the army may be tempted to get involved in policy decisions, a problematic development for democracy.

Nevertheless, there are few indications that military subordination to civilian authorities has been seriously compromised as yet. Corrupt generals can be arrested and punished. Military leaders did not play a major role in the public debate over government response to the EZLN and the EPR. The armed forces readily accepted the victory of a non-PRI presidential candidate; indeed, voting at military barracks has been nearly as diverse as in the rest of the population. Even sporadic demonstrations by small groups of officers — though a striking departure from traditional military behavior — were more directed at the internal regulation of military discipline than national policy.[75] The percentage of Mexicans expressing a great deal or quite a lot of confidence in the armed forces increased from 47 percent in 1990 to 54 percent in 2000 — making the army one of the few state institutions to improve its rating.[76]

Rather than relying on the logic of PRI control to maintain military subordination, the increasing uncertainty of Mexican politics has led to an effort to institutionalize control over the armed forces. The national security cabinet now contains not only representatives of the military but also the ministries of Foreign Affairs, Government, and the Attorney General. A Center for National Security was created for intelligence operations, separating this function from direct military control. And the army has again taken an active role in more popular activities, like disaster relief, to enhance military morale. Political competition has produced threats that may erode traditional limits on the military's political involvement. However, the military, like other actors we have discussed in this chapter, appears to have endorsed the democratic project and is unlikely to intervene unless public order is threatened by political breakdown.

CONCLUSION

However recent the rise of competitive politics in Mexico, it has transformed the political landscape. No longer does one party claim hegemony over political activity; instead, a vigorous multiparty system competes for popular support from the local to the national level. Civil society flourishes and multiple channels for making political demands have strengthened. Political competition has encouraged the development of a more balanced state, less thoroughly centralized in a single executive office. Social organizations impose checks on the ability of any single actor to dominate the political scene.

Key actors in the political system, from the smallest neighborhood association to the Mexican military, have tried to respond to this changing political situation. Some have responded more effectively than others, and many organizations are still in flux. The rise of competition itself is a factor encouraging the further spread of competition. Dramatic economic reforms contributed to the process by weakening traditional PRI alliances, while repeated economic crises limited state resources for cooptation and undermined popular confidence in the PRI. These pressures contributed to the demand for institutional reforms that in turn have made the conditions of competition more equitable. If alternation in power provides the ultimate test of this system, Mexico has passed.

Nevertheless, political competition is not yet as established, potent, and secure as democracy requires. Not all the actors gaining a greater share of power are themselves democratic. Moreover, greater power for some actors — like legislatures — makes them more attractive targets for powerful special interests. And in Mexico, compared to many established democracies, there is a greater concentration of powerful interests, some of them foreign. Ties between parties and citizens remain weak, undermining mechanisms of accountability. Power has shifted somewhat from the center to local and state governments and from the president to the legislature, but the president continues to dominate.

Finally, trade-offs are inevitable. Competition also means conflict. During the era of peak PRI strength, limits on conflict contributed to a long period of economic growth, which in turn stabilized authoritarian rule. As conflict becomes more visible during normal democratic competition, perceptions of political stability, particularly by investors, could suffer. So we come full circle: can Mexico achieve democratic stability in the light of substantial underlying sources of social and economic conflict? Must democracy involve the protection of elite interests, limited freedom of choice for the poor and marginalized, and acceptance of inequality? If so, will those left out challenge democracy? And if not, will elites themselves be tempted to overturn democracy to protect their privileges? As these questions suggest, Mexico is not guaranteed a smooth consolidation of democratic progress. Chapter 4 continues this discussion by looking at Mexico's uneven democracy, paying special attention to the extent of freedom, accountability, and political equality.

CHAPTER 4

Difficult Democracy

PROGRESS AND PROBLEMS

The rise of competitive politics marks democratic progress, and the 2000 elections helped earn Mexico the democratic label. However, competition is still plagued by limitations, and so are other necessary components of democracy. Novelist Mario Vargas Llosa now calls Mexico a "difficult democracy."[1] A happy upgrade from "the perfect dictatorship," the term aptly suggests the sense that the struggle for democracy continues.

To refer to Mexico as democratic is, therefore, to refer to a democracy encumbered with adjectives. Introduced in Chapter 1, *semidemocracy* is a term that captures much of recent Mexican politics. For Mexican politics starting in 2000, *democracy* is the superior one-word label, but our analysis deals with much more than the events since that year. Moreover, the terms *semidemocracy* and *democracy* significantly overlap, especially where the democracy in question remains as incomplete as Mexico's. Semidemocratic systems include competitive elections and extensive freedoms, whereas democratic systems sometimes include constraints on political organization, advantages for one party, weaknesses in accountability and the rule of law, and severe inequalities in participation and influence. Already before the 2000 elections most components of democracy existed in Mexico, though in partial and inadequate form. That assessment held after the 2000 elections, though with the positive side augmented and the reservations decreased. While a majority of Mexicans believed in 2004 that Mexico is a democracy (as opposed to 41 percent in February of 2000), fewer Mexicans agreed with this classification than in the euphoric period just after the July 2000 election, and 36 percent continued to believe that Mexico was not yet a democracy.[2]

This chapter focuses on three dimensions to depict the evolving Mexican democracy: freedom, accountability, and political equality. We examine how these dimensions of democracy have historically worked to ensure remarkable political stability rather than democracy, and how changes put stability at risk or force its reconstruction on a new, democratic footing. As the chapter describes shifts from qualified authoritarianism to semidemocracy to democracy with limitations, it identifies the ongoing contradictions that must be resolved for Mexico to become a clear and consolidated democracy. This chapter thus takes a "macro" look at the political system, complementing the preceding chapter's examination of Mexico's main political actors and institutions.

FREEDOM

For Mexico freedom is the strongest of these three dimensions of democracy. More than accountability or political equality, it led the way under semidemocracy by limiting authoritarianism and reaching largely democratic dimensions. Throughout Mexico's democratic evolution, however, freedom of expression has outstripped freedom of organization.[3] This juxtaposition illustrates both the progress and the problems of Mexican democratization. Semidemocracy allowed an extensive increase in the two kinds of freedom but with uncertainties especially about organization. Democracy requires the integrity of both.

Freedom of Expression: The Media

To analyze freedom of expression in Mexico, we first look at the media as a case study. Central to modern society and its degree of democracy, the media illustrate Mexico's mix of restrictions and opportunities. The restrictions have been more subtle and complex than in most authoritarian systems. The opportunities have expanded, and further expansion tends to substantiate the move from semidemocracy to democracy. Our analysis of the media treats four concerns: the role of government, the role of private ownership, the flow of information, and the audiences in question. Government in this context usually meant PRI-controlled national governments. However, as democratization and decentralization have spread, the national government has lost its exclusive prominence, and concern has expanded instead to local markets, audiences, and governments.

Government.   Even at the heyday of PRI power, the Mexican government has rarely relied on blatant control, owning only a small share of the means of communication (mostly regional television and radio stations) and engaging only sporadically in overt censorship. Instead, it has relied on the generally supportive stance of capitalist ownership and on the social underdevelopment that blocks many Mexicans from access to politically useful news. Into this mix the government has sprinkled incentives and disincentives to steer things further its way. All this has left space for free expression, avoiding the delegitimizing costs of heavy-handed repression and allowing for a valuable flow of ideas and opinions.

But PRI governments did not generally permit the freedom associated with democracy. Its arsenal of weapons occasionally included brute force. Where particular newspapers or magazines engaged in dissent considered too challenging, the government would crack down under one pretext or another, as with the daily *Excélsior* in 1976 and the weekly *Impacto* in 1986. What the government considered too challenging was not clearly defined. Much depended on the disposition of the particular president or governor. Freedom in this context has been contingent and conferred from above, not a right conquered by a society to which government leaders are bound. Such uncertainty has given courageous editors and producers room to explore the limits but has left most of their counterparts more cautious.

The government has usually tilted the media playing field with less extreme measures than physical intimidation. It has an arsenal of regulatory weapons and financial incentives. The Mexican government has been more prone than bona fide democractic governments to convert authority over radio and television licensing into punitive suspension for its critics.[4] More subtle have been the incentives offered by government ads, which still account for perhaps half the income of many newspapers. Most newsprint for Mexican papers has come through the government, which could facilitate its subsidized sale or force publishers to buy on the more costly market. Other monetary sweeteners (*gacetillas*) have flowed to media that put out government ads and statements as if they were news stories. Reporters have earned regular payments (*igualas*) and direct bribes (*chayotes*) for favorable reporting. Such corruption has been common, not exceptional. As with other facets of corruption that corrode democracy, a vicious cycle developed in which low wages have made bribes more tempting, which in turn has offset pressures for better wages and has affected who has been attracted to the profession.

Despite these manipulative arrangements, the bounds of free expression have expanded. Where once even ministers could hardly be criticized and sitting presidents were untouchable, more recent presidents (as well as ministers and sitting governors) have been criticized, ridiculed, and bluntly accused of lying. The media began to demonstrate that disrespectful (and at times unfair) antigovernment frenzy that is often associated with the modern media in vibrant democracies.[5] News stories derided traditional *priistas* (*priistas de siempre*). Just as important, national officials have engaged much less in overt attempts to intimidate the media. When the newspaper *Reforma* published a damaging letter sent by then campaign director Zedillo to presidential candidate Luis Donaldo Colosio (assassinated soon after), Zedillo denounced the publication as morally wrong but did not try to coerce the paper.

Though Zedillo could be credited for being a democrat, a more telling evaluation is that officials have lost much of their capability of choosing when to close and open the valves of dissent. A major factor limiting government ability to restrict media freedom is society's rejection of pseudodemocracy. So officials have to concentrate less on squelching opposing views in the media and more on competing with them, less on sustaining myths of democracy and more on convincing people that they are best equipped to govern well in a democracy.

All this relates, of course, to the growth of competitive politics and vigorous parties. The historic close fit between media and government is impossible where government democratically changes party and course. It becomes impossible for the media to stifle criticism of governments when it comes from opposition senators and governors. It becomes harder to avoid reporting on campaign content when different candidates command widespread support. In fact, electoral reforms directly require more media access for government critics. Leftist parties used legally allotted television time to show tough, slick depictions of how Zedillo's State of the Union address ignored women and children, students and workers, while catering to "you know who" (pictorially portrayed as big business and foreign interests). The 1994 campaign brought the first televised presidential debate, but not the last; debates seem, as in the United States, to have become expected parts of presidential cam-

paigns.[6] Americanized television campaigning now includes ads produced by consulting firms pursuing business self-interest, willing to serve
not just governments but any paying client. Whoever wins then has a
chance to build a record of noninterference with the media to contrast
with a muddier past. More difficult challenges remain at the state level,
where local media enjoy far less independence from local officials and
elites than national media. Nevertheless, as we discuss below, the main
threats to press freedom in Mexico come primarily from private actors,
with government mostly appearing in the role of ineffective protector
rather than heavy-handed censor.

In sum, government lacks the ability to restrict media freedom with
anything like the sure-handed confidence it enjoyed in the heyday of PRI
control. The undue influence it retained under semidemocracy is now also
imperiled. Whereas government long had things basically its way without
the need for heavy confrontation, its eroding ability to manage politics in
general and media content in particular has opened nongovernment space
which still needs to be further secured and vigorously utilized.

Private Ownership.   The main reason that governments over the decades
have not exercised tighter direct control is that the media have operated
mostly under very sympathetic private, elite ownership. The media have
performed more as a part of big business than a "Fourth Estate" dedicated
professionally to democratic freedom.[7] As a result, government and media
have commonly been in sync. Cooperation has outstripped coercion.
Government has enjoyed representation on the board of the main private
television concern, and with justification the Left sardonically calls for
"privatization" of the media. The key point is that democratic freedom
requires a will to exercise it, especially in both semidemocracies and
flawed democracies, where there is much less outright restriction than in
authoritarian settings but a much lower ratio of incentives to disincentives
than in democratic settings.

Therefore, a major difficulty lies with the huge concentration of media
in the hands of wealthy people who choose to support either the government in particular or the status quo in general. This stance denies voice to
the different interests and perspectives among the Mexican citizenry.
Although such criticism can be leveled in many nations, Mexico's situation
is extreme compared with that in most democracies. Cross-ownership of
different means of communication goes far beyond anything permitted by
legal restrictions against media monopoly in the United States. Mexican
law places no limits on the number of television or radio stations owned

by one organization. Thus one family (the Azcárragas) controls a large share of the Mexican news media. The Azcárraga Televisa consortium includes the great bulk of television stations and extends to interests in cable television, radio, film, publishing houses, and even some nonmedia concerns.[8]

Television's coverage of politics has historically been blatantly pro-government. Staunchly anti-Left, it has missed few opportunities to highlight the Left's failures and internal contradictions, both real and imagined. More remarkable, given television's generally rightward inclinations, has been the unfair treatment accorded to the rightist PAN. PRI governments have received preferential coverage in various ways, including time allotted, tone, and associated pictorial footage. The inequitable treatment of both Left and Right opposition reached grotesque proportions in the 1988 presidential elections, exposing the serious gap between an increasingly competitive electoral process and the traditional uniformity of media coverage. Televisa's lame defense was that it granted time proportional to votes received in the previous election. The 1994 presidential election marked a turning point, however, due in part to changes in electoral law.[9] The way was opened to more balanced coverage through most of the 2000 electoral period at the national level, as the Federal Electoral Institute (IFE) confirmed, though with much local television and radio still pro-PRI.

Because politics are more competitive and because society is more diverse and open than ever before, the private media have developed stronger commercial interests in covering a broader range of voices and in reporting the news more effectively and fairly. Diversifying private ownership also may enhance these competitive incentives. Mexico has never before had such vibrant and competitive media. The mere number of media outlets has not necessarily been a stimulus for change; Mexico City boasts more than a dozen dailies, easily more than any U.S. city, but the multiplicity has long been consistent with complicity more than pluralism. Instead, change has followed the advent of several autonomous, influential outlets.[10] Perhaps most important, the rise of privately owned TV Azteca has increased open coverage in television, the medium reaching the largest audience. Though Azteca remains allied with the social status quo, is anti-Left, and saw its image tarnished by revelations that its top investor was a business partner of President Carlos Salinas's notorious brother, its emergence put pressure on Televisa to liven up its broadcasts and cover stories reported by Azteca.

What has happened in television, radio, and the printed media is that private owners have realized that traditional blandness is bad business.[11] Unfortunately, a common substitute for blandness may be sensationalism. Sensationalism is often associated with competition in democratic settings, and Mexico is particularly vulnerable because the press and the public have yet to redefine the media's role in a democratic environment. Still, as media outlets vie with one another in the newly competitive market economy, U.S.-style ratings wars have made even morning news shows livelier. One good example of the blending of popular culture and hard news has been the unexpected emergence of green-haired Brozo the clown as an investigative reporter. Hired away from TV Azteca by Televisa in 2002, Brozo runs a morning program called "El Mañanero" (loosely translated, the "Morning Quickie") every weekday morning from 6 to 10, presenting an irreverent and often raunchy spin on the news along with entertainment segments and a scantily clad blonde cohostess. But it was Brozo's program that first broke the corruption scandal involving the Mexico City mayor's office, and in a dramatic way: airing a video that showed an official, René Bejarano, stuffing cash into his briefcase — in front of Bejarano — and then catching his stammered and unconvincing denials live on the air. Public suspicion or hostility toward government translates media criticism of government into good ratings. If government tries to pass a self-serving, exclusive inside story to one outlet, others jump up in protest. And of course the fact that government now changes hands makes it bad business to be identified with only one contestant. During the 2000 elections Televisa's president made the broader statement that democracy is very good business.

The political-economic changes that have fueled media change, making the media increasingly nongovernment and part of civil society, are reinforced by international influence. For one thing Mexican media seeking to cash in on Spanish-speaking markets in the United States, South America, and Europe must appear credible by international standards. For another thing growing access to international news through cable and satellite television renders traditional restrictions on news outdated. Moreover, foreign media cover Mexico more than they used to; the *New York Times* produces a significant piece roughly once a week. The Mexican audience capable of consuming foreign stories directly, through cable television or English-language dailies, has expanded. A more widespread impact from Mexico's integration with international markets is that a news story produced abroad has extra credibility, whereas it once had less.

Indeed, U.S. businessmen and politicians often find themselves having to explain that the appearance of a story in the *Wall Street Journal*, for example, is not proof of its veracity. The Mexican media often scramble to pick up stories initiated outside Mexico. In at least this case, internationalization appears to have a democratizing impact.

Information.   Crucial to understanding the limitations of Mexican news is the paucity of reliable information from government and other sources. One culprit has been governmental unwillingness to provide information; government, as Zedillo acknowledged, "should inform more and better." A consequence of depending on government for information is that major matters may escape informed analysis. Of course, drug trafficking and other corrupt activities by incumbents would not be easy to report on in any country; in Mexico, however, such vacuums loom large as they lie near the heart of the political system. Even on matters of legal public policy, far too few facts have been available. Observers have wondered how Mexicans manage to be as informed as public opinion polls show they are.

The flip side of silence on certain matters has been the incessant production of other types of information — mostly proclamations, commemorations, banalities, and lots of statistical data. But even the honest data often appear outside the context necessary for informed public debate. Streams of data about Mexico's problems do not by themselves advance consideration of specific policies to address them.

Independent sources of news often reflect this "safe" banality of little direct use to citizens in informed public debate. Reporting on events outside Mexico has generally been safe, though the rising interrelationship between international and domestic Mexican issues makes this trickier. On domestic issues there has been room, ironically, even for Marxist and other radical critiques heatedly blaming "capitalism" or "dependency" for deep-seated social ills; such vague criticism has been much less dangerous than specific criticism of the public policy of a particular president.[12]

Another substitute for hard news has been rumor. Although rumors fill the news in most countries, at least three points make Mexico special. First, "rumorology" has gotten greater news play than in repressive systems, which insist on tight official versions of truth, and mature democratic ones, which enjoy a freer flow of facts. Second, rumors have dominated even the most important political matters, long including the secretive selection of the next president. Third, the rumor frenzy increasingly called the traditional system's smooth functioning into question.[13]

But informational content has improved for reasons related to declining government control and increasing private competition. Governments lacking the sure control of yesteryear fragment into factions that leak different information to their favored newspeople. As opposing forces ascend to governing responsibilities, they obtain more information to publish and stronger platforms from which to do so. Governments, in turn, must compete in the information battle because they cannot resort to the near monopoly of the past. Regular news conferences by presidents and governors are a further step toward U.S.-style politics; Fox did an hour-long media show. The independent Federal Election Institute, having replaced government as the agency supervising elections, pours detailed data onto the Internet. The foreign media provide information and pressure for domestic media to follow suit. Public opinion polling gives expression to the many voices in society.

Nor are newspeople merely passive recipients. Despite all the restrictions, even some mostly compliant outlets have employed commentators who have gathered and disseminated information more independently. Editorials on current events, written by intellectuals, appear on the front pages of national newspapers and even on television; these editorials frequently match those found anywhere in the world for their insights and diversity. Investigative reporting, though still in its infancy, makes periodicals like *Proceso* and *Reforma* especially interesting. As in other democratizing countries in Latin America, investigative reports look into anti-democratic aspects of the political system, such as corruption. Where the Mexican government goes to court to argue against opening official archives, as with military archives some thirty years after the 1968 student massacre, it looks more like a democratic government battling independent media than an authoritarian controller comfortably rigging the system.[14]

One tragic development reflecting the media's increased willingness to provide real information is the growing violence against reporters and editors. Bold individuals must ponder the chilling risks of retaliation up to and including assassination. This is part of the wider paradox in which the breakdown of historic authoritarian controls, whether in the former Soviet Union or in Mexico, does not mean an immediate transition to secure democratic practice but to an uncertain and frightening mix of expanded freedom and expanded disorder. Those who report on drug traffic or human rights violations or corruption may be intimidated, kidnapped, or even murdered, by those whose interests are jeopardized. It is often impossible to identify whether the perpetrator of such crime is a government official, a private party operating with government com-

plicity, or someone outside government altogether. Whoever the perpetrators are, the threat of violence has persisted as Mexican politics opens,
showing again that democratization does not follow a neat, linear
course. Alternation in power at the national level has produced little if
any improvement in the security of journalists. Indeed, the watch group
Reporters Without Frontiers ranked Mexico ninety-sixth in the world in
press freedom in 2004, below countries like Kenya, Bolivia, the Congo,
Paraguay, and Uganda. Mexico's ranking has slipped from 2002, when it
ranked seventy-fifth.[15] Ten journalists were murdered in the first three
years and ten months of Fox's administration, a number only slightly
lower than during Zedillo's term. Most of the victims worked for local
papers in drug trafficking zones. Nevertheless, concern that government
has not done enough to protect journalists led several Mexican NGOs to
hold a national day of protest in October 2004 to demand that all levels
of government cooperate in defending press freedom.

Audience.   An inverse correlation exists in Mexico between freedom
and targeted audience: the greater the critical and informational content,
the smaller the receiving public. In this way the system has at once
avoided the closed extremes of authoritarianism and the risks of uncontrolled information to the masses. Robust democracy requires that more
information reach a much wider audience. Television has been at one end
of the spectrum. The medium least associated with open information, it
is the main source of news for a majority of the population that receives
news, with newspapers and then radio trailing far behind.[16] Newspapers
have had much more room than television for free expression but even
the largest national newspapers have a circulation of only 100,000, in a
country of 100 million; most have a far lower circulation.[17] Several million readers divide their loyalties among hundreds of publications.
Publications that have most used the room for free expression often have
lower circulation than sports dailies and tabloids. This does not make
those newspapers unimportant. Politically informed, influential Mexico
still relies more on newspapers than on television, and the elite gravitates
to a few select publications.

Weekly and monthly magazines have generally enjoyed greater room
for free expression than newspapers. Many are marginal whereas others
have important readerships.[18] On the drier side academic journals have
reached only specialized audiences with their often critical assessments.
The same might be said of books. But here too circulation grows. For one
thing the increasing population of highly educated Mexicans with money

includes some that can handle foreign works, especially in English. Meanwhile, the market increases for translations into Spanish of foreign books about Mexico or about the expanding range of worldwide political, economic, and social issues that now spark ample interest within Mexico. And Mexico's own leading intellectuals and journalists have written prolifically, with almost no government restriction, and for a growing audience, as more and more citizens seek to influence and understand the emerging democracy. Add to this the new offering of books by the confidants of top officials or by the top officials themselves — or by their ex-mistresses — as well as by opposing political figures. Some may be positive attempts to encourage democracy or biased accounts with a selfish agenda. In either case they are part of the newly contested space for political expression. Many deal with unflattering aspects of the system, from wild speculation in *Who Killed Colosio?* to a spate of politically polarized books on the rebellion in Chiapas.

Overall, then, the Mexican media show expanded freedom of expression as old restrictions have diminished. Major reasons for the change include the democratization of the political system, the strengthening of society, and the competitive, profit-driven orientation of diversifying media. However, new restrictions have emerged, largely outside deliberate government policy, which continue to make media freedom in Mexico a mixed picture, and less than what one would hope for in a democratic society.

Freedom of Organization

Compared with freedom of expression, freedom of political organization has been much more restricted. It too has grown markedly but still requires a major increase in order to achieve the vibrancy and security consistent with democracy. The PRI government would not permit, as democracies must, legally organized threats to its rule. The greater the threat of viable opposition, the more likely government would turn from flexible accommodation to repression. Although variable, limits on Mexican society's freedom to organize were extensive enough to ensure the regime's long hold on power and to mean citizens generally had an undemocratically small role in policy making.[19]

The idea that the traditional system restricted freedom when the threat of organized alternatives was greatest draws support from the previous chapter's observations about parties and elections, the standard vehicles for aggregating and organizing the preferences of free individuals. Semidemocracies have regular and competitive elections in which the lead party has too many unfair advantages. This was true in Mexico with its tight identification between one party and government and the myriad ways in which formally democratic rules have been mere trappings. However, the last chapter also showed that the rise of competitive politics has brought elections that are more fair, open, and consequential. All parties must battle for voter support. Thus the party-electoral arena indicates that even where restrictions on freedom were most crippling, democratization has been significant.

And hand in hand with the freer electoral realm, expectations of freedoms in other organizational areas have risen. The church affords us a good example. Where religious freedom is about individual expression rather than organization, it has been rather unproblematic. People may worship as they choose or not at all. That the vast majority is Catholic should not obscure the diversity of belief, with various blends of European and indigenous influence and various degrees of practice even among those who hold similar beliefs. Compared with nations where government has persecuted citizens seeking to practice nondominant religions, the very strength of government in Mexico has safeguarded individuals and minority groups from harassment by others.[20]

Where religious freedom concerns more organizational matters, however, it has been more problematic. One of the more restricted nonparty organizations historically, as Chapter 2 noted, the church was long considered a potential threat to state authority. Compared with business, the limited political voice of the Catholic Church resulted more from imposition than choice. The modus vivendi established by 1940 left the church free as a religious organization while restricting political rights. In practice, government looked the other way concerning formal violations of laws perceived by much of the population as too punitive (e.g., the running of religious schools); beyond that, many politicians were "believers at home" even as they were "anticlerics in the street," a contrast to the U.S. tendency for politicians to feign more fervent religiosity in public than they manage in private. Nevertheless, the basic idea of keeping the church out of politics has been an almost sacred public belief, at least as widely endorsed as the idea of keeping out the military. It was in fact the church's prudent unwillingness (with rare exceptions) to challenge this basic political proscription that made the government comfortable not enforcing limits on its nonpolitical organizational activity.

Yet even organizational freedoms for the church have increased in Mexico's more competitive context.[21] This change reverses Mexico's spe-

President Ernesto Zedillo's reception in 2000 of the diplomatic credentials of the Vatican's extraordinary ambassador was part of the normalization of ties between the Vatican and a regime that long prided itself on apartness. (*La Jornada*)

cial tradition of marginalizing the church from politics and instead fits a widespread tendency (in Latin America and elsewhere) for the Catholic Church to move from being seen as a mostly negative to an often positive force for democracy. The new church-state relationship is another manifestation of a kind of normalization in Mexican politics.

Typical of the transforming politics, the regime lost the smooth control it once had. The PRI itself split over Salinas's legislative reforms easing controls on the church. Emboldened by the regime's openness and weakness, and by the surge of civil society, church leaders raised their voices louder than before. To long-standing moral concerns over hunger and human rights, some boldly added a preoccupation with free elections and other aspects of democratization, challenging government. When church leaders denounced the plight of workers under neoliberalism and declared that union leaders do not stand by their members, they attacked pillars of the corporatist system. Sometimes the sharpness of church criticism has been incredible in the aftermath of decades of caution. Thus when Zedillo gave a speech depicting the church as among those institutions sharing responsibility for the plight of the indigenous, bishops shot back that he had "lost his memory" and "does not know any history." Restrictions on church involvement in politics diminish still further in

Cathedral, Taxco, Guerrero. The church represents both
continuity and change in Mexican political and social life.

light of the historical political changes of 2000 — in fact, Vicente Fox's
critics feared excessively close church-state ties.[22]

But the church hardly sweeps onto the political field as a unified organization. Involvement in Mexico's centrifugal and increasingly free politics tends to produce or expose fissures within entities. Church politics in
one region, state, or locality differ greatly from church politics elsewhere.
The whole range of political views in Mexico finds voice within the
church. This includes, of course, continued support for government by
many in the hierarchy, but government can now mean any of three parties. It also means that church critics of the government from the Left and

the Right cannot agree among themselves, except perhaps on broad principles like free elections or combating the common threat posed by the
surge of Protestant evangelicals in the southeast. The liberal church
attacks the conservative development model, its neoliberal incarnation,
and its social legacy, as it supports the Vatican's special concern for the
poor. It is itself internally divided, however, on how much to support
grassroots mobilization, the PRD, the zapatistas, and violent means to
desired ends; "liberation theology" has some backing. The conservative
church emphasizes spiritual over material issues or, in between, it
endorses the Vatican line on supporting human rights and attacking
poverty without endangering church hierarchy or social peace.

Of course, government officials have taken advantage of church splits
and played off different sides: they can welcome, for example, anti-left
invective by churches in the north and anti-right invective by churches in
the south and can isolate one side on one issue and another on a second.
For the most part, however, the church's fresh activity in the mainstream
political arena is a further sign of once-great government control yielding
to strengthened civil society and pluralism.

ACCOUNTABILITY

Freedom of organization in democracies plays a key role in linking freedom of expression to accountability. Accountability means that citizens
have the means to make the system face consequences if it violates democratic norms or otherwise fails to perform. It is thus indispensable to
linking freedom in "input" to actual policy "output." Though it is not
easy to identify what constitutes sufficient accountability to qualify as
democracy, semidemocracy is defined in part by the weakness of accountability and the rule of law. The contrast between formally democratic elections and significant freedom on the one hand and a scandalous
lack of accountability and rule by law on the other goes to the heart of
terms like *delegative democracy* that qualify democracy with negative
adjectives.[23] The applicability of this term to many countries outside a
still small pool of well-established democracies concentrated in the industrialized world is a major qualification to optimistic declarations about
global democratization. Much of the international concern to "reform
the state" is about how to make governments more responsive and less
arbitrary in dealing with citizens. We explore Mexican accountability as
it relates to three overlapping issues: leadership versus citizenship, presidentialism, and the rule of law.

Leaders over Citizens

Mexico built sturdy pillars of political leadership that contributed to exceptional stability. Instead of contributing to democracy, however, these pillars generally made the leadership too powerful relative to the citizenry.

Mass Attitudes.   Political scientists debate whether a democratic political culture is crucial for democracy. The rejection of "culturalist" views (simplistic explanations that culture determines politics) probably went too far when it minimized the role of political culture. Although a democratic political culture is neither a necessary nor a sufficient condition for democracy, it improves the odds greatly. Moreover, even where we recognize that political culture is a result at least as much as a cause of political system type, we should look at culture as a gauge of how democratic a country is.[24] How arbitrarily the political leadership operates depends in part on the political culture of the citizenry. A nondemocratic leadership is less vulnerable if the people have weak democratic values. In contrast, the sort of democratic political culture associated with strong civil society puts nondemocratic elites on the defensive, a development we have identified in Mexico. And, crucial to the evolution of semidemocracy into stable democracy, a citizenry strongly committed to democratic politics is less likely to seek authoritarian alternatives when a particular democratic government fails to produce economic results.

Scholarship has often portrayed Mexican political culture as decidedly nondemocratic. Although this is not now the dominant academic view, it is important to note certain reasonable findings that persist about negative cultural characteristics.[25] Too many Mexicans remain "subjects" rather than "participants." Some analysts see a tendency for Mexicans to wait and hope that things will improve rather than to act. "Action" often involves a petition that benevolent leaders do a personal favor, rather than citizens making demands upon accountable leadership. Even the Left's campaign spots often feature its candidate magnanimously tending to requests. But if citizens are not aggressive enough regarding their leaders, they are in some ways too aggressive toward one another. Polls repeatedly show low tolerance for opposing views and a lack of mutual trust beyond the family.[26] Moreover, Mexico ranks below the Latin American average in the number of citizens who prefer democracy to any other form of government (41 percent versus 56 percent).[27]

Most other citizen attitudes are nonetheless democratic enough to support the view that Mexico's political culture is now largely democratic. Political cultures are not immutable; they evolve. Whereas Mexico once stood out as an exceptional case in which cynicism about the political system combined with acceptance and even support for it, dissatisfaction now fuels pressure for democratic change. In survey responses citizens distinguish between a particular government's performance they dislike and the principles (free elections, the rule of law, etc.) they favor. They give lower marks to government and parties than to societal institutions such as the family, church, school, and civil society organizations.[28]

The democratizing tendencies in political culture gain momentum as interest in politics and open discussions become more common in a more competitive system. Whereas an authoritarian political system used to restrain development of democratic attitudes, an increasingly democratic system promotes such values. Moreover, democratic attitudes are most common among groups that account for a rising share of the population: urban dwellers, the middle class, the better educated. Comparative data confirm that the gap narrows between Mexico and both Canada and the United States in democratic attitudes and participation: Mexicans increasingly resemble their North American cousins.[29] The passive subject becomes less common, the demanding participant citizen more common.

Elite Networks.   On the elite level Mexico's leadership has been cooperative, collusive, and largely undemocratic. Although many studies of transitions to democracy highlight the importance of elite "pacts," noting that without elite agreements the necessary consensus on common democratic rules of the game may fall apart, elite pacts in Mexico kept things together for a stable but nondemocratic system. The keystone pacts that ended revolutionary violence and built the official party also built a corporatist system to bind the masses in controlled organizations and deny space for independent ones. These pacts proved spectacularly effective and durable. Intra-elite conflict was limited and isolated from public exposure.

One way Mexican leaders have been insulated from citizens is through structuring politics around groups connected by personal loyalties — known as *camarillas* — rather than around policy preferences. Careers have been made less by appealing to constituencies than by attaching to a group and its leader, giving service and loyalty in return for employment, security, and possible mobility. Once such a system becomes entrenched, it is hard to find enough information, resources, and support to gain power outside camarillas.[30] This functions as a rather closed system, hard for the general public or politicians with dissident views to penetrate. Competition exists within and among camarillas (and politicians usually belong to more than one), but it is more a matter of personal struggles and elite bargaining than a public contest based on policy differences.

The persisting importance of camarillas is verified by the preoccupation (of intellectuals and media as well as politicians themselves) with palace intrigue, something that goes beyond the inward-looking nature of U.S. "Beltway politics." Like other fixtures of the system, however, camarillas are challenged by a democratizing system in which people demand more openness and accountability. Candidate Fox's pledge to select "the best people" was an implicit charge that PRI-camarilla politics obeyed a different logic. Camarillas are struggling to adjust to an evolving system in which the number of positions determined by competitive election rather than appointment increases.

Observers who believe that Mexican stability has depended in part on the personal loyalties generated by largely subterranean networks worry as camarillas deteriorate as part of the broader erosion of the once powerful political class. Intra-elite conflict intensifies and goes public, into the uncertain new arena of competitive politics. As factions spread both accurate information and malicious gossip about their rivals, some fear that the rough-and-tumble politics associated with the breakdown of traditional political pillars could ultimately provoke repression.[31]

The idea that not all alternatives to elite political pacts are democratic or accountable to citizens applies also to a much-noted change in Mexico's leadership: the rise of the technocrat. Technocrats are distinguished by their specialized advanced education and their belief that technical skills can manage problems more professionally, rationally, and efficiently than "politics" can; they base their claim to rule more on expertise than political popularity. International actors who see them as having the skills and ideological commitments to tie their countries to the dominant international economic policies also prefer technocrats. Although technocrats have gained prominence in much of the developing world, at least two factors are particularly striking in Mexico. First is the strong contrast technocrats there have presented to a traditional political class with dominating skills and styles. Second, Mexican technocrats could gain special power insofar as they were not pressured by democratic politics; technocratic leadership helps explain why Mexico assumed regional leadership in pursuing internationally favored neoliberal economic policies. Despite tensions between technocrats and elements of the PRI, one-party rule shielded the technocrats. In contrast, PAN and PRD candidates have not usually followed a technocratic path. However, the evolving role of technocrats in the new competitive politics goes beyond one party; any party in power will mix in technocratic expertise in running crucial aspects of economic and internationalized development policy.

The surge of technocrats in Mexico is striking. Zedillo was the fifth consecutive president who had never held any other elective office (previous presidents had been senators or governors). In addition, the non-elective cabinet experience of those who became presidents shifted from the eminently political government ministry to the eminently technical financial ministries. This is not to suggest a 180-degree swing away from politicos, and certainly not to suggest inexorable trends. For one thing technocrats were at work in the 1920s and earlier, though not with the power they would later wield. For another, technocrats also function within traditional camarillas. Most top-level policy makers are hybrids between politicos and technocrats.

Although the mix tilted markedly for a period toward the technical side, this has changed. Zedillo found it necessary as candidate to turn to politicos to rev up his dull campaign, and as president to distance himself some from negative views of technocrats. In the internal battle to succeed Zedillo, winner Francisco Labastida had not only substantial background in the Ministry of Government but had been governor of Sinaloa and allied his primary campaign with key party operatives in most of Mexico's states. But this was not enough. His loss to a former businessman and governor, and above all to another party, shows how the growth of competitive politics spells the demise of the short era of technocratic dominance as a substitute for prior control by the traditional political machine. Most contenders for the presidency in 2006 are likely to have heavily political resumes.

The problem with technocrats, in the view of many critics, lies in their anti-democratic nature (with policies based on technical criteria rather than social choice), in the diminished social connections between leaders and people, and in diminished accountability. Though not democratically selected, Mexican leadership in the past at least used to have more contact with the masses. If modern technocrats are elected, their style of leadership may imply diminishing accountability, in the preference for technical criteria over popularity in policy choice. But technocrats in countries like Mexico and Brazil can aid a transformation from manipulated, patronizing politics — based on control and co-optation — to more accountability based on performance. Although technocrats may base their policy preferences on what is ultimately good for the people over what the people themselves want, democratic pressures may at least give people the ability to reject the results. And in some cases technocrats have seen fit to provide compensatory social welfare projects, to ease the pain associated with technocratic austerity policies.[32] Again, however, Mexico's political transformation suggests that the technocrat-politico mix viable under semidemocracy must evolve into a mix where political skills and accountability are strong.

This point is also crucial to the debate over the impact of technocratic power on political stability. Technocrats may well have sustained and revitalized the old regime by bringing much of what is required to modernize Mexico and revamp its development model. A contrary view is that their rise undermined regime legitimacy and stability. Technocrats may be less adept at political manipulations that keep conflict under control. They are more separated than politicos from the general population in their socioeconomic backgrounds and educational experiences (including private schooling and schooling abroad). This separation further tarnished nationalist claims — especially as socioeconomic policies limit populism and incline toward those favored by powerful international interests.[33]

It would be simplistic, however, to see the technocrats as the key cause of the disintegration of the once carefully groomed political class. The breakdown of prior norms and discipline resulted fundamentally from the growing gap between what the old system delivered and what the people both need and demand. Some of the new needs and demands have economic and international dimensions that contribute to the technocratic rise. Other needs and demands are largely democratic, a reality that is hostile to both the traditional political class and unaccountable technocratic rule.

Challenging Presidentialism

The undemocratic distancing of leaders from the citizenry has been epitomized in the presidency. Whereas Chapter 3 dealt with presidential power within the state structure, our concern here with accountability focuses on the relationship between rulers and citizens. We consider how the decline of powerful presidentialism raises prospects for enhanced accountability.

The Summit: From Lofty to Shaky to Promising. A wide array of powers has given the president undemocratic control over the people and the institutions that are supposed to represent them (the judiciary, legislature, local government, parties, etc.). The dominant image has been one of a nearly blank presidential check to rule for six years. This picture comes close to the truth but requires qualifications. One is our repeated observation about how the peak period of regime strength was confined to a few decades.[34] Second, some scholarship suggests that presidential power has always been more a product of informal norms than constitutional powers, opening the door for a more balanced system to evolve.[35] Most important, the growth of competition has weakened the presidency both with respect to the general citizenry as well as to other branches and levels of government; the experiences of the first non-PRI administration make it even clearer that Mexican presidents can no longer count on a blank check, and must assume a more democratic role.

The royal presidency has been eroding since the 1970s, though what now reveals itself as a secular institutional decline was often seen as merely the failure of particular presidents. When Salinas rode high, some interpreted the presidency as regally intact, perhaps revitalized. As in some sister republics, the president enjoyed widespread popularity as he acted beyond the rule of law.[36] The next few years smashed that view. Recognizing that arbitrary rule could not be reconstituted following the Salinas debacle, Zedillo coupled virtue with necessity by declaring that democracy requires respect for the principles and institutions previously left to the president's mercy. To signal an end to an imperial presidency, his inaugural address was short and without grandeur. If Salinas, López Portillo, and Echeverría had undermined the traditional presidency unintentionally as they operated imperially, Zedillo would claim to undermine it intentionally by operating more accountably. Fox (and presumably his successors) would have even less latitude.[37]

Among citizens the presidency has lost the aura that made it possible to maintain legitimacy without accountability. The president is now seen more as a leader of his faction than as a leader of the nation, a view that could be as troublesome for democratic consolidation as it became for the persistence of authoritarian rule. The golden rule of not directly criticizing a sitting president has died. Cracks appeared under Echeverría and widened substantially thereafter. Even then popular Salinas was publicly ridiculed when he portrayed himself as a splendid blend of Benito Juárez and Emiliano Zapata. Jokes about Fox and his wife are standard fare, especially on more irreverent Internet sites. The consequences of all this change in the presidency are uncertain for both stability and democracy. However much the traditional presidency served stability, a presidency combining strength, nonaccountability, and legitimacy is unlikely to re-emerge. Continued stability requires new legitimacy, which in turn requires greater democracy.

But can a more limited presidency work? This question parallels the last chapter's question about the possible antireform ramifications of decentralization. Accountability requires that a president have sufficient power to act and then be held responsible for results. Yet the overall tendency of the shrinking state leaves the president with less to give (despite important control over what to cut). Furthermore, a trimmed-down presidency may lack effectiveness within a system and culture accustomed to central authority and resolute leadership in public policy. In November 2004, Fox found himself unable to secure congressional approval for his budget. To make matters worse, PRI and PRD congressional deputies passed an alternative budget rejecting proposed taxes on food and medicine and reallocating money to states. PAN deputies walked out in protest, while Fox claimed the budget unfundable as passed and vowed to challenge the Congress's action. Legal experts disagreed on whether the president could veto the bill, whether court action would suspend the budget in legal limbo, or what would happen if Mexico had no budget in the new year. The democratic exercise of power by the Congress clashed with the president's function as agenda setter but also arguably with his democratic mandate, contributing to unprecedented uncertainty and increased potential for deadlock. Moreover, loss of the president's traditional ability to arbitrate disputes could encourage the re-emergence of historically divisive regional and local differences. Problems are especially grave when they involve difficulties in curbing violent activity by those of opposing parties or factions, inside or outside government.

More broadly, at a time when so many competitive forces are in conflict, many wonder how far reform can go unless the president remains powerful enough to stop antireformist forces.[38] The old system was based upon an undemocratically strong, lofty presidency. The democratizing system struggles to limit the presidency without fatally weakening it, to combine effectiveness with accountability.

Regular Turnover: From Renewal to Disintegration to Accountability?
The one huge limitation placed on the president in the old system concerned the transfer of power: king, but for only six years. This regular "sexennial" changing of the guard was not a periodic opening to accountability, however. Instead, in the maximum expression of their pacts, elites kept competition limited among themselves and covered up the sins of their predecessors.

The orderly transfer of power was one of the most remarkable accomplishments of the Mexican regime and a cornerstone of its unmatched political stability among Third World nations. Authoritarian regimes typically are most at risk during power transfers; extended rule, when achieved, has often rested on the longevity of individual dictators. Latin America has often suffered from *continuismo,* efforts by leaders to perpetuate themselves in power after their prescribed term. This is what happened in Mexico when the *porfiriato* collapsed in 1911. Mexico broke the pattern with its commitment to no re-election and its model for sexennial change. Nevertheless, that the turnover did not indicate accountability is shown by a signal characteristic of the process: its secrecy.[39] The identity of the anointed individual was kept under wraps (*tapadismo*) until the incumbent president chose the time and form of revelation; only then would the *dedazo* (pointed finger) identify the winner. The incumbent's control over choosing his own successor was about the surest feature of the process. Less certain were the constraints other powerholders could impose through consultation and bargaining. But the general citizenry did not share in this decision in any significant way.

The sexennial mechanism functioned in practice to bolster nondemocratic stability, not to force leaders to account to the public for their time in office. At its peak (probably 1957–75) the process involved almost no struggle for succession. For a longer period it ensured that disappointed aspirants accepted the decision and publicly supported the victor. Mobility for elites involved whole camarillas, not just their chiefs. Of course massive turnover might have destabilized the system if it cast all powerholders aside. But Mexico's turnover was not so harsh; some people who had been recycled downward for a bit could rise again as successive presidents incorporated individuals from other camarillas to build team breadth. Only outgoing presidents had to accept a complete withdrawal from public life.[40]

Furthermore, incumbents were often selected with an eye toward fulfilling particular needs of the system. This imparted a sense of pendulum swing. If one president inclined rightward, he might select back toward the center-Left; an activist might select a consolidator, and so forth.[41] Excesses could be checked in a system otherwise lacking ongoing checks on power. Even in the sensitive matter of corruption, the unusual excesses of the López Portillo and Salinas administrations were not replicated by their immediate successors. But reflecting the system's lack of accountability to the citizenry, pendulum swings were at most within the establishment's left-right spectrum and reflected needs as perceived from above. Change from one sexennium to the next was ample regarding personnel, not policy.

Both personnel turnover and policy adjustment served the system by giving it a sense of renewal. Exiting officials could function as scapegoats. New administrations created reforms or the trappings of reform, with new slogans, programs, and faces. Such activities permitted successive administrations to allow expression of simmering frustrations, consideration of good new ideas, identification of talent, and a shift of priorities to particular problems.

But neatly managed sexennial change has disintegrated. The traditional sexennial beat is fundamentally unsuited to democratic transition.

The pendulum swing first yielded to an unharmonious and unpredictable mix of abrupt shifts in personnel with a frustrating sense of continuity. Whereas key ministers had served full terms and then become precandidates, later decades saw repeated midterm realignments. Only two ministers held their posts throughout the Salinas administration. Yet major appointments were still made from on high, without accountability or even explanations to the public. The rejuvenating effect of sexennial change also weakened, as policy adjustment became minimal. Despite the turnover in personnel, key economic posts remained across administrations with such like-minded heads that critics decried functional continuismo. The neoliberal path includes so many constants in economic policy suited to international and domestic business interests that the political system has lost autonomy to juggle policy according to domestic political considerations.[42] This point may apply to sexennial change not just between PRI presidents but between parties.

Gone also are the rules of decorum that surrounded sexennial change for decades. Having enjoyed the pleasures of a system that spared them from criticism in office, ex-presidents would suffer criticism in silence when out of office. Now Mexicans have been treated to memoirs by long-retired López Portillo, angry faxes from abroad from Salinas, and bitter rebuttals to Salinas by an archrival more than two decades out of office. Ex-presidents' criticisms come, albeit in more diplomatic language, from even as steady a figure as Miguel de la Madrid. Nor can the system any longer count on bypassed candidates to fall dutifully in line behind winners.[43] In the heated primary campaigns within the PRI, some losers of local races defect to opposition parties. Gone is the era in which sexennial change epitomized sure-handed control.[44]

The healthy side of all this disintegration, whatever the risks in undoing a system that was stable for so long, is that it opens up the possibility of more accountability. Perhaps the tradition of extensive local campaigning by anointed presidential candidates really did give candidates an opportunity to learn more about the people and their problems. Perhaps a pendulum swing did help balance some interests in candidate selection. The basic issue, however, is not whether the faint features of accountability in the old process got fainter. It is how far the new democratic process can effectively make the citizenry central to the process of leadership selection. Primaries — practiced at some level in most Mexican parties — are a step in this direction.[45] Most obviously decisive, however, is that competitiveness has risen to the point at which different parties win office.

No longer can a secure political establishment simply renew itself through a set of artfully crafted and controlled practices. No longer can the sitting president anoint his successor based on his own preferences or perceptions of the national good. System renewal can come only through democratic opportunity for citizens to weigh the promises and performance of leaders who compete for their support. Losers must play their part in bolstering the system, as they did in 2000, by acknowledging the sanctity of the democratic process and the subordination of leaders to citizens. The old process of sexennial leadership selection has lost out because it clashed with modern society's demand for more participation and accountability.[46] Mexicans have reason to hope that the frightening problems associated with sexennial transitions in recent decades will prove to have been a treacherous but now crossed bridge between the old system and a democratic one.

The Rule of Law

However great the progress in democratic leadership selection, for most Mexicans the most pressing concerns about accountability center on the rule of law in matters that touch them daily. Two key areas are corruption and human rights violations. These matters represent a lack of democratic accountability in a system that has had in certain other respects (e.g., fixed electoral terms) more rule of law over the decades than Latin America's military or personalistic dictatorships. And they represent the sort of persisting problems that attach negative adjectives to "democracy" in much of Latin America; increased competition helps but does not automatically overcome such problems.

Corruption.   As an abuse of power and clear violation of transparency, corruption clashes with accountability in most nations. Unfortunately, corruption is unusually rampant in Mexico. Zedillo's attorney general estimated that 80 percent of the federal police engage in corruption; *Reforma* polling in 1995 found that Federal District residents put the figure at 98 percent. Fox's "anti-corruption czar" Francisco Barrio estimated in 2001 that perhaps 9 percent of GDP was siphoned off to corruption.[47] Corruption functioned in some ways to support system stability. Elites have stayed within the system partly because the chances for handsome rewards have been so great. The unwritten rule has been to reap the personal rewards of public office and then give others a chance; individuals cannot easily turn on the system because they or their camarilla allies have partaken of its special benefits. Furthermore, corruption gives some flexibility, through bribes and personal favors, to a bureaucracy otherwise notorious for its rigidity. It provides some responsiveness in a system bereft of institutionalized accountability. Corruption may also help the system's stability, in that poorly paid public workers can augment their incomes to decent levels.

Periodic attacks on corruption have therefore not been wholehearted, lest the attacks be suicidal for the attackers or the system overall. Such attacks may temporarily mollify a public enraged by accelerated corruption, as with de la Madrid's "moral renovation" campaign after López Portillo's corruption orgy. The attacks on corruption usually have additional political motives, including establishing one's own sexenio by undercutting key figures linked to one's predecessor or enemies. For example, Salinas went after some corrupt figures but had his own cast of untouchables. Even in the more sober Zedillo administration, which for the first time prosecuted a member of the former president's immediate family, selection of anticorruption targets appeared to follow the president's political logic (including maintaining legitimacy internationally) more than the independent logic of a judiciary. Conflict-of-interest laws remain few and weakly enforced.

Once again, however, a political phenomenon that comes to be a liability for the old bases of stability must yield to democratic accountability. International concern adds to these pressures. In an economic model that turns on competitiveness, the costs of corruption are hard to bear. Foreign investors fear putting money into countries whose economies lack transparency. The new competitive ethic also supports deregulatory policies that echo U.S. domestic efforts to allow businesses to get things done expeditiously; in Mexico that would mean reducing the ubiquity of the bribe. Three days after taking office, Fox issued a decree establishing the Commission for Transparency and Combat against Corruption as well as the Federal Agency of Investigation to reform the federal judicial police. He appointed a federal comptroller — the anticorruption czar — to examine corruption in the federal bureaucracy. Within three years, over 3,000 police were replaced and 5,000 bureaucrats were sanctioned or fired. Unfortunately, new economic realities have also provided new opportunities for corruption.[48]

More than economic necessity is operating here. Public revulsion against corruption has grown. This is rarely a puritanical movement. A candidate for local office in a major state in 1995 could still elicit a sympathetic response from his audience by congenially pledging: "Voy a robar, pero poco" (I am going to rob, but [just a] little). Revulsion is more a response to officials who callously go beyond once accepted limits and whose actions appear particularly offensive against the background of economic catastrophes. Impunity is not the certainty it once was. Some Mexican scholars have thus taken to task a popular U.S. view that corruption is the glue that holds Mexico together, arguing instead that Mexican society is morally oriented and votes against corruption.[49] Polls repeatedly find people citing police corruption as one of their major concerns.

Beyond public opinion lies the new competitive political reality. With a choice based on more information and contested elections, citizens can demand more from those needing their support. They can, for example, insist on a better accounting of how agencies spend public funds. Of course, competitive politics also means partisanship in attacking corruption, as conflict between PAN and the PRD government of Mexico City shows. Still, some evidence suggests that corruption may be lower in Mexico's most politically competitive states. Opposition parties at national, state, and local levels can challenge government accounts. New governments of one party can expose the corruption of the previous administration of another party. Whatever the historical equation between the benefits and costs of corruption for stability, and whatever disrupting dangers come with attacks on corruption, corruption is now clearly a net destabilizing force. It is too antithetical to both economic necessity and dignified democracy.

Human Rights Violations.   Corruption is but the most discussed aspect of multiple practices that add up to pervasive lawlessness. The Mexican system displays a huge overapplication of power where democratic government should not tread and a nonapplication of power against arbitrary acts by powerholders. Mexico has in fact suffered greatly from the opposite of accountability: human rights abuses. Political scientists have noted that avoidance of such abuses is one of the fairly reliable accomplishments of democracies over nondemocracies.[50] Mexican society increasingly rejects human rights abuses, but their persistence remains a major challenge.

Before the 1980s Mexico barely had a human rights movement. Church-related and domestic rights groups have blossomed since then. International support has also encouraged government response to civil pressure. After Amnesty International blasted widespread torture (and the impunity of torturers), disappearances, the use of private militias, and state-sponsored terrorism against the peasantry and other citizens, President Salinas created the National Commission on Human Rights. Although the commission commanded respect for the personal integrity of its directors, an Americas Watch report immediately found it too weak and reiterated many Amnesty charges. Mirroring its reversal on outside observance of elections, Mexico later invited Amnesty and other foreign teams to monitor inside the country, though President Zedillo was hostile to Amnesty in Chiapas. In 2001, Fox created a special prosecutor's office to investigate and prosecute past violations of human rights by PRI administrations, responding to calls for justice by groups representing families of the disappeared. He also named Mariclaire Acosta, a respected human rights activist, as Deputy Secretary for Human Rights and Democracy within the Ministry of Foreign Affairs.

Unfortunately, alternation in power alone has not proven sufficient to ensure that public officials will be committed to scrutiny of abuses once in power.[51] Two years after Acosta took her position, Fox's Foreign Minister fired her and eliminated the post. A fragmenting establishment may tempt those fearing a loss of power into increasing acts of violence, as the rash of assassinations suggests. Even where matters improve regarding a democratizing national government, state and local abuses can continue. The use of hired muscle against dissident peasants, protesting students, or professional journalists is not new. What is new is how much it clashes with demands for a decrease in such activity. In addition, governments less able to control themselves may also be less able to control the illegal activities of others. The rampant drug trade is a key example, although the line between drug lords and government is often unclear. Paramilitary activity includes murder, ambushes, kidnapping, and other intimidation. Even when it comes to street crime, governments have lost control, further weakening respect from the public, as Chapter 1 noted. Desperate citizens sometimes turn to mob justice — lynching and burning those apprehended in the act — rather than relying on a police and court system they do not trust to protect them. Public approval of such actions is surprisingly high:

over 40 percent of those polled in 2004 felt that vigilante action was justified when the authorities did not apply the law equally, when they
refused to act on reports of crimes or delayed in applying the law, or when
"there is a lot of insecurity."[52]

In turn, governments desperate to reassert themselves are tempted to
adopt anticrime measures that raise the specter of a police state. These
trade-offs exist in contexts as different as El Salvador, Russia, and the
United States. It is challenging enough to contemplate the introduction of
such steps as phone taps, elite autonomous police units, use of the military in police activities, and anonymous witnesses even into a system
with a deep tradition of the rule of law, like the United States. It is more
distressing to contemplate such steps in places like Mexico. Human
rights groups find the most serious human rights issues in Mexico involve
the justice system, including torture of accused criminals, weak oversight of police, prisons with inadequate conditions, and an ineffective
court system with long delays that can leave people in prison for long
periods of time just awaiting trial. Even judicial reform may not fix the
problem of impunity: when courts no longer protect elites or powerful
criminals from prosecution, judges themselves become targets of violence and intimidation.

Notwithstanding such deterioration, there is reason to hope that
political-economic change will bring greater rule of law. One viewpoint is
that increasingly competitive businesses cannot tolerate the lack of reliable courts to enforce contracts and regulate rivals or the broad scope of
bureaucratic abuse and arbitrary power.[53] Also, a diminished role for the
state allows other institutions to develop watchdog roles. Still, the interest of international business focuses far more on courts dealing with civil
matters (like contracts) than criminal justice; businesses may even prefer
a tough line on criminals to reduce the risk of property crimes and kidnapping of wealthy foreigners.

More hope lies on the political side: the dynamics of competition present incentives for government to control abuses within and beyond its
ranks, and focus more on issues of quality of life, insecurity, and abuse by
police. When the PRD won control of Mexico City, it discovered there
what the PRI already saw at the national level: a disgusted citizenry
would blame those in power. Thus the city's installed attorney general
would be a respected academic (with a Harvard doctorate), paralleling
the tendency at the national level.

Tough dilemmas emerge in responding to public revulsion with
abuses: What if curbing violations by local party officials means losing

pivotal support from them in coming elections? What if insistence on transparency in government expenditures reveals embarrassing evidence that becomes fodder for opponents? Additionally, sometimes government uses legally dubious means to discover and punish likely offenders. And while many applauded the conviction of Raúl Salinas for murder as a sign that prominent public figures could no longer count on impunity, others lamented that a conviction could emerge from such limited and tainted evidence. By the same token, effective campaigns against formidable criminals require substantial development of government intelligence services, which are tricky to hold accountable even in venerable democratic systems and notoriously problematic in Mexico.

THE WEAK AND THE STRONG

Established Patterns

Most of the considerations about freedom and accountability are better understood when distinctions are drawn between less and more privileged groups.[54] Privileged Mexicans are more likely to enjoy access to media freedom, organize effectively in autonomous interest groups and in elections, and become part of the decision-making leadership. They are much less likely to be the objects of the arbitrary exercise of official power. Additionally, the privileged are much more likely to benefit from the system's nondemocratic features, such as corruption and the ability to wield power in legal but inequitable ways.

Although all political systems exhibit inequality in power, this inequality is stark in Mexico. A close parallel exists with socioeconomic inequality, as poorer Mexicans are generally weaker politically. Also, the existence of some prosperity and a mixed authoritarian political system has allowed for a comparatively good situation for a significant minority of the population, including the middle class. The notion of two Mexicos — one small, rich, and powerful, one large, poor, and weak — has been quoted by everyone from Mexican academics to Subcomandante Marcos.[55] The configuration of inequality is one of the keys to the difficulty of identifying *the* Mexican political system. For the poor the system has been largely authoritarian with considerable marginality alongside corporatist controls over co-opted organizations and their leadership; inclusion has generally occurred after important decisions have been made. Human rights abuses are more common in the (poor) south than in most of Mexico. For more privileged Mexicans, however, these features are less salient and need to be weighed against the pluralism of the rather autonomous organizations and choices available. Similarly, electoral and other competition is more advanced in geographical locations where more privileged Mexicans tend to live.

To maintain its own control, the government has "needed" to repress privileged Mexico much less than unprivileged Mexico — fortunately for the government, since privileged Mexico would be more costly to repress. Moreover, the main alternative to repression of privileged groups is partnership or accommodation, whereas for mass groups it is co-optation. The PAN's electoral victory did not change much in this regard, though few Mexicans have ever seen the PAN as a champion of equality, especially social equality. Nevertheless, it is not clear that even a leftist government would be able to govern much differently: the need to keep the rich investing and the poor working is powerful.

Weaker Mexico.   Weaker Mexico comprises the much larger of the two Mexicos. As seen in Chapter 3, urban labor and the peasantry are the largest organized groups, while extreme weakness and marginalization characterizes unorganized workers and indigenous peoples. Rural dwellers are on average worse off than urban dwellers. These groups do not totally lack power, but typically have little; the power they do have has rarely rested securely on democratic bases, with legal rights and institutionalized accountability. The power of the ballot has given average Mexicans some leverage to obtain material gain in return for political support, but this has generally fallen short of active participation in agenda setting or policy formation.

On top of the limited gains weaker Mexico has managed to achieve within the formal corporatist network, it has sometimes successfully exploited government vulnerability to pressure from outside the network. This vulnerability stems from a need to maintain legitimacy and prevent greater dissidence. Strikes and demonstrations have impacts, though less often and at greater risk than protest by more privileged groups. When Salinas's 1993 legislation to lift rent controls produced protest by some twenty thousand Mexico City residents, the president put the matter on hold. Likewise, when farmers in the small town of San Salvador Atenco launched a wave of increasingly large and violent protests against the construction of a new national airport on their land, President Fox found himself forced to withdraw his proposal. Common in both urban and rural settings have been land seizures ("squatting") by those whose claim is moral more than legal. Although government may

Protests and demonstrations over poor working and living conditions have been common in Mexico, both before and during the era of expanded democracy. The scene here is the *zócalo* (central square) in Oaxaca.

repress these groups, it may also decide that the easier course is to give legal title and perhaps compensation to prior owners — or just to look the other way. Consider also the enterprising street peddlers operating without licenses in parts of Mexico City where they interfere with traffic and take customers away from legal businesses that pay rent and taxes. Business estimates that "informal sector" activity accounts for one-fifth of sales. Where police efforts to evict have led to violence, government has often backed off.[56]

Such power by the poor bears trademark weaknesses, however. First, it is mostly reactive and usually aimed at partial remedies of very difficult problems. Second, not grounded in legal rights, such mobilization depends on ephemeral calculations and forbearance by authorities or powerful adversaries. It has been an important outlet for less privileged Mexico to exert some influence but often with high risks for limited results.[57] Compared with the groups mentioned thus far, women are obviously more numerous and heterogeneous in economic and political power. Nonetheless, there are special links between women and less powerful Mexico. The worst manifestation of weakness is their vulnerability to physical abuse. More common is the challenge of managing multiple responsibilities at home and in the workplace, especially difficult for women in poverty and for those without husbands present. Political weakness extends even to economically privileged women.[58]

Stronger Mexico.   Stronger groups in Mexico include not only business but also highly skilled labor and the middle class. Skilled labor is more likely than unskilled labor to escape corporatist controls and to benefit from international trade and labor standards. For the middle class a clear example of power lies in the university. This has been the case despite the corporatist feature of near total dependence on government funding, until neoliberalism modified that in the 1990s. The public university has largely responded to the demands of its mostly middle-class constituencies. It has exercised an autonomy to make fundamental policy decisions that have conflicted with the government's own preferences regarding rapid enrollment growth, lax standards, negligible tuition, lack of ties to business, and internal electoral processes. It has also been a focal point for dissent greater than what government would permit elsewhere, whether through demonstrations, strikes, university media and cultural outlets, academic publications, or teaching curriculum.[59]

Furthermore, the middle and especially upper classes are much more likely to be able to take advantage of the individual freedoms that require economic means. These include choice over whether to use public or private facilities (such as schools, universities, hospitals, and social clubs), where to live, and where to travel. Ownership of private property is another example and assumes extra poignancy as collective land (ejidos) gets disbanded and as government sells off public property (which the masses could regard themselves as owning). As Chapter 3 showed, business has occupied a particularly privileged position over the years. Business has gotten a good deal of what it wants simply because its interests have overlapped with those of the government. Government has often gone beyond legal mechanisms to keep mass groups in line, but it has usually not gone as far as the law would allow in controlling business (or the church). Thus public policy favoring privileged groups could long take place in a context of a formally cool relationship, whereas the mass groups whom the government has affected to defend have faced a harsh public policy reality.

This differential distribution of benefits has contributed to political stability. U.S. concerns to the contrary, instability in Latin America has resulted much less from popular revolution than from revolts by frustrated elites. A crucial Mexican government role on behalf of the privileged has been to protect them from the poor.[60] All in all, the political system has in its configuration of stronger and weaker groups tailored itself to stability rather than democracy.

A Changing Picture

Long-standing patterns are under challenge, however. It is not basically that the political power gap between more and less privileged Mexico is shrinking. It is that the nature of power — its roots and expression — is evolving for both Mexicos. This alters patterns that underpinned stability and raises prospects of more democratic relationships between government and both groups of citizens.

Stronger Mexico. In the traditional model (elaborated in Chapter 3) business accepted its position as a mostly tacit partner of government. But it has organized, as its rivals do. Similarly, skilled labor — seeing its privileged position slip — has taken advantage of political opening to organize in new ways. And the middle classes have stepped forward in a variety of movements and settings, sometimes challenging political parties, sometimes leading them. For modern democracy it is not enough that privileged Mexico be involved. Yet in Mexico, where access to resources and benefits is highly unequal, the challenge of inclusiveness is daunting. As a leading scholar of democratic politics summarizes the perhaps obvious point, "If citizens are unequal in their economic resources, so are they likely to be unequal in their political resources."[61] The economic resources available to stronger Mexico convert into greater political assets and influence, which makes it difficult for weaker Mexico to make its voice heard. In addition, strong actors may deliberately oppose expanding access to weaker actors because they fear that parties that now truly depend on electoral strength may take resources away from the more privileged, indulging in "irresponsible" (populist) economic policy. This fear produces divisions within economically privileged groups, who cannot outvote the poor. Some stick with the PRI, sometimes as undeclared but dangerous enemies of democratization; others use their resources to win through the new democratic process. Privileged Mexico must pursue and exercise power differently from in the past.

Weaker Mexico. The impact of political-economic change on weaker Mexico's participation and influence is also complex. Optimists foresee opportunity for the less privileged to expand their influence over a state that is at once less repressive and more responsive. To be sure, there is evidence of groups taking advantage of new opportunities to press their case. The rise of independent labor and peasant organization and of civil society as a whole is noteworthy and in important respects unprecedented. Additionally, greater divisions within government than in the past have given more room for such organizations to play off factions against each other and win allies.[62]

On top of all this, as the new competition pressures parties to appeal for widespread support, it increases the access of underrepresented groups. One example is the recent increase in the number of women with formal political positions. By the 1990s they outdistanced their U.S. counterparts in representation in national legislatures.[63] The PRI (1997) followed the PRD (1994) in establishing a quota of 30 percent female for its candidate lists and party committees; without quotas the PAN also made substantial efforts to increase women's role. Both the PRI and the PRD approached the 2000 elections with women as party presidents. Women have likewise held important government positions, including cabinet positions and the directorship of the National Human Rights Commission. They have played a major role in nongovernmental organizations, where they hold a greater share of leadership positions than in more traditional Mexican political institutions.

A less sanguine view is that political competition, coupled with neoliberalism, tends to make Mexico's weak even weaker.[64] Political competition may create an environment that drowns out the voices of those who cannot afford to pay for media time, run polished campaigns for office, or hire professional staff to lobby the government. This danger is increased by economic policies that emphasize individual incentives and rational/technical policy making over responsiveness to political pressure or collective economic rights. Neoliberal assistance through targeted social programs is sporadic and restricted. Against this background more freedom to choose, without the material means to take action, is hollow compensation. Regarding these points, it does not fundamentally matter whether neoliberals intend to harm the poor (by forcing them to bear the burden of economic adjustments that benefit the rich) or to help them (by adopting policies that promote long-term growth and opportunity).[65] New political and economic realities, however desirable in other respects, may aggravate the gap between the two Mexicos, a serious challenge for democratic development. We explore this danger in Chapter 5.

CONCLUSION

Mexico's political system — remarkable for stability but certainly not for democracy — has yielded first to semidemocracy and then to a challenging struggle toward more ample and consolidated democracy. A system that long has allowed considerable freedom of expression has extended it to freedom of organization and democratization of leadership selection. The number of actors able to check the power of the president has increased. Other crucial matters require movement toward democratic practice rather than consolidation. A growing concern for human rights, an end to impunity, and the general rise of the rule of law are prime examples of this movement. Furthermore, on all fronts — those where democratic progress needs to be consolidated and those where it still needs to gain the upper hand over authoritarianism — democracy must become much more of a reality for the great majority of Mexicans.

Mexico's challenge is to build democratic foundations for stability, based on a more autonomous, pluralist society, in place of stability founded on extensive government control over society. Government long restricted the flow of information to citizens. It prevented organized oppositions from forming and offering citizens real alternatives in leadership and policy. Now stability must involve a much more open process of ample information, appeals, competition, and choice by citizens. It must substitute for a leadership whose once formidable pacts, procedures, and skills eroded. The erosion included the presidency itself, the stable system's command post; the imperial presidency needs to be replaced by a much more democratic yet effective presidency. Leadership selection, which can no longer ensure stability through sexennial elite circulation and renewal, must involve much more citizen participation and influence. Corruption, human rights abuses, and other arbitrary uses of power that undermine the system must yield to much more transparent, fair, humane, and accountable practices. And a system that could sustain itself through extensive corporate controls over the majority, bringing benefits to a powerful minority, requires much more pluralism and accountability for the majority.[66]

None of this movement toward democratic stability is easy. As in many other countries, Mexico's road toward democratization is lined with potholes, red lights, yellow lights, wrong turns, and very disputed speed limits. Even where progress is notable at the national level, we see that the road is often more problematic in many states and localities. A unique difficulty at the national level concerns the very strength that long surrounded the nondemocratic pillars of stability. Remove the pillars and what is left? Powerful interests build around such pillars; when put on the defensive, those interests fight change, or try to bend it to their undemocratic ends. Not all pro-change or antigovernment forces are democratic. As in other countries where authoritarian systems have broken down, risks of authoritarian turns or instability exist. These dangers grow where the extension of democracy is not accompanied by economic and social performance that gains popular support. The breakdown of public order, whether increased street and drug crime or violence by political elites, is another menacing tendency.[67] Even if eventually consummated, Mexico's democratic transition will have been comparatively slow and meandering.

But contemporary Mexico has made significant democratic strides. Freedom now includes a growing array of actors and the national electoral process itself. Meanwhile, Mexico's political culture grows more democratic. In turn, these democratic strides make the persistence of undemocratic features appear all the more illegitimate and vulnerable. Increased inclusiveness delegitimizes continued exclusions, as increased pluralism delegitimizes continued corporatism.

Mexico's recent progress toward democracy is broadly consistent with classic modernization theory. To be sure, that theory was simplistic regarding the ease and speed of democratization. It was too sanguine in its view of how different components of development would reinforce one another in upward spirals toward democracy. In Mexico various components of development long had weak or even deleterious effects on democratization, and the complicated present still suggests only uneven progression toward democracy. But perhaps enough progress has been made so that a positive web will develop as democratic changes mostly reinforce one another. And it is where Mexico is most developed socioeconomically — where it is well-to-do or middle class, best educated, and most urban — that freedoms are most vibrant and accountability advances furthest. Moreover, growing international influences appear to be having a net positive effect on democratization. The next three chapters analyze the socioeconomic and international aspects of Mexico's struggle for democratic development.

CHAPTER 5

The State and the Market

Mexico's political opening parallels a corresponding economic opening. Like many countries in the developing and postcommunist world, Mexico has moved in a startlingly brief period from a relatively closed economy with a strong state role to a relatively open economy with a still important but less activist state. Like other countries Mexico has experienced adjustment problems as a result, which affect the process of political change. A central theme in this chapter is the causal connection between economic reform and political change. In some ways the liberalization of markets contributes to political liberalization. As economic functions formerly performed by the state fall into private hands, the balance of power between state and society shifts. The growth of competition in the political market is closely associated with the growth of competition in economic markets and state withdrawal from regulatory functions. Similar patterns unfolded in other countries that adopted market reforms — an example of normalization of social and economic patterns, making Mexico less singular, less unique.

Yet at the same time, the combination of crisis, reform, and structural adjustment has reinforced the income gap between Mexico's richest and poorest citizens. As Chapter 4 discussed, this means that many citizens cannot take advantage of political opening. Inequality may also undermine democracy in the long term. The market-oriented nature of Mexico's economic model aggravates economic and social inequalities, which may lead to political inequalities even under a democratic regime.

Democracy is no substitute for comprehensive development, and the struggle for democratic development in particular could carry some internal contradictions.

Economic reform also affects the structure of government. Economic ministries have increased their power relative to that of noneconomic ministries — a fact reflected in the shift in the nature of previous cabinet experience of the Mexican presidents from political to economic ministries. Nevertheless, the main political ministry (the Ministry of Government) experienced a comeback as political unrest increased and the need for political management skills became evident.[1] This is one indicator that political reforms may influence economics as well as vice versa.

Another potential effect of political change lies in the impact of electoral competition. As parties bid for voter support, electoral pressures could cause governments to follow unwise (but politically popular) economic policies — such as excessive spending — and avoid painful (but necessary) economic reforms. PRI presidents have used this argument in the past to justify delaying and limiting electoral competition. As the pressure for liberalization grew, they attempted to insulate economic policy making from electoral pressures by taking it out of the hands of elected bodies like the Congress. Instead, they delegated key decisions either to markets or to nonelected bodies (like a more autonomous Central Bank).

In addition to these connections, several parallels exist between changes in the economic and political spheres. In the economic arena as in political life, competition and uncertainty have risen. Mexico's previous economic model protected and guided national businesses much like the PRI protected and guided social organization. In contrast, the new economic model lets markets make many decisions: internationally competitive businesses will expand; uncompetitive businesses will fail or be forced into subordinate partnerships with more competitive ones. Jobs are less secure. Many jobs are created, but many others disappear. All of this means an unpredictable and shifting economic situation, subject to cyclical economic crises and intervention by Mexico's creditors. These uncertainties, in turn, have loosened the ties linking economic interests to the former ruling party. Without stable jobs, workers have less to gain from participating in a union, much less supporting the union's party ally. The weakening of the state in economic affairs parallels the weakening of the state in the political realm. A period of successful state intervention was followed by crisis and restructuring in the 1980s. Still, although the state has abdicated some of its economic responsibilities, important elements of continuity remain. The legacy of Mexico's prior development path, particularly the economic structures and resources developed, continues to shape the choices available to Mexico. Finally, the strength of some traditional actors has diminished, while new actors grow in importance. In particular, this chapter tracks the role of international economic interests.

The chapter follows an essentially chronological structure, tracing the development of the Mexican economy and economic policy from roughly the Second World War to the present. Within each time period the analysis focuses on three areas: (1) the state-society balance and the role of competition; (2) the impact of international actors; and (3) the implications of economic change for democracy and social welfare. As we see how state managers have responded to the challenges posed by previous economic choices, the reasons behind the profound economic reforms of the past twenty years emerge, and the relationship between political and economic change becomes clearer. As the title of this book notes, it is the struggle for democratic development that most characterizes Mexico and the reciprocal effects of the struggles for democracy and development shape the possibilities of achieving both.

THE MEXICAN MIRACLE: 1940–70

Market-oriented policies were introduced into an economy that had already built an industrial base during a remarkable stretch of economic growth from 1940 through 1970, a period which roughly — and not coincidentally — matches the peak period of PRI domination in politics. The economic policies behind this growth involved considerable state intervention. Like many developing countries at the time, Mexico looked to the state to make up for the weakness of its domestic capitalist class.

State-Market Balance

The central goal of this model was industrialization. Prevalent economic theories suggested that developing countries could not create an industrial economy without a major state role, in large part because new industries had to compete with exports from developed nations. New (or "infant") industries initially have higher costs and smaller outputs, while developed industries have already become efficient through experi-

ence and have expanded their production to take advantage of economies of scale.[2] Thus until infant industries can catch up, developing countries should protect them from foreign competition and use the power of
the state to subsidize their start-up costs. This principle implied a series of
policies that involved the state heavily in economic markets.

The first and most direct role of the state in achieving the goal of
industrialization therefore involved legal protection of domestic products
from foreign competition, by taxing imports (through tariffs) and impos-
ing import quotas. The idea was to make imports more expensive than
domestically manufactured goods, in order to convert existing demand
for imports into a ready-made market for new national industries. For
this reason the model was called import substitution industrialization
(ISI); it attempted to industrialize by substituting domestically produced
goods for imported ones. Second, the state supplied cheap loans, technology, and tax breaks. Buoyed by international reserves accumulated
during World War II, Mexico's Central Bank was in a favorable position
to expand domestic credit, and public spending increased steadily as a
share of the gross national product (GNP).[3] Through loans and direct
investment in infrastructure, the public sector provided more than half of
total capital formation (net investment in fixed assets) during the initial
years, and about 41 percent of capital formation from 1940 to 1970.[4] At
the time most Mexican capitalists saw such intervention as complementary to their own investment plans, rather than as competitive, and therefore welcomed it. Only later would wariness about state involvement
ripen into outright rejection by some business leaders.

Favorable attitudes toward state intervention were particularly pronounced among national industrialists. State credit and investment heavily favored industry over agriculture, especially after 1952.[5] Between
1940 and 1950 the agricultural sector grew quite quickly (an average of
8 percent a year), due in part to agrarian reform in the 1930s.[6] But as
state investment fell, agricultural production stagnated. Between 1960
and 1965 agricultural production increased on average just 3.6 percent a
year, while manufacturing grew at more than 8 percent a year.[7] Where it
did invest in agriculture, the state favored market-oriented — and often
export-oriented — agriculture over subsistence agriculture (for home consumption). This policy complemented Mexico's overall goal of industrialization. A positive agricultural trade balance provided valuable foreign
exchange with which to fuel industrialization. Commercial agriculture
was also needed to supply the growing urban demand for food.
However, the social consequence was a growing gap between the modern

sector of agriculture and the much larger traditional sector. Only large landowners and a few peasant communities that grew profitable crops for export enjoyed regular access to capital, credit, and technology. These farms included the best land, provided with irrigation systems. They were at the heart of commercial agriculture, engaged in the large-scale production and processing of food for sale and export. Nevertheless, declining investment and slowing agricultural productivity would eventually turn Mexico from a net agricultural exporter in 1965 into a net importer of food.[8]

In addition to investment and tariff protection, the state provided industry with infrastructure and key inputs. Subsidies included cheap electrical power, transportation (highways, railroads, airports, and ports), and inputs like steel, paper, and cement. Gradually, the government assumed ownership of many strategic industries that supplied crucial inputs to manufacturing. The state also owned and operated the national oil company (PEMEX), which has had a monopoly on the exploitation of oil (and oil by-products) since its expropriation from British and U.S. oil companies by Lázaro Cárdenas in 1938. Third World countries have often mixed state ownership of key sectors with a basically market economy in this way, especially for natural resources like oil. Yet oil did not become an important source of foreign exchange until the late 1970s: after 1938, Mexico fell out of the international oil market.[9] Mexico used oil primarily to subsidize domestic industrialization. Although important, oil could not supply foreign exchange to import the technology for industrialization, the machines to fill Mexico's factories and produce industrial goods.

Finally, the state intervened in the market to ensure price stability; indeed, this is known in Mexico as the period of "stabilizing development," indicating a combination of rapid growth with low inflation. Price stability was anchored by an exchange rate pegged at 12.5 pesos to the U.S. dollar from 1954 through 1976. Pegging the peso helped keep inflation low, typically less than 5 percent a year. It also had the effect of gradually overvaluing the peso, a policy that made imports relatively cheap and exports relatively expensive. This supported import substitution industrialization, because although specific imports that competed with Mexican industrial goods could be taxed, other imports — particularly imports of capital goods — were cheap. However, the overvalued peso also hurt exports and thus undermined the financial base needed to import industrial technology. In the long term this problem would contribute to the exhaustion of the import substitution model.

International Influences

Special attention was paid to the role of foreign investment during the so-called Mexican Miracle. On the one hand, the state strictly regulated foreign investment, partly in reaction against the *porfiriato*'s courtship of foreign capital prior to the 1910 Revolution (discussed in Chapter 2). Foreign companies had to get approval from the Ministry of Foreign Relations in order to invest.[10] Certain areas, such as oil, were off limits to all private investors, domestic as well as foreign. Others, such as banking, were restricted to Mexican investors. In most economic activities foreign investors were limited to less than 50 percent of all stock. The rest had to be in Mexican hands. This gave Mexican business great leverage as protected owners or privileged partners of foreign capitalists. In addition, the approval process for foreign investment took a long time and was very unpredictable, often frustrating potential investors. Foreign direct investment as a share of the gross domestic product (GDP) shrank steadily. Foreign investment as a share of gross fixed investment had fallen to 3 percent by 1960, compared with 45 percent in 1902 and 1903, at the height of the porfiriato.[11]

Nevertheless, foreign investment concentrated on key sectors and therefore played a significant role in development. Mexico's size as well as its proximity to the United States made it attractive despite legal restrictions. Although the *share* of foreign investment declined, the total stock of foreign investment continued to grow under ISI, especially in industry. Reliance on foreign technology even in Mexican-dominated sectors remained high, as in most developing countries. Large foreign companies that could offer more money or technological expertise were courted and granted exemptions to legal limits. By 1965 firms with majority foreign ownership — one-half of 1 percent of all firms — accounted for 10 percent of industrial employment and 20 percent of production and investment.[12]

In 1965, toward the end of the period of stabilizing development, this pattern of permitting selected foreign involvement was formalized with the establishment of *maquila* zones along the northern border. These zones fall into the general category of export processing zones, common in many Third World countries, where multinational companies locate part of their production process in a low-cost labor nation, usually shipping parts into the country and re-exporting the finished product.[13] In the maquiladora sector foreign companies were permitted 100 percent ownership and given other incentives and tax breaks. Maquila zones proved a solid success: the sector expanded steadily and played a central role in export growth.

In addition to investment, Mexico sought foreign capital through borrowing. Until the 1970s Mexico's total foreign debt remained modest compared with the inflated totals it would later reach. The state relied mostly on domestic credit and savings to finance spending; taxes remained low. Yet there were signs of debt trouble ahead. After 1950, Mexico suffered a persistent trade deficit, with imports greater than exports. While Mexico imported fewer consumer goods during ISI, Mexican industries required continued imports of capital goods (factory machines). Moreover, government spending outstripped increases in revenue. Increasingly, government capacity to spend depended on securing foreign loans. The ratio of debt service payments to exports deteriorated, in part because exports declined. This meant a shrinking supply of foreign exchange to pay off the foreign debt, increasing Mexico's vulnerability to a debt crisis.[14]

Social and Political Implications

Nevertheless, the overall result of these policies was — at least until 1970 — an enviable record of macroeconomic success. Mexico achieved average annual growth rates of more than 6 percent a year for thirty years, a record comparable to that of only a handful of developing countries, including Japan, Taiwan, and South Korea. By 1970 profound changes in the Mexican economy had occurred. The GNP went up cumulatively nearly 500 percent, while the GNP per capita more than doubled.

These economic changes produced corresponding changes in social structure. Industry's participation in the GNP increased from 25 percent to 34 percent, while the contribution of agriculture dropped from 21 percent to 11 percent. The percentage of the population working in agriculture went from two-thirds to just over one-third by 1970, while the industrial labor force grew to more than 20 percent.[15] The urban population grew twice as fast as the total population, due to rural-urban migration: while 35 percent of the population in 1940 lived in urban areas, almost 60 percent of the population in 1970 did. By that year the country's mortality rate fell to less than half its level in 1940, because of improvements in housing, public services, and nutrition; life expectancy increased from fifty years in 1950 to sixty-two years in 1970.[16] A significant middle class developed, including managers and technicians who were needed in the new industries as well as professionals (doctors, teachers, etc.) who were needed to meet the demand for services from the prospering business class.

But there were snakes in this garden of Eden. First, by the late 1960s growth began to slow. At existing prices (inflated by protectionism) domestic consumer demand could absorb less new production. Because economic growth largely depended on the domestic market, this meant slower growth. In contrast to some Asian countries, Mexico did not turn at this stage to exports as an additional source of demand, nor were Mexico's infant industries forced to grow up, that is, to become competitive enough to meet international firms on their home turf.

A second set of problems resulted from the uneven social effects of ISI. Mexican industrialists clearly benefited and the middle class grew significantly. Yet job creation lagged behind overall growth, partly because Mexican industrialists imported First World, labor-saving technology to set up their new factories. While the economy grew at more than 6 percent a year, the number of new jobs increased by only 2.5 percent a year — less than Mexico's annual average population growth.[17] In 1950 about 32 percent of the population had jobs; by 1970, after two more decades of the Mexican Miracle, just 27 percent did.[18] In essence, one-quarter of the population provided for the other three-quarters, including the elderly, children (almost half the population), unemployed men, and women, who mostly did not work outside the home. A high dependency burden usually means lower rates of domestic savings and thus lower potential for investment and growth based on domestic resources.

This pattern of slow employment growth went along with rising inequality. From 1950 to 1970 the share of GDP earned by the poorest groups shrank slightly, while the share of the richest 20 percent rose. Mexico had one of the worst income distribution profiles of any nation on earth (see Table 2).[19] Ironically, public protest came less from poor Mexicans than from dissatisfied middle-class youth, who had benefited from ISI both in the living standards of their families and in their nearly free public education through the university level. The most notable example of this discontent appeared in the 1968 student movement, organized around a set of demands that included adequate professional jobs and democracy. Pressure for *democratized* development was growing but was still not the aspiration of important sectors, nor the obligatory context of political engagement.

For one thing, despite signs of trouble on the political side of the

TABLE 2. INCOME DISTRIBUTION IN MEXICO, 1963–2000
(percentage of income earned)[a]

	1963	1977	1984[b]	1992	2000
1–2 (lowest 20 percent)	3.5	3.3	4.8	4.3	3.1
3–5	11.5	13.4	16.0	14.1	37.9[c]
6–8	25.4	28.2	29.7	27.4	
9–10 (highest 20 percent)	59.6	55.1	49.5	54.2	59.1

SOURCES: Figures for 1963–77 from Levy and Székely 1987: 148; figures for 1984 from Alarcón González 1994: 87; figures for 1992 from INEGI 1993: 39; figures for 2000 from *World Development Report 2004*: 61.

a. Estimates may vary slightly due to calculations from different sources. Similar estimates for 1963 and 1977 appear in Hernández-Laos and Córdoba 1982. Slightly less favorable data are reported in Baer 1986.

b. Alarcón González's (1994) data may reflect improvement between 1977 and the onset of the economic crisis in 1981. However, her estimates for 1989 come close to government estimates for 1992 and confirm deterioration during the crisis.

c. (3–8)

equation, progress on the development side tended to stabilize non-democracy. Strong growth satisfied the immediate material needs of those sectors of the population with the most ability to protest. Even skilled workers benefited. If other sectors benefited less, many Mexicans' lives still improved compared with the difficult reconstruction period after the revolution. Though agriculture was neglected, the regime could coast for a while on the goodwill generated by extensive land reform in the thirties. Moreover, because ISI placed the state squarely in the center of economic activity, individual chances for profit and prosperity depended to some extent on state decisions. And the PRI controlled the state. Thus the PRI had leverage to convince potential opponents not to challenge its authority. As long as the economic model continued to work, this was enough not only to preserve the political neutrality of sectors like business but also to maintain the coalition behind ISI.

For thirty years ISI worked mostly as expected on the economic front, converting demand for imports into domestic demand for Mexican products. The economy grew, an industrial base developed, educational levels and standards of living rose, inflation remained low, and debt — if growing — had yet to become a serious problem. Buoyed by growth and optimism about the country's future, the PRI enjoyed strong and genuine political support. If ISI also stabilized authoritarian rule, produced fewer jobs than expected (and needed), and failed to reduce persistent inequality and poverty, the costs seemed manageable to those with political power.

THE END OF STABILIZING DEVELOPMENT, 1970–1982

These mostly positive evaluations of the political system during the Mexican Miracle began to erode in the 1970s as threats to economic growth became more serious. Some of these threats were domestic in origin, while others resulted from changes in world markets. Two consecutive Mexican governments tried and failed to save ISI. Their ultimately futile efforts would leave a lasting legacy in the shape of a vastly increased public debt, a fragile currency, and a weakened state. By the start of Miguel de la Madrid's term in 1982, business had begun to assume a more active political role, technocrats from economic policy ministries had risen to power, and the state had begun its road toward retreat from direct economic management. With these changes the stage was set for louder and more numerous demands that the state abandon its aspirations to control social organization and give way to democracy.

State-Market Balance

During the early 1970s the Mexican government's reaction to growing economic problems was to strengthen the state with respect to markets — in sharp contrast to the tack taken a decade later. Although these problems were common side effects of ISI, the government believed that the overall approach remained sound; more intervention would simply be required to get Mexico over the hump and into the next phase of growth. Thus the state's role in the economy expanded during this period.

In many countries that have tried ISI, economic growth rates tend to slow down after the so-called easy phase (of low-end consumer goods, such as textiles) ends. Typically, the next industries to develop require more sophisticated technology and more costly investment. If domestic capitalists do not have the means, governments may either allow foreign investors to provide them or take over themselves. Yet they must still finance government expenditures on the basis of the resources generated by the domestic economy — or by debt. As the Mexican domestic economy slowed, debt became the primary option for generating new capital. Public and private debt rose steadily, to pay for the budget deficits incurred by the state's commitments to subsidize industry, expand infrastructure, and provide cheap loans.

Just as later-stage products cost more to produce, they also cost more to buy and thus have smaller markets. At the high prices induced by protectionism, domestic markets for these products may eventually become exhausted, causing the economy to slow down. How long this takes depends on the size of the domestic market and the growth of domestic incomes. Mexico has a relatively large potential market (in terms of population), but its high levels of inequality, unemployment, and underemployment mean that only a fraction of its population can afford many goods. One possible solution is to expand the potential market by encouraging exports. Yet Mexican industries in the 1970s remained inefficient, unable to do without state protection. This limited their ability to export.

In this situation the government could have chosen more than one alternative. Other countries confronted with similar limitations chose different solutions, principally involving export promotion and gradual relaxation of protectionism. For example, some of the later-developing Asian nations, including Taiwan and South Korea, followed this path. Asian domestic markets were smaller and their unions were weaker, perhaps explaining why they made a different choice.[20] It would have been politically difficult for Mexico to do the same in the 1970s. Mexican governments in the 1990s came closer to imitating Asia, albeit only under the pressure of a severe economic crisis

However, Mexican leaders in the 1970s strengthened the role of the state. Instead of turning to exports, the state stepped in to provide additional subsidies, bolster domestic demand by purchasing products for government projects, and protect jobs. Worried that a shrinking economy would aggravate political unrest, President Luis Echeverría tried to spend his way out of recession. Government expenditures went in part to productive investment but also to co-opt middle-class youth by hiring them as bureaucrats. The size of the state bureaucracy doubled by the end of his term. In addition, state ownership of companies increased dramatically, in part to protect struggling companies from bankruptcy and save jobs. Before 1970 the Mexican state controlled only about 80 enterprises, most of them in strategic economic sectors, such as electricity and railroads. By 1982 the state controlled 1,155 companies.[21]

These presidents believed that by protecting Mexico's industrial base, they could generate incomes to sustain future growth. In the end they neither maintained growth nor saved ISI, although its demise was postponed for more than a decade. But they left a substantial legacy of debt and considerably expanded the state's role in economic life. Companies were protected not only from foreign competition but also from their own poor business practices. Strict regulations limited the role of foreign investors. Direct employment and ownership by the state expanded. And

state spending on infrastructure, loans, and subsidies continued unabated — all to keep the economy growing. During periods of economic
recession advanced industrial countries have often used government
spending to create domestic demand and fuel growth; such policies are
referred to as Keynesian. However, Keynesian spending may have quite
different effects on countries with fragile economies, uncompetitive
industries, and substantial credibility problems (like Mexico) than on
large countries with developed industries and nearly unlimited credit
(like the United States).[22]

International Influences

Mexico's vulnerability to external factors even under a protectionist
model illustrates the difficulty of insulating any country from the global
economy. Although the domestic problems and contradictions discussed
earlier might eventually have forced government policy makers to face
limitations to continued ISI expansion, in the end three international
events exacerbated these problems and triggered a series of crises that
ended the period of stabilizing development.[23] First, the world price of oil
increased significantly in 1973 as a result of the formation of an oil producer cartel, the Organization of Petroleum Exporting Countries
(OPEC). Second, rising oil prices triggered a world recession with inflation beginning in 1974. Developing countries suffered from the down-
turn in their principal export markets. The prices of imported goods and
machinery rose, yet their exports fell — augmenting the trade deficits
inherent in ISI. And third, as international private banks took the
deposits made by OPEC oil exporters — so-called petrodollars — they had
to lend out this money in order to make a profit. Increasingly, private
banks became substantial lenders to the Third World.

    This international incentive to lend combined disastrously with the
incentives of the Mexican government to borrow in order to finance
expansionary spending. Powerful social actors, particularly business,
resisted tax reform. Mexico was not yet a net exporter of oil in the early
1970s; hence it could not take advantage of the OPEC-led price increase
to pay for government spending. Since commercial banks had reasons to
increase lending just as Mexico had motives to increase spending, the
Mexican government took the easy way out. And because most of the
new loans came from commercial, private lenders intent on making a
profit, these new loans came at a substantially higher cost than earlier
loans from multilateral agencies (like the World Bank). If either half of

the equation had been missing, the impact might have been more limited. This internationalization of Mexican development was no step forward; indeed, the bad experience left a mark in both Mexico and the United States on public opinion about the costs of global partnership.

Mexico's foreign debt increased from $4.2 billion in 1970 to nearly $20 billion by 1976. Ironically, a debt incurred by nationalist Mexican presidents in order to fend off foreign competition would later become the main source of leverage for foreign interests that wanted Mexico to lower its trading barriers. Thus two historical goals of the Mexican regime — economic growth and national independence — turned negative, undermining its legitimacy and political stability. In addition, inflation grew, pushed by deficit spending as well as inflation in the developed countries. In sad contrast to single-digit inflation during the period of stabilizing development, Mexico developed double-digit inflation by the mid-1970s. Inflation discouraged investment and contributed to capital flight. It also led to changes in economic decision making. The time span of wage agreements was shortened from every two years to every year, raising labor costs more frequently. Nervous private investors transferred money out of production, held it in dollars, or put it in foreign banks.[24] The rational decisions made by private businessmen to protect their assets led to a collective outcome that all of them lamented: falling investment, which deepened economic decline despite the government's expansionary spending. After peaking at 8.5 percent in 1972, economic growth rates fell to 4.2 percent by 1976, barely keeping up with population growth.[25]

The peso's stability was undermined by the persistent current account deficit, inflation, capital flight, deficit spending, and growing debt. In 1975, after fifteen years of currency stability, Echeverría had to devalue the peso and begin negotiations with the International Monetary Fund (IMF). The austerity program required by the IMF resulted in a better trade balance and reduced public spending but also in a domestic economic recession. Mexico's growth rate in 1977 was the lowest since the late 1950s.

But then Mexico discovered vast new oil fields. New president José López Portillo's brief effort at fiscal discipline soon seemed unnecessary. In fact, he embarked on an unprecedented spending spree, announcing that Mexicans had outgrown the problems of capital scarcity and needed to "prepare ourselves to administer abundance."[26] Public spending grew by an average of 16.8 percent a year from 1978 to 1981, helping growth to accelerate to more than 8 percent in each of those years.[27] The decision to avoid fundamental reform of ISI seemed vindicated. Pushed by multinational corporations, López Portillo briefly considered joining the General Agreement on Trade and Tariffs (GATT), a multilateral framework geared toward the liberalization of international commerce, in order to stimulate more foreign investment and trade. But political opposition against dismantling trade barriers was very high among domestic industrialists and national politicians. High growth rates meant that López Portillo could afford to indulge them.

Yet rosy appearances cloaked persistent and even aggravated problems. Inflation continued to edge upward, to nearly 30 percent by 1981. And paradoxically, the oil boom made possible a huge expansion in debt. Used as collateral, oil made Mexico more attractive as a loan recipient. Public debt soared from $19.6 billion at the end of 1976 to nearly $59 billion by the end of 1982. A large percentage of this debt was contracted on a short-term basis, at high interest rates. The cost of this was substantial: by 1982, Mexico devoted two of every three dollars received from exports to debt service. Even more dangerous, by this time Mexico depended on oil for 75 percent of total export income.[28] When oil prices crashed in 1981, Mexico faced a serious shortfall in revenue and declared itself unable to continue debt service payments. Several other developing countries soon followed suit, and a worldwide financial crisis erupted. This forced López Portillo to devalue the peso for the second time in six years. He also nationalized the banking system (until then mostly private), in part to get a handle on inflation and capital flight. The economic crisis would last nearly a decade, and Mexico would emerge from it with a very different economic model. ISI was dead, though it would not be declared dead for several years.

International actors played a major role even at the peak of the Mexican Miracle as investors, suppliers of technology and imports, and a source of foreign exchange and loans. They continued this role during the 1970s. In addition, international bankers became increasingly important. International recessions, lending policies, and choices by the U.S. Federal Reserve to raise interest rates significantly affected Mexico. Mexico is certainly not alone in this. The lesson here is simply that Mexico's exposure to international risk did not begin with the shift toward free trade. Rather, this has been an ongoing theme.

Social and Political Implications

For the most part the social and political conditions of the Mexican people from 1970 to 1982 reflected the same trends evident during the

Mexican Miracle. Urbanization, education, and industrialization continued. More important, profound inequality continued. Indeed, perhaps the biggest story of this period was something that did *not* happen: despite state spending on social programs, direct employment, and various development schemes, things did not greatly improve for the vast majority of Mexicans. Middle-class Mexicans received more opportunities for state employment; business continued to be protected; but real wages failed to grow significantly even for the organized working class. As was sadly typical, unorganized Mexico — the larger group — continued to fall further behind. Official neglect of agriculture did nothing to lift the rural sector out of deep and devastating poverty. Indian Mexico, as always, came in last, in spite of efforts to organize by independent Indian leaders; in these mostly fruitless ventures one can find precursors of the zapatista rebellion twenty years later. At the time discontent presented no significant threat to PRI political hegemony.

Yet this apparently stagnant decade marks a dividing point, in economic as well as political terms, between the peak period of PRI control and effective state management, and the deep crisis of the 1980s that brought about major changes. The choices made in the 1970s to respond to growing challenges — choices that often seemed logical and even successful — undermined the basic principles of both economic and political spheres: in the political sphere PRI hegemony, and in the economic sphere ISI with strong state intervention. If the 1977 electoral reform comes close to a political turning point, the expansion of debt is its economic equivalent.

The 1970–82 period also provides examples of the complex relationship, noted in previous chapters, between political and economic change. In their scramble to maintain the high economic growth rates of the Mexican Miracle, successive presidents took steps that left a tragic legacy. In particular, the expansion of public debt cast a shadow over social and economic policy. Although appearing at the time to strengthen and expand the state's role, the public spending financed through debt eventually weakened the state's capacity to resist outside demands. Debt also undercut the state's capacity to provide a social safety net. Mexico was not alone: most of the large Latin American economies increased indebtedness to dangerous levels. Nevertheless, the debt Mexican policy makers acquired rather blithely, under the mistaken assumption that oil would pay for it, constrained economic and social choices.

Debt is also connected to a number of political shifts that would become more significant after 1982: the rise of technocrats to power, the

related rise of the economic cabinet within the state structure, and —
looking ahead to Chapters 6 and 7 — internationalization. Given the
importance of debt, Mexico needed leaders who understood economic
policy and who could deal effectively with international lenders. After
1970 four successive presidents had some advanced graduate study in
economics as well as experience in the economic ministries. Each was
chosen during a crisis in economic affairs.[29] Each took into office a team
of economically trained advisers, contributing to the technocratic orientation of Mexican governments. Moreover, the growing importance of
financial management resulted in restructuring of the state and particularly the administrative and policy-making responsibilities of the economic cabinet. The old super-ministry of finance (the Secretaría de
Hacienda y Crédito Público) was split into two separate ministries at the
end of López Portillo's term: a finance ministry and a budget and planning ministry.[30] In general, economic ministries (Finance, Budget and
Planning, Trade and Industry, and the Bank of Mexico) became more
influential. Whereas the minister of finance often shared policy-making
duties with other ministries during the Mexican Miracle, finance and
budget ministers increasingly became policy leaders over noneconomic
ministries. In particular, the Ministry of Government lost influence — at
least, until the management of democratic reform as well as concerns
about stability demanded more attention in the late 1990s. These trends
become stronger after 1982 but begin in the late 1970s.

At the same time politics influenced economic choices. The dramatic
expansion of the state in the 1970s owed something to the government's
fear of political instability under economically difficult conditions, a fear
given substance by the 1968 student movement and spreading guerrilla
activity. And the process of economic reform is itself political. Many
reforms eventually undertaken in the 1980s were considered and rejected
earlier because they involved painful costs or were resisted by powerful
actors. Tax reform, for instance, was taken off the table because it
involved an apparently unnecessary confrontation with business interests. Similarly, a proposal in the late 1970s that Mexico dismantle trade
protection (by joining GATT) faced stout resistance from protected
national industrialists as well as labor.

When necessary, the Mexican state was able and willing to confront
powerful actors, but in the 1970s the economic situation had not yet
become a crisis. Even strong states often postpone painful economic
reforms because of political considerations. In the early 1970s, it seemed
reasonable (if a bit of wishful thinking) to suggest that economic down-

turns were merely shifts in the business cycle — especially when growth rebounded in 1972 and 1973. In the late 1970s the discovery of oil seemed to make sacrifice unnecessary. Most other oil-producing nations from Venezuela to Nigeria assumed the same thing.[31] Nevertheless, not all Third World nations got themselves as deeply into debt as Mexico. Even at the time some voices warned against the expansion of debt and the protection of unproductive enterprises. The regime does bear some responsibility. In his final State of the Union address a tearful López Portillo apologized to the Mexican people for his administration's economic and social failures.

Sadly for him — and the PRI — the Mexican people were not in a forgiving mood, particularly as the economic crisis dragged on.[32] As discontent mounted, social actors mobilized to shape, preserve, or reform existing policy. Demands for a more accountable and democratic political system — one that could be punished for mistakes like those made in the 1970–82 period — began to grow. The struggle for development would increasingly focus on its modern aim: democratic development. But the new definition of "development" would not only be democratic but internationalized as well, reversing a key goal of the postrevolutionary regime.

THE ROAD TO THE MARKET: THE EMERGENCE OF THE NEOLIBERAL MODEL, 1982–PRESENT

During the 1980s the gathering storm finally broke. In economic terms the decade was a disaster. After the oil price crash in 1981, Mexico fell into a deep recession, with rising unemployment, plummeting real wages, and historically unprecedented inflation. A series of external shocks and natural disasters compounded the crisis. Between 1982 and 1988, Mexico's total GDP grew by just 0.2 percent — essentially, zero real change.[33] Decades of improvement in real minimum wages were almost wiped out. Even the standards of living of the privileged classes deteriorated. Other big debtor countries in Latin America experienced similar events, leading them to refer to the 1980s as the "lost decade": wasted years during which economies stagnated or actually shrank instead of making progress toward development.

Yet the 1980s also brought profound economic and political reform to Latin American countries. Most of them ended the decade with far more democratic political systems. Likewise, they began to abandon, one after another, the ISI policies which had guided them in the postwar years.

Mexico too began a tentative transition to market-oriented policies, which were expanded and consolidated during the 1990s. By 1997 a fundamentally different approach, the neoliberal model, had largely replaced Mexico's postwar economic model. Neoliberalism emphasized state withdrawal from the economic sphere, an expanded role for foreign investment, and free trade. Not since the Mexican Revolution had changes of this magnitude occurred in economic policy. And although the shift from porfirian economic principles to the ISI state had taken nearly thirty years to put in place (from 1910 to 1940), the shift back to markets took fewer than fifteen years. The economic disruptions involved in this shift are intimately tied to the social and political disruptions of the 1980s and 1990s. As the state reduced its control of the economy, the PRI's control of the political system eroded. The postwar political consensus was built around a set of expectations about the state's role in economic affairs. When these expectations were violated, the political consensus began to fall apart.

State-Market Balance

The state's weakened position relative to private actors resulted from several fundamental factors. Most immediately, the government was broke. If Mexico was to continue making payments on its foreign debt, the government had to accept severe limits on spending in order to qualify for foreign assistance from IMF and U.S. creditors. As government budgets shrank, so did domestic demand and the state's capacity to soften the blow of deepening recession. Worst of all, the debt burden was not really lifted: three years later, in 1985, foreign debt as a percentage of Mexico's total GDP remained at around 60 percent. New loans went toward payments on old debt rather than toward productive investment. And capital flowed out of the country at a frightening rate, draining the country's vital resources.

Initial responses to the 1981 debt crisis did not contemplate fundamental reforms. However, they failed to restore economic growth. To make debt payments and meet IMF budget targets, de la Madrid slashed public spending. He also laid off more than 20 percent of all state employees by July 1985 and closed or sold many unprofitable state enterprises.[34] Unemployment increased and the GDP shrank in both 1982 and 1983. A brief economic recovery in 1984 ended abruptly in 1985, as a major earthquake hit Mexico City, causing an estimated $4 billion in damage to property in addition to its tragic human toll.[35] As if this were not bad enough, world oil prices suddenly fell by half. The Mexican government lost a substantial portion of its revenue, forcing it to scrap the 1986 budget and appeal to the IMF for help. Moreover, the political system showed signs of serious strain. Popular protests against government inaction after the earthquake gave clear evidence of deep social discontent. The PRI's efforts to contain the PAN's advances in local and congressional elections in 1985 and 1986 backfired, producing civil disobedience against electoral fraud. Business leaders began to oppose the PRI openly.

Desperate times call for desperate measures. The worsening economic situation — as well as the increasing political urgency of improvement — brought key policy makers to argue that Mexico's economic problems required more fundamental reforms, not simple budget cuts or emergency loans. The crisis was not a short-term cash flow problem but structural economic weakness. After 1985 government policy began to shift toward policies that previous Mexican governments considered unnecessary or too politically costly. The danger of causing a split within the PRI by abandoning nationalist policies seemed less compelling than allowing the economic crisis to continue.

One sign of this shift was the accelerating pace of privatization. Under de la Madrid the state began to sell or close unprofitable companies it had acquired during the previous forty years. By the end of de la Madrid's term in 1988, the number of public enterprises had fallen from 1,155 to 420.[36] Incoming president Carlos Salinas expanded privatization to some of the biggest and most profitable state-owned companies. In 1989 he put the state telecommunications monopoly on the auction block, then hotel chains, steel mills, sugar refineries, fertilizer plants, and the last state-owned airline. Some of the biggest prizes — the banks nationalized by López Portillo less than ten years earlier — were sold in just over a year.[37] Foreign investors could buy stock. Huge revenues poured into state coffers — exceeding the proceeds of privatization in other comparable Latin American countries. By 1998 fewer than 150 state-owned enterprises remained.[38]

The state also withdrew from many of its traditional functions in stimulating development, including subsidies of industrial and agricultural inputs. These changes began in the context of the drive to cut budgets. Costly subsidies were an obvious target. Cuts to subsidies also shared the market-oriented logic of Mexican policy reformers and most international actors — an indication of how Mexico's policies increasingly reflected international imperatives and patterns. These reforms, by redirecting decision-making power to markets, tended to reduce the state's leverage against private actors. Markets became more central, and the state less central, to economic choices. In agriculture, for example, reform of Article 27 left private investors free to buy, sell, or rent land. Elimination of most state marketing boards removed the state from the chain connecting producers to consumers.[39] Private entrepreneurs took over their functions, from food processing to transportation and marketing.

The state did not completely abdicate its economic role, however. It remained an important investor in infrastructure and human resources. It kept ownership of the oil company (PEMEX) as a monopoly, because of its symbolic as well as financial importance. The Federal Electrical Commission also remained in state hands.[40] Finally, the state continued to regulate and license many types of economic activity, to offer tax incentives and credit, and to intervene in wage and price pacts. Nevertheless, the balance of power shifted away from the Mexican state and toward private actors.

International Influence

If the desperation of the mid-1980s pushed Mexico toward international markets, international actors pulled hard in the same direction. In some ways the crisis and international pressures simply gave Mexican economic reformers an excuse to carry out reforms they believed in anyway. But international and financial incentives cannot be disregarded either. The effect was to significantly raise the prominence of international actors in Mexican economic policy making.

The main source of leverage employed by these actors was debt. Simply put, the state — and the economy — needed a new source of capital. The Mexican economy was far from attracting new investment; indeed, it suffered massive capital flight. The state could not compensate as in the past because it too was essentially bankrupt and viewed internationally as a poor credit risk. Oil was unreliable, as the 1981 price crash had demonstrated. Tax reform implied an enormous administrative effort and was strongly opposed by business — whose support and confidence the government would need in order to generate investment and growth. This left only two sources: foreign investors and export earnings. By moving to an export-oriented model, Mexico could generate foreign exchange through increased exports and at the same time attract new investment from still hesitant investors abroad. This approach had the additional advantage that it did not require huge expenditure by the state; rather, private actors would bear the burden. Thus Mexico turned to foreign markets.

An early sign of this shift was de la Madrid's 1985 announcement that Mexico would seek entry to GATT. When López Portillo floated the same idea, he was shot down. This time Mexico joined GATT within a year. In order to win admission to GATT, Mexico agreed to reduce trade protection. But GATT failed to inspire much new investment. Investors remained skeptical of the government's ability to provide the conditions for renewed growth, and skeptical of its commitment to market reform. The government thus took further steps to convince them. The first step involved reducing inflation. Inflation typically makes predicting costs and benefits more uncertain and thus makes investment riskier. To control inflation, de la Madrid maneuvered business, labor, and peasant organizations into signing a formal Pact of Economic Solidarity to limit increases in wages, prices, and public spending. The pact illustrates how Mexico's path toward the market was paved by traditional corporatism: without its control over major labor and peasant organizations, the government would have found it difficult to reach such an agreement. Under Salinas the pact became a permanent instrument to contain inflation.

Another step involved trying to encourage investment by deregulation. The government cut down red tape and reduced or eliminated limits on foreign investment. In 1985, IBM was allowed to keep full ownership of an investment project. Then the government authorized other foreign investors to increase their share of stock in Mexican companies above the 49 percent legal limit. In both its anti-inflationary and deregulatory efforts the Mexican government clearly had in mind a foreign as well as a domestic audience. Internationalization was assuming new form and vigor. Yet de la Madrid's steps toward international markets and economic reform remained tentative. He too failed to solve the confidence problem that blocked a return to high levels of investment and growth. Debt remained a key economic obstacle, draining the nation of capital.[41] Winning over investors would take deeper and more permanent reforms.

For such reforms to take place, Mexico would need the United States to assume a more active role as a partner in Mexican development. Initially, this meant helping to relieve the burden of debt. In 1989 the Brady Plan proposed to reduce Mexico's debt through renegotiations with creditor banks. The final settlement covered close to $48 billion of public debt. Government sources estimate that Mexico saved nearly $2 billion in interest payments alone in 1990, with total savings in interest and principal reduction of more than $5 billion.[42]

Yet the most dramatic shift would require a much more profound acceptance of partnership on both the U.S. and the Mexican side. In September 1990, Salinas announced that his government would seek a free trade agreement with the United States. President Bush requested fast-track authority from the U.S. Congress and negotiations began. The North American Free Trade Agreement (NAFTA) meant reversing more than fifty years of protectionist policies — a trend begun with GATT — and deliberately seeking economic integration with the giant to the north. NAFTA committed the state to withdrawing from its traditional role as a central economic arbiter.

To investors NAFTA assured Mexico of privileged access to the U.S. market, the wealthiest consumer market in the world. Investors could reasonably expect Mexico to grow along with the U.S. economy. In addition, NAFTA guaranteed favorable Mexican economic policies, by committing all future Mexican governments — leftist governments included — to free-market policies. Similarly, Salinas strengthened the autonomy of the Central Bank, in essence to convince investors that the government had surrendered its discretionary ability to manipulate the currency's value for political advantage, just as NAFTA reduced the state's ability to manipulate tariffs for the same reason.[43] Investors further benefited from relaxation of investment regulation. More than two-thirds of the country's productive activity was opened to full foreign ownership. The approval process was streamlined. And foreign investment flowed in at a rapid rate, even during the peso-related recession of 1995 and 1996.

The reorientation of Mexico's economic policy increased the relative influence of international actors, particularly the United States. Several sources of leverage exist. First, debt remains important. Every year Mexico services an external public debt that totals more than 20 percent of GDP. In 2002, debt service costs amounted to 23 percent of the total value of all exports.[44] Thus Mexico remains susceptible to the advice of international financial institutions and creditors in the United States. Second, the decision to develop through export promotion has made access to foreign markets a critical variable. In order to assure access, Mexico's leaders surrendered protectionism. Mexican industrialists would have to compete with international companies without much assistance from the Mexican state. Strong companies would survive; weaker ones often formed partnerships with foreign companies; the weakest simply vanished. The sector most connected to international companies and markets — *maquiladoras* — exploded. Thus the government cannot use "nationalism" in quite the same way as before to win popular support at home. Chapters 6 and 7 discuss this problem at length.

Finally, reliance on foreign investment significantly increased Mexico's vulnerability to what international investors thought of Mexican economic policy, of Mexican political stability, even of Mexican election returns. Mexico's leaders tried to define their new approach as essentially nationalist, but it was clear that their definition of nationalism differed considerably from the understanding of nationalism that came out of the Mexican Revolution. Under the old model *nationalism* meant Mexican autonomy and freedom from international constraint. Under the neoliberal model *nationalism* meant an internationally linked Mexico as the only Mexico that can be economically strong.

Social and Political Implications

This tumultuous economic transition in Mexico left social and political scars. It also illustrates the complexity of such processes of change. Economic crisis and reform deeply affected social conditions and political behavior, but political behavior and social conditions also affected the management and relative success of economic reform. Economic crisis and reform brought terrible hardship to Mexicans, but it also contributed to the public's alienation from the PRI and rising political competition. Similarly, the crisis and budget constraints created by Mexico's debt problems encouraged the rise of economic technocrats and enhanced their ability to push through risky economic reforms. Some of these reforms would probably have been adopted anyway as Mexico tried to deal with the limitations of ISI. However, such corrections might not have revolutionized economic strategy so quickly and profoundly had it not been for the urgency of the crisis: halfway measures failed to convince external markets of Mexico's intent to reform between 1982 and 1986.

But the same crisis that propelled Mexico toward market reforms had also left society in a weaker position to withstand the shocks of those reforms. During any economic restructuring, some jobs are lost and others are gained. New sectors become important and old sectors lose out. Because years of high inflation and unemployment had eroded savings and wages, Mexicans were less able to wait out the transition from one job to another or from one sector to another. Unfortunately, this made the social costs of adjustment more difficult to bear. Moreover, the drastic and abrupt character of economic reforms split the political coalition that had ruled Mexico for nearly sixty years more severely than a gradual reformist approach would have. The PRI itself fractured, with its nationalist and leftist wing largely supporting the Cárdenas candidacy. The timing of this challenge is clearly linked to the government's decisive move toward a coherent neoliberal model in 1985 and 1986. [45] Thus the stage was set for the Salinas-Cárdenas confrontation in 1988.

Politics also affected the process of economic reform, again in complex ways. In some instances political conflicts contributed to the urgency behind economic reform or smoothed the path of reformers with potential international allies. Growing signs of unrest and a rising electoral Left convinced many Mexican politicians — as well as the United States — that continued economic crisis would endanger stability. In other cases politics damaged the efficacy of economic reform. Anxiety about the zapatistas provoked stock market volatility twice in 1994. Two political assassinations further eroded investor confidence. The fact that neoliberal economic reforms themselves provoked the protests that undermined their success demonstrates the dynamic interaction between politics and economics.

The peso crash in December 1994 illuminates this political and economic interaction. Because the economy had done well, Salinas was widely considered Mexico's golden boy, the genius who had brought about a remarkable turnaround.[46] Trade with Mexico's North American partners (particularly the United States) increased, and a bigger share of this trade came from nonoil exports. Consumer price inflation fell from 114 percent in 1988 to less than 10 percent in 1993. Finally, a strict commitment to currency stability kept the value of the peso steady. However, this dramatic economic improvement came at a cost.[47] Private debt increased dramatically, and consumer debt grew faster than industrial investment. Basically, as the economy got better, consumers who had put off spending during the crisis went on a shopping spree, financed mostly through credit cards and bank loans.[48] Consumers and business investors bought imported goods as falling tariffs made them cheaper, resulting in a growing current account deficit.[49] Keeping the peso steady under these conditions required substantial flows of new capital into Mexico. When investors (and lenders) lost confidence in Mexico — in part because of political problems — the peso was in trouble.

The impact of political concerns was magnified by the specific way in which the government had liberalized investment. Salinas was so anxious to get investment that he put few limits on foreign investors. Unlike Chile, which required investors to leave their money in stocks for a spec-

ified period of time, Mexico permitted high levels of speculative portfolio investment with no restrictions on when or how fast investors could
get out. Thus speculative portfolio investment far outweighed more productive direct investment in plants and machinery.[50] When portfolio
investors began to get nervous about Mexico they unloaded their hold-
ings in a matter of hours, producing an old-fashioned run on the bank.
Mexico's foreign reserves were quickly exhausted and Ernesto Zedillo's
new government was forced to devalue the peso. Less than three months
later the peso had lost nearly a third of its value.

Yet why did the government take such a risky path? Why did it not
devalue sooner and prevent such a panic, despite credible evidence that
economists within the government, the United States, and Zedillo himself
pushed for it? Again, politics seems to have influenced these decisions.
Salinas resisted a more timely peso devaluation partly to keep investors
happy, but also to support the PRI's electoral prospects for the upcoming
1994 presidential election.[51] So instead of devaluing early, the government publicly insisted that it would not devalue. Rather, Salinas sought
to raise new capital by issuing short-term bonds, indexed to the dollar in
order to reduce investment risk. In the short term the policy worked:
investors switched into *tesobonos* at a rapid rate, postponing the crash
for eight months. But by the time these bonds came due, Mexico had run
out of foreign reserves and out of options.

The combination of rising competition without strong mechanisms
for accountability both encouraged such partisan manipulation and
made it easy to cover up. Lacking inside information of their own, opposition parties and foreign investors had to accept government assurances
that no devaluation was planned. The Bank of Mexico kept Mexico's
deteriorating foreign exchange position secret by delaying the release of
data. The concealment of information from foreign investors in particular (big Mexican investors seem to have had advance notice) contributed
to high mistrust and a larger run on the bank than otherwise might have
occurred. No one was sure when the Mexican government was telling
the truth.

This experience demonstrates the complex interactions between politics and economics. The road to democratic development is full of potholes and even detours. One cannot simply sign a free trade deal and
expect to live happily ever after. Political opening increased the space for
protest and thus in some ways undermined investor confidence. Concern
about the PRI's electoral fortunes also encouraged fiscal policies that
were short-sighted and ultimately unwise. At the same time, however,

investors were most concerned by indications that Mexican democracy had not yet established itself firmly, such as political assassinations and the southern rebellion (which complained about nondemocracy). Zedillo's rapid and uncompromising acceptance of PRI defeat in 2000 produced an immediate 6 percent surge in the Mexican stock market, as investors rewarded the peaceful transition. The Salinas government might also have hesitated if held accountable by a stronger Congress, a freer press, and a more active citizenry. At the least he would have had to provide more accurate information about Mexico's financial situation, which in turn might have reduced the scope of the panic.

Another example of the intimate ties between democracy and development in contemporary Mexico is privatization. Privatization of state-owned companies did not fix the problems of corruption, inefficiency, and monopoly pricing that plagued Mexico's ISI economy. A good part of the reason seems to be that privatization took place under a semidemocratic government, not hobbled by a strong opposition or a genuinely free press. The issue of accountability looms large here. Essentially, two key problems arose.

First, privatization brought in such large sums of money that it created opportunities for corruption.[52] Mexico had company in this respect: the president of Brazil was impeached in 1992 for privatization-related corruption. The discovery of corruption at the highest levels undermined investor confidence even as the Mexican economy struggled to recover from the peso crisis. Also, the process was carried out in such haste and secrecy that some investors were able to buy shares without sufficient assets to back their bids and without a realistic evaluation of companies' true worth. Such problems would particularly harm the critical banking sector, where new owners routinely issued risky private loans in a desperate attempt to keep enough profit coming in to pay off the excessive debts incurred to buy the banks. When the economy crashed, they were saddled with worthless loans. The government had to bail them out. The parallels to the U.S. savings and loan crisis in the 1980s are striking. Second, in part because of the insider nature of these transactions, the newly "private" companies often held huge, near monopoly shares of the market. Five years after its privatization, for example, Telmex still controlled 75 percent of the Mexican market. Thus the company faced little real competition or incentive to provide better service at lower prices. Again, the semidemocratic character of Mexican politics made this outcome more likely.

In the long run, some have argued, neoliberalism should support the consolidation of democracy in Mexico. This argument makes two key points. First, neoliberalism takes many decisions out of the state's hands and thus — as we have noted before — may embolden private actors to check state power and encourage broader participation in public decision making. Second, to the extent that neoliberalism results in economic growth, it may have positive effects on the overall likelihood of democracy; as we know, wealthy societies are more likely to be democratic. Nevertheless, neoliberalism may also have negative effects on the prospects for democracy. Can neoliberalism really deliver the economic goods it promises? And even if it can, what about inequality? Can neoliberalism deliver those goods to enough people to support a broad political democracy? If the only private actors who acquire (or keep) the ability to check state power are economic elites, one could hardly call the result democratic.

Because the effects of neoliberalism will mostly be felt over time, it is difficult to determine the answers to these questions. Yet we can hardly conclude this chapter without noting some troubling problems. The transition to neoliberal economics is intertwined with fifteen years of recurrent economic crises. Both crises and reforms have left social scars, putting Mexico even deeper into the hole as far as social welfare and inequality are concerned. The poor in particular multiplied in numbers. The minimum wage lost more than half its real value between 1981 and 1989, with ripple effects on the rest of the economy. By 1986 real minimum wages had fallen nearly to their 1940 level: the wage gains of the Mexican Miracle had been effectively wiped out.[53] Economic pressures forced many families to withdraw their children from school and put them to work. Per capita consumption of expensive proteins like meat and dairy products dropped substantially, but consumption of basic staples fell too. Per capita health and welfare spending by the state fell some 34 percent.[54]

Despite some improvement under Salinas, the 1994 peso crisis further depressed wages and living standards. Macroeconomic recovery from the peso crisis was much faster than in 1982; by 1997 the economy was growing again at a robust 7 percent.[55] Most analysts attribute this recovery to the new economic model: although domestic demand shrank drastically during the recession (as in 1982), exports got cheaper with devaluation, and many export-oriented companies prospered. Mexico's overall trade balance improvement in the first quarter of 1995 was led by exports from the maquiladora sector. This sector's strong positive balance made up for a negative balance in the rest of the economy.[56]

But the recovering economy did not even restore 1994 living standards to those hurt by the 1995–96 recession. Although Mexico boasted twenty-four new billionaires, the number of poor grew to alarming proportions. Over 40 percent of the Mexican population lived below the poverty line in 2003.[57] According to World Bank estimates, some 8 percent of Mexican children suffer chronic malnutrition — higher than in Argentina, Brazil, Chile, Colombia, Peru, or Venezuela, and tied with Bolivia. Other estimates put the figure much higher — at 20 percent nationally and nearly 30 percent in some regions.[58] Both minimum and average wages have fallen with respect to historic peaks.[59]

Finally, the peso crisis shattered the illusion that the neoliberal model would usher Mexico into First World status. Neoliberalism does not guarantee protection from economic crises; in fact, it may increase vulnerability to international markets. Neoliberalism does not necessarily reduce inequality or poverty; in fact, it relies to some extent on the unequal distribution of market profits to stimulate entrepreneurship and investment. Protests against these results could undermine both economic and political stability. Thus even those who anticipate long-term gains from neoliberalism (and democracy) are cautious about the bumps ahead.

Just as the Great Depression marked the values and attitudes of a generation of Americans, the structural crises of the 1980s and 1990s — with abrupt highs and lows in employment opportunities, purchasing power, and growth — are the only reality that Mexicans forty years old or younger (the majority of the population) have ever known. This differs strikingly from the experience of Mexicans born before 1960, in a country characterized by strong growth and political stability, though not democracy. Young Mexicans are more skeptical of claims that prosperity is just around the corner, less comfortable with the Faustian bargain of stability in exchange for participation, and less willing to believe that this bargain can even be struck today. Such attitudes decrease the likelihood that any party will enjoy the domination the PRI held in the past but may also make it harder for democratic governments to win the trust and confidence of the people.

Indeed, the experience of President Fox demonstrates this point. Fox won election in 2000 largely because he succeeded in attracting the votes of young, educated Mexicans. Over half of those who thought there would be an economic crisis chose him.[60] Fox campaigned heavily on the issue of PRI economic mismanagement. No longer, he argued, could the PRI's economic competence justify the postponement of democracy.

The mass in honor of the sick (at the Basílica de Guadalupe) reflects the continued role of traditional alongside "modern" approaches to matters such as health and welfare. It is unclear what neoliberalism will mean for tradition and for those often most devoted to it: the poor. (*La Jornada*)

Short-term improvements were no guarantee of future results—witness the post-electoral economic crisis of December 1994. Working-age voters who had supported the PRI in 1994 on the basis of economic improvement under Salinas felt cheated and betrayed. When Fox took office, he promised to grow the economy by a million jobs a year. Unfortunately, the United States entered an economic recession barely a year later, which severely limited export growth for Mexico and led to a nearly stagnant economy. By 2003, nearly half of all Mexicans thought Fox had delivered less than expected; the top three reasons included complaints that Fox had not improved the economy.[61] Not surprisingly, these economic failures—linked in large part to Mexico's international economic interdependence—contributed to the PAN's defeat in the 2003 congressional elections.

CONCLUSION

In a world astonished by the fall of Soviet communism, it is easy to overlook the economic changes that have taken place in Mexico since 1982. Yet in their magnitude and rapidity, neoliberal reforms amounted to little less than economic revolution. The relationship between publicly and privately based wealth was transformed. Decisions once made by government planners were deliberately transferred to markets. A commitment to develop a nationally owned industrial sector gave way to active courting of multinational investment. The barriers against U.S. influence that were carefully erected by a generation of postrevolutionary leaders were systematically demolished by their children. Mexico's neoliberal governments have taken steps to ensure that if not entirely irrevocable, these policies will be very difficult to reverse.

Nevertheless, elements of continuity persist. While Mexico's exposure to and dependence on international economic influences and particularly the United States have unquestionably increased, it was never possible for Mexico to avoid the world entirely. Even at the peak of ISI, multinational companies played a vital strategic role. Conversely, though foreign investors increasingly dominate the Mexican economy, Mexican entrepreneurs remain pivotal players. Mexico can never be nearly as important to U.S. investors as it is to Mexican investors. Thus, though there has been a shift in the balance toward international actors, most of the old players remain on the field. Similarly, the shift away from state ownership, investment, and regulation has not emasculated the state. Though there are far fewer state companies, those remaining — such as oil companies — carry weight.[62] And although the government as yet has no formal industrial policy, its fiscal policy and its ability to manage political conflict remain important variables in investment decisions. Clearly, one cannot count the state out.

Moreover, although the balance of power between state and society has shifted toward society, not all social groups have benefited. Some have increased their power much more than others. Indeed, the privatization process resembled a transition from "state capitalism" to "monopoly capitalism" more than a transition to "free market capitalism" as classically conceived.[63] Only a small number of elite economic actors participated. Most state monopolies simply became privately held monopolies. More broadly, while the poor and unorganized have always been left behind in the process of development, they have fallen further behind under market-oriented policies. Markets tend to leave "uncompetitive" sectors largely untouched. A state that abdicates the authority to shape economic change may have to intervene more decisively through social policy in order to ensure that the inevitable consequences of "naked capitalism" do not undermine the social and political order — as the advanced developed democracies have. Yet Mexico's debt problems have limited the state's ability to pursue such social solutions. Finally, the complexity of economic change is apparent. Some of the same policies that encourage investment have side effects that make the economy more vulnerable. Rising political competition does not automatically produce responsible government, just as liberalization of markets does not point unambiguously toward stable democracy.

Indeed, in a country like Mexico, market liberalization has contradictory effects. On the one hand, it exposes Mexico to international influences from established democracies, makes individuals and firms more independent of state influence, and may create the resources for popular organization. On the other hand, market liberalization has widened the already substantial gap between rich and poor, leaving the poorest Mexicans decisively out of political decision making even as political liberalization advanced. Neoliberalism may also increase economic volatility and vulnerability to external shocks. If democratic governments cannot protect Mexico from these problems any better than authoritarian ones, Mexicans may conclude that democracy is not worth the economic cost. Generalized poverty has enlarged the subgroup of the extremely poor, increased antisystem political activity, and fueled rising crime. Such trends may encourage the sort of "authoritarian nostalgia" that has plagued post-Soviet Russia and some Eastern European nations where communist successor parties won elections by promoting nationalist platforms and a return to the "good" old days when the state provided a secure safety net. Solving the issues that confront Mexicans without returning to authoritarianism demands more thoughtful planning than markets can provide.

CHAPTER 6

Mexico in a U.S.-Led World

No observation about Mexico's place in the world is repeated as often as that attributed to turn-of-the-century Mexican president Porfirio Díaz: "Poor Mexico: So far from God and so close to the United States." Of course the statement's enduring wit plays on the unique problems Mexico faces in having such a powerful neighbor, an emerging world power in Díaz's day, the world's unmatched superpower today. However one weighs those problems against the benefits Mexico gains from that closeness, the quotation's incontestable truth is that the United States is crucial for Mexico. Indeed, U.S. influence is greater today than when Díaz first spoke those words. True, Mexico is also increasingly important to the United States, but whereas Mexico is one among several important nations for the United States, the United States is probably more important than all other nations combined for Mexico.[1]

Because this book is about Mexican development, it links the examination of Mexican foreign affairs to the central tendencies already identified in Mexico's domestic development. This chapter explores how the international and domestic contexts influence one another. One important focus is how weakness or strength at home affects Mexico's international goals and fate. Another is how the international context, deftly subordinated to domestic considerations during the period of Mexico's peak regime strength, has in recent years assumed a leading role in Mexican development. Consistent with our theme of Mexico's shift from exceptionalism to normalization, this internationalization has meant surrendering historical claims of Mexican apartness, autonomy, and even uniqueness.

Mexico's increased insertion into the world has brought some opportunity for closer relations with Europe, Japan, and the rest of Latin America. But because the world and much of its political-economic dynamics are in step with U.S. interests, or are even U.S.-led, the United States lies at the core of international influences on Mexico's contemporary struggle for development. Mexico has long been close to the United States; today it is closer. As this chapter examines Mexico and the world, it looks largely at Mexico and the United States. The two principal parts of the chapter analyze (1) patterns of Mexico-U.S. relations up to the 1980s, and (2) how these patterns have changed in recent years, particularly regarding the interaction of foreign and domestic policy. Chapter 7 then assesses specific bilateral issues confronting Mexico and the United States.

THEMES FROM THE PAST

Into the Giant's Shadow: The Nineteenth Century

Products of very different colonial heritages, Mexico and the United States had little contact with each other until the nineteenth century. Before long, however, contact was intense and conflictual. When Mexico achieved independence in 1820, it was not clear that it would end up as the much weaker neighbor, yet within two decades the United States had established superior strength. Although still roughly equal to the United States in land size, Mexico had fallen far behind in population and the overall pace of development.[2] Crucially, Mexico's brutal cycle of economic crisis and political instability in the first half of the nineteenth century contrasted with robust development and political stability in the United States. Thus, when the two nations went to war in 1846, Mexico proved no match.

Texas was the flash point. The first U.S. ambassador to Mexico actively conspired to wrest Texas away from Mexico by strongly encouraging the immigration of U.S. settlers into Texas, which was then Mexican territory. Fearing the consequences, Mexico limited the legal flow in 1830; back then it was Mexico attempting to seal the border against migrants from the United States. The measure proved impossible to enforce, just as contemporary U.S. laws fail to keep Mexicans out. "Illegal aliens" streamed across the border. In 1836, Texans declared

their independence from Mexico and soon defeated General Santa
Anna's Mexican troops.[3] The U.S. annexation of Texas in 1845 pro-
voked the lopsided war. U.S. motivations and rationalizations divided
U.S. public opinion. Critics included authors Henry David Thoreau and
Ralph Waldo Emerson and then Congressman Abraham Lincoln.
Nevertheless, the war itself was short and successful. Mexico's most trea-
sured war memory lies in the gallant if futile gesture of six young cadets
who jumped to their deaths rather than surrender themselves at Mexico
City's Chapultepec Castle. Today the Niños Héroes (Young Heroes) are
remembered throughout Mexico, in a monument near the castle itself, as
well as in street names, a metro station, and school textbooks. Today
Mexico City maintains a Museum of Intervention. The war ended but its
legacy lives.

The Treaty of Guadalupe Hidalgo in 1848 was harsh. Mexico lost
about half its territory, including all or parts of what are now the states
of Arizona, California, Colorado, Nevada, New Mexico, and Utah.
Mexico lost still more territory with the Gadsden Purchase of 1853,
when, in desperate need of money, it sold off a chunk of its land, which
would include copper mines and create an unnatural border, splitting
cities in half. The war and its aftermath hurt Mexican efforts to build
unity, stability, and prosperity. Domestic weakness led to international
weakness, which led to further domestic weakness. Mexico could not
neutralize its international environment. The war and the ensuing "land
grab" continue to influence Mexican attitudes toward the United States.
It is not that most Mexicans seethe with anger or hope to reclaim the
land. Instead, the war is embedded in the national consciousness and
remains a vital historical referent.[4] It marks the first but not the last
episode that would bring many Mexicans to judge their neighbor and
arrive at a sad conclusion: a country's internal democracy is no guarantee
of democratic or fair behavior in foreign policy.

Relations with the United States improved as Mexico next came to
suffer from French intervention from 1862 to 1867. President Abraham
Lincoln continued to recognize the government-in-hiding of President
Benito Juárez throughout the intervention, in part out of long-standing
U.S. rejection of European involvement in Latin America (the Monroe
Doctrine) and in part out of genuine admiration for Juárez's republican
ideals. Although this policy fit U.S. material self-interest, it also helped
restore faith that U.S. foreign policy would not inevitably run counter to
Mexico's democratic ideals and national sovereignty. The outstanding
claims between Mexico and the United States were settled in 1868.

Bilateral relations deepened when the *porfiriato* replaced Juarez and created just the sort of domestic environment that pleased U.S. economic interests. Unaffectionately dubbed "father of foreigners and stepfather of Mexicans," Díaz extended attractive invitations to foreign investors. He eased limits on acquiring land in border regions and on the use of subsoil resources and encouraged foreign economic activity. Most important, Díaz secured the political stability that foreign investors demanded then as now.

Historical parallels to the present are evident in several respects. One is the regime's conviction that economic opening is positive for Mexico domestically, that foreign and especially U.S. interests are integral to successful Mexican development. Another parallel is that Mexico's doors opened for Europe as well, but the United States took greatest advantage of the opportunity and established its predominance among foreigners in Mexico's economy. A third parallel is the shared concern of the regime and foreign interests for a political stability that has tended to marginalize the masses from the immediate economic benefits of policies. One difference, however, is that the dominant domestic and foreign interests of a century ago rarely saw democratization as necessary to either political stability or the international opening.

From Revolution to Accommodation

Mexico-U.S. relations predictably worsened when the Mexican Revolution replaced stability with instability and threatened foreign investment with assertive nationalism. Unfortunately for Mexico this occurred during a muscle-flexing period for the United States. The easy U.S. victory in the 1898 Spanish-American War and its construction of the Panama Canal showed America's emergence as a world power, preeminent in the New World. The political-economic context of revolutionary instability next to a preeminent regional power poised to impose its will determined more than the machinations of individual U.S. politicians. Still, individuals helped shape events and left further scars. For example, U.S. Ambassador Henry Lane Wilson was the villainous partner of Mexico's counterrevolutionary leaders in the 1913 plot to assassinate President Francisco Madero. Madero's goals as an elected (and moderate) democrat did not fit the ambassador's plan for Mexico.[5]

President Woodrow Wilson, in contrast, played the high-minded, liberal antagonist. Whereas his predecessor, Republican President William Howard Taft (1909–13), had clearly based his policy on U.S. self-interest (not on "improving" Mexico), Wilson was a human rights activist, a zealous democrat. Though not an idealist prepared to sacrifice U.S. material interests, Wilson saw democracy as favorable to the material development of both nations. In this respect one might see Wilson as a visionary whose time may finally have come. However, he resorted to paternalistic and interventionist means to promote democracy, including the use of military force and the threat of more force if defied.[6] Wilson's actions earned the enmity not only of those he opposed but also of those he favored. How could Mexicans not see further evidence at this time that U.S. democracy was no guarantee of a democratic foreign policy?

Differences of opinion exist over the extent to which the United States shaped Mexican domestic politics in the early revolutionary years. Clearly, the United States did not create all the strife but did intervene to influence outcomes. At various points the United States supported Madero, Huerta, and Francisco (Pancho) Villa, before settling on Venustiano Carranza as the figure most likely to win the military battle, establish stability, and deal acceptably with U.S. economic interests. Another sure conclusion is that, as with the Spanish colonial and later the U.S. and French interventions, domestic disunity and instability left the nation prey to blatant foreign intervention. In turn, the intervention further undermined Mexico's domestic development. Mexico could again neither control nor neutralize international actors.

Angered over U.S. intervention favoring Carranza, Villa led raids across the border. U.S. pursuit of Villa through northern Mexico, commemorated in numerous popular ballads, inadvertently contributed to his immortality. Yet additional hostilities were averted. Mexican politics stabilized, and the United States was soon preoccupied with World War I. Nonetheless, bilateral bitterness lingered. Mexico did not support the United States and its allies in the war. The main Mexico-U.S. conflict now concerned compensation for U.S. property that had been nationalized by the revolution. Carranza proved more of a nationalist than the United States had hoped. Diplomatic recognition of Carranza's successor (Alvaro Obregón) was delayed three years, until Mexico signed the Bucareli Agreements in 1923, promising not to apply certain legislation (such as the assertion of national rights to oil).[7]

But as the revolution moderated, bilateral tension eased. By the end of the 1920s no serious threat of violent U.S. intervention remained. By 1934, Mexico's economy, except for agriculture, was possibly more under outside control, certainly by U.S. interests, than at the start of the revolution.[8] And when President Lázaro Cárdenas then altered the ownership balance, nationalizing the foreign-owned railroads and oil companies, bilateral relations did not relapse into dangerous confrontation. A historical pattern was broken: the United States did not treat Mexico's assertion of sovereignty as something it must forcibly suppress.

The contrast between President Franklin D. Roosevelt's Good Neighbor Policy and the persistent domestic pressure for retaliation against Mexico was a precursor of today's reality that U.S. presidents are often more accommodating than many U.S. economic and political actors would like. Distracted by the Great Depression and an impending world war, Roosevelt could not risk costly intervention. As during the Mexican Revolution and World War I, a "soft" U.S. policy toward Mexico was motivated partly by U.S. difficulties elsewhere. World War II brought increased bilateral cooperation. The United States did not use the war as a pretext to control its neighbor and Mexico declared war on the Axis, adding to the Allies' manpower reserve. Most important, the Mexican economy accelerated its production of raw materials, and the two countries established the *bracero* program that brought Mexican workers to the labor-drained United States. These two contributions would further integrate the Mexican and U.S. economies.

As Mexico's regime institutionalized itself and implemented domestic development policy encouraging industrialization and profitable U.S. investment, grand bilateral disputes over territory, property rights, debt, diplomatic recognition, and active intervention yielded to lesser disputes, mostly economic (water rights, fishing, tariffs, migrant workers, drugs). Some of these disputes would later intensify, but during the 1940s, 1950s, and 1960s, Mexico-U.S. relations were comparatively smooth.[9]

In 1947, President Harry Truman paid the first U.S. presidential visit to Mexico City since the revolution; President Dwight Eisenhower also met several times with his Mexican counterpart. President John F. Kennedy's trip to Mexico in 1962 evoked an enthusiastic response by millions to his Alliance for Progress vision of international cooperation and his personal appeal (youth, glamour, and the status of being the first Catholic U.S. president). President Lyndon B. Johnson's early friendly contacts were later overshadowed by the Vietnam War and by both his and Mexican President Gustavo Díaz Ordaz's domestic troubles. Whereas Presidents Richard Nixon and Gerald Ford paid limited attention to Mexico, oil and Central American warfare would help make Mexico a major concern for both Presidents Jimmy Carter and Ronald Reagan. Most important, the issues highlighted in the next chapter have placed Mexico high on its neighbor's permanent agenda.

Mexican Assertiveness

Between the rather calm midcentury decades of bilateral relations and the contemporary period of increased closeness (from the mid-1980s on) lies a rather different and more assertive period for Mexico. Mexico maintained generally cooperative relations with its giant neighbor, but changes in domestic policy during the 1970s and into the 1980s affected bilateral relations. Presidents Luis Echeverría and José López Portillo both asserted Mexican autonomy in foreign policy as much as possible, given the basic characteristics of the Mexican regime and the enormous might of the United States. These two givens loomed large enough that substantial economic intercourse continued, Mexico did not threaten the superpower's fundamental world interests, and the United States maintained its support for Mexican political stability. Still, Mexico's assertiveness in this period is noteworthy for indicating both the possibilities and the limitations of the nation's independence from the United States. The tug between the efforts to achieve greater independence and the constraints encountered therein is a major theme in Mexican foreign policy.

One continuity throughout all periods is Mexico's proud sovereignty in formulating the portion of its foreign policy that deals with the world beyond the United States. On the one hand, that portion has been rather limited; on the other hand, Mexico strove to expand it in its period of maximum assertiveness, leading to more Mexico-U.S. confrontations. Central to the tradition of assertiveness has been a universalism, even a "leftism," at odds with slavishly U.S.-oriented policies. Universalism invokes the idea of one standard of just treatment for all nations, powerful or not. In contrast, a foreign policy obedient to U.S. leadership would befriend U.S. allies and reject U.S. foes. Mexico's repudiation of such obedience is proclaimed in the Estrada Doctrine of 1930: Mexico grants diplomatic recognition to any government. It does not judge other governments as the United States continually has judged Mexico and others.[10] The sense of leftism arises, at least as perceived from the U.S. side, when Mexico's universalism winds up defending leftist antagonists of the U.S. government. It arises even more strongly when Mexico subordinates aspects of universalism to defend those antagonists.

Echeverría worked zealously to increase Mexico's profile beyond the United States. Though previous presidents had also used travel partly to show independence, Echeverría — dubbed the "around the world in eighty days president" — literally outdistanced all his predecessors combined. Although he strengthened relations with Japan and Western

Europe, what most marked Echeverría's break from the past was his Third World focus. Most predecessors had displayed relative indifference to developing nations; two decades later President Carlos Salinas would identify Mexico with aspirations to join the *First* World.[11] Both approaches argued, pragmatically, that the developed economies simply had more to offer. In contrast, Echeverría sought to place Mexico as a political leader within the group of non-aligned Southern nations. He condemned superpower politics, multinational corporations, and indiscriminate openness to foreign investment, proudly accepting the wrath of U.S. elites. But many Mexicans, notably in the business and middle-class communities, also saw him as impulsive, irresponsible, dangerously leftist, and ultimately ineffective. The cumulative backlash showed that Mexico's assertive foreign policy had ventured beyond where it could go with impunity. Realizing this, López Portillo projected greater moderation in the initial post-Echeverría years. This did not mean acquiescence to U.S. foreign policy, however.[12] Moreover, López Portillo was assertive in direct meetings between heads of state.[13]

The most sustained bilateral confrontation came over Central America. Especially for the Reagan administration, Central America was a significant Cold War battleground where local leftists represented Soviet/Cuban infiltration and a serious national security threat to both the United States and Mexico. Mexico did not see it that way. Even neutrality consistent with the noninterventionist Estrada Doctrine would have annoyed the United States, but what thrust Mexico into deep disfavor was a vigorous activism that sometimes benefited opponents of the United States. Mexico gave strong public support to the Sandinista insurgency against Somoza's dictatorship in Nicaragua and severed diplomatic relations. It also supported the insurgent Left in El Salvador, until the guerrillas' 1981 offensive failed to topple the regime.[14]

THE CHANGING RELATIONSHIP
BETWEEN FOREIGN AND DOMESTIC POLICY

Putting Mexico First: Home Is Where the Heart Was

The zenith of Mexico's assertiveness was short-lived. The overarching reason goes to the core of the relationship between foreign and domestic policy: such assertiveness did not serve Mexico's domestic development, the long-standing bottom line of Mexico's foreign policy. While there is room for debate on how well assertiveness served prior to the mid-1980s, we show why policy makers could think it was rational for their domestic ends.[15] Only afterward, as both the international context and domestic policy itself changed, would an assertive foreign policy be blatantly illogical and counterproductive for domestic policy. Presidents have latitude, but major changes in Mexican foreign policy stem mostly from attempts to preserve — under changing conditions — the basic relationship between foreign and domestic policy. Let us see first how the formulation operated classically at midcentury and then how it has evolved.

During its decades of maximum domestic strength (1940s–1960s) the regime clearly and successfully ran foreign policy to serve domestic policy. Of course, most governments try to design foreign policy that is rational for their domestic goals. What stands out for Mexico, however, is how strongly domestic development dominated. Another point is how well the regime managed the formula, succumbing neither to Mexican interest groups with clashing foreign policy agendas nor to U.S. pressure for greater conformity with U.S. foreign policy. Mexican foreign policy was so subordinate to domestic policy that some claim there really was no foreign policy. We prefer to emphasize that foreign policy lacked an inner cohesive force apart from its service to domestic development. Moreover, it was fundamentally defensive. A key concern was to shield Mexico from outside influences that would undermine the regime's ability to direct the course of Mexican development. By staying out of most matters beyond its borders, Mexico was usually unaffected by how those matters played out.[16] In this respect the foreign policy of these decades contrasted with the assertive period that followed in the 1970s.

Nevertheless, the logic of assertiveness neither begins in 1970 nor ends in the mid-1980s. Although we concentrate on the assertiveness in its peak period — because it is clearest there and came closest to undermining domestic policy — we also hark back to precedent.

Why Leftism?   The assertive strain in Mexican foreign policy has carried it beyond the endorsement of noninterference to the semicontradictory endorsement of leftist movements outside Mexico. Why did a regime that was conservative at home inject such leftism into its foreign policy? Genuine conviction is part of the picture. Given its revolutionary history, the Mexican government tended to see leftism elsewhere as essentially nationalist and popular, where the United States saw such movements more through a Cold War lens, as dangerous radicalism. To dismiss the notion of genuine conviction is to indulge in a hypercynicism that is both unfair and inaccurate. But because convictions inconsistent with perceived material interests usually have limited impact on policy making, we concentrate on the ways in which Mexico's leftist assertiveness strengthened the regime at home. As we do so, however, we must keep in mind that the rationales and actions depicted here best characterize Mexico in the postwar decades; leftist assertiveness has declined since the mid-1980s.

First, leftist assertiveness displayed independence from the United States. This resonates in the context of a tragic bilateral history and unshakable political, economic, and geographical constraints on Mexican independence. In a sense the reality of constraints increases the need for pointed assertion where possible in order to maintain political identity and legitimacy. Closer to the United States, Mexico asserted its independence in foreign policy in ways that many Latin American nations would not. An extension of the paradox has arisen whenever increased Mexican coziness with the United States has required an act of defiance to placate public opinion.[17]

Second, while leftism aimed to increase legitimacy among Mexican citizens in general, a particular target was the Mexican Left. Assertiveness appealed to its convictions. It energized the nationalist Left within the basic PRI (Partido Revolucionario Institutional) coalition and dampened the opposition of some outside the coalition, including many in the educational and artistic communities. Comparatively left-leaning administrations could naturally denounce dependency and bilateral inequities to good political effect. But most administrations have been far from left leaning in general, so their ability to attract some leftist support through foreign policy has been especially helpful. By the 1990s, however, the ruling PRI party would make fewer even symbolic gestures to the Left. When the PRI finally yielded power after the 2000 elections, it was to a rightist party that had usually condemned populist and defiant foreign policy.

Third, another key audience has been the foreign Left. Here too the reason is a mix of conviction and deft calculation by the actors involved. The regime's vaunted ability to co-opt has extended beyond Mexico's borders. In return for its support of leftists elsewhere, the government has secured their lack of opposition or even their outright endorsement. As we discuss shortly, recognition of the Castro regime tended to reduce Cuban support for Mexico's own leftist opposition. The effect, notable for decades, decreased as Latin America had fewer significant antisystem leftist movements than before. Yet a new dimension arose as the PRI faced increasing challenges for its revolutionary mantle by independent leftist movements after 1980; to undercut this the Left has been especially important to neoliberal presidents of Mexico from de la Madrid through Vicente Fox.

Fourth, populist foreign policy involved relatively low costs compared with the sacrifices the regime would incur for populist domestic policy; if foreign policy diverts attention from regressive domestic policies, that is an added pay-off. Denunciation of undemocratic politics elsewhere was often less threatening to Mexico's rulers than moves toward democracy at home. Indeed, support for leftist non-democratic governments like Cuba played into leftist suspicion of democracy as a bourgeois trap and justified in some sense the PRI's own slow progress toward democracy. The unenviable comparison between Mexico and the United States regarding democracy at home could be partly offset for some by drawing the foreign policy contrast between Mexico's support of national self-determination and U.S. authoritarian-imperialism. Next to 1968 demonstrations against Mexico's own lack of internal democracy, the two biggest Mexico City demonstrations in the 1960s and 1970s were against the U.S. role in Vietnam and the 1973 coup in Chile; costing the Mexican government nothing, these demonstrations provided opportunities for popular rhetoric.[18]

Much about the global context has changed since the late 1980s. The fall of Soviet communism and the weakening of Cuban internationalism made Mexico's leftism more acceptable to the United States. Moreover, Mexican governments with more electoral legitimacy did not need to resort to invocation of leftist ideals as an alternate justification. What has not changed are Mexican concerns about balancing the influence of their northern neighbor. Most Mexicans condemned the September 11 attacks on the United States, but they also condemned U.S. attacks on Afghanistan and Iraq. The U.S. government assertion that it must 'hunt down the terrorists wherever they are' does not necessarily make Mexicans feel safer. Instead, Mexicans perceive the arrogance of a superpower determined to pursue its security at the expense of other, mostly innocent, bystanders. More vitally, cooperation with the United States in the war on terror could only increase Mexico's risk of attracting the notice of international terrorists. Thus, just as previous Mexican presidents defied U.S. pressure in order to criticize U.S. military interventions against leftist movements in Central America in the 1980s, President Fox defied U.S. pressure and criticized U.S. military interventions against dictatorships halfway around the world in 2002 and 2003. The party in power in Mexico had changed. The U.S. target had changed. But Mexican incentives to demonstrate independence from the United States and to reject the extension of its military influence remained powerful.

Cuba.   The domestic logic of foreign policy leftism has been on display longest in regard to Cuba. Since Fidel Castro's takeover in 1959, the U.S. government has treated Cuba as a threat to the region's stability, but the Mexican government turned the Cuban issue into a plus for its own stability and legitimacy. Mexico was the only Latin American nation not to break diplomatic or commercial relations with Cuba, despite strong U.S. pressure. It opposed the 1961 U.S.-sponsored Bay of Pigs invasion (although it prudently refrained from criticizing the United States in its showdown with the Soviet Union over missiles in Cuba a year later). It helped persuade the Organization of American States (OAS) to lift sanctions against Cuba in 1975. It thus gained credit at home for defending national sovereignty and asserting its independence from the United States.[19]

The Cuban case also shows how the Mexican government skillfully used foreign policy to handle its own Left. It denied the Left an exclusive appeal to sympathetic Mexican public opinion and bolstered its own revolutionary credentials. Yet it did not simply give in to the Left. It allowed Mexican conservatives to conduct an anti-Cuba campaign in the early 1960s, taking the opportunity to smooth relations with the foreign and domestic business community and to secure part of the sugar market opened by the U.S. embargo on Cuba. Moreover, when pro-Cuba demonstrations criticized the Mexican government at home, the government clamped down: the Cuban revolution could not become a rallying cry for changes in Mexican domestic policy. This point has been well understood by Castro himself. He has more than once humiliated and angered the Mexican Left, as when he attended Salinas's inaugural ceremony. Castro's attendance gave legitimacy to elections in which the Mexican Left had declared itself robbed of victory. Questioned about this, Castro pointedly responded: "My friends are the Mexican government and Carlos Salinas de Gortari and if with my presence I lend some more help, for me it is an honor." He proceeded to meet with Mexican business leaders and invited them to Cuba.[20]

As Mexico's foreign policy assertiveness waned, Mexico became more circumspect in dealing with Cuba. By the 1990s, with the collapse of the Soviet Union and of Cuba's image as an alternative development model for Latin America, Cuba lost much of its importance for Mexican politics, on occasion looming as an albatross.[21] President Ernesto Zedillo in fact turned the Cuba issue around: less keen than his predecessors to attack U.S. policy, and interested instead in presenting Mexico as on the road to democratized, internationalized development, he attacked Cuba for resisting the democratic tide. Fox has continued this trend. In February 2002, Fox's foreign minister agreed to meet officially with anti-Castro dissidents. In March 2002, Castro walked out of a U.N. conference on development financing one day before President George W. Bush was expected to speak; a month later, an irate Castro made public a tape of a private conversation with Fox himself, asking Castro to leave before Bush's arrival so as not to embarrass him with the Americans. Fox ordered the Mexican representative to vote in favor of the annual U.N. resolution condemning Cuba's human rights record in 2002 and 2003, and in 2004, recalled Mexico's ambassador to Cuba after Castro publicly lambasted the Mexican government for betraying its traditional friendship with Cuba. Things had clearly changed. Cuba had become more of a liability to Mexico's policies of economic integration with the United States. With Soviet support withdrawn, Cuba posed little potential threat to domestic political stability in Mexico. Even Mexican leftists had begun to express cautious disapproval of Castro.

Central America.   Whereas Cuba provides the longest-standing case of Mexico's leftist foreign policy, the principal case during the period of Mexico's maximum assertiveness was Central America. Again, as with Cuba, the main concern of Mexico's foreign policy was its own domestic policy and, more specifically, defensive protection of the Mexican political system. Just as the United States wants a stable Mexico on its southern border, so Mexico wants a stable Central America on its southern border. Of course, U.S. policy also aimed at stability in Central America, but it saw stability there threatened by communist insurrection; in contrast, Mexico's view in the 1970s and 1980s was that Central America's status quo was doomed, and attempts to preserve it would be as destabilizing as they would be unjust. Central America needed profound domestic change to be stable. Mexican policy makers stubbornly resisted the suggestion that the same equation applied to Mexico itself.[22] In addition, Mexico saw a danger to its own sovereignty in the U.S. principle of dealing with regional conflicts as Cold War confrontations; forceful U.S. action in Central America could justify intense pressures on Mexico.

Just as Central America would need to change to save itself domestically, so Mexico would have to become more active in its foreign policy to achieve the domestic goals once assured with less active diplomacy. If

Mexico did not help bring a viable peace to the region, armed conflict might spread across the border.[23] A more immediate impact was the influx into Mexico of hundreds of thousands of refugees fleeing civil war in their own countries. This raised sensitive issues, parallel to those of Mexican migration to the United States. And although U.S. policy makers feared a "demonstration effect" on Mexico from Central American revolutions more than Mexican policy makers did, the physical presence of Central Americans in Mexico created domestic strains. The Mexican government was lucky that by the time the *zapatista* rebellion erupted in 1994 in southern Mexico, Central America had already turned more peaceful and stable. However, there were dangers in possible though unproven links between zapatistas and Guatemalan rebels who had been "guests" of the Mexican government in the south. But ten to fifteen years earlier, when Central American insurgency was at its peak, Mexico stuck to a strategy of courting rebels enough so that they would not support antigovernment movements within Mexico.[24]

The Mexican government was also concerned that protracted regional conflict could dangerously polarize Mexican politics, violating the principle that foreign affairs must not cause divisions inside Mexico that could threaten stability. On the Left, grassroots clergy involved with the poor and the refugees were hard to co-opt or otherwise placate. On the Right, the government had to deal with increasingly vocal and confrontational voices that complained about the effect of leftist foreign policies on their interests. The Right served notice that it no longer regarded foreign policy as marginal to its interests or as the province of an establishment that inclines left of center on such issues. The media and business, staunchly anticommunist, opposed assuming the burden of Central American refugees and warned against unduly alienating the United States. Even the government itself showed a vulnerability to polarization. While Mexico's Ministry of Foreign Relations remained generally in charge, the Ministry of Finance expressed reservations about the economic costs of helping refugees and the Ministry of Government feared growing political conflicts.

Further evidence that Mexican policy was about rational self-protection much more than leftist ideology or even symbolism is that Mexico did not routinely side with the region's rebels. Instead, it pragmatically calculated who had power and what consequences could result for Mexico. Sometimes that meant support for rebels, sometimes for a moderate Left, and sometimes for governments against the rebels. Oil aid, for example, would go to leftist Nicaragua and Cuba but also to anticommunist

Honduras and Guatemala. Mexico's strong endorsement of Nicaraguan Sandinistas did not come until it was clear that they would gain power. Later, Mexico would restrain the Sandinista government, which resented the strings Mexico attached to its aid.[25]

So what the United States often saw as Mexico's naive or intentional provocation was in Mexican eyes a pragmatic policy. Although it included benefits for the regime's legitimacy at home and for handling the domestic Left, its essential purpose was to protect Mexico from spillover effects from outside Mexico. Two different factors explain Mexico's waning assertiveness in Central America by the mid-1980s. One has to do with a tactical change for strategic continuity: as the regional situation itself changed, it called for a different Mexican response in defense of basic domestic interests. The other reason, however, was that both the world and Mexico's own domestic development model were changing. The new model required a new strategic relationship with foreign policy.

Closer to the United States: The Increased Dependency of Domestic Development

As Mexico's development model and its relationship to the world changed, so did the relationship between foreign and domestic policy. Foreign policy was traditionally subordinate to domestic goals and essentially defensive. When foreign policy sought to do more than neutralize external events, it was usually to utilize them for domestic gain.

With the Salinas administration, Mexico began to subordinate its domestic policy to international forces. In some bottom-line sense the goal remains to serve domestic ends, as almost any country's foreign policy would. However, to serve its new development model Mexico must submit to international forces — indeed, must embrace them — in ways it would not have dreamed of before. National development is defined as integration into the world, specifically and spectacularly including unprecedented integration with the United States. This goes well beyond the degree of unavoidable dependency that existed before. Pre-1990s Mexican governments generally considered political sovereignty and economic dependence contradictory. Under neoliberalism Mexico's nationalism, sovereignty, and autonomy yield to a vision in which integration into a U.S.-led international environment is the only viable route to development.[26] If anything, alternation in power only enhanced this tendency. Unlike the PRI, the PAN has not had the restraining force of a leftist wing in its foreign policy.

This section first outlines Mexico's new U.S.-led international imperative. It then shows how this plays out in Mexico's need to appeal to and listen to its northern neighbor. From there it considers whether closer bilateral relations mean better bilateral relations. Throughout the section one central conclusion emerges: with its fate tied to international imperatives in which the United States is central, Mexico (poor Mexico or not) becomes even closer to the United States.

International Imperatives.   In the twenty-first century, Mexico strives to fit into the world not stand apart from it. Mexico's neoliberal presidents have sought to limit Mexico's exclusive dependence on the United States by pursuing economic investment and trade with Europe, Japan, and Latin America. However, they do so in the context of an explicit recognition that their primary relationship is and will be with the United States. Other deals are negotiated within a context framed by what is acceptable to the United States. They surrender Mexico's cherished claim to exceptionalism, however much they would hate to put it that way and however much they repeat that national sovereignty remains their first principle of foreign policy. Indeed, they feel compelled to proclaim how well they are fitting in, a far cry from the traditional proclamation of unique protection of sovereignty and progressiveness within Latin America's foreign policy arena. In this key respect, then, foreign policy provides further evidence for this book's portrayal of a normalization of Mexican politics.

As usual, several overlapping factors explain the change. Fundamentally, Mexico changed its domestic development model and therefore had to change its foreign policy. The emphasis here, however, is that Mexico changed its development model in large part because of international imperatives (or at least the reasonable perception of such imperatives). Policy makers concluded that domestic policies were failing because they were out of line with these international imperatives. They concluded that economic growth, as well as social and political stability, would be doomed if they did not get into international step. Appreciating the decisive role of foreign investors — the U.S. government, and international financial agencies such as the International Monetary Fund and the World Bank — they saw a need to redefine national development in terms appealing to those powers.[27]

Mexico's perception of these international imperatives reflected, in turn, its weakened position — and the United States's strengthened position — with respect to the rest of the world. Thus Mexico's multiple crises in the 1980s and 1990s increased its vulnerability to outside pressure, especially when U.S.-led international bailouts or loan guarantees were required. Meanwhile, the United States emerged from the Cold War as the world's lone superpower and enjoyed phenomenal economic strength.[28] Salinas and Zedillo could not deal with Bush and Clinton the way that López Portillo had dealt with Carter. Nor would the United States accept an assertively nationalist Mexican policy that had previously been tolerated as a necessary irritant.

But the international imperatives for change went well beyond any shift in the balance of power between the United States and Mexico. Even at the height of Mexico's economic recovery and Salinas's political strength in the early 1990s, the new international orientation of Mexico's policy was clear. Some commentators have ventured that the Salinas years saw a change in foreign policy more radical even than the change in Mexican economic policy.[29] It is preferable to emphasize the inexorable connection between these changes. Mexican policy makers believed that economic crisis would continue if the country maintained policies such as import substitution, protectionism, and large state ownership, and would ultimately bring the regime down.

"National security" would lose meaning without economic strength, and strength required increased international investment, business partnerships, and trade. This neoliberal-style national security required not only a smaller state but also a pointedly nonrevolutionary one. Where national security used to be seen from a domestic perspective centered on internal order, and required keeping the world at a distance, now national security requires involvement in the world, and the domestic-international lines blur. Instead of relative isolationism, Mexico embraces multilateralism that puts world markets and the United States front and center, severely weakening (though not abandoning) the principle that Mexican sovereignty should be protected by holding U.S. influence in check as much as possible.[30] By the close of the century, there was even sporadic talk of dropping the peso in favor of the U.S. dollar. Meanwhile, an increasing number of financial transactions take place in dollars.[31] Reflecting on U.S. influence, Mexico's finance minister spoke words in May 1999 that were striking for their contrast to historical rhetoric: "We happen to live in the right neighborhood." Lucky Mexico, so close to the United States!

There is room for debate about the degree to which U.S.-led international forces have imposed change versus how much Mexican policy makers have chosen it, within the economic realities confronted. There is also room for debate on how much these policy makers have then imposed their will on a reluctant or sympathetic society, though the PAN victory in 2000 and the huge national majorities for the PAN and the PRI combined suggest a society that is on board. But even where imposition has come from a narrow power structure, the impacts reach deeply into society, as the next chapter will illustrate.

Appealing and Responding to the North. More than ever, Mexico listens to its northern neighbor when making policy. This does not mean that the United States barks out orders to subservient Mexican counterparts. On the contrary, the U.S. government arguably barks less than its overwhelming strength might suggest, because the "big picture" is favorable on matters of greatest material importance. What it does suggest is an unequal partnership, in which Mexico, now embarked on a new course, rather naturally listens and appeals for U.S. support in ways once unimaginable. For example, the PRI puts great effort into packaging information to polish its image in the United States, whereas it used to call attention to its distance from the United States. A tradition of blaming the United States for Mexico's problems has not disappeared overnight but is now counterbalanced by the view that U.S. involvement can be helpful.

A visit by President Zedillo to Washington, D.C., in 1995 highlighted this new relationship. Not calling attention to Mexican uniqueness, Zedillo emphasized his similarities to Clinton: two presidents in their forties, with advanced degrees (both from Yale University), able to communicate in English and flanked by "modern" first ladies. Mexican critics lamented that convergence moved exclusively toward becoming "American" and complained that Zedillo seemed more accountable to the gringos than to his own people. After 2000, the new presidents of both countries continued to emphasize parallels rather than differences: two boot-wearing ranchers reaffirmed their common interest in strengthening ties between their countries. George W. Bush made a point of mentioning family ties to Mexico (a Mexican sister-in-law), while Fox talked about his American grandfather.

When interests conflict, however, most of the concessions have come from the Mexican side. Mexico has begun to extradite Mexican citizens to the United States, albeit on a case-by-case basis. It permitted a visit by the U.S. secretary of defense, which was previously disallowed as offensive to Mexican sensibilities and sovereignty. Moreover, Mexico's United Nations voting record has come more into line with U.S. positions. Or consider the criteria used for high-level appointments important to one's neighbor. Outside of perhaps the drug czar, top-level U.S. appointments rarely have much to do with what Mexico will think. The point has arguably held even for the U.S. ambassadorship to Mexico.[32] In contrast, no Mexican president would try to impose an unpopular ambassadorial choice on the United States.

Mexico has had to appeal more to the United States than before. As Mexican development has assumed a new economic and international orientation, elevating the financial ministries, those ministers must also stand up to scrutiny by U.S. economic and political circles. These same criteria have even stretched to more political ministries such as the attorney generalship and the Ministry of Government, traditionally home to a nationalist; today the government minister must convince the United States that Mexico is both stable and politically open. The president's selection once simply had to avoid antagonizing the Giant but increasingly no presidential candidate in Mexico can credibly promise the voters a future of successful economic management without demonstrating at least basic acceptability to key U.S. interests as well as international markets. Thus, even though competitive politics has thrown decisions more into the public's hands, with less room for a political elite to calculate how Mexico should court U.S. support, all candidates for national office find themselves in the same predicament: having to reassure foreign audiences in order to win domestic support. In 2000, all three presidential candidates (including Cárdenas) made public commitments to continue NAFTA as part of this strategy. Governors and aspiring presidential candidates make trips to the United States to meet their U.S. counterparts, or invite U.S. consultants to take lucrative deals advising their local administration. In short, these politicians have reasoned that highlighting experience and closeness with the United States is good politics, both domestic and bilateral.

However much critics may denounce the Mexican government for its turn northward, the government is not alone. Many sectors of Mexican society increasingly take their cue from their U.S. counterparts and seek legitimacy from them. All this adds up to a move away from leftist nationalism. Especially striking is that the Left itself casts its eyes and ears northward. It does so because of U.S. power but also because it has learned that within the pluralistic U.S. government and society, the Left can find international allies who support its particular point of view. To oppose its own government, the Left carries its case to factions in the U.S. government, law enforcement, media, educational communities, labor,

NGOs, and public opinion. This may involve Mexican opposition parties meeting with U.S. government representatives or it may involve an effort to gain the support of U.S. labor unions for labor rights in Mexico.[33] The point holds as far left as the zapatistas, who have looked to the U.S. government and public opinion to inhibit the Mexican government (fearful of losing precious legitimacy) from repression of dissidents.[34]

The Left's acceptance of partnerships with U.S. audiences is quite a concession for a movement that historically downplayed the existence and meaning of U.S. political ("bourgeois") democracy. Of course it partly reflects the Left's own embracing of political democracy and its general moderation. Changes within the United States have also made such partnerships more acceptable to Mexicans across the political spectrum. In the first place, the United States has become more open to leftist leadership as the end of the Cold War and the rise of terrorism has reoriented its definition of what constitutes a threat to U.S. national security. Where once the prospect of a leftist president aroused fears of Communist expansion, the new threat is Muslim, not class-based. Secular leftists could be allies in this new battle rather than enemies. In the second place, U.S. audiences have become increasingly convinced that democracy in Mexico suits U.S. self-interest. U.S. pressure for democracy has precedent, with Wilson and Truman's mild prodding for a two-party system, but such advocacy was usually subordinated to political stability and economic growth. Today democracy in Mexico is portrayed as integral to these other goals: a stable Mexico for economic investment must also be a democratic Mexico. When to emphasize or downplay democracy is, of course, a major question in U.S. policy toward many countries. With justification the international watchdog organization Human Rights Watch criticized the Clinton administration for burying concerns over the Mexican government's abuses as long as it toed the economic line. Anti-NAFTA forces made a similar case regarding labor rights, elections, and environmental policy. The United States remains willing to tolerate considerable imperfections in the democratic institutions of countries that accept the basic parameters of U.S. economic interests.

If the U.S. government speaks inconsistently about Mexican democracy, other voices speak more clearly. Various NGOs exert pressure through their advice, information, or opposition. International observers have played an important role in evaluating the honesty of elections, though the 2000 elections showed a role reduced more to affirming the validity of Mexico's own safeguards.[35] The U.S. media have repeatedly weighed in with often the most trusted and influential accounts of what is going on in Mexico. A common pattern, reflecting U.S. leadership and Mexican dependence, has been that Mexican media discover a story, or feel they have the protective cover to transmit it, only after it appears first in the U.S. media. Mexico's true democrats (as well as pretenders) from the Left, Right, and Center all use the U.S. media to increase two vital but scarce commodities: information and legitimacy (born of honesty). They also receive and disseminate information by multiple means of communication, including mass mailings and the Internet. U.S. polling agencies join in by gathering and publicizing data on public opinion; they operate alongside Mexican agencies modeled after them or incorporated into international polling networks.

So although the increased competitiveness of Mexico's domestic politics might sometimes force Mexican policy makers to avoid appearing too compliant with U.S. interests, that same competitiveness can stimulate increased U.S. influence on Mexico, as Mexican groups seek to gain an edge domestically by bringing in U.S. allies or information. Moreover, competitiveness means a splintering of control over Mexican foreign policy. The president still towers above all others but is no longer unchallenged. Interest groups, parties, and the legislature, previously "extremely limited," are now involved and can impose political costs for unpopular presidential actions.[36]

Two sorts of Mexican lobbying of U.S. interests thus have grown greatly and mark dramatic departures from traditions of insularity. One is Mexican lobbying of U.S. actors who can put pressure on Mexican institutions, like government ministries. Another is Mexican lobbying to affect decisions by U.S. institutions — governmental, business, media, educational, and so on — whose actions heavily affect Mexicans.[37] Courting U.S. favor is a tricky political play, for it runs up against historical convictions and emotions about the insidious effects of U.S. influence on Mexican sovereignty. Despite the risks, all sides in Mexican politics now turn to the United States to win new friends or expose old enemies. This reflects a key dynamic of competition: even where you may not like the cumulative consequences of the actions engaged in, you find it necessary to engage in them yourself. The old wall of political protectionism, constructed on doctrines of sovereignty and national security, has crumbled.[38]

Finally, Mexico has reduced strident criticism of the United States. To be sure, many Mexican political voices remain quite critical, especially in relation to alleged U.S. responsibility for Mexico's troubles. Moreover, many of the historical reasons for Mexican suspicion remain, joined by the effect of increased domestic political competition that rewards assertiveness. Mexican government policy appears basically locked in and pro–United States. Criticism falls far short in both tone and volume from the peak period of assertiveness. Some criticisms have been dropped and others have softened, as Mexican policy makers search for issues that carry political weight domestically but are not considered central by U.S. policy makers.

"Mexico-U.S. Relations Have Never Been This Good."   No wonder the U.S. government proclaims that Mexico-U.S. relations have never been this good. Mexico has become more open to the world in general and to the United States in particular. As integration, imitation, a desire to please, and direct lobbying have increased, political protectionism, public criticism, assertiveness, and defense of Mexican distinctiveness have decreased. A democratizing Mexico treats the United States less as a dangerous force to be kept at some distance and more as a positive force for domestic development.

No wonder the Mexican government, PRI or PAN, also says Mexico-U.S. relations have never been this good. The new development model forces the Mexican government to make the bilateral relationship close and friendly and to state this publicly in order to convince the United States as well as the international financial community. Beyond just saying it, however, the Mexican government has reason to believe it. Its agenda and that of the U.S. government overlap more than ever before. Cooperation has expanded greatly between cabinet counterparts, including attorneys general and finance ministers as well as the more traditional foreign minister–secretary of state link. Cooperation between chief executives is strong. Meetings between the presidents are occasions for announcements of further agreements. First President Bush and then President Clinton came to the Mexican government's assistance each time financial-political crises emerged. They downplayed conflictual points.[39] Basically, the U.S. government sees reason to accept bilateral glitches as long as the Mexican government has the will and the strength to pursue a development model that, on balance, suits U.S. interests. And as long as U.S. policy remains favorable, the Mexican government sees relations as good. Also, although conflicts over drugs and migration remain, Mexico's changing development model has expanded the official bilateral agenda into new areas, many of which are essentially cooperative.

But the statement that Mexico-U.S. relations have never been this good is a partial truth. Closer is not always better, and good at the top is not good all the way through. It holds for the relationship between administrations, often including gubernatorial administrations, as well as for many aspects of the expanded commercial, educational, and cultural contact. It does not hold, however, for the totality of the bilateral relationship and not even for all intergovernmental affairs. There is also evidence of some worsening relationships. Sloppiness about whom or what is the subject of the generalization leads to nearly simultaneous proclamations that U.S.-Mexican relations have never been better and have never been worse.[40]

Whereas U.S. presidents usually portray a Mexico on course for prosperous democratic development, others portray a Mexico wracked by corruption, poverty, pollution, drugs, severe political conflict, repression, and violence. There is some truth in both portrayals. But many U.S. actors have trouble paying attention to Mexico without denigrating it. Popular U.S. images of Mexico, historically negative, are sometimes worsened by increased attention to Mexican troubles on the part of international agencies, NGOs, church groups, scholars, and media. Such increased attention is natural given the growing bilateral integration and Mexico's public commitment to change. Increased openness and political competitiveness further encourage this scrutiny. Ironically but predictably, however, increased attention to matters that are on balance improving also brings attention to the inadequacy of improvement to date.

More than the executive branch, U.S. political parties and Congress often reflect negative perspectives rampant in American society. U.S. legislators have expressed harsh views about Mexican "backwardness," consistent with public opinion that views Mexico largely as a problem, often not meriting U.S. help.[41] Though polls find Mexican public opinion more favorable to the United States than many scholars have imagined, negative and loudly expressed U.S. opinions quite naturally offend many Mexicans. Mexicans often feel that their substantial efforts to accommodate U.S. interests are met with contempt or indifference and certainly are not reciprocated. The Clinton-led bailout of Mexico in 1995 was opposed two and one-half to one at home; the president had to use rare executive authority to circumvent Congress.

In part, these mixed messages result from the open and competitive nature of U.S. politics. Presidential administrations like to emphasize that support for their Mexican policy is bipartisan. True, but so is opposition. Organized labor, liberal advocacy groups, and groups hurt by drugs and migration pit much of the Democratic Party against its more centrist pro-trade wing. On the Republican side the pro-trade establishment finds itself opposing vocal conservative forces that are largely hostile to Mexico, often emphasizing social over economic concerns.

The gap between official U.S. policy and other U.S. interests is especially dangerous for Mexico to the extent the U.S. president's hegemony over policy toward Mexico weakens. As Mexico becomes more visible and salient for U.S. interests, more actors get involved. The era when a few individuals shaped U.S. policies toward Mexico is ending. Polls show that a substantial majority of U.S. citizens express interest in relations with Mexico over drugs, jobs, migration, energy, trade, and the environment. The main reason is clear: they care greatly about these powerful domestic issues, and they are not inclined to defer to government on these matters as much as on more remote foreign policy issues.

By distracting the U.S. president from paying attention to Mexico, September 11 left U.S.-Mexico relations largely in the hands of non-state actors, a situation that has tended to make U.S. policies toward Mexico less coherent, more contradictory, and less favorable to Mexico as a whole. Early indications that Bush and Fox might strike agreements to expand legal immigration, for example, receded in the aftermath of the terrorist attacks. As the U.S. government focused on the war on terror, presidential leadership for advancing integration with Mexico was missing. Meanwhile, strong local opponents of immigration in various states engaged in policy making on the ground, without an overarching national framework.

On the Mexican side, decentralization of the control over the U.S.-Mexican policy agenda has also occurred, mostly due to the rise of Mexican civil society, NGOs, and congressional independence rather than presidential disinterest. Divided government, where one party controls the presidency but not a legislative majority, carries it further. No longer can the president assume nearly unchallenged control over even government policy in affairs with the United States. Such efforts drove Fox, largely against his initial instincts, to take public positions against U.S. actions in Afghanistan and Iraq. Of course, decentralization of foreign policy (on both sides) does not always increase bilateral conflict. Many expanding bilateral relationships are largely positive. Although this point is explored in the next chapter, one vital trend must be highlighted: the convergence of values between the Mexican and U.S. publics. Though many differences remain, they are diminishing. Very much fitting our themes, however, convergence mostly involves Mexican shifts toward U.S. beliefs, including toward democratic values.[42] Again Mexico becomes less distinct. Again Mexico comes closer to the United States.

To sum up, Mexico-U.S. relations have become much more intense and multifaceted in the past several decades. In the process they have become better than ever in many respects but worse and more problematic in other respects. When it comes to neighbors, closer can mean both better and worse simultaneously.

Mexico and the World

Although Mexico's new international imperatives center on the United States, they also play out in Mexico's relationships elsewhere. Mexico increasingly ties itself to the world. To appreciate the shift away from political protectionism, we compare Mexico's more recent tendencies with its historical patterns in remote global relations, including South America, as well as in more historically important relations with Central America and the Caribbean. From there we look at Mexico's evolving relations with the developed world.

Mexico hopes that broad internationalization can limit its dependency on the United States. This might be yet another area in which the best realistic prospect for Mexican development is that short-term challenges will then be followed by long-term improvements. The difficulty is that Mexico's thrust lies in integrating Mexican development with dominant international influences, and "dominant" translates mostly as U.S. influences. Accordingly, Mexico's increased closeness to the world complements rather than undercuts increased closeness to the United States. The reality for the foreseeable future is that "Mexican relations with other countries are, in good measure, a derivation of its relations with the United States"; for Mexico, "the U.S. economy is the world economy."[43]

Globalism: From Remoteness to Participation. Mexico's foreign policy combined, historically, a rhetorical sense of globalism with the substantial reality of remoteness. Mexican globalism has been expressed by its championing of several interrelated principles as valid worldwide. These include national sovereignty and self-determination, equality among nations, universalism, nonintervention, arms control, opposition to nuclear testing and proliferation, and peaceful settlement of disputes. Thus, for example, Mexico has opposed veto power for Security Council members at the United Nations, instead favoring increased membership on the council or greater weight for the General Assembly, in which all members have equal representation. Mexico has been one of the nations readiest to honor the Latin American tradition of asylum for political refugees — a "friend of all," as official Mexican propaganda characterized it.[44] Yet such universalism has been consistent with resistance to deep involvement (by Mexico in others' affairs or allowing others into Mexico's affairs) and with the essentially defensive nature of Mexican policy.

Mexican participation in international organizations has reflected its brand of broad but thin globalism. Mexico has been a member of the OAS, the Inter-American Development Bank, and the Association for Latin American Integration (formerly the Latin American Free Trade Association), and beyond the Americas, the United Nations, the International Monetary Fund, and the World Bank. But Mexico has tried to balance participation with independence. Unlike other oil producers Mexico would not join the Organization of Petroleum Exporting Countries (OPEC). Nor would it join the movement of nonaligned nations. Mexico has become more of a joiner as its development model changed, making its international ties more robust. Mostly, Mexico strives to join international organizations central to the dominant international economy. Mexico's 1986 entry to GATT was a milestone and led to its inclusion in GATT's replacement: the World Trade Organization (WTO). In the 1980s Mexico assumed a seat on the United Nations Security Council for the first time since 1946. Reflecting the primacy of economic goals over political ones, Mexico declined a Security Council seat for 1992–1994 because it did not want to risk public clashes with the United States at a time when it sought U.S. approval of NAFTA. Mexico accepted a Security Council seat again in 2001–2003. The timing proved unfortunate for Mexico in that it repeatedly found itself in conflict with the United States over Afghanistan and Iraq. Since leaving the Security Council, Mexico has urged reforms in the United Nations to focus less on security and more on global human development; it organized a group to encourage this shift called the Friends of the United Nations.

This globalism sort of moves away from criticism of the political status quo, away from mere defensiveness. Mexico's new globalism "wants in." It expresses a normalization in which Mexico de-emphasizes its uniqueness and instead emphasizes how it is ready and worthy to take part in the big game.

From Old to New in Latin America. The traditional remoteness of Mexican foreign policy was manifested even in relations with Mexico's cultural and historical brethren in Latin America. Mexico's hemispheric policy was at the service of Mexican domestic concerns and usually defensive, preoccupied with how U.S. foreign policy could be a threat to

Mexico. South America was remote to Mexico's main political and economic concerns. Mexico has traded relatively little with its southern neighbors. Moreover, South America was not the target of such frequent, direct, and forceful U.S. intervention as Central America and the Caribbean. While Mexico espoused the same principles of nonintervention throughout the Americas, these principles did not require much action in South America. Nor did Mexico have to protect itself from events in South America or from U.S.–South American relations.

Where Mexico did express its global principles, distancing itself from the United States, it was more a maverick than an inter-American leader. When Mexico championed redistribution of world resources from north to south, it became a leader more to some African and Asian countries than Latin American nations. As Mexico consistently opposed U.S. attempts to create an inter-American military force, it prided itself on standing apart more than on gaining support for its cause.[45] Further remoteness from Latin America resulted from Mexican recognition of U.S. dominance within inter-American organizations. Given that reality, a Mexico concerned with keeping the Giant as distant as possible would have to limit its own role in these organizations. That is why Mexico was more comfortable dealing with the United Nations, where the United States has been less powerful, than with the OAS. Increased participation in the OAS since the 1980s has stemmed partly from more balanced leadership within the organization and partly from Mexico's declining interest in avoiding U.S. influence.

Within Latin America, Mexico has been least remote when it comes to its own backyard: Central America and the Caribbean. Geography accounts for that. Yet even there we see that a defensive Mexico has sought mostly to prevent disputes from spilling over into Mexico and to prevent U.S. interventionism from setting precedents dangerous for Mexican sovereignty. It is in this region that Mexico has most often invoked the principle of nonintervention against U.S. action. Examples include Guatemala in 1954, Cuba in 1961, the Dominican Republic in 1965, and Grenada in 1983 — all U.S. military actions to thwart leftist forces. Mexico denounced each as a blow to the sovereignty of vulnerable nations.[46]

With the end of the Cold War and the new thrust of Mexico's foreign policy, Central America and the Caribbean have declined in relative importance for Mexico. Mexico is no longer driven by the same urge to restrain U.S. influence. At the same time Mexico's new model drives it to turn increased attention to more economically and politically powerful regions. This reshapes the engagement with Latin America; where Latin America fits into the international economy, ties with Mexico can be increased. Since 1994, Mexico has signed free trade agreements with Colombia, Venezuela, Bolivia, Chile, Costa Rica, Nicaragua, Honduras, Guatemala, El Salvador, and Uruguay (as well as Norway, Switzerland, the European Union, and Israel). Mexico also signed preferential trade agreements with MERCOSUR, Brazil, and Panama. The logic is compelling: much of Latin America is pursuing internationally oriented economic development models similar to Mexico's. Indeed, Mexican leaders set aside traditions of not criticizing other governments, to lecture those who defy neoliberal, international trends.[47] Mexico's new policy is a far cry from exceptionalism.

The Developed World.   Mexico's new policy is mostly aimed toward the developed world, not Latin America. Latin America cannot offer Mexico large amounts of investment, rich markets, or cutting edge technology. Outside the United States, this mostly means Canada, Europe, and Japan. The dream that other developed countries will provide a counterweight to U.S. influence remains alive at some level. But "outside" the United States hardly means "apart from" the United States. For one thing those countries' interest in Mexico is basically "triangular," tied to Mexico's access to the U.S. economy. For another, partly as a result, Mexico's path toward the developed world runs through the United States. Where "diversification of markets" once implied a means of distancing Mexico from the Giant, Salinas (and his successors) have actively touted Mexico's closeness to the United States as a selling point for diversification abroad — turning the traditional meaning on its head.[48] To enter the OECD (Organization for Economic Cooperation and Development) in 1994, for example, U.S. support was crucial. Mexico's increased closeness with the developed world outside the United States goes mostly along with, not against, increased closeness with the United States.

The Mexico-Canada relationship has epitomized the difficulty of escaping the Giant's shadow. If desire could nudge aside material realities, Mexico would achieve more balance in its involvement with its two northern neighbors, thereby limiting dependence on one. Moreover, Mexico and Canada share certain concerns about the United States regarding fishing rights, cross-border pollution issues, and especially cultural and economic influence. Both feared implications of a North American common market, yet they court U.S. investment. While Mexico has only recently developed into one of the United States' three main trading partners, Canada has long been by far the biggest. Like their Mexican counterparts, many Canadian workers depend on U.S. business, and tourism is a major industry. Like Mexico, Canada has often resented over-bearing U.S. policy in the hemisphere.[49] As in Mexico, concern about the effects of free trade has become an issue in Canadian electoral campaigns.

The hard reality for both U.S. neighbors, however, is that they must deal with the Giant between them as a giant. Although Canada shares many development characteristics with the United States, it does not afford Mexico an important counterweight to U.S. power. NAFTA has been mostly a matter of U.S.-Mexico and U.S.-Canada relations, not Mexico-Canada relations. For all their common interests Mexico and Canada cannot jointly minimize their dependence on the United States. Canadian Prime Minister Pierre Trudeau once famously remarked that sharing North America with the United States was like the situation of "a mouse in bed with an elephant . . . no matter how friendly . . . one is affected by every twitch and grunt." Unfortunately, he added, "If Mexico climbs into the same bed, it merely means that two mice will be sleeping with the elephant."[50] NAFTA brings Mexico and Canada closer than ever. Nonetheless, this closeness is tied to the United States.

Although Mexico is farther away from Europe than Canada, the reigning concepts are largely the same. There is some effort to build non-U.S. space, culminating in negotiation of a free trade agreement with the European Union in 1999. Mexico joined — as Latin America's first full member — the OECD, an organization with a mostly European membership. Mexico's entry into the Asian Pacific Economic Community obeyed a similar logic.[51] Nevertheless, these organizations are far from acting as counterweights to the United States. The United States belongs to both the OECD and APEC.

Europe supports generally the same kind of Mexican development that the United States favors. Economically, this means international opening and international agreements. Politically, its influence is largely pro-democratic. If much more remote than U.S. influence, European concern about democracy tends to be more consistent, as it is less offset by fears about instability.[52] European agencies and citizens add to the weight of NGOs, electoral observer teams, media coverage, and so forth. Nevertheless, U.S. and broader international influences basically work together.

CONCLUSION

If an internationalizing Mexico is closer to the United States than ever before, this represents an increase over historical closeness. Mexico has been connected with the United States throughout its postcolonial life, while major involvement with other countries has been sporadic. Often depending on Mexico's internal strength, the Mexico-U.S. relationship has produced mixed legacies, with both benefits and problems for Mexico. In historical perspective the bilateral relationship has been comparatively positive for more than a half-century. Even in the 1970s and 1980s tensions would not at all approach the magnitude of the kind of military bullying demonstrated in actions like the 1914 seizure of Veracruz. A sense of history puts recent difficulties into perspective. As a general principle, bilateral relations are better when Mexico's domestic policies have brought political stability, economic growth, and investment opportunities rather than turbulence or radical reform. Now democracy can be added to the list of Mexican achievements that promote closeness. In any event official relations between the countries have become unusually cooperative.

This new cooperation is basically the result of the significant changes in Mexico's development model. Mexico's foreign policy has always aimed to serve domestic development, but the historical pattern did not require the current level of cooperation. Rather, domestic policy developed as a result of internal dynamics, and foreign policy was created to complement these domestic objectives. This explained both Mexico's essential defensiveness and its spurts of assertiveness in the 1970s and 1980s. Today domestic policy is largely based on U.S-centered international imperatives. The new relationship between foreign policy and domestic development has brought Mexico closer to the United States principally on matters involving the two countries but also on matters where Mexico interacts with the rest of the world.[53]

What we see is less a convergence where two sides have moved to a midpoint than unilateral movement by Mexico toward an "Americanization" in foreign as well as domestic policy. Mexico finds it necessary to build its new foreign-domestic policy mix around policies that appeal to the United States and to gain acceptance in the powerful international arena. And so closeness, cooperation, and U.S. influence grow. This growth goes far beyond government-to-government relations, especially as Mexico democratizes and its civil society is invigorated. These Mexico-U.S. tendencies manifest themselves in the key bilateral issues examined in the next chapter.

CHAPTER 7

Bilateral Issues

APPROACHING THE KEY ISSUES

Because the relationship with the United States remains fundamental to Mexico, in this chapter we focus on key issues in the Mexico-U.S. relationship to understand how these issues affect Mexican foreign and domestic policy. Specifically, we look at drugs, migration, tourism, and trade to examine the main bilateral interactions, motivations, perceptions, and impacts. General patterns identified in Chapter 6 play out in concrete form in these issues. Each issue illustrates both Mexico's increased closeness with the United States and the revamped domestic policy–foreign policy nexus. Each issue also illustrates how increased closeness does not guarantee smoother relations. Cooperation is widespread and increasing, but conflict also runs deep. Although Mexico's foreign policy orientation is mostly favorable for major U.S. interests, it leaves many bilateral difficulties unresolved.

Asymmetry is another theme that carries over from the last chapter. The changed relationship between domestic and foreign policy involves Mexico's attempt to integrate itself into U.S.-led international contexts, and this means increasingly emulating U.S. norms and appealing for U.S. support. The two countries have joined in greater partnership than ever before, but this partnership is quite unequal in leadership and power. This chapter deals with how asymmetry manifests itself in specific bilateral issues. Although asymmetry is a historical theme in U.S.-Mexico relations, the concrete manifestations of inequality have shifted as Mexico itself has developed. And as bilateral interactions have become more extensive (covering more issues), the impact of inequality has become more extensive and pronounced.[1]

Mexican policy makers obviously believe that getting closer to the United States even in asymmetrical relationships is advantageous for their country. This chapter takes an issue-by-issue look at who wins and who loses. The drug trade is overwhelmingly negative, damaging both nations and contributing to difficult international relations; trade and tourism are mostly positive, bringing benefits to both countries in a largely cooperative vein, while migration lies somewhere in between. Yet the aftermath of September 11 has affected the management of migration policy more than the other three issues. While the potential for positive mutual gains persists, much will depend on how U.S. actors weigh security interests and readjust policy along the border. Trade and tourism thus show how increased closeness with the developed world in general and the United States in particular can benefit Mexico, whereas the drug issue shows how it can hurt.

At the subnational level of analysis each issue produces clashes and winners and losers on both sides of the border, whatever the net effects. Rarely is it simply "Mexico" against or with "the United States." "Bilateral" can be a misleading concept. Reflecting our earlier discussion of centripetal foreign policy tendencies in both nations, the executive branches do not speak as authoritatively for their country as they once did and are themselves often divided. Other participants, including private actors, are often at odds with their own governments and one another. Thinking of Mexico-U.S. relations solely as administration-to-administration affairs was always a simplification; today it is more so. For this reason it is impossible to identify neatly what "each side" thinks or does. Nonetheless, we focus on governments insofar as they make important policies that set the context for interaction in the wider bilateral mix of conflict and cooperation. Another qualification to any simple bilateral formulation comes where key Mexico-U.S. issues tie into interactions with other countries. Drugs, migration, trade, and tourism are broad international issues; even the intense Mexico-U.S. interactions sometimes affect and are affected by the wider international context.[2] Yet, consistent with the last chapter's argument, where Mexico-U.S. issues tie into interactions with other countries, they mostly reinforce Mexico's dependence on the United States.

The key bilateral issues are too complex for thorough analysis and evaluation here. Certainly, this chapter cannot provide clear solutions to problems. A more feasible objective is to identify fundamental aspects of these issues and to see how they change as Mexican domestic and foreign policy is recast. Additionally, we highlight contrasting Mexican and U.S. perceptions of the enduring disagreements. Most interests and perspectives that underpin Mexican positions remain constant, before and after the historic alternation in power that took place in 2000. Although disagreements result more from opposing interests than misunderstanding, better mutual understanding may lead to more willingness to face common problems squarely rather than simply trying to shift the blame to others.

DRUGS

Drugs head the list of specific bilateral problems. Although other issues also create major negative consequences and concerns, these must be weighed against the considerable legitimate benefits simultaneously produced. Drug traffic produces some benefits, but these are fundamentally illegitimate and illegal. Meanwhile, the damage done to both Mexico and the United States is huge. Drugs exemplify the tendency for bilateral issues to be driven by multiple domestic forces outside the scope of governments. They also exemplify the tendency for international issues to influence domestic issues. Moreover, drugs exemplify how increased closeness with the United States can be negative in poisoning the broader bilateral relationship and in bringing overall material injury, even while some material interests in both countries are served.

Our analysis of the drug problem focuses on the following: (1) why simple perspectives misstate the problem; (2) the evolution of the drug flow and various campaigns to combat it; (3) the reasons U.S. efforts have failed to yield better results; (4) Mexico's serious efforts; and (5) why Mexico tries and how it increasingly suffers.

False Simplicity

Why is the devastating problem of drugs not solved or at least substantially tamed? Finger-pointing is a common substitute for an adequate explanation. With few exceptions outside academia, U.S. actors have pointed mostly, sometimes exclusively, at Mexico. Mexicans range from blaming the United States to the more reasonable view that both countries contribute to the problem. To be sure, there is ample blame to go around. But the common jump from that truth to the assumption that goodwill and genuine effort would reverse the problem is misleading. Although it may increase psychological comfort or win political points, it is lazy thinking.

The blame game ignores a crucial point: those with goodwill and vigor — on both sides — lack sufficient leverage over those who support the drug trade and derive benefits from it. The increased closeness of the two countries facilitates greater efforts at solution but is also part of the problem: while government officials cooperate more, so do their antagonists. The results do not diminish the problem overall, and ephemeral gains often come at considerable personal, social, economic, and political cost. But poor results are neither proof of weak effort nor justification for abandoning efforts. Many costs increase in the absence of intensified efforts; standing still is not a viable option. We need to understand not only bad motivations but also the benefits and power that lie at the root of the problem.

Some in the United States subscribe to a piece of this argument about conflicting interests but identify secret sympathies as a problem exclusively affecting the Mexican side and understate the antidrug incentives inspiring Mexican efforts to beat back those interests. The reality is that each country has those who try to solve the problem and those who battle against solutions. Some in each society, though agreeing in principle that drugs are bad, think the drug war comes at too high a cost. Were both governments fully committed to fighting the drug problem, their impact would increase. Even then, however, their efforts would be resisted by those who object to any policy that might diminish the drug flow that provides themselves pleasure, escape, income, influence, or jobs.

Quantitative and Historical Dimensions

Mexico is the top drug exporter to the United States. Its move from a more peripheral role to the leading role is a sad example of "close" becoming "closer" and then "closest." Mexico first vaulted into prominence in this capacity when World War II interrupted heroin supplies from the Middle and Far East; a historical irony is that the United States actually requested increased (legal) Mexican production of marijuana and opium, then used as a common pain medication, for the wounded Allied soldiers. A similar leap "forward" resulted in the 1970s from opportunities created by diminished supply elsewhere after heroin producers such as Turkey cracked down on poppy growing, law enforcement weakened the "French connection," and the communists took over in Vietnam. A third shift took place in the 1980s, when law enforcement progress against Colombian cartels produced an opportunity for Mexican drug traffickers. Already a lesson had emerged: where demand is strong, the suppression of one source often opens the door for another.

The drug traffic from Mexico is varied in composition and impact and shifts over time. Mexican marijuana exports to the United States go back at least to the 1930s; since at least the 1970s, Mexico has been the primary foreign supplier of marijuana to the U.S. market.[3] Heroin exports have also varied. In part because it tends to be of lower purity than heroin from Asian sources, Mexican "black tar" heroin has never represented more than 6 percent of world supply; nevertheless, virtually all of Mexico's heroin heads to the United States. Even when less heroin than marijuana is in the country, heroin looms larger because it is a more dangerous and costly drug. In the 1980s, however, cocaine became the major concern. In cocaine, unlike in the marijuana and heroin trade, Mexico is primarily a transporter and distributor. By 2000, Mexican cartels were responsible for 65–70 percent of cocaine entering the United States from abroad. Ties with Colombian cartels have bolstered the strength of Mexican drug dealers. By the mid-1990s, Mexican cartels were taking up to half of the cocaine they transported in payment for their services. While this eased the problems associated with transferring large cash payments, it also ceded to the Mexicans a growing share of distribution networks within the United States. When it comes to drugs, Mexico's ties to a part of the Third World contribute to the problem and lie largely beyond the legitimate activity of governments. Recently, Mexican cartels have emerged as the top methamphetamine suppliers in the United States. U.S. authorities seized 1,370 kilograms of Mexican methamphetamines in 2001, compared to only 6.5 kilograms in 1992. This, too, reflects the expansion of international ties: importing precursor drugs from Canada or other Third World sources, producing methamphetamine in large industrial labs in California and Mexico, and using existing distribution networks to corner the market.

In a perverse display of decentralization — with sobering implications for those who see contemporary decentralization as a key to democratized development — Mexico's major cartels are known by the city, state, or region in which they dominate: Tijuana, Sinaloa, the Gulf, Cuidad Juárez, and the Pacific cartels, among others. The U.S. Drug Enforcement Administration (DEA) and the Customs Service have periodically launched damning attacks on allegedly corrupt, inept, and cowardly Mexican officials. Yet the reality is that the drug trade has grown despite antidrug campaigns by both governments. More conflict historically arises from programs that involve a direct U.S. presence within Mexico, or from unilateral action dictated by the hard-line U.S. view of the drug problem.[4] But as we discuss in this chapter, Mexico has allowed much more extensive joint antidrug efforts, as befits the new era of a closer bilateral relationship, with greater Mexican subordination and the need for U.S. approval.

The antidrug actions produce many victories in the so-called war on drugs. Yet the war is not won. Nor is the overall tide clearly favorable. Victories are like the visible battles organized armies win against guerrillas over whom they cannot gain a lasting upper hand. They provide welcome but temporary material relief as well as temporary political gains. Sometimes the victories are politically timed, as with Mexican government arrests just before elections or just before U.S. authorities are to make important decisions on aid for Mexico. As in the Mexican fight against corruption, new presidents nab some offenders but others go untouched and still others move into favored positions.

It is not all smoke, deception, and shifting characters, however. Mexican and U.S. authorities also in good faith capture and punish some offenders without getting into bed with others. They make large confiscations and demolish transit routes. But with supply temporarily reduced and demand steady or growing, price increases and so do the incentives for new suppliers to take the risks involved. The pattern plays itself out at the top rungs of cartels and in local neighborhoods. In fact, it has played itself out repeatedly for decades, but public opinion and policy makers usually continue to ignore the lesson.[5] New campaigns are innovative in name and detail more than conception, and few serious reasons are offered for why the "new" should succeed where the "old" has failed.

Why U.S. Efforts Fail

Those who believe that Mexican production and trafficking create the drug problem think that U.S. efforts must concentrate on persuading or coercing Mexico. But however one judges Mexican actions, the drug problem does not originate in Mexico, and so U.S. efforts will never be effective unless they can change behavior inside the United States itself. Put another way, although drug use may be less than it would be without police efforts, policies that do not change U.S. consumer behavior will continue to fall far short of expectations and proclaimed goals.

Demand is the heart of the problem on the U.S. side. Mexico tends to see this as the heart of the problem overall: with no demand, there would be no reason to produce or distribute drugs. Diminished demand would lead to diminished supply. Millions of U.S. consumers are ready to pay billions of dollars for their illicit pleasures. The demand reflects the ills of U.S. society as well as the wealth of the U.S. economy — so many can pay so much. In this example increased Mexican contact with the United States is not a positive influence on Mexico. U.S. demand explains why even a relatively inexpensive drug like marijuana brings a Mexican peasant more income for a few pounds than corn does for a ton and why drugs stand as Mexico's leading cash crop.[6]

The Mexico-U.S. case fits into international studies that repeatedly find that suppressing drug supply is very difficult when demand is strong. Just as suppression of the flow from one country usually increases the flow from another, so suppression of one supply route within a supplying country usually creates a new flow. If Mexican and U.S. authorities make helicopter transport more difficult, drugs increasingly arrive overland. Supply diversion is much easier than supply suppression. When confronted with the demand-supply reality, few in the United States deny it. Yet they repeatedly ignore it. Major bilateral conflict sometimes has less to do with direct clashes over facts than with radically different emphases on which are the root causes. President Bill Clinton spoke to U.S. citizens about punishment, rehabilitation, and personal responsibility, even echoing former First Lady Nancy Reagan's "Just Say No" campaign. But he also managed to talk about the "two fronts" in the bilateral drug war as production sites and transportation routes; eradication on one front and interdiction on the other were the "new" solutions. His attorney general hailed big drug busts as hitting the problem at "both ends," Colombian production and Mexican distribution. Something is missing there.

Embittered by the omission of the United States itself, Mexicans usually redirect the scolding finger back at U.S. demand. The president of the Mexican Episcopal Conference, for example, proclaimed the unjustness of blaming peasants for growing crops that U.S. citizens snap up. Angered at a U.S. Senate vote condemning Mexico for the bilateral drug problem, Salinas reportedly shot back that the United States is a nation of drug addicts. Exaggerated, of course, but not without a painful element of truth. Some estimates place regular illegal drug users in the United States at around thirty-eight million, double that if irregular users are added. Surveys from the late 1980s found U.S. citizens about ten times more likely than their Mexican counterparts to use illegal drugs; though Mexican use has grown substantially as U.S. drug use diminished, Mexicans produce and transport drugs overwhelmingly for a U.S. market.[7] U.S. efforts regarding the drug problem are doomed as long as they do not significantly diminish U.S. demand.

U.S. demand creates a market for Mexico largely because of geography. The negative consequences of this closeness are plain. Mexico sits right next to the world's top drug market. Nearly all of Mexico's drug exports go to the United States. The flow obeys economic laws of supply and demand facilitated by the low cost of delivery. It is similar when it comes to U.S. demand for Mexican workers, prescription drugs, prostitutes, or other illegal services; Mexican demand for guns (legal in the United States but not Mexico) produces illegal trade in the reverse direction. Inevitably, drug traffickers move into otherwise legitimate businesses through which they can move their illegal products.[8] Not only does this allow drugs to penetrate further into the whole Mexican economy, from vegetables to tourism, but it also hampers efforts to check legal commerce at the border — such as Operation Hardline in 1995 — and may negatively affect legitimate business and thus pose high costs. Of course, NAFTA (North American Free Trade Agreement) supporters argue that improvements in Mexico's legal economy will eventually more than offset any short-term negative results from increased drug trade.[9]

U.S. forces driving the bilateral drug trade and benefiting from the geographical juxtaposition go beyond consumers alone. They range from the wealthy crime leaders to common street pushers. It is important to identify who profits most. So much of the multibillion-dollar annual drug revenue accrues to U.S. interests. This is another fact U.S. fingerpointers often ignore when blasting Mexico. U.S. efforts that aim at Mexico thus bypass much of the problem. "Corruption," a term commonly and properly applied to the politics of drugs in Mexico, applies to the United States as well, in a double sense: the morally corrupt society that demands drugs and the criminally corrupt society (sometimes including police corruption) that allows such plentiful trafficking.

Given the powerful forces that push U.S. drug involvement, U.S. policy is woefully inadequate. Classifying drugs as illegal is clearly not a sufficient deterrent. As with alcohol during Prohibition, the laws do not stop use as much as they push it into illegal channels. Whether the United States should legalize certain criminal drugs is a complex issue beyond our scope, but one reasonable view is that legalization might diminish the cost of the drug war at unacceptable social costs. Thus, although accepted antidrug measures may be ineffective, more effective measures may be unacceptable.

Indeed, when the U.S. antidrug debate goes beyond blaming Mexico, it sometimes involves claims that wrongheaded political opposition at home blocks potentially effective measures. Liberals insist that their government does not invest enough in prevention, education, and rehabilitation; more broadly, it does not do enough to create jobs and otherwise diminish the poverty and hopelessness that make drug use likely. Conservatives, however, insist that government and society lack the will to set clear moral standards and to pursue and punish criminal drug activity with appropriate zeal. Conservatives do not believe the liberal proposals would work and certainly are not ready to finance them; liberals see repression and inequity at the heart of conservative proposals. In other words much more vigorous government or societal action of the liberal or conservative kind would entail costs (in finance, citizens' rights, and political conflict) that the United States has been unwilling to incur.[10]

Unprepared or unable to cope with its own fundamental contribution to the drug trade, U.S. policy reverts to leaning on Mexico. Flawed as far as winning a drug war, the policy is often a political winner domestically. Distortion of complex bilateral issues to play for short-term domestic political gain is a game played by U.S. as well as Mexican politicians. In practice, U.S. policy has usually been more restrained than the rhetoric. This restraint could be reinforced by heightened concern for Mexican stability as well as by tighter ties between U.S. and Mexican administrations. U.S. pressure on Mexico stems partly from reasonable expectations about what Mexico should do but partly from inadequate acceptance of how extensive, influential, and intractable diverse and negative U.S. interests are.

Mexico's Real Efforts

The attitude that Mexico does not make much effort in fighting the drug trade is widespread in U.S. public opinion. It helps drive hard-line positions. Like many other U.S. beliefs about Mexican failure, however, it is as misleading as it is true. There is much to criticize in the inadequacy, ambiguity, and sometimes phoniness of Mexican policy; and Mexico should have done more, earlier, to encourage legitimate agricultural alternatives, fight drug traffickers, run honest antidrug campaigns, and cooperate with the United States. Yet the image that no serious and substantial efforts have been made is false.[11]

Compared with all other Latin American drug-producing nations, Mexico spends the highest percentage of its national budget, including the majority of its justice ministry's budget, on fighting drugs. It may make the most aggressive control efforts arguably close to the maximum of what the United States should realistically expect.[12] Many actions have been undertaken against powerful forces that exact costly retribution. Also, with political risks the government has increasingly brought armed forces into the fight. Some of these Mexican efforts are in fact bilateral efforts in that special units receive U.S. training. Increasingly sensitive to voters, factions in each of Mexico's parties demand to know why the Mexican military must put itself and society at risk while the U.S. military is kept out of the U.S. drug war at home. Mexican security forces overall have risked and lost their lives far more than U.S. forces have; Mexico's military has, for example, captured more drugs and put more land out of drug production. U.S. deaths, by contrast, come much more from drug use than from drug enforcement. When Mexicans sacrifice so much to combat a problem that otherwise primarily claims U.S. lives, it is not difficult to understand their chagrin over the charge that they are not making a real effort.[13]

Another Mexican sacrifice that is unappreciated by the U.S. public is Mexico's acceptance of greater U.S. involvement in antidrug efforts. Here again this official closeness reverses revolutionary Mexican nationalism that kept a distance from U.S. efforts and garnered political support for doing so. Intergovernmental cooperation and closeness has increased. The Miguel de la Madrid–Ronald Reagan Operation Alliance in 1986 meant increased personnel, funds, and measures that "drastically modified" bilateral cooperation.[14] Cooperative actions have expanded to include permitting the use of U.S. helicopters in Mexico to identify drug fields (previously banned), aerial spraying of crops, allowing DEA agents to operate in Mexico, sending Mexican military officers for U.S. antidrug training, and accepting a U.S. Department of Defense invitation to join in as an observer in hemispheric military antidrug action. In 1996, Mexico turned over a drug kingpin to U.S. authorities for the first time. (In other cases involving U.S. law enforcement authorities, however, Mexican reaction has ranged from mild protest to extensive expression of protest or efforts to curb the U.S. action.)[15] In 2000, the outgoing Zedillo government signed a bilateral agreement to facilitate tracking of large sums of money from the United States to Mexico. The Fox administration then went even further, earning praise from U.S. agencies for "unprecedented cooperation between Mexican law enforcement and U.S. counterparts."[16] Mere weeks after Fox's inauguration, the Mexican Senate approved an expansion of its Extradition Treaty with the United States —

right on the heels of a ruling by the Mexican Supreme Court validating the principle of extraditing Mexican nationals. Extradition remains a sore point for Mexico, is time consuming, and is still largely reserved for cases where the defendant does not face either a death sentence or life without parole (both unconstitutional in Mexico). Nevertheless, growing numbers of druglords have been extradited to the United States: from 1 in 1996, the number increased to 12 in 2000, and 25 in 2002. And the Fox government expanded efforts to prosecute drug traffickers on its side of the border, in 2001, even arresting a former governor of Quintana Roo for drug trafficking and money laundering.

Although the U.S. public largely ignores the Mexican government's acceptance of increased U.S. intervention, the Mexican public does not. Thus, the government's effort is more impressive than it might otherwise appear. For the Mexican government this is, in a sense, the worst of both political worlds. It seeks domestic political cover by continuing to proclaim what it still does not allow — such as U.S. pursuit of narco traffickers across the border — and thereby offends U.S. legislators who seek to make such concessions a condition of their support. But as the list of what is off limits shrinks, the Mexican government offends and outrages defenders of the old "sovereignty" line. Neither audience gives the government much credit for concessions it makes to its side. The shifting line between what Mexico does and does not permit still allows negotiation of bilateral disputes, and domestic public opposition gives Mexican policy makers some leverage to be assertive as well as genuine in proclaiming the popular principle of national sovereignty when the United States overreaches.

None of this alters the fact, however, that Mexico generally acquiesces in a more active U.S. role. So the Mexican government increasingly portrays fighting drug traffic as an issue of *domestic* national security in order to make antidrug actions appear to reflect Mexican self-interest rather than subservience to the United States. In fact, self-interest and compliance blur. Closeness with the United States has become central to Mexico's self-interest; in addition, as we discuss next, Mexico has some incentive to fight drug cartels even without U.S. pressure.

However real the Mexican government's effort to fight drugs, it is ultimately inadequate. The inadequacy contributes to a stereotypic U.S. view that the effort is not credible. This view unfairly assumes that genuine effort is sufficient for success. By that standard U.S. efforts are also not credible. Mexican drug control efforts are inadequate largely because they can neither solve the U.S. (demand) side of the problem nor escape the economic and geographical forces that carry the problem to Mexico. Inadequacy does not mostly reflect lack of good intent.

Antidrug efforts also are frustrated because they come up against Mexicans who have vested interests in the drug trade and who take advantage of painful vulnerabilities in Mexico's evolving political-economic life. Failure in Mexican official policy represents triumph for some Mexicans. There is truth in the U.S. argument that the drug trade produces enormous revenues for Mexico. The Mexican government estimates that drugs account for perhaps 2.5 percent of Mexico's gross national product (GNP) and 8 percent of Mexico's export earnings. True, the wealth concentrates in the hands of the cartels, but it also is invested in the stock market, banks, and real estate. Even individual peasants receive drug money for their products, including bribes to grow drugs instead of food. In mafioso style, local drug lords may gain popular support by building hospitals and schools and providing other social assistance. Domestic gains from the drug trade raise the costs of official efforts to combat drugs. A charitable perspective is that this makes the official efforts that do take place even more impressive; a tougher perspective emphasizes that the costs severely limit the government's incentives to curb the drug trade.

Why Mexico Tries — and the Cost It Pays

Explanations of the Mexican government's genuine efforts to diminish the drug trade are essentially twofold: U.S. pressure and Mexican recognition of the trade's pernicious effects on Mexico. Not all antidrug activity relieves these pernicious effects, however; in fact, some antidrug activity makes matters worse. Yet whether helpful or harmful in ultimate impact, the motivations for action reflect Mexico's vulnerability both to U.S. pressure and to deterioration within Mexico itself. The idea of U.S. pressure as a stimulus to official Mexican action has already been introduced. This pressure has increased as U.S. suffering from drugs has worsened while its leverage over Mexico has grown. Additionally, the ability of the U.S. president to direct policy toward Mexico has weakened; this is important because modern U.S. presidents have been more ready than other U.S. actors to understand the difficulties confronting Mexico and to contain drug conflicts within a larger bilateral picture. The growing role of other U.S. actors has therefore placed extra pressure on Mexico.

No one should cast aspersions on those U.S. media avenues that try to present the fullest truth they can, but there are incentives to present sensationalistic exaggerations about Mexican efforts as well as to emphasize injurious truths. The media often portray noble U.S. efforts stymied by Mexican treachery. Partly because they still lack full appreciation of the decentralized, uncoordinated nature of U.S. politics, many Mexicans see such reporting as official U.S. pressure on Mexico. Meanwhile, the U.S. Congress becomes another high-profile arena for denouncing Mexican policy. A painful annual ritual unfolds when the U.S. government has to decide whether to certify that Mexico is cooperating in the drug war, a legal requirement for Mexico (and all other drug-producing nations) to receive U.S. aid. In 1988, for example, the Senate voted over two to one for sanctions, but the president came to the rescue with a "national security" exemption; in 1996, a different president, from a different party, had to do the same thing.[17] Reflecting the primacy of economics in bilateral affairs, the U.S. Treasury has replaced the State Department as the main force for blocking sanctions.

As subordinate partners often do, Mexico has found room for maneuvering and shielding itself from U.S. pressure. Just before the 1997 congressional certification vote, Mexico picked up one of its major drug dealers, as it has done more than once, but the dramatic last-inning play has been wearing thin. So, however, has the certification process itself. Many on the U.S. side recognize the futility of threats that bring little tangible result, either because Mexico cannot easily do more or because the costs of punishing Mexico would be too great to U.S. interests.

At the same time Mexico's motivation for antidrug action is domestically and bilaterally rooted. Drugs badly damage Mexico internally. This reality is often missed in popular U.S. portrayals, which tend to highlight Mexican profits and U.S. losses. Argument over which country suffers more is largely pointless, as both countries suffer greatly though differently.[18] The reality of Mexican suffering is also understated and twisted by Mexicans who portray the drug problem as a U.S. problem that becomes a Mexican problem simply because of U.S. pressure.

A general sense of social breakdown has provided fertile ground for increased drug abuse in Mexico. The increase has alarmed Mexican policy makers, especially because it has reached the privileged classes. Use in Mexico has remained low compared with that in the United States, but has grown rapidly. Treatment centers, antidrug campaigns, and drug searches of students all have become part of the landscape, a chilling example of Americanization.[19] Moreover, for societies as for individuals it is much easier to fall into a serious drug problem than to escape it. Thus recognition that some Mexicans gain from the drug trade should not obscure the fact that the net impact for most Mexicans is negative. Because of this book's focus, we highlight the political problems. Drugs undermine not only the system that was once so strong but also efforts to build responsible democracy.

One key problem, for instance, is the way in which bilateral U.S. pressure may actually weaken the Mexican government and thus its ability to stand up against the cartels. To the extent that Mexican antidrug efforts appear as just responses to U.S. pressure, they are humiliating. Mexican weakness is exposed and even aggravated. The perceived ineffectiveness of these efforts then raises the specter of punitive U.S. action, which in turn increases the need, but not necessarily the ability, for Mexico to act effectively. All this contributes to the growing feeling that Mexico is incapable of preventing problems from undermining domestic development.

The debilitating picture gets worse when the mafioso forces gain credit for specific good deeds of social construction while government is decreasingly associated with such construction. Any popular perceptions along these lines can undermine both political stability and prospects for democratic legitimacy. The drug trade brings wealth so vast that it creates alternatives to central power. There is money to buy weapons, to bribe officials, to intimidate people. As with corruption in general, the drug trade brings benefits (economic reward and enhanced political influence) to individuals in government while, for the system, the destabilizing impacts far outweigh the benefits.

Also, the term "government" is a simplification if it implies a unified actor, for government is internally divided such that earnest policy makers struggle against others who defy official policy. No amount of firepower by army and police can solve this problem. The frenzy of charges, arrests, and reshuffling of officials over drug policy sometimes comes from government efforts to impress its anxious public and certainly U.S. policy makers. But it sometimes comes from dead-serious struggles for power within a political system in which many old rules and forms of control have eroded while new ones have yet to be institutionalized. Some of those struggles have to do with the breakdown of the old political system, others with the rise of competitive politics, which gives new incentives to discredit opponents. The drug problem painfully illustrates how the government is no longer able to contain its internal differences and keep them from leading to visible ineffectiveness and weakness.

It is not then drugs *versus* government as much as drugs *infiltrating* government. In this sense Mexico risks becoming more like Colombia, Bolivia, and Peru, as it fails to keep drugs from penetrating the heart of national and local politics. Political assassinations are often either drug related or, reflecting a sense of breakdown, are widely thought to be.[20] By 1999 there was evidence of drugs penetrating Mexico's elite U.S.-trained drug-fighting unit. Various state governors, mayors, and congressmen have been accused of ties to the cartels. Judges have "accidentally" released druglords captured by the police, or given advance warning of raids. Off-duty federal police have been caught serving as bodyguards to drug traffickers or security forces for their shipments. Drugs undercut the strength and stability of a political system that long rested on power in the hands of rulers who could agree upon and impose a common set of rules, rulers who could paint themselves as the peaceful alternative to violence and chaos.

Mexico's political system is particularly vulnerable as it confronts the challenges of shaping its new competitive forces. This creates opportunities for illegitimate interests as well as legitimate ones. Candidates who once could have prevailed in sham elections must actually persuade voters; in elections that increasingly imitate U.S. counterparts in their media orientation, competitiveness rests on being able to finance expensive campaigns. Yet Mexico lags badly in its ability to monitor the sources of campaign money. Drug money purchases advertising and other support as well as intimidation and selective protection. It is difficult to shake the ends-justifying-means temptation: If our unworthy opponents do it, how can we afford not to? Moreover, as drugs increasingly penetrate the legal economy, it is hard to tell where "legitimate" money leaves off and "drug" money begins—creating the option of plausible deniability. To date, hard evidence on drug money in Mexican elections is lacking, but stability may be imperiled where parties have incentives to turn in evidence on their enemies, or to allege it, even recklessly, with knowledge of its falsity.

Problems like corruption and drugs go far beyond government alone, let alone any one party. And if a system built on central control could not deter drug dynasties, additional difficulties emerge where law enforcement requires action within a competitor's territory. Thus, as drugs contribute to the erosion of the old system's political strength, they infect and undermine the democracy that is crucial to replacing that system. Accumulated illegal wealth and power are strong alternatives to the will of the people. Increased illegal economic activity handicaps efforts to build legal activities. The rule of law has trouble taking root where security forces struggle against deadly enemies and sometimes cannot or simply do not bother to distinguish between perpetrators and innocent bystanders.

The criminal justice system is too weak to handle the drug problem, and it grows still weaker as judges and prosecutors are bribed and appointments bought. Mexicans themselves are cynical about the judicial process, at least unless it gets linked with Swiss, U.S., or other foreign authorities. The picture of Mexicans testifying against other Mexicans in foreign courts vividly illustrates the delegitimation of a Mexican government that needs to look outside its own system for credibility and accountability, even while such cooperation with foreign authorities still brings damaging charges of being an antinationalist sellout.

And a special danger regarding law enforcement involves increasing military participation. We have already mentioned the loss of life (as well as public funds) and the specter of capitulating to U.S. pressures. Additionally, the military's new role contrasts with the proud history of the military's relative absence from most aspects of Mexican politics, a key feature of Mexico's unique civilian rule. This is a "normalization" of politics that could be very dangerous. Whatever reluctance the military has, it appears to welcome the rationale for increased spending and upgrading and argues that its antidrug role should be permanent.[21] Military efforts to track down drug traffickers may lead to increasing involvement in spying on Mexican citizens, as well as violations of human rights. At a time when Mexico's struggle for viable democracy requires greater accountability to the citizenry, the military must maintain that a good part of its activity should be secret, reducing its public accountability.[22]

The drug problem epitomizes Mexico's shift from confident state-directed development to a loss of control. Drug-related violence surges. Government efforts to fight drugs increase, but internal division and the power of harmful forces outside its control also increase. Government appears ineffective. It loses legitimacy. It loses ground to both legitimate democratic opposition and to illegitimate predators. It is unable to protect Mexico's domestic development from negative external forces. Thus the drug problem is simultaneously a bilateral as well as a serious domestic problem within both the United States and Mexico. It reflects both the heightened cooperation and the friction between the two countries. It shows increased U.S. leverage over Mexican policy makers and the difficulties of translating leverage into solutions for either country. It demonstrates the increased closeness of the two countries and the sometimes negative consequences of that closeness. Among those negative consequences are the ways in which drugs make it difficult for democracy in Mexico to fill the political space left by the erosion of traditional government control.

MIGRATION

Similar to the drug issue, migration also shows how close the two countries have become. Again, closeness brings conflict, oversimplified views, stereotyping, and finger-pointing. Again, law enforcement efforts produce flashy campaigns which, nonetheless, fail to stop economically inspired and geographically facilitated movement. Additional parallels with the drug issue include the presence of winners and losers on both sides of the border and the character of bilateral issues as domestic political issues within both the United States and Mexico.

There are also notable differences between drugs and migration. On migration the Mexican law enforcement effort is much weaker, reflecting its perception of migration as a lesser problem. Migration is advantageous for millions of Mexicans and a strong net plus for Mexico. Whereas drugs undermine stability and prospects for democratic development, migration may help on both counts. Mexico is much more united on migration than on drugs and much more united than its northern neighbor. Migration affects some U.S. interests positively, others negatively, and conflicting positions pit major parts of the U.S. government against other parts. Such division notwithstanding, migration yields many more widespread benefits (in both countries) than the drug trade, and these benefits are both legal and illegal. Even the illegal benefits, as well as the costs, rarely resemble the brutal ones associated with drugs. So, in contrast to the drug issue, efforts to curb migration are resisted by legitimate, socially responsible interests, and it is not clear that more curbing equals better public policy.

This section on migration considers three matters: (1) which Mexicans migrate to the United States and why; (2) the impacts of migration on both countries; and (3) the efforts, largely frustrated, to curb the flow. The section emphasizes the conflicting perspectives that emerge when interests clash; the facts are often ambiguous and complex.

Who and Why

Debate over migration and what causes it is so divisive that the two countries fail to agree even on what to call those who trek from Mexico to the United States. U.S. government, media, and citizens routinely refer to "illegal aliens." Mexicans argue that framing the debate in terms of those who cross without authorization unfairly portrays all Mexican migrants in the U.S. as lawbreakers. In fact, Mexico is the largest source of *legal* immigration to the United States, with twice as many migrants as the second-place provider (India). Moreover, Mexicans believe that the very term "illegal alien" portrays a basically economic question as a legal one, and that it debases the human identity of its citizens and blames them for causing the problem. Mexicans prefer to speak of "unauthorized workers." This term, in turn, is too benign for common U.S. usage: many Mexicans migrate in violation of U.S. law, and not all are workers. We refer here simply to "unauthorized migrants" (or just "migrants"), a label that is inclusive and nonjudgmental though limitedly descriptive.

Nor is there agreement on the numbers involved. Mexicans have charged that U.S. opponents of immigration hysterically exaggerate. The Mexican government has usually refrained from giving estimates or has favored lower ones. On the U.S. side, higher numbers usually provide justification for anti-immigrant policies. However, serious observers as well as both governments have arrived at a ballpark figure of about 7 million unauthorized migrants in the United States, about two-thirds of whom are Mexican.[23] Mexico's estimates, which include legal migrants, suggest that 8.5 million Mexican-born citizens lived in the United States in 2000, a whopping 8.7 percent of the total population of Mexico residing in Mexico.[24] In any case the figures are huge. One country is the world's leading receiver of migrants, the other the leading sender.

Yet the raw numbers fail to capture the dynamic and fluid nature of Mexico-U.S. migration patterns. Not all unauthorized migrants in the United States are permanent residents. Rather, many individuals cross the border repeatedly. They try after they fail to cross, or they try again after a successful work stint. "Circularity" is common and there are "migratory careers." Much of the traffic is seasonal. Border Patrol agents can apprehend more than a million people a year and still fail to stop the flow. For one thing border agents catch only about a third of the Mexicans who try to enter. For another, migrants who are caught and deported frequently wait only a matter of days before trying again. Mexico's most important "export" to the United States is arguably not drugs, food, or oil but people. Most Mexican migrants go to a few states, although the flow diversified in the 1990s.[25] Moreover, whereas the historical inflows arrived in discrete waves, migration is now ongoing — and more and more Mexicans stay permanently.

Everyone recognizes that Mexicans come mostly for economic gain. U.S. critics of Mexico make two arguments in this respect. One is that improved law enforcement must prevent the motivation to migrate from translating into actual migration. The other is that the motivation itself is rooted largely in the failures of Mexican domestic development. Decades of extraordinary population growth coupled with an economic policy that failed to generate needed jobs produced an excess workforce. Repeated economic debacles in the 1980s and 1990s contributed to labor flight. U.S. unions and other critics add that neoliberalism has ushered in a new and ugly chapter in Mexico's history.

The general assertion that Mexican economic failures contribute to migration is valid. As with the drug issue, however, validity dissipates when critics argue that if Mexico would just undertake sound policy the problem would be solved. In reality, the development gap at the root of migration will continue for a long time, regardless of Mexican policy. Moreover, there must be demand on the receiving end. Someone in the United States wants the migrants, just as someone wants the drugs. U.S. critics too often restrict their explanations to factors that "push" people out of Mexico, skipping over the economic factors that "pull" people to the United States. U.S. critics also often miscast the illegality as one-sided. It takes illegal action by U.S. citizens to make illegal action by Mexicans viable. U.S. laws forbidding migration and employment of migrants are like laws against prostitution, gambling, or unauthorized drugs. Enforcement is hard because it runs counter to strong incentives. Laws do not stop the flow of people northward largely because they do not stop those who illegally hire factory workers, agricultural workers, and nannies.[26]

Thus, as Mexico emphasizes the economic over the legal dimensions, it stresses explanation over blame. Backed by abundant empirical and comparative evidence, it sees the economic motivation to migrate as a natural, nearly inevitable phenomenon where wealth lies proximate to its absence. There is massive migration within Mexico itself as well, from poorer to richer regions. In Mexico's view, if Mexicans must suffer all the natural disadvantages of closeness to a colossus, and of internationalized development, they should not be begrudged the corresponding benefits — any more than U.S. retirees should be denied their migration southward to stretch their savings by moving to a lower-cost environment.[27] However, Mexico has been much less sympathetic to Central American migrants heading northward into Mexico for similar economic reasons.[28]

In the Mexican view migration would be a two-way street even if high Mexican unemployment were the main causal factor. But variation in unemployment does not explain most variation in migration rates. Instead, the key has generally been the binational wage differential: a massive ten to one. Although the effective figure is smaller because migrants concentrate at the lower rungs of the U.S. wage ladder, it is still large, and Mexicans know they can earn more away from home. If Mexicans migrate more when their economy weakens, they have also migrated more when, for example, the California or Texas economy has strengthened. Individually they have done quite well: U.S. work experience often translates into higher wages if they return to Mexico.[29]

U.S. policy has taken economic dynamics into account in this matter, but its own economic dynamics; it has adjusted to shifts in U.S. demand. Mexicans perceive that as a crass manipulation of the flow, whereas the United States naturally emphasizes its sovereign right to fix the number of legal entrants. Until the late 1920s unrestricted immigration fit U.S. needs for more workers, or at least employers' desire to hold down wages by making labor abundant. World War II then brought the *bracero* program to compensate for U.S. workers' exodus to the war effort. Predictably, the bracero program was cut back almost immediately after the war, although Mexicans were legally admitted to harvest crops until 1964.

The bracero period marked the only era in which the two governments managed the migratory flow by mutual agreement. In 1954, Operation Wetback entrusted to a U.S. military general the task of deporting more than one million "excess" Mexican workers. Quotas on immigration from Mexico and other Latin American nations would also become more restrictive. Mexican migration soared in the 1970s, but just as Mexico fell into deep recession in 1982, rising U.S. unemployment provoked Operation Jobs, a roundup and forced deportation of thousands of Mexicans. No wonder this has been called the flower-petal policy: "I need you, I need you not, I need you. . . ." Reflective of public opinion (more favorable in times of growth, more hostile in times of recession), the flower-petal policy also operates widely at the micro level when employers hire and fire with impunity.

Mexico has often called for U.S. policy more favorable to Mexico's domestic job market, denouncing U.S. trade barriers as an obstacle to Mexican business and a source of unemployment for Mexican workers in Mexico. Such official denunciation has waned as U.S. barriers drop and bilateral trade integration grows; this softening also reflects declining Mexican assertiveness. As with the drug issue, estimates of the impact of NAFTA on migration have conflicted. Mexican policy makers and U.S. pro-NAFTA forces hoped that NAFTA, by removing most trade barriers, would spur the domestic Mexican economy and slow migration, while critics argued that NAFTA would lead to increased migration. In the short term, however, NAFTA appears to have been a wash.

A look at *who* the migrants are helps us understand why they migrate. The majority of Mexican migrants (especially the short-termers) have historically been males in their twenties. Though about half the male migrants are married, they have tended to come alone. This is a classic pattern for job hunters. But these are not mostly people who have failed to find jobs in Mexico. They are not the poorest Mexicans, contrary to the stereotypes of impoverished victims of failed Mexican development. Most U.S.-bound migrants have come from central-western states, as well as from Baja California and Chihuahua, not the poor southern states. They have come largely from middle-sector rural and semiurban settings, not the most depressed peasantry, and they have had above-average educational backgrounds and the money to migrate.[30] This is the profile of enterprising migrants seeking to improve their economic station.

The migrant profile has changed and become more complex since the 1980s. Today more migrants come from major urban areas and have professional skills. If this shift further challenges U.S. stereotypes, it lends credence to U.S. fears about job competition. Also, today's migrants have increasingly spread out beyond their traditional concentrations in the U.S. Southwest. Although Texas and California remain the top recipients of unauthorized Mexican migrants, states like Georgia, North Carolina, and Colorado have experienced large percentage increases.[31]

Another striking change is the increased presence of women and children migrants.[32] Mexican migration remains predominantly a phenomenon of young men. Nevertheless, women may be more likely to settle for longer periods, to avoid the risks of repeated crossings. Family movement, though it often follows upon the male workers' lead, undermines the traditional profile of migration as young men coming mostly for temporary employment. Longer-term residency, with children, adds to U.S. fears about both job competition and social expenditures for dependents. At the same time more women are moving by themselves. Socially, this is dramatic, a kind of liberation. Economically, it is largely a replication of what men have been doing for a long time — seeking better employment.

Finally, the changing socioeconomic profile reminds us that although economics lies at the heart of migration, it is not the only element. Men who traditionally came for economic reasons would leave their families behind and plan to return to them. Whereas U.S. economics have been a magnetic attraction, U.S. society can also be a repelling force. Partly, this follows from the difficulties of language and other cultural differences, partly from a rejection of what often seems to be immoral U.S. social life, especially where migrants cannot easily escape low-income areas wracked by drugs, violence, and family disintegration. But the social picture is in fact mixed; as the migrant profile includes more families than ever before, educational opportunity becomes an attractive factor.

Unfortunately, as on the economic side, there is a social push factor alongside the social pull factor. Mexicans increasingly associate social deterioration with Mexico itself, with home. The longer-standing reality has usually been this: Mexicans have come to the United States for short-term economic gain, while social factors restrained the frequency and permanency of their movement. Economic motives have had to overcome social reluctance.

Impacts

U.S. critics generally emphasize that Mexico benefits from migration. They see the migrants themselves but also Mexican policy makers as acting out of self-interest, dumping a problem on their prosperous neighbor. This of course parallels the charge made regarding the drug problem, but it is more credible here given the much more favorable benefit-cost ratio for Mexico concerning migration. The most obvious benefit to Mexico is financial. Unauthorized — and authorized — workers send important revenue (known as "remittances") back to Mexico. As much as 10 percent of Mexican workers earn most of their income in the United States. In 2004, the Bank of Mexico estimated that remittances from Mexicans living abroad would total 17 billion dollars — more than revenue from crude oil exports or income from visiting tourists.[33] Whether it makes sense to see this money as basically pulled out of the U.S. economy, it is critical income for Mexico. Moreover, the migrants provide some relief from unemployment in Mexico as their absence opens spaces for others. Yet not all the economic impacts for Mexico are clearly positive. Remittances do not convert much into the savings and investment Mexico needs, instead going overwhelmingly to family consumption. Meanwhile, the Mexican economy loses some of its skilled and enterprising workers. That said, however, the net economic impact for Mexico appears strongly positive.

Social impacts are harder to calculate. They depend partly on whether the focus is more on Mexicans in Mexico or on Mexicans in the United States. What happens when migrants return home after expanding their horizons or suffering traumas? What happens to their children in their absence? Many rural towns have almost no young adult males and almost no productive economy. Both materially and symbolically this is depressing. And, as more families migrate, children are exposed to new opportunities but also to tough social and psychological environments and discrimination. Sometimes parents conclude that it is better to send their children back home, even if to incomplete homes. Sometimes schooling is badly disrupted.

For Mexicans in the United States there are the problems of adjustment and social disruption. Americanization can mean erosion of values such as respect for elders. The neighborhoods are often difficult, as poor migrants end up in low-cost areas with fewer services, worse schools, and sometimes violence. And migrants experience discrimination and hostility from the "host" population. In 1996, for example, television images of U.S. police beating captured unauthorized migrants led to revulsion in Mexico.[34] More recently, the focus has turned to the rising numbers of Mexican immigrants who die each year attempting to cross the border.[35] It does not help that, according to some surveys, most U.S. citizens think most immigrants are illegal. Another disturbing trend has been the emergence of private vigilante groups who hunt down migrants attempting to cross "their" land (though other groups have sought to provide humanitarian assistance — water and medical treatment).

It is wrong, however, to portray simply an ugly social picture, endured by those who choose to migrate only because of meager economic benefits or ignorance of what lies in store for them. Recent research makes two important counterarguments. One is that within a generation or certainly two, Mexican immigrants in the United States tend to do well. A big gap lies between longer-term immigrants and new arrivals regarding income but also health standards, life expectancy, educational attainment, biculturalism, and other positive indicators of social life. Indeed, these indicators are positive compared not only with recent arrivals but also with much of the U.S. domestic underclass.

The other counterargument is that U.S. society often turns out to be more welcoming than first depicted. Immigrants find employers eager to hire them. Some employers actively recruit Mexican workers, with Spanish ads. Of course, even short of exploiting migrants' vulnerable legal status, employers may welcome workers whom they can pay less and offer fewer benefits. Among their neighbors many migrants run into ignorance more than hostility. When the California job market became saturated, migrants were welcomed in small U.S. cities in nontraditional settling grounds. This welcome extends to women and children and helps explain why Mexicans increasingly build their families in the United States. Research also indicates that good news about life in the United States filters back to Mexico and stimulates further migration.[36] Although all this should not whitewash problems, it does reinforce the view of migration as a mostly positive phenomenon.

On the political side the strongest benefit is the "safety-valve" effect: migration has long served to relieve pressure on employment, population, agriculture, and so forth—contributing to Mexican stability. The effect is especially noteworthy because those with the courage and initiative to migrate may have been among those potential rebels less likely to accept a disappointing status quo at home.

But like other issues migration becomes a political wild card as the system has grown more competitive and uncertain. Time will tell how the migrants themselves fit into the political picture as participants, contributors to campaigns, or popular issues for competing parties to highlight. Where once Mexican governments could largely ignore (at least publicly) the effects of U.S. immigration policy, parties today can capitalize on frustrations over Mexican treatment abroad. They also increasingly attempt to seek support (both financial and political) among Mexicans in the United States. Mexican remittances have become a more important part of political fund-raising. The impact of migration on democracy in Mexico would only increase if—as proposed—the Mexican government extends the right to vote to Mexicans living abroad. While many logistical challenges remain, the idea (already passed by the Mexican Congress) would allow Mexican citizens in the United States to vote in presidential elections by mail, with proof of Mexican registry. If successfully implemented, the votes of an estimated eight million eligible Mexicans would surely raise the significance of issues related to immigration for politicians in Mexico.

Still, the impact of migration on Mexican democracy is unclear. On the positive side, migrants have direct exposure to, even immersion in, U.S. life. But democracy is not the only political example the United States displays. A sad reality of migration is human rights abuse (both for those crossing and those already in the United States). Some in the United States equate Mexicans' lack of legal status with lack of rights, or at least realize that they can act with impunity.

Moreover, a major problem with migration as an issue in domestic politics is that Mexico has relatively little control. The Mexican government registers complaints on behalf of its citizens abroad. But it faces a dilemma posed by its new domestic and bilateral situation: just as competitive politics within Mexico exact a toll for inadequate defense of Mexicans' rights, it becomes harder to confront the United States. As a bilateral issue, migration reminds Mexicans of their nation's relative weakness and of the unfulfilled promises of domestic development. Mexico's subordination shows itself each time its neighbor launches a unilateral action; sometimes this leads to a rather unproductive Mexican cycle of responses: surprise, indignation, a search for some Mexican actor to blame, and then resignation to the effects of bilateral asymmetry.[37] Again, we see how Mexico's intensified dependency on the United States for its own domestic development presents problems for legitimacy and stability.

On balance, the net impact of migration on Mexico has been positive. Although this book's purpose does not include an exploration of impacts on the United States, we consider briefly how these impacts, or perceived impacts, condition U.S. immigration policy. Most economic studies have indicated a positive effect for the United States as well, but that conclusion is not so widely shared by U.S. citizens. U.S. employers benefit by having industrious workers and paying lower wages and benefits than they otherwise would. Some business leaders credit migrants for contributing to the U.S. economic boom in the 1990s. There may also be a rising need in the United States for the kind of relatively unskilled labor Mexico has generally provided. For years Mexican migrants have been crucial to meeting the southwest's demand for seasonal farm labor, resulting in lower-cost farm products.[38]

U.S. consumers also benefit from lower prices for goods and services (clothes, housecleaning, childcare, home repairs, etc.) more cheaply produced by low-wage migrant labor. Some studies argue further that taxpayers gain insofar as most migrants pay U.S. taxes (e.g., sales taxes) while not claiming ample social welfare benefits (at least when they come without families, for short stays, or refrain from claiming entitled benefits out of fear of exposure). Mexican workers have helped build the U.S. economy, traditionally concentrating in jobs unattractive to U.S. workers and filling in for shortages of working-age citizens. But migrants are not "only" low-wage labor: they also start businesses and contribute their entrepreneurial skills and industriousness.[39] As the international economy has become more open, migrant labor has probably helped U.S. business compete and move abroad less than it otherwise would have. Additionally, by providing a safety valve for Mexican labor, migration has allowed Mexico to pursue the sort of economic development model generally favorable to powerful U.S. interests, as opposed to a more labor-intensive alternative.

But there are also harmful economic impacts. Mexicans who take low-paying jobs can increase unemployment and exert downward pressure on the poor's wages and benefits (a problem that U.S. welfare reform may aggravate). At the same time the better-educated Mexicans arriving in urban areas compete for more desirable, skilled jobs. When Mexicans bring their families and stay on, they place burdens on schools, hospitals, and law enforcement agencies. Such charges used to be based mostly on impressions or prejudice, but those who dismiss the charges as pure scapegoating or xenophobia must themselves overlook the research evidence that immigration no longer brings the clear net positive effects it once did. The changing international economy depresses wages for U.S. unskilled labor, and individual states' expenditures on migrant families climb.[40]

Beyond the mixed economic picture, social matters show how critics often selectively portray migration's impacts. For although the United States has a history of receptivity to immigration, it also has a history of antipathy to it and, as in Western Europe, there are often racist reactions to the migration associated with globalization. Popular opinion (sometimes accompanied with a deafening silence from government authorities who know better) overstates the amount of crime committed by migrants. What nobody knows are the net social effects of the migrants on their host communities. Much of course depends on one's views about immigration in general and about the value of diversity. Migrants have surely brought much to the rich U.S. cultural mix.[41]

Instead of blaming the migrants for deep-seated domestic problems or denying that migration exacerbates any problems, we should try to understand the interactive, bilateral nature of the problems as well as the benefits. The point holds for health problems, from tuberculosis to AIDS, as well as for cultural effects. Mexican migrants are part of a huge transnational movement wherein norms, beliefs, and behaviors are carried from one culture to the next and back, leading to impacts including assimilation, integration, and hybrid cultures. The process is not totally positive or benign. Neither is it, as America First zealots claim, a tragic destruction of U.S. culture. Second-generation Mexican-Americans come closer to U.S. norms in general and tend to care more about local (U.S.) issues than Mexican or even Mexico-U.S. issues.[42]

Conflicting U.S. perceptions of migration's impact predictably reflect conflicting interests of different regions and groups. The opposition is most intense in states with the largest migrant population; support is also the strongest in these states. In other words, the issue is most contentious there. One huge debate concerns access to public services, notably hospitals and schools. While courts and human rights groups hold that denial of services is unconstitutional, cruel, and ultimately more costly, public opinion is disinclined to assume the tax burden and reinforce incentives to migrate. Equity considerations enter. Is it fair for poor citizens to subsidize those who compete with them for jobs and benefits? Should the most affected states be relieved of welfare burdens by the national government (which fails in its responsibility to control the border), or should they gain autonomy to make their own policies as the national government cuts back on public benefits to migrants?

Some of the most powerful opposition to migration comes from organized labor, led by the American Federation of Labor and Congress of the Industrial Organizations (AFL-CIO). Labor advocates stiffer penalties against employers who hire unauthorized workers. African-American groups have also been wary of the Mexican influx.[43] More striking is the opposition by much of the U.S. Latino population, including Mexican-American citizens. They face a similar squeeze regarding employment and social services and, additionally, the problem of spillover discrimination. Heightened antipathy toward "illegal aliens" blurs with general antagonism toward "Mexicans." Even legitimate measures to try to limit the influx and hiring of the unauthorized often lead to humiliating harassment of *legal* workers, or even to the conclusion that it is safer and easier not to hire Latinos at all. Although Mexican-Americans staunchly defend the rights of those who have already migrated, they are split about further migration; their mixed position on California's controversial and punitive "Save Our State" Proposition 187 (which called for stripping public benefits, including schooling for the children of illegal migrants) illustrated the point in 1994.[44] In sum, certain U.S. groups lament the bilateral closeness manifested in massive migration and seek to impose greater distance.

Outside the most directly affected groups, opposition to migration is less intense but widespread. Measures like Proposition 187 have considerable grassroots support. This is reflected in the U.S. media and the Congress, in sharp contrast to the mainstream view in the U.S. academic community, and again belies the claim that Mexico-U.S. relations have never been better. Those who adopt a friendly or neutral attitude toward migration are usually less vocal than opponents. Exceptions include religious and human rights groups. Consumers are rather unorganized or unaware of the benefits they reap. Business tends to work quietly with its allies in places such as the Department of Agriculture. Support has often, though decreasingly, come from the Departments of State and Justice, as well as the presidency, which fight harsh measures on the basis of their negative effect on the bilateral relationship. Again, we see evidence that U.S. policy toward Mexico is driven, often in contradictory fashion, by swirling forces more than by one central authority.

And, as Chapter 6 showed, both supportive and opposition camps have a bipartisan composition. In favor of migration, Republican economics-first conservatives and their think tanks such as the Cato Institute find themselves allied with Democratic liberal academics and human rights advocates against Republican cultural values–first conservatives and labor and minority-group Democrats.

U.S. Immigration Policy

In a context of conflicting U.S. incentives and strong if inconsistent Mexican pressure, U.S. immigration policy has ranged from supportive attempts to legalize the migration that does occur to militarization of border control. Amnesties for undocumented migrants in the United States for a long period of time are followed by renewed efforts to crack down on future immigration. Nothing stems the flow of migrants for long, in part because migration is more a boon than a problem for so many. For others migration is at least not a big problem, and controlling it would involve costs. These costs range from direct expenditures (e.g., money for border enforcement, deportation, or inspection of employers) to indirect costs (e.g., higher prices) to infringements on personal freedoms. The Mexican government's effort is limited as it calculates the benefits reaped versus the small price paid. But as the United States gains leverage over Mexico and raises the price of inaction, the most basic reason for relative inaction is clarified: there has been little the Mexican government could do. That attitude infuriates U.S. critics who blame Mexico for the migration problem and regard inaction as irresponsibility. Thus government efforts to curb migration, unlike efforts to curb drugs, are mostly U.S. efforts.

One set of U.S. government efforts can be called hard line. Focused on interdiction, as in the case of drugs, these efforts respond to those who see migration as a scourge. While aggressive, they fail to grapple with the causes of migration and therefore have a limited impact. As with the capture of drugs, the capture of people brings short-term political boosts but migrants try again or reroute. Fence building and other increasingly high-tech efforts fit the pattern. Periodic attempts to tighten border control by restricting the flow of tourists likewise fail to weaken migration, and reduce tourist income, provoking business complaints. As with the drug problem, efforts like the 1995 Operation Gatekeeper in Southern California simply do not undo the basic laws of supply and demand that drive the behavior.

Election year 1996 showed the pressure for hard-line U.S. policies. Calls for a "Tortilla Curtain" did not attract a Republican majority but pushed moderates to toughen their positions. President Clinton supported tough measures even while assuring liberals he would make amends after the election.[45] Legislation in 1997 on welfare reform included provisions to cut back benefits even to legal immigrants. Defenders of the legislation pointed to perverse national policy that encourages excess immigration through the promise of quick access to benefits that balloon in cost, while critics denounced cold-hearted if popular policy aimed at a politically vulnerable group.

U.S. hard-line efforts lead to deterioration of relations. The Mexican government denounces U.S. militarization, simplification, and finger-pointing. It fears massive deportations of Mexicans from the United States. But, reflecting its increased ties with the U.S. government, it tends to protest with caution. It also joins in bilateral border control efforts previously resisted in negotiations. Or Mexico takes on the soft job within a loose joint program; for example, a 1996 pilot program used U.S. money to fly captured border-crossers to central Mexico, where they would be farther from another try at crossing and where they would be helped by the Mexican government. A second set of U.S. policies, more moderate, also takes unauthorized migration as a problem, but it focuses less on pure law enforcement and more on complex incentives for migration. Attention to U.S. political rhetoric and media coverage alone would underestimate the importance of moderate policy.

The main effort of moderate policy during the Carter and Reagan years was to legalize the status of many migrants already working in the United States and likely to remain. Initiative for such legislation has come mostly from Congress. The Simpson-Mazzoli-Rodino Bill, passed in 1986, granted legal amnesty and status to those who had been in the country continuously since at least 1982 (though denying them public social services for five years). This proposal was coupled with law enforcement measures against further migration, but it aimed at the U.S. "takers" as well as the Mexican "comers." It raised sanctions against employers hiring the unauthorized and required use of identification cards. Reflecting the curious ideological battle lines on migration, the card was anathema to conservatives worried about employers' freedom for efficient action in the face of overbearing bureaucratic inspection and to liberals worried about human rights abuses against both unauthorized migrants and Latino U.S. citizens.

There is room for honest debate about the net impact of these policies, but they have not transformed the fundamental dynamics of migration. The 1986 bill led to the quick legalization of some two million people, thus becoming a rare public policy that lowered the unauthorized population. But not for long. New unauthorized migrants soon arrived. Some came to work. Others came to join a newly legalized family member who scrapped plans to return home. Additional unintended but predictable consequences drove impacts further off course. Employers accepted fraudulent identification as it would not be easy for government to prove they had done so knowingly. Or, intimidated by potential penalties, employers found it safer to steer clear of Latino workers, no matter their legal status. Yet unauthorized workers from Mexico kept coming, despite the increased risks and costs and diminished public services. Sometimes they turned to short-term or part-time jobs that are harder to police. Meanwhile, newly legalized migrants flooded local job markets and thus hurt some U.S. workers.[46]

Along these lines, the electoral victories of Fox and Bush in 2000 led to hopes that closer U.S.-Mexican relations would bring a groundbreaking deal to legalize many forms of temporary migrant labor in the United States, an extension of economic integration to labor which Fox called "NAFTA plus." As a former governor of Texas, President Bush prided himself on his understanding of the economic interests involved for migrants, taxpayers, and U.S. business, and was receptive to the idea. On September 5, 2001, Fox opened his first state visit to Washington D.C. with a press conference; with Bush by his side, he announced Mexico's intention to seek a new immigration deal, including amnesty, "by the end of the year," an idea cautiously supported by the Bush administration.

Six days later, that immigration agreement vanished in the smoke of the collapsed World Trade Center. Not only did the attention of the U.S. president shift to the Middle East, but migration itself — and, more specifically, border control — became key elements in the war on terror. "Expedited removals" of unauthorized migrants, with fewer procedural requirements, increased significantly. Mexican nationals constituted 81 percent of such removals.[47] Worried about the possibility that terrorists might use the porous U.S.-Mexico border to sneak lethal weapons or operatives into the United States, the U.S. government stepped up recruitment of Border Patrol personnel. In November 2002, Bush authorized a law folding the old Immigration and Naturalization Service (INS) into the new Department of Homeland Security. Immigration and border control had become matters of national security, not just economics. Meanwhile, the cooling down of the U.S. economy increased — as usual — pressures from states and local governments to curb migration. Thus, despite continued interest on both sides in legalizing certain kinds of (temporary) migrant flows, the costs and risks involved have limited the ability of the U.S. government in particular to pursue new directions in migration policy.

The shortcomings of current policy must be gauged against the realistic alternatives, including what would happen in the absence of limits. This perspective allows a place within the policy mix for law enforcement. U.S. government ability to slow illegal border crossing through greater manpower and technological sophistication has grown.[48] But intelligent enforcement policies require more attention to realities than emotions or political pressures. Academic studies and expert bilateral commissions suggest increased quotas for legal seasonal migration, occasional amnesties, and the tempering of law enforcement with judiciousness and mercy. In addition, they note, in the context of an aging U.S. labor force, excess Mexican labor may be increasingly needed over time. These views resonate strongly with opinions in key policy circles, though domestic U.S. politics — especially in the U.S. Congress — may continue to make implementation difficult. Evidence on negative effects of increased job competition with unskilled U.S. workers and the burden of families on social services gives rise to proposals that legal permission to immigrate be based less on family ties and more on skill and educational levels. Others propose not restrictions but liberalization of migration, a parallel to proposals regarding legalization of drugs.[49] Further study on the why, who, where, and how of migration can help in designing policy aimed at what is really happening.

It is important to learn the lesson that no simple or low-pain solutions exist to what is simultaneously a problem for some and an opportunity for others. This realism will, at a minimum, limit the damage from feel-good rhetoric that falsely raises expectations or concentrates on blame and unhelpful punishment. Measures that would address the root problems (e.g., the creation of more and better employment) are not feasible to the extent that they lie outside the logic of the nations' basic development models. Very harsh restrictive policy by U.S. authorities would also be rejected even by much of the U.S. public that is unfriendly to immigration. Migration is a matter of more or less, not all or nothing. Changes that make home more attractive and abroad less attractive can mean less migration than would otherwise occur.[50]

Finally, migration is the ultimate example of multiple forces not directed by two national administrations. Policy is effectively made less by governments than by literally millions of participants: the migrants, the employers, the ranchers who organize vigilante patrols and the human rights groups who monitor migrant security, the businesses who market increasingly to migrants, and the consumers who do not normally see themselves as actors making migration policy.[51] The bilateral exchanges that occur among these participants are more cooperative than conflictive, even when hostility characterizes cross-national public opinion or government-to-government rhetoric.

TOURISM

Like the other bilateral issues, tourism shows both the long-standing and increased closeness of Mexico and the United States. A key difference, however, is that in tourism this closeness manifests itself overwhelmingly in cooperation. Asymmetry between the two countries is certainly still evident and exacerbated by Mexico's shift toward more U.S.-dependent development. Conflict, contrasting perceptions, and even hostility surface in many individual interactions. But tourism is the one major issue in this chapter that is rarely considered by public opinion or policy makers in either nation as a bilateral problem. The impact of tourism on Mexican economic development and political stability continues to be generally positive. In contrast especially to the drug problem, for tourism geographical proximity is fortuitous. As a legal activity, tourism does not create the same crucial concern with law enforcement as do drugs and migration. When it comes to tourism, there are fewer major losers and fewer illegal winners.

The less troublesome nature of tourism as compared with other bilateral matters should not, however, make tourism appear unimportant. Tourism has huge consequences for Mexican economic development as well as less clear ones for political and social development. Growth in numbers of tourists and in income generated has been phenomenal in the past few decades. The following sections on tourism deal with bilateral benefits and asymmetry.

Bilateral Benefits

In tourism, closeness is dramatized even more than in other bilateral matters by the juxtaposition of citizens' massive participation to relatively limited policy making by government. The Mexican government plays a direct role in developing tourist sites and promotional activities, but its major role is indirect in contributing to Mexico's overall attractiveness, and the U.S. government role is more indirect still. It is predominantly businesses, workers, families, and individual tourists themselves who make their own decisions and, in so doing, determine what bilateral tourism is.

Sheer numbers begin to give an idea of the magnitude of the interactive participation. Mexico ranks eighth in the world for international tourism—first in Latin America, and second among all developing countries (behind China). In 2002, 19.7 million international tourists visited Mexico, nearly 90 percent of them from the United States.[52] Mexico is the second leading U.S. destination overall, behind Canada and ahead of all of Europe combined. What is often obscured is that tourism is a massive two-way street. Mexico ranks second (after Canada) as a source of tourism to the United States. Mexicans visit relatives as well as Disney World, Las Vegas, New York City, and other attractions. Because it is less important to Mexican development, we give less attention to Mexican tourism to the United States than to U.S. tourism to Mexico, but both contribute to close and favorable bilateral ties. One reason for the difficulty in counting is that no clear line separates tourism from other intense human movements across the border. When are Mexicans crossing as tourists, just quick shoppers, or migrants that might extend their visit? When are U.S. Mexican-Americans crossing the border simply to shop or visit family? Counts of border crossings often run very high, especially because some people cross regularly. Thus there may be as many as three-quarters of a million crossings daily.

Expenditures confirm intense interaction. In 2002, foreign tourists in Mexico spent $8.9 billion. Overall, tourism (including Mexican internal tourism) accounts for 8.3 percent of Mexico's GDP and 5.5 percent of its employed population.[53] Meanwhile, Mexicans have accounted for a sizable portion of U.S. tourist income.[54] Beyond such numbers is the enormous cultural impact that stems from the movement, albeit temporary, of millions of people from one society to another.

The positive impact for the United States is almost unquestioned. As host, the country receives significant income. As guests, though some U.S. tourists have a disappointing experience in Mexico and many suffer from temporary stomach problems, the huge number who make repeat trips is testimony to their mostly positive experiences. Indeed, Mexico's attractiveness for tourists is easy to understand. Geographical closeness translates into easy, low-cost travel, especially from populous areas such as Southern California and Texas. The development gap also boosts tourism as it attracts those from each country who are interested in seeing and experiencing something different. In fact, Mexico's attractiveness to U.S. tourists is multifaceted. Mexico offers beautiful beaches, archeological treasures, fascinating folk experiences, and modern entertainment.

Whereas the migration and especially the drug issues harm many U.S. citizens who see themselves as hapless victims, when it comes to tourism in Mexico, U.S. citizens are participants by choice. When visitors engage in "sex tourism," gambling, or other activities often illegal or expensive back home, the harm is usually limited, though arguably there is a negative social impact on Mexico.[55] U.S. citizens can usually determine for themselves whether they want to get involved. This also helps explain why tourism does not produce serious U.S. antagonism against Mexico.

Tourism also does not produce irritating U.S. pressure on Mexico comparable to that seen regarding drugs and migration. The positive economic impacts of tourism on Mexico are rarely offset by negative politics. Tourism means jobs. Tourism also provides opportunities for both large and small Mexican businesses. Increasing binational economic integration often means that U.S. and Mexican interests benefit simultaneously. U.S.-based hotel chains, for example, have developed partnerships with major Mexican business consortia to cater particularly to the U.S. traveler, especially on the luxury end of the hotel trade.[56] Because tourism is good for both U.S. and Mexican interests, the Mexican government makes supportive policy a priority, building infrastructure and maintaining strong tourist bureaus to prevent mistreatment of tourists. It advertises avidly and skillfully, pitching to what U.S. tourists want to hear.

Looking ahead, tourism has the potential to expand and even to contribute to broader development. Tourism has historically built up undeveloped places but, typical of Mexico's unequal growth patterns, benefits have accrued disproportionally to a few showcase projects, with little benefit to surrounding areas. For example, while Acapulco was transformed from a small town to a world-class vacation spot, the rest of the state of Guerrero remains tragically poor. As these locations become more overcrowded and prices rise, tourism might sprout in smaller and more diverse sites.[57] Increased nature-oriented tourism ("eco-tourism") could bolster rural areas and the ecology while attracting new environmentally oriented tourists. In turn, a more diffuse tourism could contribute to Mexico's decentralized development. If successful, that would help counteract the lamentable tendencies of Mexico's new development

Acapulco remains a leading attraction of Mexico's important tourist industry as well as a painful example of Mexico's stark inequalities. (Mexican Tourist Council)

model to lead to increased concentration of benefits. And since the fortification of fragile democracy depends partly on socioeconomic performance, positive socioeconomic impacts from tourism could at least indirectly help the prospects for democratic development.

Asymmetry

Whatever tourism might become, however, it has to date fit largely into a development model in which benefits are highly and inequitably concentrated. Some even argue that average Mexicans come out worse off, for example, through inflation. Beyond economics, a reasonable critique is that tourism has epitomized development policy suiting privileged Mexicans and the United States. Some Mexicans articulate the theme of subordination or dependency in the tourist relationship. In this view policy caters excessively to tourist desires and investment. In some cases the government moves forcefully, even brutally, to suppress local disturbances that could frighten away tourists. Coastal regions are "denationalized," as foreign investors rush to develop them, and even national investors try to cater to U.S. tastes. Though *ejidos* (collective property) were historically restricted from participation in part because small communal landholdings were difficult to develop as tourist sites, neoliberal reforms open up the possibility of converting them into private property. Negative consequences of tourism can thus reach into the ecological, political, economic, and social realms. Though not the root cause of difficulties, tourism may aggravate them.

Then there is a broader psycho-cultural argument shared at least in part by many Mexicans. U.S. tourists are walking symbols of the binational development gap and Mexico's need to serve. The symbolism is especially denigrating when "ugly Americans" imperiously demean local society.[58] Like migration, tourism brings examples for and against the view that increased contact translates into positive feelings. It is less the inappropriate behavior of some tourists than the overall context of subservience that is troublesome. Although tourism is a two-way street, it is hardly free from the extreme asymmetry that characterizes Mexico-U.S. relations. Mexican tourism is very nice for the United States, but U.S. tourism is vital to Mexico. When U.S. citizens travel, they take Mexico as only one of their destinations, but when Mexicans travel, the United States is the destination perhaps 85–90 percent of the time. For the United States, Mexican tourists are one among several large groups from around the world, whereas Mexico depends on the United States alone for roughly 90 percent of its tourists and for the vast majority of its precious tourist income.[59]

The bilateral asymmetry also plays itself out politically. Long a reality, it has sharpened since the 1980s in keeping with Mexico's tendency to be less assertive about sovereignty as it pins domestic development ever more on the gratification of U.S. interests. Tourism is a handy pressure point for U.S. policy makers to threaten Mexican policy makers in matters such as drugs or trade. When orders come for U.S. officials at crossing points to step up searches and thus make U.S. citizens wait in their cars for hours to reenter their country, the effect is crippling on the border tourism and commerce that Mexico needs.

Finally, the success or failure of Mexico's domestic development will be crucial to U.S. tourism. Mexico's vulnerability grows if its own domestic viability erodes. Even in the past, tourism suffered from U.S. media portrayals of tourist incidents involving violence or extortion as well as general portrayals of Mexican crime, disease, or inefficiency; the mere threat of a "tourist advisory" from the U.S. government about a lack of safety can make Mexico tremble. When internal disorder, crime, and violence increase, Mexico appears less attractive to tourists. But democratic elections and more vigorous Mexican government declarations of kinship with its northern neighbor help present a picture to potential tourists of a Mexico that is credibly on the road to peaceful, democratized development.

TRADE AND NAFTA

Trade parallels in critical ways the other bilateral issues discussed in this chapter.[60] It illustrates the extent to which increased closeness brings increased opportunity for conflict as well as cooperation. To a significant degree, trade conflicts — and cooperation — take place among private actors, outside the direct interactions of the two national governments. In this respect trade issues more closely resemble tourism, where private actors also dominate, than either drugs or immigration, where governments face off against private actors engaged in behavior they consider inappropriate. Trade also involves important asymmetries of interest and power. As in tourism, the asymmetry of interest leaves Mexico significantly more dependent on trade with the United States than the United States is on trade with Mexico. This is not an enviable position for Mexico to be in: both more eager to sustain trade and less able to control and direct it.

Yet although feelings run high, trade has not generated a consensus on either side of the border about its long-term implications. Is trade a problem or a win-win situation? The answer seems to depend on the sector of the economy, the time frame, and even the specific companies involved. The potential costs to Mexico are more significant than they are in tourism and immigration, but the potential benefits are also much greater; the costs of drug trade are significant and expanding, but both its costs and benefits directly affect a smaller percentage of the population than trade. Protests against trade have been more numerous and threatening to stability. At the same time trade may have some positive effects on democracy and stability. Whereas drugs have a far more negative impact, trade affects prospects for democracy in profound and complex ways.

At the bilateral level trade has largely buffered the impact of heightened conflicts over drugs and immigration. For example, recertification of Mexico as a cooperating country in the drug war owes no small debt to concern about the economic effects of disrupting the trade relationship; though trade with Mexico represents a relatively small part of the

United States economy as a whole, it is important enough to key economic actors (and regions) to put pressure on the U.S. government. Similarly, concern about the effect of strong anti-immigrant policies on bilateral economic opportunities figures in discussions of migration in states such as California and Texas. In this sense trade reminds us that the issues discussed separately in this chapter interact in practice to shape the overall bilateral relationship. We are also reminded of trade's capacity to generate a constituency for cooperation that is broader than on any of the other issues.

The Formulation of Bilateral Trade Policy

In a 1997 account of the NAFTA negotiations the head of the Mexican lobbying effort in the United States called the NAFTA process a "rediscovery of common interests among three countries that have often parted ways over the years."[61] In large part, however, this "rediscovery" entailed a Mexican journey from protectionism toward free trade. U.S. academics had floated the idea of a free trade initiative for some time; President Reagan also discussed the issue. However, negotiations took place only after President Salinas made a proposal to President Bush in August of 1990. The trade initiative reversed his own previous refusal in the 1988 election campaign to consider a trade agreement and continued Mexico's move away from sixty years of defensiveness against foreign penetration. From the Mexican perspective it was a risky move. Although Mexico had a lot to gain, it "had departed from commonly held traditions" and "had more to lose."[62]

The decision to seek a free trade agreement with the United States resulted largely from the reorientation taking place in Mexico's economic model, the neoliberal revolution discussed in Chapter 5, and the general move toward internationalization discussed in Chapter 6. Once the Mexican government decided to turn to markets, to stress exports and foreign investment, integration with the United States was almost inevitable. Even under import substitution policies, two-thirds of Mexico's exports and imports went to the United States, most foreign investment came from the United States, and production integration began in the maquiladora sector in the 1960s. Several years before NAFTA negotiations, entry into GATT (the General Agreement on Trade and Tarrifs) required Mexico to dismantle many trade barriers. Mexico's top tariff fell from 100 percent to 20 percent, and its average tariff fell to 10 percent. Increased trade and integration with the United States would have occurred — and was already occurring at a tremendous rate — with or without NAFTA.

However, Mexico risked the political fallout of departure from tradition in order to secure a formal agreement. Why? First, Salinas wanted the agreement to bind domestic political opponents to free trade. Second, NAFTA would guarantee access to the large U.S. market, protecting Mexico from future protectionist sentiment in the United States. Thus NAFTA would work politically to preserve free trade and reassure foreign investors that a favorable investment climate would continue. Ironically, the negotiation of NAFTA provoked in the short term what the governments had hoped to prevent in the long term — the formation of a cross-border alliance against trade. However, NAFTA's passage has changed the terms of future debates about market access and integration. Finally, NAFTA created mechanisms for dispute resolution in the areas of trade, labor, and environmental protection. NAFTA neither resolved potential conflicts nor offered Mexico equal standing in disputes with the United States. Nevertheless, argued Mexican proponents, "the new framework defined by NAFTA is better suited to address new, and old, problems than the ancient one of mistrust."[63]

To secure a deal, Mexico had to make several unwelcome concessions to an increasingly restive U.S. Congress. While successfully resisting moves to include drug cooperation, Mexico lost its battles to leave out oil and environmental protection.[64] Mexico also had to make last-minute concessions to U.S. and Canadian lobbies that demanded protection in sectors where Mexico had expected to compete effectively, particularly sugar and citrus. One of Mexico's most significant exports to the United States — its migrants — was entirely omitted. The Mexicans understood that this would be a deal-breaker for the United States.

This kind of concession demonstrates the asymmetry of power between the United States and Mexico but also the impact on both sides of political change in Mexico.[65] When Salinas began negotiations, Mexican politics were not yet free. Opponents to free trade within Mexico were ineffectively organized and politically marginalized. Salinas could count on a loyal legislature to approve the treaty without respect to its content. In fact, PRI legislators turned down opposition requests for regular updates on the progress of negotiations. In the end the Mexican Congress approved the agreement essentially without debate. Thus Salinas risked little in domestic political terms by accepting concessions. NAFTA might well have failed to pass in the U.S. Congress by 1997, however, after the political upheavals of 1994 and the Mexican peso crash. The agreement approved by the U.S. Congress in November 1993 is hundreds of pages long, but several basic principles appear throughout.

First, NAFTA's primary goal is to reduce tariff barriers below the levels established by GATT. This goal was understood by all participants from the beginning and was largely accomplished across a broad spectrum of economic activity.[66] At the same time it was clear to negotiators that Mexico could face serious adjustment problems: Mexico had farther to go to bring its tariffs into line, and as a poor nation, Mexico was behind in terms of infrastructure and technological competitiveness. Thus the United States and Canada agreed to delays in phasing in tariff reductions for Mexico.[67] A special fifteen-year transition period was granted to the critical corn and bean sectors, to make the shock of adjustment less abrupt for two million inefficient Mexican peasant producers. Such delays constitute the main concession by the more developed partners to Mexico's economic status. However, this concession pales in comparison to the financial assistance to poor nations within the European Union, which are paid for by richer members.

A second key principle was the adoption of rules of origin — different in each sector — in order to mitigate concern that non-NAFTA countries might use Mexico as a platform to export products into the United States tariff-free. Some of the strictest rules apply to the automotive sector, where U.S. companies fear Japanese and German competition. From Mexico's perspective these rules represent a potentially substantial cost in lost investment from Japan and Europe. Once again, internationalization has meant entering the developed world through the United States and largely on its terms.

A third principle was the establishment of institutional mechanisms for coordination of policy (to head off potential conflicts) and for dispute resolution (when conflicts occur anyway). The main coordinating body is the NAFTA Free Trade Commission, which is responsible for the operation of twenty-four committees and working groups.[68] However, these "enforcement" mechanisms lack strong independent capacity. NAFTA encourages independent arbitration and mediation to settle commercial disputes prior to hearings by the official panels that deal with complaints. Similarly, separate commissions to hear disputes in the areas of labor rights and environmental cooperation have little ability to enforce decisions. Committee and commission membership is determined by the governments of the respective nations, and thus lack substantial independence from official policy. In this sense the NAFTA institutional mechanisms are far weaker and less comprehensive than the European Union's administrative structure. Nevertheless, they offer significantly broader opportunities for communication and cooperation than previous interactions between Mexico and the United States.

Prior to NAFTA, contacts between the two governments took place primarily through their foreign ministries. Today the networks of communication have increased in complexity and directness, running through different functional and sectoral offices. These networks may enhance the efficiency of cooperation on specific matters but also complicate the coordination of overall national policy. In essence, U.S.-Mexican relations are managed (to the extent that they are managed by governments at all) by an increasingly diverse set of actors inside each state.

Finally, NAFTA required institutional protections for foreign investors. Among the most significant were adjustments to Mexican law involved liberalizing rules regulating foreign investment and reforms to strengthen the protection of intellectual property — copyrights and patents.[69] The 1993 foreign investment law abolishes most restrictions on foreign investment.[70] Growing numbers of companies operating in Mexico have no Mexican shareholders. However, certain "strategic" activities, including oil, remain reserved for the state.[71]

Within NAFTA, islands of protectionism remain. Nevertheless, NAFTA largely accomplished what it intended to do, establishing conditions for freer trade among the North American nations. NAFTA locked in, and further reduced, tariffs that had already gone down under Mexico's new economic strategy. Between 1982 and 1993, before NAFTA took effect, Mexican tariffs on U.S. goods declined from over 25 percent to around 12 percent, while U.S. tariffs on Mexican goods averaged about 2 percent. By 2003, Mexican tariffs had declined to an average of just 1.3 percent, while U.S. tariffs fell below 1 percent.[72] The result has been not only an expansion of trade but broader economic integration through investment and production.

The Economic Impact of NAFTA

The debate over how NAFTA affects both Mexico and the United States has been heated, with complex and often technical evidence. In some cases the evidence tends to support one side, but in many other cases the evidence is extremely murky. Both pro-NAFTA and anti-NAFTA advocates often exaggerate the strength of their case. And it is easy to select particular examples on one side or the other, in part because the process of economic change has winners and losers as well as costs and gains — even for the winners. Three major issues have dominated the debate over NAFTA's economic impact: trade, investment, and jobs. In each case the issue of asymmetry becomes an additional matter for dispute, with NAFTA advocates stressing the mutual benefits of trade and integration, while NAFTA critics raise troubling questions about the implications of asymmetry for Mexican sovereignty and for the less privileged in both countries.

Volume of trade — the first indicator most people look at — is a good example of how proponents and opponents can select particular indicators to support their case. Overall, U.S-Mexico trade has increased. Between 1993 and 2001, annual Mexican exports to NAFTA partners increased by 225 percent, accounting for more than half of real GDP growth in Mexico. Exports to the United States grew on average by 10 percent annually prior to NAFTA; after NAFTA, exports to the United States grew by 16 percent each year.[73] NAFTA advocates therefore cite trade volume as proof of NAFTA's success. Recent World Bank estimates suggest that Mexico's global exports would have been 25 percent lower without NAFTA.[74]

Furthermore, the content of trade diversified considerably, with a much heavier contribution coming from manufacturing exports and services, as is logical with the integrated production made possible by freer trade.[75] Indeed, much of the expansion in trade reflects an expansion in *intra*-industry trade — essentially companies trading with themselves — as production and assembly of a single product increasingly takes place in multiple locations in multiple countries. Meanwhile, reliance on oil declined. In 1980 oil represented nearly two-thirds of total exports. By 2003 oil provided only 16.5 percent of the total.[76] Although oil income remains important, Mexico's reliance on a single export is a thing of the past. In this sense at least, free trade has reduced Mexico's vulnerability to changes in export markets.

Yet critics of NAFTA also find trade data to support their position. For example, increased trade has asymmetrical effects. Mexico's already substantial dependence on the U.S. market has increased even further under NAFTA. In 1980 the United States accounted for just under two-thirds (62 percent) of total Mexican exports and imports. By 2003 the United States accounted for an astonishing 89 percent of Mexican exports and 62 percent of imports.[77] Mexico has also become more central for the United States. It is the second or third largest market for U.S. goods, depending on the year. However, the size of the U.S. economy limits the effect of this shift. Because the GDP of the United States is more than twenty times that of Mexico, even substantially increased bilateral trade is a drop in a large bucket. Moreover, U.S. trade is much more diversified globally. U.S. trade with Mexico has grown faster than U.S. trade to the rest of the world, but Mexico's share remains small.[78] This means that any disruption to trade would have far more profound effects on Mexico than on the United States. It puts Mexico in a weak bargaining position to renegotiate aspects of NAFTA. It also leaves Mexico especially vulnerable to recession in the United States, as Fox found out. As an old Mexican proverb has it, when the United States catches a cold, Mexico catches pneumonia.

The positive side of trade asymmetry is that when Mexico suffers a domestic recession, it can turn to the U.S. market to cushion the blow without excessive concern that it will trigger a recession in the stronger partner. During the debt crisis of the 1980s the Mexican economy suffered years of persistent recession, with a severe contraction of total demand. By contrast, the Mexican economy recovered relatively quickly from the recession of 1995, led mostly by a strong export sector.[79] Moreover, strong trade growth should have a greater impact on the smaller Mexican economy, pulling GDP growth forward, whereas the impact of increased trade on the huge U.S. economy is more minor.

A second measure of NAFTA's impact is investment flows. To advocates, NAFTA had a galvanizing effect on foreign investors: seen as the "ultimate pledge of good behavior," NAFTA "gave rise to a veritable Mexican gold rush."[80] Foreign direct investment went from an average of $4 billion a year in the pre-NAFTA period to an average of more than $13 billion a year since NAFTA took effect.[81] Foreign direct investment accounted for more than 10 percent of total gross fixed investment in 1995, compared with 2 percent in 1990.[82]

But in investment data too, critics find some cause for concern, particularly with respect to the asymmetry of effects. U.S. investment has played a particularly important role, going from 47 percent of accumulated direct investment in 1994 (the first NAFTA year) to 65 percent in 2003.[83] Mexican investment in the United States has also increased, but again the respective size of the two economies means that the impact on the United States is minimal. Thus Mexico's economy has become substantially more dependent on U.S. investment, while the United States remains relatively impervious to decisions by Mexican investors. As earlier chapters have argued, this makes Mexico vulnerable to the opinions and preferences of U.S. investors, particularly regarding economic policies but also regarding Mexico's nascent democracy and indicators of political stability, in a way that obviously is not reciprocated on the U.S. side. U.S. policy makers can still afford to be insensitive and even offensive to Mexican sensibilities; Mexican policy makers usually cannot afford to offend the United States, even at the cost of Mexican sensibilities.

Finally, the most unreliable data — and thus a fertile source of "information" on both sides — involves NAFTA's impact on jobs. Much of this data comes from econometric guesstimates of NAFTA's role in overall increases or decreases in jobs. Few job gains or losses can be attributed directly to NAFTA. No company's decision about whether to relocate can depend exclusively on NAFTA, nor is it clear how to determine what proportion of any decision depended on that factor. Estimates from the Mexican government — which of course has a motive to inflate the number of jobs from NAFTA — suggest that NAFTA has created approximately 1.7 million jobs in Mexico.[84] These tend, on average, to be better paid than nonexport jobs. U.S. trade officials — who have the same incentives to maximize estimates of job growth from NAFTA and minimize the number of jobs lost — find that the "great sucking sound" prophesied by businessman Ross Perot in his opposition to NAFTA never materialized, but neither did great gains.[85]

Here asymmetry seems to favor Mexico. If these estimates are close to the mark, Mexico has gained more jobs than the United States under NAFTA, as most economists anticipated. For Mexico these jobs are potentially significant, though with a million new Mexican workers entering the job market each year, NAFTA alone cannot meet the increasing demand for work. For the United States, in contrast, even worst-case scenarios suggest that job shifts connected to NAFTA have been insignificant relative to the size of the U.S. labor market as a whole. Moreover, trends in job creation in Mexico since about 2000 suggest that Mexico itself has begun to lose jobs to even cheaper labor sources abroad, such as China.[86] Nevertheless, the sectoral and local effects of NAFTA on a given community or industry are significant. Thus, while both Mexico and the United States may have a lot to gain through trade, individual groups and sectors may also have a lot to lose. The loudest complaints have come, not surprisingly, from Mexican farmers: as delayed tariff reductions for key staple crops begin to take effect, their own competitiveness has declined. Thus, as in the areas of drugs or immigration, conflict (and cooperation) will largely involve nongovernmental actors: multinational companies, domestic industries, unions, farmers, environmental groups, and so forth. Indeed, given the nature of economic activity, most conflict or cooperation over trade under the new market-oriented policies has taken place outside the governmental sphere.

The Politics of NAFTA

NAFTA contributes to political change within Mexico as the neoliberal package has redistributed economic power and reshaped relations between society and the Mexican state. Many of these effects have been discussed in preceding chapters. This chapter focuses on how NAFTA affects the relationship between Mexico and the outside world and particularly between Mexico and the United States.

The most direct political consequence of NAFTA was the generation of cross-border coalitions to support, or oppose, NAFTA's passage. Many of these actors had little contact with or interest in each other prior to NAFTA negotiations. On the pro-NAFTA side private actors received support and encouragement from the Mexican government, which established an office in Washington, D.C., to run its lobbying effort. This office spent much of its time coordinating private supporters in the United States.[87] The main organization of the pro-NAFTA business groups was the U.S.-NAFTA Coalition, which included more than twenty-three hundred corporations and corporate lobbying groups. The coalition created a grassroots organization in each state to manage the public relations effort (though all but one of the fifty state captains came from the country's five hundred largest firms). The coalition also had privileged access to NAFTA negotiations through representation on several advisory committees. The Mexican lobby provided the coalition with information, encouragement, and lists of U.S. companies with Mexico contacts, especially in swing districts where the congressperson might vote in favor. It also conducted an analysis of media markets in critical districts and tried to influence the editorial boards to favor NAFTA. It organized an intensive public speaking campaign and claims to have provided Vice President Al Gore with "copious notes" for his debate on NAFTA with Ross Perot.[88] Finally, the Mexican government made an intensive effort to reach out to the Hispanic community in the United States.[89] Such efforts have continued under President Vicente Fox.

Mexican lobbying of the U.S. government illustrates several themes of this chapter. First is the Mexican government's growing need to intervene in the U.S. political process in order to achieve its objectives. This led to a much more aggressive and sophisticated lobbying effort. Second, even during the treaty negotiations — intergovernmental in nature — private actors mattered and figured in government strategies. Third, internationalization occurred in the blending of actors from Mexico and the United States into a pro-NAFTA coalition.

Similarly, cross-border coalitions also formed. The anti-NAFTA coalition included environmental groups, the AFL-CIO, independent Mexican labor unions and political parties (especially the PRD), a number of U.S. Democrats, diverse human rights organizations, and some business interests.[90] Billionaire Ross Perot and leftist politician Cuauhtémoc Cárdenas make very strange bedfellows in most respects but found themselves on the same side in the NAFTA debate. The fight over NAFTA's passage became a prototype for other cross-border coalitions, including the pro-zapatista coalition (forged by the Internet and television) that spanned from remote rural Chiapas to Washington, D.C., France, and Italy. The key to understanding these efforts lies in the perception that if decisions are no longer made at the local or even the national level, successful organization must target the international level, preferably with the cooperation of international allies affected in the same way.

Private coalitions are also involved in bringing issues to NAFTA dispute resolution committees and in ongoing efforts to influence political events in Mexico and the United States. On the anti-NAFTA side groups like Global Exchange and the Mexico Solidarity Network engage in cross-border politicking, including everything from poll watching in Mexico to congressional lobbying in the United States. Fund-raising to support like-minded progressive groups is an important part of many networks' activities, with most money flowing from the United States to Mexico. These networks are increasingly linked via the Internet and electronic mailing lists, in order to respond quickly to events.[91] However, progressives are not the only ones to discover the Internet or to develop cross-border cooperation. One of the key players in promoting business cooperation on trade has been the U.S.-Mexican Chamber of Commerce, which not only lobbies both governments and holds conferences on trade and business issues but also directly stimulates joint business ventures and educational exchanges.[92] Many other companies and government offices offer assistance to potential investors in Mexico. More generally, pro-trade organizations like the Heritage Foundation and the Cato Institute publish reports on Mexican trade and lobby to support the expansion of NAFTA to other nations.

The Future of Trade

It is difficult to imagine a major reversal of economic integration. Disentangling two countries that have become so deliberately entangled would entail significant costs.[93] Similarly, returning to protectionism would not only require abrogating an international treaty but would also cut off basic lines of supply. Many products are produced in a binational fashion already, as much in Mexico as in the United States. Fundamental asymmetry of power and interests will also continue to characterize the trade relationship. Mexico is too far behind, too small, and too dependent on the United States to catch up quickly. The United States must pay more attention to Mexico than ever before. Nevertheless, the United States continues to matter much more to Mexico than Mexico does to the United States. The very asymmetry of the relationship is likely to perpetuate asymmetry, as the United States attempts to protect its interests by heading off significant challenges to its power from the Mexican side.

Finally, the growing trading relationship is unlikely to settle into a purely consensual one. Just as in the other bilateral issues considered in this chapter, both conflict and cooperation will remain part of trade, in part because trade has such differential impacts on sectors within each country's economy. Trade provides new sources of irritation, such as conflict over cultural content in mass media and over the loss of sovereignty implied by integration. Moreover, as with our other issues, the security concerns raised by September 11 make trade more difficult in some respects. For example, control of the long U.S.-Mexico border may be needed for security reasons but could impose higher costs on legitimate trade. Yet at the macroeconomic level — where governments operate — the potential benefits of trade have motivated considerable efforts (particularly by the presidents of both nations) to play down conflicts of interest in other areas if they threaten the trading relationship. In this sense trade has helped temper other causes of conflict and offered a path toward the identification of more common interests than either country has been willing to acknowledge in the past.

CONCLUSION

Important bilateral themes emerge repeatedly, though not uniformly, in consideration of drugs, migration, tourism, and trade. These themes could be identified in other Mexico-U.S. issues as well. Although we cannot elaborate here, the environment provides an example of an issue of rising importance on which cooperation increases.[94] Each of the issues in this chapter shows increasing bilateral closeness. Each involves south-north and north-south flows, though migration and drugs mostly involve the former; simultaneous bidirectional flows underscore the point that each issue is, in a broad sense, a trade issue. And on each issue governments play important and often debated roles, but most of the players sit outside government.

Close interaction brings bilateral conflict. The degree of this conflict varies greatly, not only between governments but also among a range of other actors. All the issues except tourism show considerable domestic conflict within both countries. Both the bilateral and the intranational conflict are logical as different interests are involved and the issues generally involve winners and losers. In all these issues an asymmetry in development and power is obvious. The asymmetry leaves room for Mexico to put forth its own views and to resist certain U.S. pressures, either because these pressures are themselves contradictory, exerted by conflicting U.S. interests, or because pressures are for policies that are impossible to implement or enforce.

But popular and policy attention on points of conflict or asymmetry risks missing what is mostly a positive picture. With the key exception of drugs, the major bilateral interactions make for more winners than losers on both sides of the border. This is clearest for tourism and powerful (if more complex) for trade; most evidence also suggests a positive net impact of migration on the United States, and a strongly positive one for Mexico. Although the biggest winners on these issues are often privileged interests, the benefits are not limited to them. Except for drugs, all these issues can have a salutary influence on Mexico's democratizing and internationalizing development.

Moreover, bilateral cooperation is ample and increasing. Even more than Mexico's development model of more than half a century, Mexico's revamped, internationalized model ensures the sort of domestic Mexican policy that suits key U.S. interests. This effect is least controversial for tourism and perhaps most notable on trade. In turn, cooperation in these areas tends to facilitate intergovernmental cooperation on the still confrontational issues of drugs and migration. And as contacts between private actors increase exponentially, the potential for both conflict and cooperation also increases; however, the sense of shared and overlapping interests among many actors makes harmonious bilateral relations increasingly vital to key actors on both sides of the border. Indeed, the border itself becomes less of a dividing wall. A landscape that includes so many winners on both sides, as well as conflict within each nation, should not be viewed mostly as Mexico versus the United States.[95]

CHAPTER 8

The Struggle for
Democratic Development

During the period from 1988 to 1994 — a time of relative economic recovery in Mexico — a survey found an average of eleven books per year published about Mexico (in English and Spanish) with the word *crisis* in the title. These books portrayed an era of rising uncertainty, crisis on multiple levels, and questions about Mexico's economic and political future. During the first four years of the Fox administration, *only* four books per year contained the word "crisis" in their title. Instead, more authors focused on "democracy" and "transition" as central themes for understanding Mexico's trajectory.

This book was one of them. We have argued in now both editions of this book that the last two decades of the twentieth century witnessed a broad assault on the traditional bases of politics and development in Mexico. But this assault and subsequent breakdown permitted the emergence of something new in Mexican history: Mexico by the turn of the century had drawn closer to viable political democracy than at any other time in its lively and remarkable past. The same decades saw the fundamental transformation of Mexico's model of economic development. With the exception of postcommunist countries, few nations have made such a decided transition in such a brief period of time — from protectionism and state intervention in the market to an internationalist posture based on free trade with a dramatically reduced state role. Throughout the course of these changes Mexico's relations with its northern neighbor have intensified. Where once Mexico counterbalanced inevitable aspects of closeness and dependence with efforts to assert independence, Mexico today embraces its neighbor and defines its future through integration with the world by way of the United States. Even opponents of economic integration seek alliances within the United States more and more frequently, expanding Mexican debates into increasingly bilateral affairs.

Finally, the structure of contemporary Mexican society differs substantially from Mexican society at the peak of PRI hegemony, despite some tragic continuities. Deep and persistent inequalities that predate the Mexican Revolution survived not only the revolution but also subsequent decades of economic growth. Economic reforms have failed to alter this situation so far, and debate rages about whether they will do so at all. But Mexican society has also become more urbanized, educated, diverse, and organized. At all levels and among nearly all social groups we have seen an increase in both the number of voices and their capacity to articulate demands politically, through voluntary and increasingly independent organizations. These groups dispute control over the political agenda and policy making with the state and various political parties. Mexican governments of every party have to take into account this multiplicity of actors.

In characterizing this process of domestic and international change, we have emphasized two principal themes. First is the shift toward democratic politics and its complex relationship to economic and social change. Over time the struggle for democracy has become ever more central not only to political development and stability but to economic development as well. Today prospects for economic development rest in part on the successful consolidation of democratic politics. But while some aspects of political and socioeconomic change reinforce one another in mutually positive ways, other aspects involve trade-offs and contradictions. Second, we note the extent to which Mexico has — in both politics and economics — become more internationalized. The combination of these trends presents us with the picture of a Mexico converging in many ways toward patterns common in other nations, including developed ones. Instead of exceptionalism, we see more "normal" patterns, in both a positive and negative sense.

In presenting this perspective, we do not argue that even the successful achievement of alternation in power — though a historic and enormously positive step — has ended the struggle for democratic development. On the contrary, although freedom and political competition have increased in Mexico, both remain uneven across social classes, demographic groups (notably, the indigenous), and regions. Alternation establishes one fundamental condition for democratic accountability, but accountability requires more than regular and fair elections. It requires establishing the rule of law during as well as between administrations. Mexico cannot expect to consolidate a vibrant political democracy by coasting on its past achievements. Civil society, political parties, and government at all levels and branches must work actively to build on and to consolidate the progress that has been made.

THE STRUGGLE FOR DEMOCRACY: VIRTUOUS CIRCLES AND VICIOUS TRADE-OFFS

The central political shift in Mexico over the past twenty years has involved movement toward democratic politics. Many aspects of this shift have reinforced one another in a "virtuous circle." Within civil society, as groups have emerged and gained strength in one sector of society, they have contributed to broadening opportunities and liberties for other sectors. Sometimes this results from direct cooperation as organizations seek safety in numbers and work together for various causes. For example, as church-sponsored political activity has become more acceptable, local church-related groups have sponsored the formation of new organizations, which in turn support the church's rights.

Sometimes the effects have been more indirect. The increased number of independent groups has destroyed the PRI regime's once famous leverage. It is harder to co-opt one hundred organizations than five organizations, especially with limited resources, and harder to repress one thousand organizations than one hundred. Thus increased freedom has created space for independent groups and parties, while the growth and strength of these groups and parties has in turn strengthened public protection of freedom, making it more of a right and less something doled out by the government at its own discretion. Any temptation to engage in repression that governments may feel — from local PRI caciques in Oaxaca to PRD mayors in Mexico City to the PAN president — face the potential costs of public protest and international scandal, including negative investor reactions. Indeed, domestic groups often count on such reactions in order to put pressure on governments. This tends to increase governmental accountability.

Positive connections also link changes in civil society to the electoral arena. Mexican elections have gradually become more credible and free. Where once the PRI controlled all states and almost all local governments, by 2000, the PRI held onto 61 percent of states and 57 percent of municipalities.[1]Support from civil society has played a key role in this process, by pressuring the government for legal reforms that have increased the fairness of elections, by cooperating in election monitoring, and by developing political leaders.

In turn, civil society may gain influence and access as electoral competition grows. Where once independent organizations felt they could get the regime's attention only through protesting, their options today include multiparty bargaining. Perhaps most crucially, when elections matter, parties must compete for votes by paying attention to public opinion and living up to more of their campaign promises. Even as the PAN celebration unfolded on the night of Vicente Fox's historic victory, the most common plea from the jubilant crowd was simply this: "*no nos falles* — do not fail us." The development of such claims on the part of voters becomes a crucial link in the strengthening of citizens' ability to hold government accountable. In addition, competition may affect organization and accountability within civil society and political parties. The alternatives represented by independent organizations have pressured leaders of traditional unions to be more responsive to their members. In a related way traditional media outlets have found themselves increasingly compelled to adopt critical reporting in order to compete for market share. No government in the future can count on a slavish pro-government line; again, this should enhance accountability as citizens obtain more information about their government.

Liberalization in the economic sphere also has some positive effects on political liberalization. As the state pulls back from a central role in economic decision making (through privatization, deregulation, and free trade), it turns over many decisions about profit and resource allocation to the private sector. Actors who do not need state approval for their economic success are more inclined to reject state interference. The association that developed in the 1980s between some business owners and the PAN is one example of how this effect can strengthen party competition. More indirectly, business pressure can bolster democracy by supporting the rule of law — a basic requirement for democratic accountability. Business has an interest in strengthening the judicial sector's ability to enforce contracts and administer punishments according to a set of predictable rules. A more independent, less discretionary judiciary can also protect those who disagree with the government. Finally, as business pressures the state to minimize political turmoil, it may encourage government responsiveness to popular pressures.

Within popular sectors, market reforms reduce or eliminate the ability of any government to make use of the incentives that the PRI once offered to encourage cooperation. In the peasant sector, for example, the end of land reform eliminated a key benefit for PRI-affiliated peasant organizations. Reductions in credit, the decline of marketing boards, and the end of protection for some export crops have a similar impact. The state's smaller role in economics has created opportunities for organization less subject to manipulation by government. A leftist government might make an effort to reverse some market reforms and recover some old incentives, but even then it would face institutional constraints like NAFTA and the opposition of those who have benefited from reforms.

Despite some positive and mutually reinforcing effects, the process of political and economic reform also involves negative dynamics, a vicious cycle undermining the virtuous one. Expanding freedoms for prodemocratic organizations may expand opportunities for less democratic ones as well, like guerrilla groups and paramilitary organizations.

Similarly, freedoms do not expand at an equal rate for all groups, leaving democracy on rather narrow bases. Formal democratic institutions do not necessarily improve the situation of the marginalized. New opportunities open up, but the poor are least able to take advantage of them. The freedom to organize and the ability to organize effectively are two different things. Those who have the advantages of money, time, education, and political connections have a better chance of making their voices heard, even when they seem superficially to have the same freedom to speak as the less advantaged. This problem is common in democracies, but Mexico faces an acute version, which the neoliberal model may aggravate. The mammoth changes in Mexican politics and development must not blind us to the fact that the vast majority of Mexicans remain unorganized, disunited, and scattered. They have fewer resources and are less likely to create successful organizations than both wealthy and middle-class groups. Although parties have incentives in a competitive environment to appeal to unorganized masses, they also face lobbying by powerful special interests. And as the centrality of parties to policy making increases, elite groups intensify efforts to control them. Democracy opens new channels of access without changing this central problem.

In addition, satisfying the demand for democracy may imply sacrifices or delays in the achievement of other goals, including economic growth, stability, national sovereignty, and equality. Many of these were historically goals of the PRI regime, as Chapter 2 detailed. Yet democracy does not necessarily maximize all other goals, and in certain ways, at certain times, it may undermine them. For example, democracy requires government to make concessions to social groups, but some concessions may slow economic growth. Electoral pressures may lead politicians to promise policies that, while popular in the short term, have harmful macroeconomic effects later on. When an election is coming up, it is hard for any party that wishes to be re-elected to cut the budget or devalue the currency, though postponement may have more negative consequences in the long term.

Likewise, democracy does not always provide ideal conditions for economic growth, at least from the point of view of investors. In the case of the 2000 election, democracy brought to power a conservative pro-market candidate. Investors were thrilled. But elections can also bring leftists to power, on the basis of social demands for state services and protection, rejection of some neoliberal reforms, or a preference for less internationalized development. Investors may be less thrilled with such outcomes. Do elections offer a more solid basis for legitimacy and stability — or do they create new sources of unpredictability and instability in government policies? Perhaps both. Under the PRI's authoritarian rule, powerful presidents could implement major policy reforms with little public accountability. The mechanisms of controlled succession limited the magnitude of the swing in any one election, though they allowed a degree of policy shifting within the established model. Democratic elections can increase the magnitude of such swings by creating opportunities for more extreme electoral alternatives. The constraints imposed on economic policies by internationalization could limit this risk by limiting the range of viable alternatives. Yet here, economic stability may come with a cost for democracy: if voters sense that international actors limit what any elected government can do, the scope of democratic politics may shrink to an unsatisfactory and ineffective middle ground. Support for democracy may decline.

Nor does democracy guarantee stability. Democratic advocates argue persuasively that Mexico cannot remain politically stable without democracy. But democracy — especially in the developing world — has been a fragile thing. The freedom necessary for democratic competition can be abused. Some conflicts of interest seem impossible to resolve through compromise. Some games are zero-sum. Some stakes are too high to accept defeat. Even in the best of circumstances, democratic politics is messy. The pressure of competition can tempt actors to behave badly: cheating, lying, and intimidating their opponents. Corruption

President Vicente Fox (2000–2006) faced many questions — and high expectations — regarding his plans for the country's future. (*La Jornada*)

scandals are more likely to become public and damage the legitimacy of the government. Public disillusionment can then grow, undermining the stability of democracy.

And Mexico does not enjoy the best of circumstances. Mexico must deal with the aftermath of decades (if not centuries) of authoritarian rule: deeply rooted authoritarian behavior, lack of experience with democracy, and a long list of unresolved grievances against repressive and corrupt PRI governments that would tax even the most capable and dedicated reformers. Mexicans must also confront potentially intense social conflicts that could put stress on democratic politics. Throughout this book we have repeatedly noted Mexico's profound social and economic inequalities. At least in the short run, neoliberal policies will not significantly reduce inequality and may increase it. Democratic theorists have long worried that the "principle of numbers" could lead to the breakdown of democracy in unequal societies. Because the poor outnumber the rich, they can outvote them, and if unjustly excluded from economic opportunities, they may use their votes to redistribute wealth.

In Latin America business has often encouraged military coups for these reasons. Thus scholars from Aristotle to Alexis de Tocqueville to Seymour Martin Lipset have argued that stable democracies should be characterized by equality and the presence of a strong middle class. Mexico lacks both. Small wonder that novelist and amateur politician Mario Vargas Llosa called the task facing Fox nearly titanic. Vargas Llosa's own nation, Peru, made a transition to democracy only to see the popular desire for stability and economic progress override the desire for democracy; Peru's president (Alberto Fujimori) dissolved the Congress and manipulated the Constitution to re-elect himself but long enjoyed popular support because of his success in repressing Peru's Maoist guerrillas and restoring economic growth.

None of this means that democracy is not worth the risks, however, or that it is incompatible with internationalized development. After all, virtuous circle effects exist too, and all established democracies are broadly capitalist. The argument developed throughout this book has emphasized the importance of democracy as a central goal and an integral part of development. Many of the problems we raise have long and tragic histories that cannot be blamed on democracy or neoliberalism. Yet we need to sound a cautionary note. Democracy cannot maximize all desirable goals. Nor is neoliberalism the solution to all problems. Democratic development will not occur without thought and considerable effort, and even its achievement in Mexico would leave major issues unresolved.

THE STRUGGLE FOR DEVELOPMENT: INTERNATIONALIZATION

Mexico's struggle for economic development has always involved significant connections with foreign markets; no country sharing a border with the United States could avoid that. Most postrevolutionary governments recognized the potential advantages of Mexico's geographical position and sought capital and markets in the United States. However, Mexico under the classic PRI regime was wary of the potential disadvantages of this connection. Where possible, the Mexican state protected Mexican business from competition in trade, regulated foreign investment, and avoided enthusiastic emulation of U.S. political, cultural, or economic models. The political corollary of this nationalist position was a distinctive party system, claiming a unique Mexican approach to "democracy" which involved less electoral competition but an inclusive and even pluralist dynamic within the party itself.

In contrast, Mexican governments of the past two decades have followed a more outward-looking approach, an approach compatible with a conservative and pro-market PAN. Rather than protecting Mexican business from foreign competitors, administrations have opened the economy to trade and have encouraged exports. Rather than demanding Mexican control of national enterprise, they have stimulated foreign investment. And rather than insisting on the traditional definition of Mexican national sovereignty, they have redefined (critics say, cynically, manipulated) "nationalism," as strengthening Mexico through integration with the world. Mexico's emergence from behind its protective economic screen has brought it closer to the developed economies of North America. Not coincidentally, evolution toward common norms often brings Mexico especially close to a U.S. model.

Regarding politics, where Mexico's postrevolutionary political regime often seemed unique among the world's political systems, political behavior and institutions today more closely resemble those of other countries, for better but also for worse. The term *normalization* as we have employed it signals Mexico's closer resemblance to patterns of political interaction found elsewhere and contrasts to the "exceptionalism" typically applied to the study of Mexican politics in the past. Mexicans have increasingly endorsed traditional Western definitions of democracy as involving, principally, free and fair elections with broad participation and meaningful competition. In addition, though not always noting the connection, many Mexican actors have sought to imitate other U.S.-centered characteristics of democracy, including support for checks and balances, strong federalism, civil liberties, and accountability (a concept often referred to in English, reflecting its shallow roots in Spanish legal tradition). Mass surveys also show convergence in political and social values.

Mexico has also become more typical in negative ways. Successive PRI governments seemed ever less able to manage political conflict with a sure hand. The mantle of secrecy once discreetly covering over corruption and conflict among elites has fallen away. Ugly evidence of these realities contributed to the sense of outrage and social breakdown that led to Fox's victory, as he campaigned on the simple slogans of "today" and "enough already"—enough of the PRI, enough of corruption, enough of the past. Yet the exceptional political system that limited popular participation also subordinated the military, offered political order, contained inter-elite conflict, and bolstered stability. Today's more open and democratic system lacks these internal restraints. However reluctantly, Mexico has turned with increased frequency to the United States for assistance in meeting many of these challenges: accepting U.S. military training, requesting financial and technical assistance in fighting drugs, crime, and corruption, and taking advantage of U.S. aid to encourage institutional development. Some "domestic" problems are increasingly joint problems for which bilateral solutions can be sought.

The full effects of this closer integration are complex and will not play out completely in the short run. In the near term, U.S. actors assume an increasingly powerful role in Mexican domestic debates on everything from labor law and environmental policy to tax laws and the national budget. Mexico also occupies an increasingly prominent position within U.S. domestic debates, especially on trade, migration, security, and drugs. Ideas, resources, and experience flow back and forth across the border, bringing internationalization into more and more areas of social, economic, and political life.

DEMOCRATIC DEVELOPMENT
IN THE TWENTY-FIRST CENTURY

While social scientists take risks when they predict, readers legitimately want answers and ask them to speculate about the inevitable question: What does democracy imply for Mexican politics and economic development? While we can identify few certainties, the weight of the trends established over the past twenty years points more strongly in some directions than others. Most important, the rise of political competition, the increasingly broad preferences for democracy, the exercise of political freedom, the growth of independent civil society, and the acceptance of alternation in power point most strongly to a democratic political system in the near term. Democratic competition would be difficult and costly to reverse. Absent some kind of (unlikely) military coup, no elected government will enjoy the control the PRI wielded at its peak or display its sure-handedness in directing Mexican development. Democratic governments must negotiate and persuade rather than dictate; a government lacking a majority in either house of Congress must rely even more on such skills. The virtuous cycle has created a network of support for democracy that is broader and deeper than any historical counterpart.

At the same time building on this foundation toward a more meaningful and consolidated democracy will not be easy. First, democracy confronts profound social inequality — as Mexican intellectuals often put it, there are two Mexicos. One Mexico — wealthier, internationally connected, educated, and urbanized — is strong enough to make its voice heard within a democratic context, while the other Mexico — poor, isolated or hurt by internationalization, less educated, frequently rural and indigenous — remains marginalized even within an open political system.

Accountability and the rule of law often fail to reach this Mexico. The inadequacy of electoral democracy alone in reaching and meeting the needs of the second Mexico could result in protest outside democratic channels. At a minimum the need to address issues like inequality, opportunities and services for the poor, protection from the effects of internationalization, and political autonomy for indigenous people, will put democratic institutions under considerable stress.

The second major problem confronting democratic consolidation is that the institutions which support democracy have yet to develop roots as deep as those that long sustained authoritarianism. Two competing forms of politics exist together uncomfortably. Although the aspiration for democracy has become widespread and deeply held, democratic norms, practices, and institutions have not gained clear supremacy over authoritarian ones even among "pro-democracy" advocates. Among reluctant converts — like many leaders of the post-2000 PRI — control of the presidency could lead to unwillingness to implement democratic reforms or even attempts to reverse some of them. And these efforts might find a degree of support among other factions of society looking to re-establish stronger social controls.

The theme of development, like politics, shows a relatively strong central trend toward an internationalized and market-oriented model but with unresolved areas of conflict. The institutional and structural changes in Mexico's economy since the 1980s make it difficult to reverse the neoliberal economic model even if some party in power should want to try. At the same time this model poses significant constraints on the Mexican government's ability to address the issues of inequality, poverty, and the distribution of gains and losses; all solutions must confront steep challenges of compatibility with NAFTA mechanisms. The renationalization of privatized industries would face severe resistance from new owners. And discussions of progressive taxation and regulation take place in an internationalized arena where multiple and multinational actors participate.

Still, internationalization in the broadest sense has become an increasingly defining factor in Mexico's future political and economic development. For Mexico internationalization takes the form of integration with the world mostly as a function of increasing closeness with the United States. This causes trouble, discomfort, and friction. Yet definition of any matter as "national" has become more a tactical decision than an unalterable principle, even for "nationalistic" actors. The anti-NAFTA zapatistas have shown no hesitation in reaching out to foreign audiences for assistance, even within the United States. Both the leftist Cuautémoc Cárdenas and the conservative Vicente Fox campaigned in and frequently visited the United States. The Mexican army accepts training courses and exchanges of military information (not to mention aid and equipment) from the United States. Mexican election law officially welcomes U.S. election observers. The Mexican media mine U.S. news outlets for information. Mexican-owned business actively seeks foreign technical assistance, investment, and advice and lobbies the U.S. government in defense of its interests. Environmental cooperation, health care networks, feminist exchanges, NGO fund-raising, antidrug cooperation (and drug distribution!) become international. Migration itself expands family decisions onto an international stage. While the U.S. government must still avoid the appearance of meddling, internationalization has expanded well beyond government-to-government interaction.

CENTRAL CHALLENGES

Although these trends toward democratization, markets, and internationalization appear as hallmarks of Mexican development in the new century, each involves struggles and serious challenges. If not managed well, these problems could lead Mexico toward less likely outcomes, like authoritarian reversal or isolationist economic policy. Here we highlight four particular challenges: achieving broad and steady economic growth, deepening institutional development, containing anti-system threats, and managing choice.

Economic Performance

Like all political systems, Mexico is vulnerable to declines in economic performance. The PRI did not experience severe challenges until the economy, a source of stability during the Mexican miracle, began to falter. The stability of Mexican democracy may hinge in part on whether the neoliberal economic model can deliver promised jobs and economic growth. A Mexico wracked by repeated economic crises, unemployment, devaluation, and slow growth is less likely to sustain a stable political system of any sort. Even if the economy grows, however, its social impact presents a difficult challenge for democracy. How will the benefits of growth be distributed? If there are few winners and many losers, political conflict may be difficult to resolve, especially in a democracy, where numbers matter. And if Mexican governments do little to soften the adjustment process, the political risks grow. Democracies may have advantages here, since losers can press their claims for assistance within existing legal structures. But if democratic institutions fail to address these claims — either through lack of will or lack of capacity — losers may be tempted to take more extreme and destabilizing actions.

Judgments about Mexico's political future often depend on judgments about these social aspects of economic policies: Can neoliberalism provide enough jobs, growth, and flexibility in distributing economic costs? Optimists, while acknowledging short-term adjustment costs, foresee the emergence of a coalition of winners who will support both stable democracy and neoliberalism. They argue that an open economy requires an open political system, based on the principle that choice in the economic sphere supports demands for choice in the political sphere. As long as the neoliberal economy offers enough material security to meet most legitimate demands (and they think it will), democracy will endure. This group sees hope in Mexico's relatively rapid export-led recovery from the 1994 peso crisis and in U.S. willingness to provide emergency credit assistance. In this view internationalization tends to protect Mexico by ensuring U.S. support (and the U.S. market) as a hedge against extreme economic or political instability.

Pessimists, in contrast, see neoliberalism as incapable of providing enough jobs, growth, or flexibility to generate a broad coalition of winners. Instead, there will be a few wealthy winners (many of whom will not be Mexican) and a large number of impoverished losers, especially in the countryside. Additional pressure on the democratic compromise is furnished by the inability of markets to guarantee short-term economic stability: there will be stock market panics, runs on the currency, and vulnerability to recession abroad — as Fox found out to his chagrin in the first years of his administration. For pessimists the spectacle of repeated if short-lived crises in the 1990s raises troubling questions about Mexico's future. Politically, the growth of guerrilla movements and paramilitary right-wing groups suggests polarization, while the weakness of party links to society constitutes an additional source of concern. Scenarios range from revolution to authoritarian repression.

However, the most likely outcome may fall somewhere between these stylized points of view. Mexico's political future probably should not be evaluated as a stark dichotomy between democracy and collapse: while collapse may be unlikely, it does not necessarily follow that the only other alternative is a robust democracy. A consolidated and healthy democracy may require generating a significantly greater number of winners than economic policies alone can offer, especially in the short term. Continued pressure for more popular participation without more broadly distributed rewards could lead to a compromise that limits the scope of democracy. From this perspective one possible outcome is the consolidation of democracy with adjectives: with continued inequality, limited accountability, uneven freedom, and unstable patterns of competition. Such a democracy would be limited in the kinds of issues it could address without risking deadlock or breakdown but would be hedged in as well by the potential for protest if issues are ignored. It might limp from crisis to crisis without falling apart but also without meeting popular expectations.

Another intermediate (and more optimistic) scenario involves expansion to a democracy with fewer crippling qualifications. This would allow for an effective political system and socioeconomic benefits for a broadening middle class—possibly even a majority of citizens—but would still leave a significant minority behind. Mexico's history of relatively stronger social organizations, including multiple parties, as well as its longer experience with market economics tends to point more in this direction. Yet much will depend on how Mexican society and government respond.

Institutional Development

The second major challenge is institutional development. When economic crisis and conflict occur, political systems respond differently. Mexico's weak link is the embryonic state of the political institutions and processes that manage political conflict in a stable democracy. A country with such a limited democratic history does not develop these practices and structures quickly. The same holds for democratic political norms, though these are already much more widespread than many imagine. We have analyzed not only the lack of democratic institutions and practices but also the strength of nondemocratic alternatives through much of the twentieth century. Hierarchy and authoritarianism have pervaded major representative institutions, including unions and parties. Habits developed under authoritarianism—such as isolation from mass bases, elitism, personalism, or vague ideological programs—are deeply ingrained. Democratic alternation does not fix these problems automatically. Popular distrust of all parties and many government institutions remains high. Parties and other institutions will have to work hard to develop the ability to represent and mediate among various social demands.

Similarly, the Mexican state has been lopsided, leaving presidents too strong and other branches unprepared to take on policy-making responsibilities. The deficiencies in this respect are tremendous and cannot be fixed simply by weakening the presidency — or replacing the president. Without a simultaneous building up of other institutions, a president who abdicates authority deliberately and with the best of intentions may simply leave a power vacuum. The pressure on the president to step in and fill the gap could then become tremendous. Likewise, the development of freedom, accountability, and the rule of law — challenges explored in Chapter 4 — depends upon the development of alternative institutional channels and civil society. Such institutional changes require an evolution in norms and expectations in that citizens must look increasingly to themselves, a variety of civic and social bodies, and several countervailing political institutions more than to a strong president as the initiator of reforms and the provider of results. For example, the growth of political diversity in the Mexican Congress has given congressional politics greater prominence, but representatives from all parties still lack the resources, staff, and preparation to take part effectively and consistently in policy formulation. Legislative reforms might help build a congressional support staff capable of assisting new legislators in their duties, but the prohibition against re-election continues to block development of expertise in any legislative area.

Another major institutional weakness lies in state and local governments, long dominated by the central government. Democratization and decentralization challenge local authorities to deal with local problems. Yet most state and local governments lack the resources and the administrative capacity to develop effective solutions. Their weaknesses limit the people's ability to fairly hold governments accountable for their promises, since they may fail even when they make honest and intelligent efforts. Furthermore, under internationalized economic development, regions benefit quite unequally. What can the national government do to compensate those left behind in development and services? And how will efforts to compensate poor states affect wealthy states that resist national redistribution of resources? A context of growing local autonomy could make these problems worse. Mexico has yet to develop new methods to reach compromises among states while accommodating drives for decentralization. Neoliberalism complicates the process further: in the past the revolutionary legacy gave legitimacy (though insufficient reality) to the principle of redistribution, but the logic of markets does not provide strong justification for this goal. U.S. models of federal democracy may not prove adequate to the task of dealing with such severe inequalities and limited resources; even in the wealthy United States, claims of states' rights have complicated the implementation of social reforms intended to help poor states improve economically.

These tasks alone are daunting, especially as the underdevelopment of democratic institutions exists alongside overdeveloped authoritarian institutions that do not conveniently disappear to clear the way for democracy. And internationalization complicates the task of developing domestic political accountability. International financial institutions (the International Monetary Fund, the World Bank, the World Trade Organization) and U.S. institutions (the Drug Enforcement Administration, the Federal Reserve, or the Homeland Security) are increasingly "Mexican" institutions as well, at least according to their impact on Mexico. Yet these institutions are even further removed from domestic democratic accountability than parties, the court system, or the media.

Anti-system Threats

A third major challenge concerns threats to the national state. Some of the traditional threats to Latin American states seem weak or absent in Mexico. Guerrilla forces often threaten to overthrow the state; nevertheless, because the will to overturn the state does not necessarily imply the capacity to do so, we argue that Mexican guerrilla groups do not represent a significant threat. If a guerrilla group emerged with this capacity, U.S. assistance would probably tip the scales in favor of the Mexican government. In contrast to Central America, where the United States never brought its full military power to bear, a threat to Mexico would inspire substantially more concern. Another potential threat to stability — military coup — does not seem imminent. Trends toward military politicization are worth watching but have not advanced far enough to cause Mexican presidents or ordinary citizens to lose a lot of sleep.

The most serious threats to the state in Mexico arise indirectly, from the growing strength of actors who undermine the rule of law. Drug cartels and crime rings thrive in an environment of weak judiciaries and impunity for the well connected. Part of the Mexican formula for stability allowed for ample corruption to soothe the ambitious and pay off the dangerous. Yet at the PRI regime's peak, corruption was regulated by the centralization of control over opportunities for corruption. Ironically, democracy threatens the regulatory system for corruption. There are no natural limits to corruption; at the same time democratic competition

The televised presidential debates for the 2000 election reflected agreement that Mexico must further democratize to develop economically and socially but disagreement about what are the best choices to those ends. From left to right: Vicente Fox, Cuauhtémoc Cárdenas, and Francisco Labastida. (*La Jornada*)

may reward those who expose corruption and thus potentially provoke the corrupt to take desperate measures to defend themselves against prosecution, including violence. This is one of many examples where democratic development offers considerable hope and yet troublesome uncertainty.

Efforts to develop democratic accountability come up against the independent and uncompromising illegality of some modern sources of corruption. The traditional political system could accommodate the "ordinary" corruption implied by bribe taking, moderate embezzlement of government funds, and the sort of kickbacks also associated with U.S. politics during the late nineteenth and early twentieth centuries. Withdrawing the state from economic activity reduces certain sources of corruption, but where corruption involves crime rings or drug cartels, it may escape the ability of the system to control without considerably ratcheting up the level of violent confrontations between these actors and the state.

In addition, because such actors cannot be easily integrated into the legal political system, they may have an interest in undermining it. As drug cartels have become more powerful, they have threatened to derail efforts to strengthen the judiciary. Similarly, where drug lords attempt to threaten and/or corrupt anyone in a position to harm them, honest politicians often do not survive long, even with popular support. But in consolidated democracies nobody should be able to alter the outcome of public policy by threatening violence. And the public could become disillusioned with democracy if it finds that politicians who start out honest quickly lose their integrity.

Choice

The final challenge is perhaps the least predictable, because it refers us to choices. The situation we have described is far from deterministic. Factors that support certain outcomes, including democratic development, must be weighed against undermining factors. This leaves ample room for choice to play a role. Will elites behave responsibly, or will they accept the risk of destabilizing the political or economic system in order to maximize their own gains? The responsible behavior of Plutarco Elías Calles and Lázaro Cárdenas helped build a uniquely stable civilian reign against a historical backdrop of irresponsible elite actions. Can the same now be done to build stable democratic rule? The decision of President Ernesto Zedillo and the losing PRI candidate Francisco Labastida to accept defeat on election night 2000 contributed to a peaceful transition. The actions of defeated parties can have as much of an impact on the emerging rules of the game as the actions of victorious parties. What will future leaders of political parties do?

Social leaders—unions and peasants, business and social movements—also have strategic choices to make. Will actors accept democratic norms—even when these norms seem incomplete, inegalitarian, or fixed against them? Or will they reject the rules as soon as they seem to favor the adversary? And U.S. actors—governments, multinational companies, and private NGOs—have the option to insist on maximum concessions or compromise with hard-pressed Mexican counterparts. The visions of the future pursued by different actors lead to complex interactions, difficult to predict. Actors often fail to foresee what other actors plan to do, assess what their own relative power really is, or anticipate the effect of their actions. "Leaders" may misinterpret the strength of their support among mass audiences, leading where they are not followed, or fail to anticipate shifts in public opinion. They may overplay their hands or underplay them. Politics—notably including democratic politics—is as much a game of poker, ruled by bluff and uncertainty, as a game of chess, ruled by logic and skill.

Nezahualcoyotl School: What education and what future for Mexico? (*La Jornada*)

Even under conditions of perfect information, however, actors would seek to pursue different and at least partly incompatible visions of the future. Fundamental disagreements remain about the definition of democracy and the type of economic and social development that democracy requires. Furthermore, some actors respond to democratic competition in violent or authoritarian ways rather than putting democratic rules ahead of their particular interests. These actors certainly include figures within the PRI and some business and union leaders but also include supposedly democratic actors in the PAN and PRD. Nor are social movements exempt: for some, democracy means mostly freedom from external regulation, not accountability. At the same time radically democratic groups demand more than liberal representative democracy would offer. For such groups parties and elections are a pale imitation of democracy. They advocate direct participation in all decision making, including economic decisions in firms and factories. They argue that neither civil liberties nor markets nor even competitive elections are an adequate substitute for inclusive and meaningful democracy.

Similar divergence can be seen in debates over economic development. Political parties, the church, unions, business, foreign investors, and environmentalists are constrained by NAFTA and neoliberalism. Yet their economic and social priorities differ. Whom should development serve most? What degree of market regulation is acceptable or desirable?

These are contentious questions in a lively and ongoing discussion among an array of domestic and international interests. And there are implications in these debates for social policies. How should the state serve the poor? Through social welfare, subsidies, or market incentives? What kinds of educational priorities make sense in a Mexico determined to become internationally competitive? What should be the relative effort on primary, secondary, or university education, and to what extent should Mexico use public tax revenue to provide access? The answers to such questions will have profound impacts on the ability of Mexican youth to contribute to democracy and development.

Because of the elements of strategy and choice, we cannot assume that the strong always win. For example, the decision of some Chiapas peasants to take up arms in 1994 had an effect on national policy, whether or not they benefited personally. As states (and parties and other interests) try to win public support, they may find themselves listening to the weak against the inclinations of the strong. Similarly, the United States does not always get its way — partly because the increasing complexity of interactions has left the definition of "U.S. interest" even more vague than before, but also partly because of the very asymmetry of interaction: the outcome of conflicts frequently matters more to Mexico than to the United States. Thus political outcomes are rarely fully determined. Because of the complexity of political change, outcomes result from strategic calculations based on incomplete, uncertain, or even incorrect information. The end product may be something that no actor intended. Even where we can assess the relative likelihood of one outcome versus another, we cannot be sure of the outcome in any particular case.

CONCLUSION

We have argued that Mexico's most likely path in the near term includes democracy, neoliberal economic development, and internationalization that features strengthened ties with the United States. Mexico shares many of these characteristics with other countries in the developing world and indeed, with most economically developed nations as well. Overall, we have struck a rather optimistic note, with reservations. Most important, we must remember that Mexico has been, is, and will continue to be plagued by the challenges of poverty and inequality. And the combination of democracy and inequality may prove a more unstable and unwieldy one than the combination of authoritarian rule and inequality. Much will depend on the choices made by actors on both sides of the border and on the capacity of the neoliberal model to deliver results to as many as possible. It will also depend on the will and capacity of the state — indeed, of the Mexican and U.S. publics at large — to help those left behind in internationalized development. Stability and development, we have argued, require democracy. But Mexican democracy, to fulfill its promise and to ensure its viability, must also promote broad-based Mexican development. If this hope fails, then many others will as well.

Notes

1. In the 1950s and 1960s many scholars saw a democratic imperative, but the preexisting Mexican political system obviously proved more persistent than they had imagined. See, for example, González Casanova 1970: 158–97 and Paz 1972: 45. In the 1970s, 1980s, and 1990s other scholars saw a liberalization or "glasnost" within authoritarianism as the regime's chosen and perhaps viable (if undesirable) option between democracy and harsh backlash. See, for example, Loaeza 1994. Today the advent of formal democracy does not necessarily mark an irreversible path, as the experience of many countries has shown.

2. Dahl 1971 is widely cited in modern political science. For an accessible overview on democracy in contemporary Latin America, see Camp 1996. For a broad comparative view with cases (including Mexico), see Diamond, Linz, Lipset 1995 as well as Diamond et al. 1999, a series volume on Latin America.

3. Semidemocracy is Diamond, Linz, and Lipset's (1995: 7–8) label for systems with the following features: elections are competitive and regular but fall short of true popular sovereignty because of entrenched advantages for the leading party; freedoms are extensive but uncertain because of serious constraints on liberty that block some interests from peacefully organizing; and accountability and the rule of law are too weak to qualify as democratic. Although the 2000 elections tip the balance toward labeling Mexico a democracy, most of these characteristics of semidemocracy persist to some significant degree. The authors cite Malaysia, Senegal, Singapore, Thailand, and Turkey, in addition to Mexico, as examples of semidemocracies. Semidemocracy clashes with "authoritarianism," which has been common in these countries since at least the 1970s. Rejecting the hope that had dominated the modernization school's view that developing societies would convert socioeconomic gains into democracy, the authoritarian thesis was that Mexico had merely the trappings

of democracy (e.g., opposition parties). See, for example, Reyna and Weinert 1977. Citing Mexico's historical uniqueness and thus validating a view of exceptionalism, other scholars have eschewed the democratic-authoritarian dichotomy and referred to more concrete defining characteristics. Thus Needler (1994: 383) wrote of a near consensus that the system was run by a "self-perpetuating elite trying to rule with an economy of force." Among the greater number of analysts who qualified the term *authoritarian,* Camp (1999b: 9) reasonably used the term *semiauthoritarian* to depict a system still fundamentally authoritarian and corporatist despite growing openness. But our use of semidemocracy portrays a different mix, including substantial pluralism alongside the corporatism. See Levy and Bruhn 1999.

4. For Krauze (1986), democracy must meet demanding criteria regarding voting, tolerance, restraints on official power, citizen participation, and so forth. From 1945 to 1985, Mexico placed between third and seventh place among twenty Latin American nations on the best-known rankings of democracy (Johnson and Kelly 1986: 19–22), but that was largely by default when militaries ruled in many nations; their move to civilian rule is what lowered Mexico's comparative ranking. These are not precise rankings.

5. Internationalization sometimes poses problems for democratization by promoting policies much of the populace sees as imposed and inequitable. Democracy, in turn, sometimes poses problems for internationalization, as when political parties are unwilling to pay the electoral price for supporting policies more popular abroad than at home. Fortunately, many important aspects of democratization and internationalization are today mutually supportive

6. This carries us back to the modernization thesis, its time perhaps now come; Camacho (1994: 36) writes that democracy would be the new basis of stability. On the idea that factors commonly linked to democratic stability produced stability without democracy in Mexico, see Levy and Bruhn 1999.

7. The party was even identified as the longest ruling party in history (Molinar Horcasitas 1996). Although we use state, regime, and government to refer to formal political rulers, state typically gives the broadest sense of such rule, regime refers to a type of government (e.g., authoritarian), and government sometimes refers to a particular administration.

8. As Mexico democratized, Vargas Llosa (2000) dropped the characterization; then, in the wake of the 2000 elections, he contrasted the perfect dictatorship and the newly democratic Mexico, now a "difficult democracy" (see Chapter 4, this volume).

9. Perpetuation became less about robustness than the lack of a viable alternative. If the fragility of most Latin American regimes since the 1980s has related to an inability to consolidate new democratic regimes, Mexico's related largely to erosion within an old, nondemocratic regime; with the democratic transition of 2000, Mexico faces the challenges of consolidation, but these are affected by how elements from the old regime fade or reassert themselves. On the frequency of perpetuation through lack of viable alternatives more than through the legitimacy of rulers, see Przeworski 1986.

10. Morris (1995: 190–91) analyzes the cycle of crises, correctly noting that

some observers saw "crises" where the system was still strong enough to handle them. See Prud'homme 1999 on centrifugal forces and Rochlin 1997: 1 on a "cauldron of chaos."

11. In the case of the slain party official, the victim's brother, who was appointed to head the investigation, soon resigned in protest over cover-ups and later committed suicide; the slain official's own brother-in-law — himself the brother of recently retired President Carlos Salinas — was convicted of masterminding the murder. However, a tragicomedy of mismanaged investigation, including disappearing witnesses and planted evidence, left doubt about the extent and nature of conspiracy. The arrest of the ex-president's brother prompted the discovery of evidence of financial shenanigans; when his wife was detained trying to withdraw some $84 million from a Swiss bank account, citizens had more evidence of the deep penetration of "narco-trafficking" into Mexico's highest political and economic circles.

12. Lorenzo Meyer, "Una rebelión al fin de régimen," *Reforma,* January 11, 1996. There is a parallel to Cuba in the 1950s: Fidel Castro's rebel force was small but Fulgencio Batista's regime was too decrepit to beat it back. Although Mexican rebels could not topple their own vastly more powerful regime, they contributed to uncertainty about its ability to rule. Mexico has a rich history of guerrilla activity and the previous wave, in the late 1960s and early 1970s, polarized politics with a rash of kidnappings, some ending in assassination, others in releases (probably through secret agreements), all leading to a perception of government weakness. The single most infamous episode weakening the regime went beyond guerrillas: in 1968 the government slaughtered more than three hundred protesting university students. It never fully recovered its legitimacy.

13. In East Asia, too, political stability long seemed associated with delayed or absent democracy. Problems in its development model burst upon the international scene when economic crisis hit in the late 1990s, but such countries as South Korea and Taiwan have also made significant democratic progress.

14. The issue of stability is more complicated than a dichotomy of maintaining the status quo regime or overthrowing it. Intermediate outcomes are possible. Historians who look back on Mexico in the 1980s and 1990s may disagree about how much the regime persisted, perhaps with deft accommodation to heightened challenge, or fundamentally changed. Although the 2000 elections mark more of a breaking point, only the future will tell how much of the old regime survives.

15. Such academic fields as comparative politics and Latin American studies came into their own during this period, and so Mexico became known in these fields by leading development characteristics of the time.

16. There is no one-to-one relationship between development and democracy, and at certain points development may correlate more with dictatorship (O'Donnell 1988). Nonetheless, the gross development-democracy correlation is strong enough to warrant belief that growth in productivity, urbanization, education, middle-class population, and so forth pushed Mexico into a higher zone of probability for both the democracy achieved to date and the more robust democracy Mexico needs. Although the modernization school's optimism for

Mexico (Scott 1971) greatly underestimated the challenges and alternatives to democracy, it may still have been right in some very broad strokes.

17. On the lack of a design for social improvement, see Urquidi 1994. Regarding social consequences of the economic crisis of the 1980s, see González de la Rocha and Escobar Latapí 1991.

18. On the capitalists, Camp (forthcoming) cites the figures; *La Jornada* reports that in 1999 the one hundred richest Mexicans controlled businesses worth roughly 29 percent of the GDP (Roberto González Amador, ".0001% de la población domina la economía, May 27, 2000). Philip Russell (1994: 280) cites the *Forbes* figure, and Mexico was reportedly still fifth in 1999. On Indian incomes, see Bartolomé 1996: 301.

19. Thus, for 1997, with nine phone lines per hundred thousand people, Mexico ranked just behind Brazil, Colombia, and Venezuela and well behind Uruguay, Argentina, and Costa Rica. With its 0.5 Internet host computers per thousand inhabitants, however, Mexico surpassed Brazil, Colombia, Venezuela, and Uruguay, although it badly trailed Chile and Costa Rica. Data from *IDB America,* November 1997, 8.

20. www.nationmaster.com.

21. Del Valle 1995.

22. On the survey data, see Inglehart, Nevitte, and Basáñez 1996: 77–104. As in the United States, a division exists between a political-economic Right (favorable to neoliberal policy) and a political-social Right (unenthusiastic and hostile, blaming neoliberalism for social deterioration). The social Right is concerned, for example, when the country's profile of income distribution by family stagnates as average wages sharply decline and women increasingly enter the workforce. See Urbina Fuentes and Sandoval Arriaga 1993: 201–3.

23. See, for example, the editorial in *La Jornada,* "Fuerza del Estado," September 12, 1996.

24. Sometimes divisiveness is grounded in conflicting interests, such as peddlers versus shop owners or motorists. Religion exemplifies rising divisiveness in citizen-to-citizen interactions and in public policy debate as society becomes more religiously pluralistic and competing political parties appeal to the beliefs and prejudices of different factions.

25. Abortion remains illegal (except in the state of Yucatán), and some estimates are that more than two million illegal abortions occur annually, resulting in more 150,000 deaths. It is predictably the poor who suffer the most from terrible medical attention, often dependent on just massages or herbs, and who mostly account for the four hundred thousand babies born to mothers younger than twenty years old. These statistics make abortion perhaps the fourth leading cause of maternal death in Mexico.

26. Bray and Wexler 1996: 217–18. See also www.semarnat.gob.mx.

27. www.semarnat.gob.mx.

28. "Unsafe" here refers to over 200 IMECA points; unsatisfactory to over 100. These are the Mexican government's break points, based on international standards. Data from www.semarnat.gob.mx.

29. www.inegi.gob.mx.

30. On ecocide, see Rochlin 1997: 12–33. On water problems, see Bennett 1995. While poorer Mexico worries about getting any water, wealthier Mexico worries about shortages of hot water. Exclusive clubs in Mexico City post locker-room signs reminding members that it is not a matter of money or a bribe: there just is not much hot water. Meanwhile, it is very costly to keep increasing the city's water supply, especially as three-quarters of the water comes from the ground, and the city keeps sinking.

31. This figure falls if we do not count transfers on public transportation. More than half of these trips are made on buses (and "microbuses"), about 17 percent by car, and 14 percent by metro. By 5:00 a.m. nearly a quarter-million people are on the move, increasing to 2.7 million by 7:15 a.m.; because many Mexicans return home for lunch, the maximum figure is nearly duplicated at 2:00 p.m.

32. Javier Beristain (1996: 392) provides figures claiming that nearly all Mexico City households have drinking water, sewage, and electricity, and official census figures are also high in such respects. These figures appear too sanguine and cover only private homes, however; newspaper surveys give more sober figures.

33. Kandell 1988; Pick and Butler 1997. The 1990 census indicated that some eighty-nine million live in Mexico City proper — the Federal District — whereas the rest live in suburbs legally attached to other states and given municipal governments of their own. The entire metropolitan area is highly interconnected, however, with residents of suburbs commuting to jobs in Mexico City or vice versa. Many of the suburbs are also located within the environmental basin of the Valley of Mexico, and thus so physically connected that it is impossible to tell where they begin and the Federal District ends. See INEGI 1993. Guadalajara, Mexico's second largest city, has roughly four million people.

34. Figueroa Perea (1996: 193–97) and Urbina Fuentes and Sandoval Arriaga (1993: 192–95).

35. www.inegi.gob.mx.

36. Probably the most cited analysis that drew political conclusions was Paz 1972. Also see Reavis 2000. An additional Indian influence on Mexican culture overall is language. Indian words have found their way into the national Mexican lexicon. Even "Mexico" probably comes from a root such as Mexica, one of the Aztec tribes, or Mexitl, an Aztec epithet for God. Indian names mark many of Mexico's geographical places, streets, and so forth, and mestizos take such names as Cuauhtémoc and Xochitl.

37. Although Latin America's evangelical movement is widely regarded in stereotypic terms (ultraconservative or elitist, or, on the positive side, grassroots democratic), empirical study casts doubt on these terms.

38. Some Mexican intellectuals argue that Mexico lacks the twentieth-century immigration that made certain South American countries more open and less xenophobic societies. For more on this, see www.oncetv.ipn.mx/Primer Plano/primerplano.htm (accessed on the Internet on December 27, 1999).

39. See, for example, Alatorre 1994. Prejudicial attitudes are rather routinely stated. For example, when an opposition party won the city of Tuxtla Gutiérrez

in 1995 and proclaimed why it would not lose in the next election, as had happened after its 1976 victory, spokespeople attributed the earlier loss to having a female candidate.

40. Cosío Villegas 1964: 7, 162–71.

41. For documentation of stereotypes held by U.S. elites, see Aguayo 1998 as well as Coatsworth and Rico 1989. On lack of attention, Aguayo (1998b: 51) points out that among the memoirs of U.S. presidents, only Jimmy Carter's devotes more than a few lines to Mexico.

42. For an analysis of U.S. media coverage, see Laichas 1980: 582–94. See also Lajous de Solana and Velasco Márquez 1985: 31–42. Regarding U.S. academic institutions in Mexican studies, the main one is the Center for U.S.–Mexican Studies at the University of California, San Diego. The University of California school system hosts another center and boasts a vibrant network of activities related to Mexico. Georgetown University's Mexico Project is another unit of note, and the Woodrow Wilson Center is among organizations that have recently started programs with foundation support. (Meanwhile, Mexican interest in studying the United States, and not just Mexico-U.S. relations, has also taken great strides.) Typically, knowledge has increased in certain circles of academia, government, business, and nonprofit organizations, while it remains lower in the general public. A sad if amusing reminder of the need for greater knowledge came in 1994: A U.S. national security project survey of the federal government's perceived needs for information on foreign countries discovered that officials were confident of their expertise on Mexico. A few months later, however, officials were stunned by Mexico's economic crisis and political uncertainty.

43. Carter established a major presidential commission on Mexico during his presidency, an indicator of special U.S. attention to one nation, and the United States and Mexico established a consultative commission that went beyond any of its bilateral predecessors reaching back to 1960. The commission was reorganized in 1979 into eight policy-oriented groups and then renewed by the Reagan administration. In 1986 a Bilateral Commission on the Future of United States–Mexican Relations reflected the rise of private bodies concerned with bilateral policy. Pastor and Castañeda 1988: 61. A deputy assistant secretary of state for the Bureau of Inter-American Affairs noted that he spent approximately 70 percent of his time on Mexico (*Georgetown Latin American Newsletter* [winter 1996–97]).

44. The Castro family in Oscar Lewis's classic study (1959) illustrated this tendency even years ago: pancake-mix breakfasts substitute for tortillas, fried beans, and chili; U.S. cosmetics and toys become "necessities." It would be ludicrous, however, to believe that U.S. influences have negated Mexican culture. For one work on "Mexican-ness" in the modern age, see Monsiváis 1996.

45. Lowenthal and Burgess 1993: vi. Chicanos' economic clout means that businesses increasingly target them. On Mexican-Americans, including differences within the group, see Connor 1985. At the same time some half million U.S. citizens, mostly retirees, live in Mexico, and many others have vacation homes there.

46. The San Isidro (California)–Tijuana point alone is the site of perhaps some seventy-five million crossings annually. For an overview of border issues,

see Lorey 1999, Williams 1986: 211–34, and Herzog 1992. For an account of life on the Mexican side of the border, see Ruiz 1998.

47. Lines at the border have reflected the development gap. Entry into the United States often involves long lines, delays, and tedious inspections (especially for Mexican and Chicano citizens suspected of seeking illegal entry). In contrast, entrance into Mexico was usually immediate, with almost no inspections, but delays have become more common in this direction too, reflecting the upsurge in bilateral interaction.

CHAPTER TWO

1. Probably few countries celebrate so many holidays, partly because defeats after victories necessitated future victories. As Paz (1979: 148) wrote: "Mexico has a plurality of pasts, all present and at war within every Mexican's soul."

2. On abortive democratic efforts, see Guedea 1996. On the generally negative political, social, and economic outcomes, see Safford 1974: 72, 91–92 and Tenenbaum 1975: 7–9. For recent books on nineteenth-century Mexico, see Murray 1997, and for a partial challenge to negative interpretations, see Rodríguez 1997.

3. Some liberals hoped that U.S. involvement would help their side; appeals for U.S. support became important in Mexican politics by the 1990s, after a period of greater national independence.

4. Santa Anna's most consistent preoccupation was self-interest. Among his self-designations were Most Serene Highness, Father of the Country, Savior, and Perpetual Victor. A sad commentary on Mexico's political instability from the 1820s to the 1850s is that this last title had some validity.

5. Vázquez 1998.

6. Cosío Villegas 1964: 10; Cosío Villegas 1965 remains a leading work on the Reform period. On nineteenth-century liberalism, see Hale 1989.

7. Tannenbaum 1950: 154.

8. The modern regime was uncomfortable with parallels that highlighted its undemocratic and nonrevolutionary nature. With turns toward both neoliberalism and greater candor in recent years came an attempt to improve the mostly negative portrayal of the porfiriato in school textbooks (Gilbert 1997).

9. Díaz referred to his Congress as "my herd of tame horses." For all the similarities between the regimes, the porfiriato was more exclusionary and repressive.

10. Lessons also concern provision for elite mobility. Aging regimes denying rotation in elite positions or access for rising groups risk overthrow. Porfirian economic growth spawned new interests that felt thwarted by the dictatorship. Matters were aggravated when Mexico fell into an economic depression and the government responded with harsh policies (e.g., calling in loans), alienating even some of the elites. Mexico's contemporary political elite may fear the destabilizing role, nearly a century ago, of economic failure after decades of economic growth.

11. Smith 1979: 163.

12. Hollywood has produced colorful movies about the Mexican Revolution and its leading personalities; unfortunately, most reveal more about Hollywood than about Mexico. For a concise history of the revolution, see Hamnett 1999,

and for a monumental one, Knight 1986. Rodríguez 1990 looks at recent interpretations of the revolution; recent work has given considerable attention to revolutionary struggle in individual regions (Fowler-Salamini 1993) and has been more attentive to the role of ordinary citizens. Also see Hart 1997.

13. Political leaders would continue to come heavily from the northwest. The official party's electoral weakness there as Mexico democratized was a key sign of its precarious position.

14. Labor rights included a minimum wage, the right to strike, collective bargaining, an eight-hour day, workmen's compensation, maternity leave, freedom to shop at other than company-owned stores, and even some employer responsibility for health, housing, and educational opportunities.

15. As governor in the 1920s, Cárdenas had established his commitment to agrarian reform. He dramatically demonstrated this commitment, while deepening his mass support, by campaigning for president throughout the country for one and a half years.

16. Cárdenas strengthened the presidency both when he assumed and when he vacated the office. First, he expelled Calles, the man who had appointed him but who then persisted in trying to undermine him. Later, bypassing leftist leaders within the party to appoint a moderate as his successor, Cárdenas in effect chose to institutionalize rather than to intensify the revolution.

17. The cartoon appeared in *Los Supermachos,* January 23, 1975. Novelist Carlos Fuentes (1964) described the emergence of this more pragmatic and opportunistic style of leadership; title character Artemio Cruz subordinates revolutionary to material goals and uses state power to repress rather than help the less privileged. In Zebadúa's (1994a: 356) analysis "who won the Mexican Revolution was the middle class." Even judged as early as 1929, the bloody contest could be seen not as a revolution over the ownership of property, including foreign property, but as a political transformation. This transformation was not democratic: mostly it was about the ascension of elites who had not held extensive property, and partly it was about divisions among elites that allowed some space for incorporation of mass groups — but under elite control.

18. See Turner's (1968) account of revolutionary nationalism and even xenophobia. Also see Vaughan's (1982) account of persistent dependence on foreign thought.

19. For example, see López y Fuentes (1996). José Vasconcelos wrote of the mission of the cosmic Ibero-American race as a fortuitous blend of Indian, European, and African roots. Architects associated ornament with bourgeois decadence and strove instead to transmit a more common sense of Mexican reality.

20. Fuentes 1996: 67. Fuentes also notes that unlike the Chinese and Russian revolutions, Mexico's did not silence its creators or critics. On popular culture and the state, see Joseph and Nugent 1994.

21. Despite the contrasts among administrations, a fundamental moderateness in economic policy persisted. Sheahan (1987: 271–72) contrasts this to more aggressive state action on the one hand and greater reliance on free trade on the other; he believes that Mexico's responsible policy helps explain why the country would outperform sister nations in economic growth and avoidance of more repressive authoritarianism.

22. Echeverría probably deviated from the alemenista model less because he was an irresponsible radical adventurer (as some detractors would have it) or because he was a dedicated revolutionary (as some supporters would have it) than because he saw serious crises within the existing development model.

23. But there is disagreement on when the revolution died or even whether it ever lived. Standard reading includes Ross 1966; for a review essay on institutionalization, see Benjamin 1985.

24. Some implicate Calles in the assassination of Obregón (Needler 1995: 9–10). Parallels could be made to the implication of Salinas in candidate Colosio's assassination almost seventy years later. Both Calles and Salinas were public promoters of the assassinated candidates. One event occurred before the period of stable development; the other occurred after it.

25. Violence continued to surround most local and national elections. Three contenders were killed in the 1928 presidential campaign. Religious warfare with violent intensity was unabated. On top of this, the world depression was bound to exacerbate discontent. Mexico's powerholders needed political order.

26. González Casanova 1970: 34.

27. For a detailed account of Cárdenas's efforts at party institutionalization, see Cornelius 1973. Naturally, a concern for institutionalization and stability began before 1929.

28. Collier 1992: 9–37, 156; incorporation of labor marked a "critical juncture" in Mexico's institutionalization.

29. At the same time the military suffered from the weakness that it had not won a war and thereby gained popular legitimacy; on the contrary, it had suffered a terrible defeat by the United States in 1846–48.

30. Furtak 1978: 217–18. For a well-known historical account of military institutionalization, see Lieuwen 1968. The most thorough recent work with pertinent data and analysis is Camp 1992. For example, Camp reports that only 2 percent of the top political posts (and only 4 percent of the total executive branch positions) under Salinas were held by those whose profession was the military; some civilian jobs are held legally, others are not.

31. For a detailed account, see Larin 1968. For an English-language source on the state-church issues, see Bailey 1973. In the 2000 elections candidate Fox harked back to ideas and slogans of the cristero rebellion.

32. Grayson (1992) found the church to be the only national organization not getting government funds or control. This marks an important exception to the corporatist tendencies of Mexican politics. For a broad account of the role of the church today in Mexican society and politics, see Camp 1997. One indication from Camp that the modus vivendi has worked well is that government leaders have a positive view of the clergy.

33. "The state should control education at all levels, from elementary to university. . . . University youth is 80 percent or more reactionary and tries to . . . dislodge the revolutionaries from power and thus keep them from combating . . . capital and the clergy." Quoted in Mayo 1964: 261–62. Our account of the university draws on Levy 1980: 24–28.

34. The presidents granted autonomy partly to placate university opposition, partly to justify withdrawal of public funds that might have undermined the uni-

versity to the point where a revolutionary institution could replace it; Cárdenas also established a government-run National Polytechnic Institute to serve the revolution, as the university would not.

35. The military represented the greatest threat, followed by the church. The party that the regime created was of course not a threat, but its creation overcame real challenges from a fractured party system, regional caciques, and independent labor and peasant movements.

36. The "corporatism" described here, as well as the shift toward greater pluralism, is fleshed out in Chapters 3 and 4.

37. For a lengthy yet readable single-volume overview of Mexican history, see Meyer and Sherman 1995. Also see MacLachlan and Beezley 1998. A leftist overview appears in Cockcroft 1998. A comprehensive source on Mexican history is the series *Historia General de México* (published by El Colegio de México).

CHAPTER THREE

1. Diamond, Linz, and Lipset 1995: 27. Typically, "what distinguishes these groups from other collective actors in society is that civil society organizations are concerned with and act in the public realm, [and] relate to the state (without seeking to win control over it)." Thus, parties are excluded because they try to win control over the state through elections, and firms are excluded because they are organized for profit.

2. The first and probably most influential of these scholars was Alexis de Tocqueville, who wrote that such associations were "necessary to democratic nations." See de Tocqueville 1969: 515.

3. Encarnación 2003: 178.

4. Huntington 1991: 72–85.

5. Inglehart et al. 2004: Items E069, E079, E080, E082.

6. This pattern is common in most large organizations. As they institutionalize, such organizations develop a stable and relatively small group of leaders who as incumbents tend to maintain their power over time — the "iron law of oligarchy." See Michels 1962.

7. For example, parties may have trouble maintaining voting discipline in legislatures. This happened to the PRD in Mexico City when civil society (nonparty) legislators, elected to the local city council, blocked the PRD mayor's legislative reform program.

8. www.ezln.org.

9. Collier and Collier 1991: 3. In Mexico's type of labor incorporation, radical populism, "both the working class and the peasantry were mobilized electorally and organized into functional associations, such as unions, linked to the reformist . . . party." This resulted in a more stable, less polarized, and integrative system. Collier and Collier 1991: 196.

10. For definitions of state corporatism, see Schmitter 1974: 86, Collier and Collier 1991: 51.

11. Initially, the CTM controlled a majority of Mexico's unionized urban and industrial workers. By 1948, it held 21 percent of unionized (federal jurisdiction)

labor, and by 1978, about a third of organized labor (Middlebrook 1995: 91, 118, 152). Other estimates suggest that over a third of all organized workers are federal employees, and thus outside the CTM *per se* (Camp 1999: 141).

12. Still, Mexico is more densely unionized than eleven of eighteen European countries for which statistics are available. www.ilo.org, see also Norris 2002: 174–175.

13. Martínez 2000.

14. The closed shop privilege required all workers in a factory to belong to the union. Thus, expelling a worker from the union essentially cost him his job.

15. Gutiérrez Garza 1988: 152–153. Changes in the minimum wage are relevant to understanding conditions for organized labor; unorganized labor was less likely to receive salaries pegged to the minimum wage.

16. In the 1950s, some primary school teachers challenged the National Education Workers' Union (SNTE) in a series of strikes and protests. In the 1960s, teachers participated in the Movement for National Liberation and the student movement. In the late 1970s, dissident teachers organized to demand union democracy and higher wages. For the history of teachers' unions, see Cook 1996 and Foweraker 1993.

17. Gentleman 1987: 55.

18. The members of UNT include the unions of telephone workers, bank workers, airline pilots, flight attendants, some university workers, and the public social security system. UNT remains the primary independent union confederation, though several smaller ones (notably, the National Association for the Transformation Industries, ANIT, and the Federation of Mexican Unions, FSM) also formed in the late 1990s. Both are close to the PRD. The UNT has rejected an exclusive alliance with any political party.

19. Javier Aguilar García, *La población trabajadora y sindicalizada en México en el período de la globalización* (Mexico City: Fondo de Cultura Económica, 2001): 380.

20. Besides the SNTE and the SUTGDF, departing unions included the Mexico City subway workers, air traffic controllers, and federal unions of workers in the Ministries of Agrarian Reform; Social Development; Agriculture, Fishing, and Livestock; Statistical Research (INEGI); and Communication and Transportation. Fabiola Martínez, "Rompen 17 sindicatos con la FSTSE," *La Jornada*, December 6, 2003: 8. Accounts of the same event in the rival newspaper *Reforma* cite a figure of twenty-one unions departing, but *Reforma*'s list includes several dissident factions of unions that officially remained within the FSTSE. See Claudia Salazar and Carlos Reyes, "Viven burócratas cisma," *Reforma*, December 6, 2003: A1, A4, A5.

21. Aguilar García 2001: 379.

22. For example, Salinas arrested the leader of the powerful oil workers' union on corruption and weapons charges, and removed the head of the teachers' union. The new oil union leader agreed to massive layoffs, while the new teachers' union leader agreed to implement educational reforms previously resisted.

23. For descriptions of peasant incorporation, see Cornelius 1971, Hamilton 1982, Becker 1995, Córdova 1974.

24. See Ross 1971: 19–20, 12–14.

25. For an analysis of the impact of these reforms, see Cornelius and Myhre 1998.

26. State marketing boards bought the majority of the crop, then stored, transported and marketed it. Without these boards, small farmers were often at the mercy of local capitalists for such services.

27. Fox 1994, Harvey 1998.

28. See for example Smith 1979: 191–216, Camp 2003.

29. In order to persuade politicians to accept prohibitions against re-election, the system tacitly permitted some illicit enrichment in office, which could finance a business career. Thus, the pattern of politicians later going into business has been seen as an indication of the pervasive corruption that greased the wheels of the political system.

30. On the intellectual roots of this business organization, see Luna and Tirado 1997.

31. A parallel with the United States is that business turned to a more direct role in mainstream political competition after feeling increasingly challenged by the Left in the 1960s (see Himmelstein 1990), though business has long been more involved in politics in the United States than has its counterpart in Mexico.

32. The exception is Diego Fernando de Cevallos — a business lawyer. Manuel Clouthier, the PAN's candidate in 1988, entered politics during the post-bank nationalization furor and was a former president of the CCE. Clouthier, in turn, helped recruit both Ernesto Ruffo (a successful auto distributor who became the first opposition governor), and Vicente Fox. Fox rose from a job as a Coca-Cola route driver to the head of Coca-Cola's Mexican distribution network; he also had experience exporting agricultural products. For more information on this period, see Mizrahi 1994.

33. Episode recounted in Oppenheimer 1996: 106–110.

34. On the role of elections and political liberalization, see Drake and Silva 1986, especially chapters by Middlebrook, Molinar Horcasitas, and Cornelius.

35. After the adoption of limits on party registry, the number of parties went from eleven in 1946 to an average of four in each of the ensuing twenty years. Molinar Horcasitas 1991: 42.

36. The reasons for the 1977 electoral reform included fears that continued exclusion of the Left would produce more guerrilla movements like those of the early 1970s, and the PAN's failure to offer a presidential candidate in 1976 (due to an internal split, in part over whether to participate in elections). This left the PRI without any competitors.

37. The same basic division — three hundred majority seats, two hundred proportional — continued through the 2000 election. The method of allocation changed over time to give the PRI a share of proportional seats; as opposition parties gained ground, these seats compensated the PRI for its losses and helped maintain its control.

38. This formula tends to favor larger parties. In addition to the historical two senators per state (a total of sixty-four), half of the additional senate seats go to the second-place party in each state; the rest are national senators, distributed proportionally on the basis of each party's national vote.

39. On the 1996 reforms, see Prud'homme 1998, de Swaan, Martorelli and Molinar 1998.

40. On the split within the PRI, see Garrido 1993, and Laso de la Vega ed., 1987. For its evolution into the PRD, see Bruhn 1997.

41. *La Jornada,* July 3, 2000: 1.

42. For accounts of the formation and functions of the PRI during its classic period, see Story 1986, Garrido 1982, Partido Revolucionario Institucional 1990.

43. On PRI adaptation to competitive pressures, see Hernández Rodríguez 1998: 71–94. Ultimately, the PRI accepted the mobilizational structure as a supplement to — but not a replacement for — the traditional sectors.

44. Candidates for high office (like presidents and governors) were required to have belonged to the PRI for at least ten years and held at least one elected position. Under this rule, not one of Mexico's five presidents from 1970 to 1994 would have qualified.

45. In its first three years of operation, Solidarity funded over 150,000 projects, bringing drinkable water to 8 million Mexicans, new classrooms to 1.4 million students, and electricity to 11 million in over 10,000 communities. Nearly as many communities (92 percent) got electricity in the first three years as during de la Madrid's entire six-year term. The number of land titles surpassed the total for the previous ten years. Salinas also opened 1000 kilometers of new federal highways — more than in the previous forty years — and issued 1.2 million legal titles to land, many during a three-day blitz shortly before the 1991 congressional election. Solidarity also included soft credit to small producers, scholarships, and food baskets, which could often be seen piling up in municipal government offices in the month before the 1991 election. On public works, see Secretaría de Gobernación 1991a: 48–9, Secretaría de Gobernación 1991b: 2–4, on titles, see Secretaría de Gobernación 1991a: 49, on roads, see Macías 1991.

46. For early history of the PAN, see Mabry 1973, von Sauer 1974, and Barragán 1997; for a full history to 1997, see Loaeza 1999.

47. For instance, one PAN mayor criticized billboards showing models wearing only their Wonderbras. Though Mexico is heavily Catholic, an increasingly secular urban culture is reluctant to follow Church authority over social mores; influence from U.S. media contributes to this trend. The extent of these policies — linked to a couple of PAN mayors — has been greatly exaggerated. Nevertheless, the PAN's experience illustrates the vulnerability of parties to image problems in an era of rising competition.

48. In 1992, several national leaders — including two ex-presidents of the PAN — resigned in protest against cooperation with the PRI, which they saw as a sellout of the PAN's independence. For an analysis of the PAN's struggles to absorb new activists, see Mizrahi 1998.

49. www.parametria.com.mx.

50. This gain is only a little misleading. In 2000, the PRD ran under an umbrella coalition, which allocated some candidacies to other parties within the coalition rather than to the PRD. In 2003, the PRD picked up five of these forty-five seats at the expense of its former alliance partners, and the other 40 at the expense of the PAN.

51. On convergence and moderation on the Mexican Left, see Carr 1985, Martinez Verdugo 1985.

52. For discussion of this process, see Bruhn 1997.

53. Ironically, Cárdenas is not known for his personality — usually, he stands out for his dignified demeanor and rather boring speaking style. It was considered major news in 1997 when his campaign poster showed him smiling. His stiff style worked against him as the importance of modern media exposure has grown, helping charismatic communicators like his PAN rival Vicente Fox. Sometimes offsetting that is the popular perception that Cárdenas's low-key style is an indication that he is different — more earnest and honest — than traditional politicians.

54. López Obrador's problems with corruption could affect voter support. However, his conflicts with the federal government could make him ineligible as a candidate. The issue involves a disputed piece of land that López Obrador expropriated to build a road to a hospital. The owner won a court injunction reversing the decree. López Obrador defied the court's decree to stop construction, apparently believing he had the right to continue construction while he appealed the court's decision. PAN strategists want charges brought against him for defying this court order. In April 2003, a PAN-PRI coalition of congressional deputies voted to remove his constitutional protection against prosecution as an elected official, effectively removing him from office and clearing the way for the filing of formal charges. If López Obrador loses, or even if his case is unresolved by January 2006, he would be forced out of the 2006 presidential race. López Obrador argues that hundreds of other politicians have routinely defied court orders with no consequences, thus, his case amounts to politically motivated prosecution. PRD-sponsored protests defending López Obrador have involved thousands of people. As of this writing, the outcome of the case is undecided.

55. For analysis of the PRD's performance in the 1997 election, see Bruhn 1998a.

56. On decreased party identification, see Basáñez 1990.

57. See Mainwaring and Scully 1995, on advantages of stable party systems with modest volatility. Overall, Mexican volatility — measured by the stability of party vote from one election to another — remains relatively low for Latin America, but higher than all party systems in Europe prior to 1977, except France.

58. For a discussion of the uses and abuses of polls see Camp 1996.

59. Some studies, based on aggregate analyses of voting results, find modest associations between these variables (e.g., Klesner 1995). Challenging this view, one well-known study of 1988/1991 electoral polls found that support for the PAN was associated (negatively) with union membership. However, the PAN vote was also associated with negative evaluations of the economy and the PRI, as well as with the previous PAN vote (party loyalty). Similarly, the Cárdenas/ PRD vote had few demographic associations, although church attendees and professionals were slightly less likely to support him. The authors of this study interpreted these results as the effect of a two-stage voting process: first, voters decided whether or not to support the PRI, and only then did they decide among the opposition parties (Domínguez and McCann 1996, especially pp. 104, 138).

The effect of a two-stage voting process has diminished as the PRI has lost its incumbent status. See Domínguez and Poiré 1999.

60. The PAN has dominated in northern states, as well as Jalisco, Guanajuato, Puebla, and the Yucatán, the PRD in the central states of Michoacán (Cárdenas's home state), Guerrero, and Morelos, as well as Oaxaca and Chiapas.

61. In 1997, a united PRD-PAN candidate would have won in 44 percent of congressional districts actually won by the PRI. Calculation from IFE 1997.

62. Article 72, *Constitución Política de los Estados Unidos Mexicanos*, available at www.conggro.gob.mx.

63. For instance, he needs congressional approval for trips abroad, and for many appointments.

64. Instead, conventions were used to name candidates to the three hundred majority districts — with candidates of unity (or single aspiring nominees, named from above) predominating. For the proportional representation list, the party president simply released lists.

65. Camp 1999: 169.

66. These changes give the Senate more power than the previous version, which gave the Senate only ten days as opposed to the current thirty, and required a simple majority. The extension of proportional representation to the Senate also gives the PRI a less secure hold on the process, as it expands the number of opposition senators. The Judicial Council is charged with overseeing the "administration, vigilance and discipline" of courts and setting their budgets (except for the Supreme Court, which sets its own). It contains representatives of the Supreme Court, other court circuits, two nominated by the Senate, and one by the Executive. All reforms from the *Constitución Política de los Estados Unidos Mexicanos,* Articles 96–105, at www.conggro.gob.mx.

67. However, the Mexican Supreme Court's right to declare a law unconstitutional is limited: cases may only be brought by a one-third vote of the legislature (which passed the law), the Attorney General, or (in the case of electoral law) a registered party, but not by citizens, as in the United States.

68. This calculation counts only the 2000 municipalities with elections on a party basis in 1996. In addition, 412 municipalities in Oaxaca were elected by *usos y costumbres* — according to traditional indigenous practices. They have no formal party affiliation. Rodriguez 1997, p. 55.

69. Presidents de la Madrid and Salinas both claimed to favor decentralization. The de la Madrid reforms expanded the responsibilities of *municipios,* including police and regulatory powers, far more than they expanded the resources local governments could use. Salinas also argued that decentralization cut down on corruption (because local people could monitor better) and used state funds more efficiently. Zedillo implemented reforms to make Mexico City's government more autonomous and more democratic. And Fox came under heavy pressure to improve local autonomy from both his party colleagues and PRI local authorities demanding more local autonomy. On decentralizing reforms, see Rodríguez 1997, Nickson 1995, Beltrán and Santiago Portilla 1986.

70. For analyses of municipal governance, see Cornelius, Eisenstadt, and Hindley 1999, García del Castillo 1999, Rodríguez and Ward 1995, Ziccardi

1995. For analyses of state governments, see Ward and Rodríguez 1999, Espinoza Valle 1998, Rodríguez and Ward 1994, Guillen López 1993.

71. Cornelius 1999: 11.

72. Vicente Fox (PAN) governed Guanajuato, Francisco Labastida (PRI) governed Sinaloa, and Cuauhtémoc Cárdenas (PRD) governed not only Mexico City, but — while still a PRI member — Michoacán. Within the PRI, pre-candidates with gubernatorial experience include Roberto Madrazo (Tabasco) and Manuel Bartlett (Puebla). The PAN made this transition earlier than other parties, as it relied on candidates with local reputations.

73. For analyses of the military, see Camp 1992, Serrano 1995, Wager and Schulz 1995.

74. Military expenditures went from 2 to 3 percent of GDP per capita to an average of 5 percent under Zedillo; their size also increased from 170,000 in 1986 to about 240,000 in 1999. Camp 1999: 131. However, World Bank data suggest that by 2002, military expenditures had fallen back to 3.2 percent of the national budget. *2004 World Development Indicators,* 2004: 283.

75. For example, the fifty officers who demonstrated as the Patriotic Commando for Consciousness-raising of the People focused on protection for soldiers accused of violating military regulations.

76. Inglehart et al. 2004: E070. By way of comparison, confidence in the police, the legislature, the civil service, and the political parties all declined.

CHAPTER FOUR

1. Interview with Mario Vargas Llosa, "De la dictadura perfecta a una democracia difícil," *Reforma,* July 3, 2000. The contrast between the perfect dictatorship and a difficult democracy fits our theme of Mexican "normalization."

2. www.parametria.com.mx

3. The contrast is consistent with philosopher Isaiah Berlin's observation about the ample freedom individuals sometimes exercise in fundamentally private matters (such as choosing where to live, work, worship, or travel), even when freedom is less vibrant in public affairs.

4. Cinema has also been regulated.

5. When Zedillo attempted in October 1995 to draw a distinction between Mexico and other countries requiring a total overhaul to achieve democracy, he was roundly ridiculed (and demeaned by use of his first name) for pretending that Mexico was democratic by critics who portrayed the questionable and exaggerated claim as preposterous.

6. The 1994 debate can be compared with the U.S. Kennedy-Nixon debates in 1960 in that, although the number of changed votes was limited, the debate marked an irreversible entry into the age of television politics; for U.S. politics this meant a changed style of democratic politics, but for Mexico it represented a significant step forward in recognizing the public's right to information about all presidential candidates.

7. In fact, in the past less dissent aired on private than on public radio and television. When administrations swayed leftward, as during the Central American conflicts of the 1980s, private media outdistanced government in ardent

defense of the conservative status quo. The growth of public television in the 1970s also undermined the comfortable government- (private) media modus vivendi; fears of nationalization led private owners to distance themselves a bit more from government (Baer 1988). This parallels the broader business trend toward political independence set in motion by the antibusiness posture of Echerverría.

8. Together with just two more families (the O'Farrills and Alemáns), the Azcárragas account for a huge share of Mexican media; the privatized TV Azteca, although a more recent addition to the television ownership group, belongs to a billionaire. See Adler 1993 on media ownership and Orme 1997 on collusion mixed with a rise of independent outlets. It has been difficult for well-intentioned newspeople to defy owners or editors.

9. See Bruhn 1997: 280 on 1994 and Domínguez and McCann 1996: 153 on 1988. While the media gave the PRI very excessive coverage early in the 1994 campaign, opposition complaints to the IFE — and direct IFE intervention — resulted in more equal coverage thereafter. The 1997 congressional and Mexico City elections brought Mexico further toward fair media treatment.

10. Among dailies, *Reforma* and *La Jornada* lead the way. The latter's willingness to open its pages to the views of dissidents like the zapatistas is a landmark signal of change, while *Reforma* has broken several major corruption scandals. Magazines include the liberal *Nexos,* the leftist *Proceso,* the conservative *Vuelta,* and the pluralistic *Este País.*

11. See, for example, Trejo Delarbre 1996: 23–24.

12. In the newly open political system another substitute for legitimate news is irresponsible accusation and propaganda by opposition as well as government — knowing that the falsity of charges cannot be proven.

13. Along with the suddenly shaky presidential selection process itself, the unsavory brew has included drug trafficking and assassinations. In a system long on rumors and short on sources of objective news, arbitrary or partisan selection of stories often results in widely varying headline news, as well as different coverage of the same stories in different media outlets. Mexican news stories often require decoding from contradictory texts, a process requiring considerable knowledge and limiting the potential audience. See, for example, Adler 1993: 168. Even skilled decoders are left playing a guessing game as to why a person or policy was chosen over others.

14. See Aguayo 1998a. Short of investigative reporting, many outlets in each medium gather and report more information than before. A typical example was a television feature on the tenth anniversary of another momentous event in Mexico's political evolution: the 1985 earthquake. The feature started with background and shot to an on-site reporter, who added further information orchestrated with pictures and then successively interviewed past and present government officials along with independent academic figures regarding how many perished, what the government should have done differently, and whether subsequent actions have left the city less, more, or equally vulnerable to future quakes. In general, stories provide increasing information about a range of policies. Meanwhile, media transmit real political petitions, including ones that denounce the government or appeal to legislators. And whereas the media were tradition-

ally almost mute on the implications of news items for democratization, they are now fairly consumed by them.

15. www.rsf.org. The first year of rankings was 2002.

16. The importance of television explains the chagrin of a leading adviser to Lázaro Cárdenas when the candidate insisted on personal campaigning in remote areas rather than turning to television (Castañeda 1994: 139).

17. Lawson 2002: 211.

18. At times a few comic books held a unique place for their thinly veiled political satire (e.g., ostensibly simple folks asking beguiling questions about how the elite prospered while the masses suffered).

19. The contrast between freedom of expression and restrictions on freedom of organization is consistent with our point that media restrictions have been greatest when dealing with mass audiences or the information required for formulating credible alternatives to government policy. Because freedom of assembly, for example, occupies terrain between individual expression and organizational activity, it has received a mixed treatment like that accorded the media. Demonstrations in Mexico have been far more common than in most authoritarian regimes, but the riskiest have been those appearing to pose a credible alternative to the government. If peaceful co-optation did not disable the threat, demonstrators faced stiffer responses.

20. By the same token, the weakening of the government may now be a problem in connection with minorities who have been persecuted in other nations, as the new strife between Catholics and converts to Protestantism may suggest. As with rising violence against the media, the breakdown of strong nondemocratic government opens space for "freedom" to persecute and harass even as it opens space for democracy.

21. The loosening of political restrictions on the Mexican church is often traced in part to permission for papal visits starting in 1979; politicians noted the size and enthusiasm of the pope's crowds. Under Salinas the government introduced further historic changes, including the attendance of religious leaders at Salinas's inauguration; more concrete changes came with ensuing legislative reforms. Like political change at the time, the substance of this opening up was more consistent with democracy than were the means — initiatives by government rather than active, effective demand from citizens. Indeed, the closed nature of the process means that explanation of the government's action involves speculation. Mexico's adept authoritarianism has often allowed for some responsiveness to public opinion, even as a kind of reward for its lack of organization and direct challenge. It is also possible, however, to attribute changes in church-state relations to a fresher element at play: the rise of competitive politics leading government to seek broader bases of public support. Already bishops in some states had strongly suggested that their followers avoid votes for "atheism" and "corruption" (referring to the PRI and favoring the PAN). When Salinas hosted the pope in 1990 (though in "personal" rather than "state" receptions) and began sending a representative to the Vatican, he might have relished splitting the Left, cornering some into attacking the breach of constitutionalism. And when neoliberal policies cost support from traditional constituencies and President Zedillo was at a low ebb in popular support (in 1995), fresh support came from evangelicals.

22. Fox, a graduate of the Jesuit Ibero-American University, is the most publicly religious president modern Mexico has had. As a candidate he made much of his faith, used the Virgin of Guadalupe in campaign material, prayed to her on election morning, and promised to expand freedom for church schools, though he also promised to abide by the Constitution's guarantees of laical public education.

23. See O'Donnell 1994. Related terms include *degraded democracy*.

24. See Diamond 1998.

25. Such points could reinforce stereotypic views from the U.S. side, as seen in the popular media and legislators' attitudes. Ironically, some negative or traditional Mexican cultural orientations increasingly parallel trends in the political culture of developed societies like the United States, where political apathy has risen (as long as the system delivers material goods) along with higher expectations of dishonesty and arguably diminished interest in political and social participation.

26. The classic study putting Mexican political culture in a negative comparative light was Almond and Verba 1963, but improved and more balanced analyses include Craig and Cornelius 1989. For a summary of findings on beliefs and trust, see Camp 1999b: 59; he reports an increase in trust of fellow citizens, though from a low starting point. Also see Needler's (1995: 51 and passim) discussion.

27. Seventeen percent think an authoritarian government might be preferable to democracy in some circumstances, and 22 percent think the type of regime makes little difference "to people like me." www.parametria.com.mx

28. On these assessments, support for party competition, and other mass attitudes, see the analysis of polling data in Camp 1999b. A Mexican tendency to agree that a few strong leaders can help Mexico more than laws and rhetoric may be undemocratic, but it may also reflect an accurate appreciation, not necessarily an endorsement, of national political reality.

29. On the North American data, see Inglehart, Nevitte, and Basáñez 1996: 83–99. Also on democratizing political culture in Mexico, see Booth and Seligson 1984: 106–124, Domínguez and McCann 1996, Camp 1999b, and Craig and Cornelius 1989. A civil society that demands and successfully fights for democratic government arguably makes for a firmer, enduring base for modern democracy than elite "pacts" alone. The euphoria surrounding Mexico's 1997 and 2000 elections reflected a feeling of popular conquest not unlike the feeling in Chile in 1988, when the electorate began to turn out the military government. Some analysts have been skeptical about how much civil society strengthening has paralleled Mexico's state weakening (Cavarozzi 1994).

30. See Langston 1995: 243–77 on what makes camarillas tick. Even low-level officeholders have owed their jobs to designation (Hansen 1974: 113), but this is changing. For a classic treatment of camarillas, see Smith 1979.

31. See Hansen 1974: 165 on the behavioral and personnel underpinnings of stability; see Rochlin 1997: 4 on repression. The bizarre and ugly Salinas family soap opera mentioned in Chapter 1 is not the only incident involving prominent figures. In 1999 a well-known TV comic was assassinated, drugs were suspected, and government-inclined television immediately blamed Mexico City's PRD gov-

ernment for the crime wave. That same year a banker, jailed in Australia, told of huge payoffs to the PRI, and while the attorney general investigated, opposition parties called for a special prosecutor. Although the last aspect has a familiar U.S. ring to it, the spectacle of bitter accusations by prominent Mexicans on foreign soil illustrated the erosion of Mexico's political class.

32. Chapter 3 discussed how democratic pressures might compromise economic planning and why some PRI members distance themselves from technocratic policies. On the antidemocratic tendencies of technocrats, see Centeno 1997, Bartra 1989: 63, and Zermeño 1993; for other Latin American countries, see Conaghan and Malloy 1994. On the positive mix of technocratic and democratic, see Domínguez 1997. A pioneering study on the Mexican technocrat-politician mix was Camp 1985.

33. As the technocratic trend became a liability to the PRI and as opposition parties ran candidates who had held elective office, PRI insiders responded with the 1996 reform that future presidential candidates must have had elective experience. Camp 2002 highlights the expanded social distance between elites and masses in recent decades as elites are more middle class, urban, and educated (including many U.S. doctorates), but he also writes that the PRI's newest political leaders come more from the provinces, with more party and electoral experience and closer ties to the grassroots. It is fair to note that both Zedillo and the fallen candidate he replaced (Colosio) were from rather modest backgrounds, whereas Salinas grew up in an influential politico family. Fox is from a comfortable but still modest background without strong political family ties. On the weakened political class, see Prud'homme 1999.

34. Other qualifications have included the following: the president could be no more powerful than the government overall; even presidentialism has allowed for interactions with groups and actors, and the picture includes confrontations and compromise rather than consistently easy imposition. Vernon (1963) wrote of a presidency struggling to balance interests and to control its own bureaucracy. Philip (1992: 167–72) contrasted a despotic power to tell others what to do to a weakness in mobilizing resources for effective policy. While debate rages on how powerful democratic presidents should be in mobilizing resources, no doubt exists of the need to curb their despotic power. On the great strength of Mexican presidents, see Carpizo 1996 and Krauze 1997 as well as Brandenburg's 1964 classic.

35. Lawson 2001.

36. Morris 1995: 149. See Márquez 1995: 55 on the paradox of how Salinas's personalized approach made the presidency appear stronger while it was really becoming weaker. Zedillo gave his first State of the Union address without his wife and children at his side, arguably an expression of a newly austere image.

37. Opponents suspected President Vicente Fox of authoritarian personal tendencies. But confronting divided government and a democratized citizenry, his administration could not have anything like the massive unaccountable infrastructure that prior presidents dominated.

38. In Mexico debate about how active the president should be is a large part of the overall debate about how active the state should be in democracies. Neoliberal democrats call for a smaller but more efficient and responsive state,

while critics argue that neoliberalism allows an escape from the responsibilities a democratic government should have to its people. President Zedillo's education plan won praise for breaking a forty-year pattern in which national government decided what to do and how; instead, it left a major policy role to plural actors including states and teachers (Latapí 1996).

39. The dean of *sexenio* studies dismissed claims by U.S. specialists to understand the turnover process (Cosío Villegas 1975: 9-36); on the meaning of sexennial change for the system, see Basáñez 1991 and Smith 1979.

40. When an outgoing president did jockey for continued influence, the system accorded his successor all the necessary power to put him in his place, perhaps with an ignominious appointment to a remote ambassadorship. In fact, power started shifting from the time of selection. So much attention went to the turnover process that some observers claimed presidents had only two years to concentrate on public policy, a serious qualification to the powerful presidency. For the two preceding years they had to install themselves, and for the last two they engaged heavily in making the transition work.

41. Purcell and Purcell 1980.

42. But as government loses autonomy to civil society, it may be forced to modify neoliberalism by selecting leaders who are also able to address issues of democratization and social justice. On the neoliberal requirements, see Hinojosa 1988. The idea of a two-tier cabinet parallels a U.S. tendency in which key economic posts mostly go to established figures while other posts are more open to considerations like minority representation.

43. Chapter 3 noted that PRI hard-liners have often rebelled when "their" guy has been sacrificed to uphold the democratic legitimacy of elections or to appease the opposition. At the presidential level Manuel Camacho coyly refused to back Colosio's 1994 presidential candidacy and later fell reluctantly into line behind Zedillo. For more on the intrigues and rumors centered around Camacho, Salinas, and Colosio, see Márquez 1995. Fuentes (1996: 86-127) calls 1994 "the year of living dangerously." Also on sexennial crisis, see Basáñez 1991.

44. Culminating in 1994, transitions came to epitomize how sexennial change could offer more uncertainty than renewal of the system. Efforts to repair problems created in the outgoing administration could lead to fierce new problems, as failures do not fly off as easily with exiting presidents but instead stain the system. The scapegoating game partly wore thin when five presidents in a row exited in the public's low esteem. Enrique Krauze has observed (in "¿Qué le queda a Salinas?" *Reforma*, January 14, 1996) that Salinas exceeded even López Portillo in damaging the system by rising so high in popularity and then so betraying the public trust that he stole off into hiding. Krauze called López Mateos, who left office in 1964, the last ex-president to walk the streets to cheers, while de la Madrid was the only one of the last four able to leave office without jeers. At least some 1996 official ceremonies on television limited their snapshots of former presidents to the same two. Incoming President Zedillo enjoyed no honeymoon, but his departure six years later in good standing represents a reversal — a historic democratic reversal — of the period of undermining transitions. The Mexican stock market jumped 6 percent the day after Mexico's 2000 elections.

45. The search for accountability leads some to question the sacred principle of no re-election. No re-election ostensibly prevents leaders from holding power so long that they become remote from citizens. This is largely the argument for U.S. term limits. Critics argue, however, that citizens should have the right to judge the performance of leaders and decide which ones to retain. Also, with accumulated experience from multiple terms, Mexican legislators might exercise their power more responsibly and effectively. Re-election is currently proscribed for all federal elective offices, though sometimes with provision for nonconsecutive service (in nonexecutive positions). Similar rules prevail at the local level.

46. Perhaps a shift to democratic normalization in transition periods is found in electoral bombast, and Mexicans expressed disenchantment with it; as Carlos Monsiváis has written (in "Por mi madre, bohemios," *Jornada,* March 15, 1999): "The most frequently heard demand" is to "let whoever wins win, but let the noise factor end."

47. www.publicintegrity.org

48. Business organizations, including media, have long engaged in corruption. Privatization brought fresh opportunities, as in countries like Argentina, Brazil, and Russia, proving that the turn to a less state-run economy does not spell a quick end to corruption. The sale of TV Azteca and most notably of the telephone company took place at below-market prices to favored business associates who would handsomely reward the officials by providing windfall profits.

49. A particular target of criticism was Riding's (1985) harsh analysis. Some Mexicans refrained from buying López Portillo's memoirs so as not to reward the devil who therein acknowledges without apology such facts as the gift from the oil workers union of a house in Acapulco.

50. Dahl 1971.

51. The presidency is of course the main institution wielding arbitrary power. It has failed to defend citizens' dignity, rights, and accountability, as a democracy requires. It has also operated de facto according to extraconstitutional privileges that are not strictly legal. Paradoxically, even when the president has acted to effect a reform, it has often been through the exercise of uncontrolled power, as in the removal of abusive or politically problematic governors. Whereas most presidents in the past half-century removed from three to six governors, Salinas booted ten. On the dismissals, see Hernández 1994: 204–5; for one view of Salinas's actions as essentially reformist, see Grayson 1992: 67. For a study of how even desirable presidential reforms effected by unaccountable authority are troublesome for democracy, see Elizondo 1995. On the president's extraconstitutional as well as constitutional powers, see Garrido 1989: 420–26.

52. www.parametria.com.mx

53. Business increasingly sees that liberty must extend beyond private property to become a general principle for Mexican society. NAFTA reinforces concerns that foreign interests count on transparency in Mexican courts and effective protection of their enterprises, executives, and assets against crime (Rubio 1994).

54. Of course, great variation exists within each of the two groups, and more precision could come by dividing the population into more than two categories.

55. This has contributed to what Jorge Castañeda characterized as a plural nation, but which reflects the pluralism unfairly. See Castañeda 1994: 154.

56. See Cross 1998: 18. He estimates there are around two hundred thousand vendors, with more at Christmastime. Leaders of vendor associations adeptly exploit divisions within government as well as new opportunities presented by competitive politics to avoid harsh, effective crackdowns. On government reaction to land seizures, see Gilbert 1989, and on government vulnerability to pressure from the lower class, see Brachet de Márquez 1994. Rising independent demonstrations may be compared with a more closed tradition in which many demonstrations have been displays of support more than protest or have supported one tendency over others within merely the limited options permitted.

57. Mexico's most privileged groups usually have ways to protest and influence without recourse to the streets, though middle-class groups fall somewhere in between. But demonstrations seem increasingly out of step; in Mexico City, for example, the number of demonstrations fell after the 1997 election of an opposition mayor. For one thing the system has opened space in the party and electoral arenas; for another, neoliberal policy makers disdain the traditional politics of doling out resources to mollify protesters in economically irrational ways. To many once sympathetic observers, demonstrations have become less a noble effort to persuade public opinion to a cause than a tiresome part of corroded politics — and a serious traffic problem. This perception mirrors growing dissatisfaction with ritualistic muscle flexing, petty rivalries, empty echoes of populist slogans, and disruptive petitioning of government.

58. As of 1989, women represented about 5 percent of the political elite — 58 women of 1,113 political elite members — and rarely held the most important positions (Centeno 1997: 115).

59. See Levy 1980, though government has excercised influence through repression, appointment of high officials, and the budget. In 1999 a decision by authorities at the National University to charge tuition, already imposed in other public universities and repeatedly recommended to decrease state subsidization, provoked a crippling student strike. Despite official retreat from the tuition policy, the Democratic Student Coalition continued to strike, fighting what it considered authoritarian neoliberalism. Students again demonstrated their power to block change by making the political costs high, especially as the national election season loomed. Many disgusted Mexicans blasted a government so cautious to avoid trouble and international opprobrium that it undermined democratic responsibility and the rule of law not by using excessive force but by refraining from using any (Elizondo 2000).

60. Labor's low wages and lack of independent power to organize make a climate comfortable for business. With its vague doctrine of "economic democracy" (supporting those in government who are less neoliberal than others), organized labor still sets itself against independent labor and a fundamental break with traditional state corporatism.

61. Dahl 1985: 68–69. Dahl continues in a vein that could have relevance for Mexico if neoliberal economics and competitive politics lead to increased inequality: "In the extreme case, a minority of rich will possess so much greater political resources than other citizens that they will control the state, dominate the majority of citizens, and empty the democratic process of all content."

62. The federal government has long assumed the role of arbiter between popular organizations (or groups) and hostile local governments. Exploiting government factions has been a dissident strategy, but government factions can also play complex political games.

63. Women held roughly 15 percent of seats in Mexico compared with roughly 10 percent in the United States; the figure varies from under 3 percent to more than 33 percent in other developed democracies (Fernández Poncela 1995). Representation decreased with the PAN victory in 2000. Camp (1999b: 90) cites survey data showing that while Mexican women discuss politics much less than men, they hold fairly equal views of their ability to be influential.

64. The critics hold that neoliberalism, technocrats, and so forth lead to greater concentration of political-economic power, not to pluralist, competitive distribution of power (Teichman 1995). Many critics are therefore dismayed at the lack of major protest as neoliberalism strips common citizens of "historic conquests" such as the *ejido*.

65. Another debate that highlights contrasting views of neoliberal change concerns the indigenous population. Progressives argue for special treatment to overcome legacies of oppression, a kind of affirmative action. Neoliberals argue that the indigenous should be given equal opportunity to democratic processes and then be treated like other citizens who become responsible for their own well-being.

66. The PAN in national power must prove it champions freedom and accountability as much as it claimed when it was out of power, and it must show a similar concern to deal with political inequality.

67. On the one hand, such uncertainties may strengthen those who fear democratization. On the other hand, whereas Mexicans' much noted fear of instability once reinforced a markedly nondemocratic system, it may help protect Mexico's fledgling democracy from some of the risks of polarization and unwillingness to compromise, particularly in light of broad popular rejection of an antidemocratic retreat.

CHAPTER FIVE

1. Three of the four contenders within the PRI for its presidential candidacy in 2000 were essentially political managers — former governors with substantial experience in dealing with political conflicts. And the fourth had a long history of party experience.

2. Economies of scale result from the expansion of the productive capacity of a firm or industry, leading to decreases in the cost of production per unit of output. So as a firm expands its market share and increases its output, its costs — and prices — should go down.

3. Singer 1969: 23 and Ross 1971: 102.

4. Levy and Székely 1987: 133.

5. Initially, public investment in agriculture slightly edged investment in industry, but after 1952 industrial investment doubled, tripled, or even quadrupled the share of agriculture.

6. Under agrarian law land not under cultivation and over a certain limit could be transferred to peasants. To keep their land, landowners had to use it; unused land transferred to peasants was also brought into production. However, at the peak of land reform, state investment in agriculture was also higher, and this contributed to growth.

7. González Casanova 1970: 225.

8. Izquierdo 1994: 133.

9. In part, this reflected international boycotts of Mexican oil; more fundamentally, it reflected the difficulty Mexico had in running the oil industry after the departure of most of the British and U.S. engineers formerly employed by the oil companies.

10. After 1967 approval was transferred to the Ministry of Industry and Commerce. On Mexican regulatory practices, see Whiting 1992.

11. Ibid.: 32.

12. Companies with *some* foreign participation (just under 1 percent of all manufacturing firms) accounted for 16.9 percent of the industrial workforce, 32.2 percent of the value of production, and 35.4 percent of invested capital. Ibid.: 65–69.

13. In Mexico's case the maquiladoras were set up in large part to avoid U.S. tariffs. Assembled maquila products could be exported to the United States with duty paid only on value added — typically quite low. On the maquiladora sector, see Sklair 1993.

14. By 1970 debt service took up nearly 25 percent of the value of exports, the highest debt service–to-exports ratio in Latin America. IDB 1980: 101 and World Bank 1980: 134–55.

15. As in many countries the most rapidly expanding sector in Mexico has been the service sector — including everything from restaurants to banking. GNP calculations from 1940 to 1968 are in constant (1950) pesos (Ross 1971: 82); Solis 1970: 220. Demographic data from Nacional Financiera 1977: 5, 13–15.

16. López Acuña 1979: 181 and Izquierdo 1994: 272.

17. Population growth from Izquierdo 1994: 139; other figures from Secretaría del Trabajo y Previsión Social 1979; Secretaría de Programación y Presupuesto 1979; IDB 1980.

18. Levy and Székely 1987: 147.

19. World Bank 1980: 156–57.

20. This, at least, is part of the explanation proffered by Haggard (1990). Curiously, these Asian countries ultimately preserved more protectionism in their economic policies than Mexico. It is interesting to speculate whether the economic consequences of the 1970s made it harder to keep significant parts of ISI than if Mexico had adapted earlier.

21. Secretaría de Hacienda y Crédito Público 1991: 15.

22. The largest debtor country in the world is the United States. Investors feel that the U.S. economy is strong and stable. The U.S. government is thus allowed to carry a higher debt, just as individuals with a good job get credit cards with higher limits. Investors are more likely to panic when fragile countries acquire debt.

23. ISI refers to a trade policy, which would not end until the late 1980s.

What ended during the 1970s was really the combination of rapid growth with low inflation — the "stabilizing development" recipe.

24. In a six-year period the share of deposits in the domestic financial system that were made in dollars increased from 17 percent to 40 percent of the total. Even easier was simply depositing money in foreign banks. Bazdresch and Levy 1991: 243–44.

25. Ibid.: 232.

26. Monsiváis 1987: 35.

27. Bazdresch and Levy 1991: 236, 288.

28. Levy and Székely 1987: 138, 241.

29. While negotiating with the IMF, Echeverría chose as his successor the head of the Mexican Finance Ministry (Hacienda). In turn, López Portillo chose de la Madrid, an economist from the financial ministries, to succeed him during the 1981–82 debt crisis. De la Madrid's minister of programming and budget (Salinas) became the PRI candidate in 1987, one of the worst years of crisis; and Zedillo's doctorate in economics was a plus in his selection by Salinas to replace the assassinated PRI candidate in 1994.

30. Salinas would later fold the Budget Ministry — his former portfolio — back into the Finance Ministry, recentralizing control over financial matters.

31. This paradox is explored in Karl 1997.

32. In fact, for many years López Portillo could barely go out in public without people barking at him — a caustic reference to his 1976 promise to "defend the peso like a dog." It did not help that he was widely viewed as one of the most corrupt presidents in history (until the Salinas clan), having enriched himself while in office.

33. Secretaría de Hacienda y Crédito Público 1991: 35.

34. Gentleman 1987: 51.

35. After the earthquake the IMF reversed its earlier decision to suspend Mexico's drawing rights because of poor progress in meeting budget and inflation targets. But the restored funding fell far short of Mexico City's reconstruction needs, let alone investment.

36. Secretaría de Hacienda y Crédito Público 1991: 15.

37. The state kept about 9 percent of total banking stock but sold the rest of its stock to thirteen financial groups and five individuals.

38. During the last half of the de la Madrid administration (1985–89), privatization brought in just over $1.2 billion; under Salinas privatization brought in $24.4 billion from 1990 to 1994. The other top privatizers in Latin America (Argentina and Brazil) received $15.4 billion and $8.6 billion, respectively, in the same period. SALA 1998: 887 and Secretaría de Gobernación 1998: 49.

39. Marketing boards bought crops from producers, transported and stored them, provided assistance in their preparation for market (for example, building drying facilities for raw coffee beans), and helped market the crop. They dominated the purchase of a crop, often paying subsidized prices. From ninety-four boards in 1982, Mexico went to only ten by 1990.

40. PEMEX production still represents a significant source of income for the state. However, pride also plays a role. The government initially planned to sell petrochemical plants which process Mexican oil, but protests by PEMEX work-

ers and others forced it to reconsider. As of 1997, the state still held 51 percent of shares in petrochemical plants. Plans to partially privatize the Federal Electrical Commission in 1999 and again in 2003 were successfully resisted by labor unions and elements of the PRI.

41. After six years of "restructuring" under de la Madrid, the foreign debt surpassed $100 billion, more than 58 percent of the GDP. Close to 9 percent of the GDP and almost 45 percent of Mexican export earnings went toward debt service — almost the same percentage, proportionately, as in 1982. Fuentes-Beraín 1992 and Aspin 1992.

42. In 1989 the threat of a leftist Cárdenas presidency in 1988 may have sharpened U.S. concern about failure to relieve Mexico's debt burden. Banks themselves favored a negotiated solution, because orthodox rescheduling had failed to eliminate the threat of default. The World Bank and the IMF were willing to agree as long as the government accepted economic reforms. As cabinet minister under de la Madrid, Salinas had long promoted an economic strategy that coincided effectively with these proposed economic reforms. Thus the actors with a direct interest in Mexican debt had come closer to each other in their perspective. Under the Brady Plan, which they negotiated, Mexico's creditors exchanged around $22 billion in debt for the same nominal amount in bonds with lower fixed interest rates, and $20 billion for bonds at a 35 percent discount off the original value, but with floating interest rates. The discounted loan option could have backfired if world interest rates had risen, but Mexico was lucky: interest rates remained stable, and the government saved money. Average savings were projected at around $4 billion a year. Secretaría de Hacienda y Crédito Público 1991: 22, 20.

43. Ironically, Salinas then turned around and pressured the Central Bank prior to the 1994 presidential election to delay the release of figures that might have foreshadowed the impending peso devaluation. He also repeatedly denied that any devaluation would be necessary, even as his administration privately discussed the timing of devaluation.

44. The calculation from 1997 and 1998 is available on-line at www .odci.gov/cia/publications/factbook/country.html; SALA 1998: 907. One Mexican government calculation, adding the cost of the internal debt assumed by the Mexican government to bail out the troubled Mexican banking system in 1997 (known as Fondo Bancario de Protección al Ahorro, or Fobaproa), calculates the total cost of public debt at around 40 percent in 2000. González Amador 2000b.

45. See Bruhn 1997 on the relationship between economic reforms and the split in the PRI.

46. Between 1989 and 1992 the GDP grew at an average of around 3.5 percent a year, compared to an average of less than 1 percent during the previous five years. Industrial production grew even faster, more than 5 percent a year (OECD 1995: 186; Secretaría de Hacienda de Crédito Público 1991: 38). By 1994 manufacturing accounted for 83 percent of exports (compared with 18 percent in 1981). INEGI 1995: 110; for the 1981 figure, see SALA 1998: 649. On inflation, see INEGI 1995: 81.

47. For a discussion of many of the factors behind the peso crisis, see Roett 1996 and Santiso 1999.

48. From 1987 to 1994 consumer bank lending grew by 458 percent (in constant pesos). More than 70 percent involved credit card debt, and the rest involved loans for such durables as refrigerators, homes, or cars. Lending for housing grew 967 percent. By contrast, lending for manufacturing grew only 131 percent. See Ramírez de la O 1996: 13.

49. The current account deficit increased from $4 billion in 1989 to nearly $29 billion by 1994 — some 8 percent of the GDP. Secretaría de Hacienda de Crédito Público 1991: 18; Ramírez de la O 1996: 12, 25.

50. In 1993 of some $30 billion in net capital inflow, $25 billion went into portfolio investment. See Ramírez de la O 1996: 12.

51. Nobody likes inflation and most Mexicans dread devaluations. Given Mexican demand for imported goods and inputs, devaluation made everything more expensive. And Salinas expected Cárdenas to run again for president in 1994. Two further reasons to wait may also apply. First, Salinas may have felt some obligation toward the United States; having promised no devaluation in order to win U.S. approval of NAFTA in November 1993, he may have been reluctant to devalue within two months. Then PRI presidential candidate Luis Donaldo Colosio was assassinated in March, and by the time markets recovered, the election was less than six months away. Finally, insider reports indicate that Salinas wanted to become president of the World Trade Organization. Devaluation would have tarnished his reputation as an economic genius.

52. President Salinas's brother Raúl allegedly accumulated millions of dollars in Swiss bank accounts through bribes offered by investors bidding on state companies. Major companies (like Telmex and several banks) ended up in the hands of close Salinas friends (and wealthy investors) such as Carlos Slim and Carlos Hank González.

53. González de la Rocha and Escobar Latapí 1991: 5.

54. High school and junior high graduation rates dropped 50 percent between 1982 and 1986. Between 1982 and 1988 per capita consumption of rice fell by almost 60 percent, beans by 44 percent, and corn — the core of the Mexican diet — by 40 percent. Health statistics from Cordera Campos and González Tiburcio 1991: 32–34.

55. See www.odci.gov/cia/publications/factbook/mx.html.

56. INEGI 1995: 122.

57. www.cia.gov/cia/publications/factbook/.

58. Cruz 2000: 36.

59. According to some estimates, real wages have declined by about two-thirds since 1980, and average wages by nearly a quarter of their value. Santiago Levy 1994: 15–111. Also see SALA 1998: 388. All wage estimates adjust for inflation. If 1990 is indexed at 100, the value of the real urban minimum wage in 1996 would be 71.1 (that is, 71.1 percent of the value of the 1990 wage); by way of comparison, the 1980 minimum wage index is 252.9, or more than two and a half times the 1990 wage (ibid.: 362).

60. "Gana México urbano y educado" 2000: 8A.

61. www.parametria.com.mx.

62. In 1994 the state still depended on oil for a quarter of its income (INEGI 1995: 170). However, the state attempted to circumvent political opposition to

full privatization of oil by creating joint state – private sector ventures in the sector. Thus the importance of private actors has increased even in the strongest bastion of state-owned enterprise.

63. Womack 1996.

CHAPTER SIX

1. Of Mexico's seventy consulates in foreign countries, fifty-two are in the United States. The U.S. Embassy in Mexico is nearly ten times the size of the Mexican Embassy in the United States.

2. Schmitt 1974: 44–50. Also, on Mexico's potential strength, see Cosío Villegas 1964: 35. For a brief overview of the history of Mexico-U.S. relations, see Vázquez and Meyer 1985.

3. Although President Andrew Jackson recognized Texan independence in 1837, Texan requests for annexation and statehood were initially rejected. Abolitionists opposed the addition of another slave state, and there was concern not to provoke Mexico excessively. Pressures built, however, and President James Polk was a zealous advocate of U.S. expansion. Mexico might have been better off allowing Texan independence to avoid a confrontation with a country that seized the opening to rip away vast territory; indeed, the results might have been even worse had the United States not been sinking into its own Civil War, and had it not feared absorbing a large indigenous alien population (Meyer 1990: 254–55).

4. "Wounded nationalism" has served as a foreign policy bargaining chip: Mexican policy makers could tell their U.S. counterparts that sensitive public opinion demanded tough negotiation. That approach has diminished since the mid-1980s.

5. Although democracy was not the widely recognized imperative that it is today, one could argue that support for dictators only fanned revolutionary winds and ultimately condemned Mexico to another century of considerable authoritarianism and inequality. Perhaps a democratic beginning, however initially restricted in participation, would have been worth support, though one could debate how viable it would have been.

6. Another view is that President Wilson used the minimum force realistically possible, given the nature of the Mexico-U.S. clashes and the powerful demands for intervention by U.S. business interests (Knight 1987: 103–14). In any case Wilson helped topple the Huerta government (which the United States had helped install). On the U.S. role overall, see Katz 1983.

7. Only a short era of good feeling would follow, however. By 1925 Mexico's new president, Plutarco Elías Calles, toughened national policies on ownership of oil and land (see Meyer 1977 on the importance of revolutionary nationalism in Mexico-U.S. conflicts). Additionally, Calles unleashed a brutal attack on the Mexican church, provoking conservative Catholics in both nations to solicit U.S. intervention. However, an anti-U.S. strain has traditionally existed within Mexico's Catholic Church, involving a rejection of U.S. Protestantism, liberal individualism, and materialism. One reason for a decline in this sentiment in the twentieth century was the church's support for the U.S.-led anticommunist crusade.

8. Cornelius 1973: 399.

9. The Cárdenas-Roosevelt era marked a transition from continual wrenching conflict. Schmitt (1974: 193) described the 1945–70 period as more "harmonious and carefree" than any previous period in history, with the possible exception of the porfiriato.

10. Aguayo (1998b: 49) notes an unwritten corollary to the nationalistic, nonjudgmental approach: Mexican officials do not praise foreign countries either, though they do praise foreign leaders and other individuals. In any event Mexico's piety is not convincing to Central Americans who believe that Mexico tries to dominate them.

11. In 1975 alone, Mexico established diplomatic relations with thirty-three developing nations. It championed Third World positions, though neither this nor attempts to broaden relations with communist nations yielded much tangible result. Echeverría strengthened relations with Castro's Cuba. His enthusiastic support for Chile's Marxist government went beyond traditional commitment to nonintervention, and Mexico then branded Chile's ensuing military regime a pariah and broke diplomatic relations (not restoring them until Chilean democracy returned in 1990). Mexico also welcomed an influx of Chilean refugees. So Mexico went beyond universalism to assertive support for friends and opposition to enemies. Earlier, nonrecognition of Franco's Spain had been a unique example of negative foreign policy toward another government. Mexico did not initially recognize Communist China but did so well before the United States did.

12. One caustic clash involved Iran. In 1979 militant Iranian students seized the U.S. Embassy in Tehran and demanded the return of the toppled Shah in exchange for release of U.S. citizens they had taken hostage. The Shah had been living in Mexico for most of the year, benefiting from that aspect of universalism. The Shah then came to the United States for medical treatment and expected to return to Mexico, but Mexico refused entry. The United States felt betrayed in an hour of grave need, since it wanted neither to force the Shah back to Iran nor to incur all the security risks of his presence in the United States. But Mexico wanted to avoid terrorist retaliation and insisted that its foreign policy must serve its own needs. See Levy and Székely 1987: 201–3. Consider the contrast to Mexico's policy in the region a decade later: the Mexican government supported the 1990 U.S.-led military intervention against Iraq, though many in the media and society dissented. Still, Mexico has not become a consistent supporter of its neighbor, as seen in 1998 when U.S. threats of attacks on Iraq were decried as unjustified; in both Iraq cases Mexico stood with most of the world — once with U.S. policy, once against it. In 1999, when U.S.-led NATO forces acted to halt Serbian racial atrocities, Mexican statements were low-key, balanced denunciations of Serbian policy and assertions that the UN rather than NATO was the appropriate international body for such conflicts and that conflicts should be settled by negotiation rather than force.

13. At least that was one way to read the calculated coolness, snubs, and lectures that humiliated President Carter on a visit to Mexico. Carter had opened his visit with surprisingly undiplomatic remarks. The Mexican government, meanwhile, argued that it merely spoke frankly, and that the stunned U.S. reaction reflected persisting "gringo" colonial attitudes.

14. On occasion Mexico appeared so sympathetic to guerrillas that Latin American nations denounced Mexican interventionism. Usually, however, Mexico called for restraint, dialogue, and compromise.

15. Ojeda (1977: 33) claimed that jarring assertiveness may ironically have led to "much more dependence on the exterior," thereby illustrating limits on zealous independence.

16. Aguayo 1991 and Green 1977: 1–9. The main qualification to the principle of holding foreign influence at bay arose when the United States was too "close" or vital to Mexican development to be marginalized or when the United States saw its own national interest at stake. Deference to the superpower helps explain why Mexico's international relationships within Latin America and beyond were often more ceremonial than important. But affairs beyond the vital aspects of the U.S.-Mexico relationship allowed assertiveness. This explains how Mexico could have (until recently) a UN voting record quite at odds with U.S. votes.

17. In other cases the boost from opposing U.S. policy is sought when government popularity is low for domestic reasons (as when Echeverría entered office in the aftermath of the domestic violence of 1968).

18. Another example: López Portillo refused to attend the 1977 signing of the Panama Canal treaty, protesting its inadequate protection of national sovereignty and the attendance of South American dictators. The general foreign-domestic policy paradox was captured in the satirical comic book *Los Agachados* (March 17, 1976). In the book a Mexican leader pontificates that Mexico will resume diplomatic relations with Spain (then under dictator Francisco Franco) only when democracy is established, to which the Spanish general replies: "In Mexico." In fact, Spain became democratic in the late 1970s, much earlier than Mexico.

19. López Mateos and Echeverría fit Cuba policy into their overall leftist or populist claims. López Portillo used Cuba policy to offset his usually conservative posture at home.

20. *Proceso* (December 12, 1988). Castro's ties to Mexico date from the legendary time he (and Che Guevara) spent in Mexico preparing their revolutionary takeover; they were not, however, official guests. For an account of Mexico's Cuba policy during the volatile first decade of Castro's rule, see Pellicer de Brody 1972b. Similarly, official Mexican relations with the Soviet Union bolstered legitimacy while undermining Mexico's communists.

21. For example, when Cuban refugees arrived in 1993, Mexican plans to deport them led to pressure from Miami's Cuban exiles at a time when Mexico wanted Florida's support for the passage of NAFTA (Covarrubias Velasco 1994). President Salinas eventually turned a deaf ear to Castro and met with Cuban exile leaders (Baloyra 1995: 221).

22. Only later, in the face of increased civil strife, economic catastrophes, and social decay, would many Mexican political leaders come to see that Mexico needed to change fundamentally in order to be stable. Even then some resisted the idea that this change must involve either democratization or the sort of resource redistribution advocated by insurgents in Central America.

23. This threat has been a reason, perhaps sometimes a pretext, to modernize

Mexico's military and allow it an expanded role in national security issues, thus arguably jeopardizing the civilian control that has been a pillar of Mexican development.

24. When the Mexican Left complained about the coziness of Nicaraguan leftists with Mexico's conservative government, Nicaraguan revolutionary leader Daniel Ortega responded even more sternly than Castro: if the Mexican Left chose to play at silly electoral politics and failed to realize that the only true change comes through armed struggle, it would have to live with the consequences.

25. Support for the Salvadoran guerrillas declined once the government showed electoral strength and the guerrillas showed military weakness. And Mexico never supported the guerrillas in Guatemala, where they were comparatively weak; instead, it tolerated Guatemalan army incursions into Mexico. Subsequently, to the delight of the Guatemalan government and dismay of the guerrillas, Mexico moved refugee camps away from the border. By 1993, Mexico worked with the "Group of Friends" to promote the Guatemalan peace process. Mexico's role in the Contadora peace process (with Panama, Venezuela, and Colombia) also showed moderation, irking both gringos and Sandinistas. In general, by the mid-1980s Mexico could again be seen as more of a passive than assertive middle-range international actor (Jauberth et al. 1992). Also on Mexico's Central American policy for domestic ends, see Ojeda 1985 and Levy 1986b: 235–64.

26. See Zebadúa 1994a. If avoiding economic interactions (in the name of sovereignty) leads to national weakness, it could undermine sovereignty.

27. See, for example, Gereffi 1996: 100.

28. Mexican assertiveness was possible when the Vietnam War, the Watergate scandal, and economic challenges from Japan and Western Europe plagued its neighbor. As pundits proclaimed a transformation from a bipolar world headed by the United States and the U.S.S.R to a multipolar one, the Mexican government spoke hopefully of the "activism of middle-range powers" and of breaking fatalistic attitudes of dependence.

29. See Garza Elizondo 1994.

30. The U.S.-led international imperative is acknowledged not just by neoliberals but by some nationalist figures within the PRI and even the moderate Left. On the new concept of national security, see Bagley and Aguayo 1993, and for an expansive critical view, see Rochlin 1997. At the same time, Mexican democrats credibly argue that Mexican security and strength in its foreign dealings are enhanced to the extent that Mexico strengthens its democracy and therefore its legitimacy. Many commentators noted how the 1997 elections, with their peaceful leftist victories, fortified stability, counteracting Mexico's otherwise increasing weakness in its dealings with the United States (and boosting the Mexican stock market).

31. That dollar transactions are reality for many businesses but not when it comes to workers' pay illustrates the gulf between internationalizing Mexico and marginalized Mexico. Polls show Mexican support for dollar transactions, once more indicating that anti-U.S. sentiment is often exaggerated and that many Mexicans "want in" and (considering that other Latin American countries have pondered or even adopted "dollarization") that Mexican exceptionalism further

declines. However, dropping the peso for the dollar appears unlikely unless provoked by further crisis; opponents see such a change as a loss of sovereignty or fear that Mexican economic policy makers could get lazy and rely on their U.S. counterparts to impose financial discipline. Another possibility is the substitution of a monetary council for the Bank of Mexico, a change that could in effect sacrifice Mexican handling of its currency in favor of tying it to the dollar.

32. Both U.S. parties have made unpopular appointments. The first President Bush appointed as the U.S. ambassador to Mexico John Negroponte, who was seen in Mexico as a hard-liner whose selection stigmatized Mexico as a security problem. Clinton's appointment of a former stock market president, James Jones, might also have qualified as unsympathetic except that it could be seen as a signal of U.S. confidence in Mexico's new policy of business development. However, Clinton's nomination of William Weld as Jones's successor showed that many U.S. politicians cared little about pleasing Mexico: despite Mexican support, Weld was blocked by U.S. conservatives for domestic political reasons, amid loud and insulting complaints about corruption in Mexico, and the ambassadorship remained vacant for more than a year.

Earlier, Democratic President Carter had appointed an ex-governor with little background pertinent to Mexico; after the ambassador's tenure — and then an extended vacancy — the first Mexican-American was appointed but was regarded as hostile by many Mexican foreign policy makers. Republican conservative President Reagan then appointed John Gavin, an ex-actor (like the president), who was greeted with considerable dismay and ridicule, although his mother was Mexican and he was fluent in Spanish and had some pertinent educational and diplomatic experience; Gavin undiplomatically raised questions about Mexican political stability and stirred dissatisfaction. (Ironically, Gavin was vilified in the early 1980s for advocating Mexican entry to GATT and a North American common market — a sign of how much Mexico's foreign policy has changed since the Gavin years.) With successor Charles Pilliod, an ex-businessman, controversy diminished.

33. Carr 1996: 226–27. At the height of the Cold War, mainstream U.S. unions favored Mexico's government-controlled unions but now relations are more diverse, as we discuss in Chapter 7.

34. Leftist candidates seek to allay foreign concerns by meeting with businessmen and visiting the U.S. Congress (Castañeda 1994: 69). Cuauhtémoc Cárdenas looks northward as no prior leader of the Left did; if he does so with personal reticence, the underlying dynamic that compels him to do so is forceful, and future leftist leaders may plunge into the act more vigorously. A further sign of Mexico's and the Left's new openness to U.S. influence is the Mexican legislature's project for receiving technical assistance on legislative practice. Under the heading of strange bedfellows comes the leftist PRD's provision to ultraconservative U.S. legislator Jesse Helms of information he could use, as head of the Senate Foreign Affairs Committee, to undermine causes pursued by the Mexican government. The Left's foray northward is dangerous, in that the Right is usually in a stronger position to play the U.S. card. The Left has allies in NGO and intellectual circles but the Right has more powerful allies.

35. Prior to the 1994 elections, PRI candidate Luis Donaldo Colosio rejected the idea of foreign observers as an intrusion, but soon a limping regime needed

the foreign stamp of legitimacy. Molinar Horcasitas (1996: 35) writes that the government feared leaving the task to more radical individual scholars or "tourists." So it allowed "foreign visitors" while denying access to "foreign observers." Sensitivity about international monitoring remains but the PAN and the PRD have claimed there is insufficient observation in rural areas.

36. Chabat 1989: 84.

37. On Mexican lobbying in Washington, D.C., see Dresser 1993.

38. Mexicans have (with historical justification) perceived a threat to national security when they are disunited on foreign policy issues (Rico 1989: 120). The perception obviously concerned the United States above all. Mexicans feared direct U.S. intervention as well as the peril of sitting next to a nuclear power that could get involved in deadly conflict. U.S. citizens almost never think of their country as a national security threat to Mexico, but Mexicans do. By the same token, Mexicans do not see Mexico as a security threat to the United States, but some U.S. policy makers have repeatedly perceived such a threat from Mexico's economic deterioration or potential political instability. Bailey and Aguayo 1996 note a weakening of Mexico's national unity–national security viewpoint, however. Although Mexicans continue to worry about U.S. threats to national security, they are less focused on them and more focused on building ties that bolster development.

Another view is that unity traditionally has come from a degree of Mexican xenophobia. Like other political matters that get into cultural and psychological territory, this one is sensitive, hard to prove, and easy to exaggerate as a way to belittle Mexico. On the other hand, given Mexican-U.S. history and the contemporary reality of asymmetry, a degree of xenophobia, like a fear of disunity, might well be expected. By the same token, expanding education, development, and international contact should in the long run diminish xenophobia. A less debatable reason for Mexico's relative unity on foreign policy has been the authoritarian noncompetitiveness of the domestic political system. This reason has obviously declined significantly.

39. Even the Reagan administration, which largely preceded Mexico's new policy and which was generally hard line in foreign policy, split on how to react to Mexican assertiveness and was mostly tolerant. Some right-wingers in the Republican Party, the CIA, the National Security Council, and federal drug agencies portrayed Mexican policies as deeply threatening to U.S. interests and favored a hard line against independence in Mexican foreign policy. The hard line included pressure for changes in Mexico's development model (toward democracy in some formulations and toward a more open market economy in all). Though sympathetic to this position, Reagan on balance upheld the traditional guidepost of U.S. policy toward Mexico: bilateral differences are tolerable as long as Mexico maintains a stable regime that preserves peace, trade, and investment (Castañeda 1985–86: 287–303). The Reagan administration distanced itself from Senator Jesse Helms's punitive approach, extended aid, and even sporadically praised Mexico's regional peace-making efforts.

40. A *New York Times* story ranked relations as at the "lowest point in years." Julia Preston, "U.S. Trying to Smooth Mexico's Path," *New York Times,* April 20, 1997. To some it is the best of times; to others, the worst of times.

41. On Congress, see Schoultz 1989: 43. Even in leftist U.S. grassroots organizations, one sees a tendency to treat Mexico more as a problem than a source of ideas, and a "striking asymmetry" exists as initiatives flow north to south (Carr 1996: 210).

42. See Inglehart, Nevitte, and Basáñez 1996. The authors downplay U.S. dominance as they emphasize a modernization and North Americanization in which Canada may be something of a leader. However, if one focuses on the Mexico-U.S. pair, it is hard to escape the view that the major secular changes mostly involve Mexican shifts toward U.S. norms of capitalism, social authority, and democracy. The growth of Mexico's nonprofit sector also fits the notion of convergence; a 1992 amendment to Mexico's tax laws draws on U.S. definitions and provisions, thereby further facilitating cooperation between Mexican and U.S. NGOs.

43. Garza Elizondo 1994: 540. See also Roett 1991.

44. Of course, exceptions have qualified the "friend of all" approach. Mexico has even refused to grant diplomatic recognition to some states, as noted earlier. In recent years Mexico has been more selective and limited in offering asylum. More generally, the vagueness of such platitudinous principles has given Mexico's president great flexibility. He has been able to justify almost any foreign policy by reference to some consecrated principle. Universalism provided a sure rationale for ignoring the U.S.-led boycott of the 1980 Moscow Olympics in the aftermath of the Soviet invasion of Afghanistan, but had Mexico wished to boycott, it could have claimed to be defending Afghanistan's national sovereignty.

45. Even Salinas continued to oppose U.S. ideas for inter-American defense treaties.

46. In the 1970s and 1980s, when Mexico exercised its maximum assertiveness, this defensive concern remained a major reason for vigorous criticism of U.S. military intervention in Nicaragua and El Salvador. Mexico also opposed Guatemalan moves to assert its territorial claims over tiny Belize, independent from Great Britain only since 1981. Mexico itself had territorial claims in Belize, to the point that hostilities with Guatemala seemed possible in the mid-1970s, but later renounced its claims as inconsistent with nonintervention and self-determination.

47. Whereas prior deviations from noncriticism tended to buttress leftist foreign policy, Zedillo would denounce leftist policy (as when he criticized the political economic policy in the Brazilian state of Minas Gerais while defending the policy of President Fernando Henrique Cardoso). Chile is the Latin American leader in neoliberal reform. Mexico's admiration for Chile's internationally oriented capitalist reforms contrasted to Echeverría's praise of Chile's prior socialist experiment.

48. Mabire 1994.

49. Mexico and Canada acted together at important junctures during the Central American conflicts. They joined again in the mid-1990s, with OAS backing, to oppose the U.S. Helms-Burton trade restrictions against countries trading with Cuba.

50. The original quotation from Trudeau appeared in *U.S. News and World Report*, March 9, 1981, cited in Castro 1994, and expanded in www.mapleleaf

web.com/features/economy/us-canada/sleeping-elephant.html. Whereas unity between López Portillo and Trudeau represented the brief peak of Mexico-Canada cooperation with an anti-U.S. policy focus, the new and more substantial Mexico-Canada contact has a pro-U.S. policy focus. And yet, Canadian Prime Minister Jean Chrétien repeated the same sentiment in a 2003 speech in Mexico: "Now, we are two mice." See www.wsws.org/articles/2003/mar2003/chre-m04 _prn.shtml.

51. Relations with Israel also highlight the evolution of Mexican foreign policy. For decades relations were friendly but limited. Under Echeverría, Mexico supported a UN resolution equating Zionism with racism. Both the vote and Mexico's subsequent retreat from it discredited Mexico and marked an unprecedented and unrepeated deviation from friendly relations. Mexican sales of oil have helped carry relations with Israel to greater heights than ever before. Echeverría wanted Mexico to identify more with Arab countries, but contemporary Mexico looks more to democratic and developed Israel.

52. In Eastern and Central Europe the often-troubled drive for democracy in former communist countries presents parallels for a Mexico also trying to make a transition from decades of undemocratic stability; Western Europe obviously presents more substantial democratic models.

53. At what point does closeness slip into integration? In one Marx Brothers' routine the rich divorcée judges a wooing Groucho's intentions by the passion of his embrace. "Closer, closer," she implores. "If I get any closer," Groucho observes, "I'll be behind you."

CHAPTER SEVEN

1. Pastor and Castañeda (1988: 139) make "disproportionate influence" thematic to their study, pointing out that what is a minor bureaucratic decision in the United States may hit Mexico hard, whereas Mexico still has trouble getting its neighbor's ear. Since publication of their book, however, Mexico has become more visible on the U.S. agenda.

2. Internationalization contributes to the decline of Mexican exceptionalism and arguably to declining exceptionalism in the bilateral relationship. Scholarship on the bilateral relationship is increasingly informed by research done on a more inclusive geographical scale. In turn, works specifically on Mexico-U.S. relations have informed the wider literature on drugs, migration, and trade.

3. At some points Mexico may have accounted for 95 percent of the U.S. marijuana market (Reuter and Ronfeldt 1992: 91–94). Another good English-language overview of the bilateral drug problem is Toro 1995.

4. For example, President Richard Nixon's Operation Intercept in 1969, with its onerous border searches, angered Mexicans and hurt the nation economically, slowing tourism and border trade and showing the asymmetry of bilateral power. Within days, however, a less offensive substitute was put in place. By the mid-1970s the bilateral Operation Condor brought Mexico's military and judicial forces into action in combination with U.S. money and reconnaissance technology.

5. This statement applies mainly to the U.S. side. Mexicans tend to be more

resigned (be that realism or fatalism or both) to the intractable aspects of the problem.

6. Toro 1995: 39.

7. Drugs like cocaine, though much more expensive than alcohol, are within the purchasing power of many citizens in a rich country, and others put themselves into the market by engaging in profitable crime. On the Mexico-U.S. contrast in use, see ibid.: 47.

8. Andreas (1998) notes the general phenomenon, for which both drugs and migration offer examples, of how free trade paradoxically increases the need for government law enforcement.

9. In Operation Green Air, for example, U.S. agents uncovered a unique marijuana smuggling operation that exclusively used FedEx. After bribing FedEx employees to accept packages containing marijuana and apply false labels, the drug suppliers shipped their product via regular FedEx planes with no questions asked. As the DEA reported, with unaccustomed humor, "like the majority of the shipments handled by FedEx, the illegal packages were picked up by 4 p.m. and delivered by 10 a.m. the next day." http://www.usdoj.gov/dea/major/greenair .htm. If, for example, U.S. tariffs on legal goods like vegetables have hitherto increased the incentives for Mexican farmers to cultivate drugs, now growing the legal products may make more sense. Policy makers will still have to confront two problems, however: drugs will likely remain more lucrative, and shortages of credit make it difficult for farmers to switch to legal crops (whereas, for drug production, cartels often provide credit at little or no interest).

10. Budget data (Pastor and Castañeda 1988: 267) do not support charges by Mexicans and U.S. liberals that U.S. government efforts concentrate on policing more than prevention, but the U.S. inability to handle its drug problem despite its two-pronged effort further suggests how deeply rooted its problem is.

11. Also misleading is the impression that, while drug traffic has perpetrators on both sides, only one government has resolved to confront the problem; this overlooks both the limits on U.S. resolve and the stiffening of Mexican resolve.

12. Reuter and Ronfeldt 1992: 90 and Toro 1995: 67.

13. See, for example, Fernando Benítez, "El flagelo de las drogas," *La Jornada,* January 21, 1996. In another sense, however, the visibility of Mexican efforts comes partly because Mexican corrective action must focus on government, whereas U.S. corrective action must more diffusely include consumers. In 1996, Mexico fired seven hundred federal police at once.

14. Toro 1995: 64. Other manifestations of increased U.S. influence are less blatant but not necessarily less potent than military measures. As the attorney general becomes an increasingly important Mexican post that must earn U.S. government support, de la Madrid, Salinas, and Zedillo all appointed figures that were seen as independent of the government; for example, Salinas named a respected scholar who had headed the commission on human rights and publicly criticized the attorney general's office, while Zedillo named as his first attorney general an opposition party member.

15. In the 1996 case Mexico chose to accept the U.S. interpretation that the suspect was by birth a U.S. citizen; within Mexico the act was widely seen as a

sellout of national sovereignty. On the other extreme Mexican officials strongly protested Operation Casablanca in 1998. They also protested the 1990 kidnapping of a Mexican citizen within Mexico by the U.S. DEA, an action later upheld by the U.S. Supreme Court. The suspect was accused of participating in the 1985 murder of a U.S. DEA agent inside Mexico; rancor for that murder ran deep, and U.S. officials blamed Mexican government officials for protecting the perpetrators. All bilateral drug programs were suspended, but they were almost immediately reinstated as President Bush assured Mexico that there would be no further such kidnappings. Though a federal judge later dismissed the case for lack of evidence, freeing the suspect to return to Mexico, the legal precedent remains a potential source of future conflict. Bilateral flare-ups continue but so do the quick damage control and accommodation between administrations, reflecting how close the bilateral relationship has become at the official level.

16. http://www.usdoj.gov/dea/major/trifecta/index.html.

17. See, for example, Weintraub 1990: 175. Individual congressional representatives get to advertise popular votes without facing the responsibility for the bilateral consequences because they know the president will probably overrule them. Meanwhile, however, the administration can further pressure Mexico by portraying its own proposals as the minimum to prevent victory by U.S. hard-liners. This is an ironic echo of the way Mexican administrations have historically bargained bilaterally by citing the restraining force of Mexican public opinion. A key difference is that the Mexican ploy helped offset asymmetry, whereas the U.S. ploy reinforces it.

18. On drugs as a rare bilateral issue that hurts the United States much more than Mexico, see Pastor and Castañeda 1988: 242–50. Recently, however, the institutional threat posed to Mexico by drug trafficking has increased significantly, as has domestic (Mexican) drug use.

19. Mexico's health ministry reported a four-fold increase among twelve- to nineteen-year-olds in just a six-year period. The DEA now estimates that cocaine has overtaken marijuana as the drug of choice among young Mexicans who use drugs. Though still relatively few, at 5 percent of the Mexican population, the number of Mexican cocaine users has grown by 500 percent since 1991. www.usdoj.gov/dea.

20. Reuter and Ronfeldt (1992: 132) distinguish Mexico from the most drug-damaged South American countries as recently as the late 1980s, but on the increased penetration of drugs into Mexico's political system, see Lupsha 1994. Speculation about the cardinal's assassination in 1993 suggests that his murder might have been retaliation for church attempts to take formal title of land it had previously entrusted to other hands, including drug hands, before the 1991 constitutional change once again allowed outright church ownership.

21. This remarkable statement appears in an internal military document that was leaked; Camp 1999a: 13–14.

22. While the military role can negatively affect Mexican politics and society, so Mexican politics and society can negatively affect the military. There is the temptation for civilians to turn loose military force against opponents and the temptation for certain military leaders or units to side with certain political factions, a problem that has haunted democracies elsewhere in Latin America.

23. These estimates come from the U.S government as well as many scholars. Other scholars would put the total figure of unauthorized migrants moderately lower. Figures typically exclude children born in the United States to the unauthorized (since, under the U.S. Constitution, these children are U.S. citizens). Mexicans account for a much higher proportion of the unauthorized than of the legal migrants. According to estimates based on the 2000 U.S. census, unauthorized migration is increasingly Mexican: of those who entered illegally between 1990 and 1999, nearly 80 percent were Mexican. But unauthorized migrants account for only about a third of the Mexican-born U.S. population and a tenth of the Mexican-origin population. Most Mexicans who gain legal entry do so because they have family members already in the United States. See Bean et al. 1998: 80, Baker, Cushing, and Haynes 1997: 151, Gelbard and Carter 1997: 117; Freeman and Bean 1997: 24, and Arroyo, de León Arias, and Valenzuela 1991: 51. Martin (1996: 147) refers to 1–3 million seasonal workers. Three valuable, detailed books on migration are Bean ed. 1997, Suárez-Orozco ed. 1998, and Binational Commission 1998.

24. http://www.inegi.gob.mx.

25. However, the great majority of Mexican immigrants live in a few states, led easily by California and then Texas, with smaller populations in Illinois and New York. See Greenwood and Tienda 1998, Lowenthal and Burgess 1993, and McCarthy and Vernez 1997. On circularity and migratory careers, see Bustamante et al. 1998; this and other studies in Bean et al. 1998 also show the different geographical and employment patterns of those who come from different parts of Mexico.

26. The issue was thrust before the U.S. public when Clinton appointments for high office were found to have employed nannies or housekeepers who lacked legal documentation. Should blame fall on meagerly paid Mexicans or on wealthy and middle-class U.S. families trying to avoid paying legal wages and benefits for their childcare, housecleaning, and handiwork?

27. Of course, U.S. migration is comparatively small and does not violate Mexican law. Its future would be jeopardized by Mexican social, economic, or political instability. Underscoring the naturalness of migration where economic differences and geographical proximity mix is the reality of heavy migration in contemporary Europe; beyond legal guestworker programs, many emigrate from less developed nations to find jobs in capital-intensive societies that demand cheap labor not legally entitled to costly social services. See Cornelius, Martin, and Hollifield 1994.

28. The migration of Central Americans into Mexico reinforces the idea of natural migration in the face of economic disparities in geographically contiguous areas, though the Central American flow has also had much to do with political repression. Figures reach into the hundreds of thousands. The idea of natural migration supports the Mexican case against U.S. finger-pointing. But the Mexican government treats the migrants as a problem, draining scarce public resources and creating tension where poor Mexicans resent migrants' competition for resources and jobs. Moreover, the concentration of Guatemalan Mayas in the largely Mayan state of Chiapas raises government fears of an ethnic challenge to Mexico's dominant identity (Nash 1995). So the Mexican government

has engaged in hard-line policies, including expulsion of about eighty-five hundred migrants in some years (e.g., 1989 and 1995), more in others (e.g., 1990). Along with employers and other citizens, it also engages in human rights violations. International criticism of these violations hurts Mexico's already shaky legitimacy. Criticism also comes from Mexico's increasingly democratic society, including television reporting and statements from the church. Mexican human rights violations against migrants are sometimes depicted as fitting a general authoritarianism as well as a subordination to U.S. pressures to beat back a flow that often ends up heading through Mexico to the United States (Cabildo 1996).

29. See Smith 2000: 130 on the flow depending more on the U.S. than the Mexican economy. Sometimes, however, Mexicans migrate northward even when the U.S. economy slows, an indication of the strength of push factors (Pastor and Castañeda 1988: 350). On the lack of employment, see Roberts and Escobar 1997: 48–62. On major wage differentials between the two countries, see Díaz-Briquets and Weintraub 1991; on increased income in Mexico, see Zahniser and Greenwood 1998. Arroyo, de León, and Valenzuela (1991: 51–53) find that it is difficult to slow the migration even when Mexico enjoys short-term growth, because the existence of migration networks with contacts in the United States tends to reduce and stabilize the cost of migration as well as limit the risks. The border wage gap is smaller than the general binational gap, but even it is often put at between 4 to 1 and 8 to 1.

30. Migration from rural areas or small towns to large cities within Mexico often aggravates Mexico's urban problems.

31. See Suárez-Orozco 1998 and U.S. Census data, available at www.census .gov. Particular school districts can rather suddenly have a major Mexican-American population.

32. Ibid.

33. http://www.mexidata.info/id317.html. See also Martin 1996: 145 on the 10 percent figure. The amount of remittances has been steadily increasing. Lozano (1998: 1210–11), for instance, finds that remittances may have run close to $3.5 billion in 1995, contrasted to roughly $2 billion in 1990. On the difficulty of gauging migration's impact on Mexico, see Verduzco and Unger 1998.

34. Migrants often suffer horrible abuse from "coyotes" who promise to guide their difficult passage across the border to safety and employment. Illegal by Mexican law, coyotes are used by most migrants without family contacts and are further examples of the limits of law enforcement where economic incentives are strong. See López 1998: 965–74.

35. Improved enforcement at traditional crossing points in San Diego and El Paso has shifted migrant traffic into the more dangerous and unpatrolled desert regions. Abandoned by their guides, or simply unprepared for the difficulty of the trek, many die of thirst and heat exhaustion. In 2003, 340 Mexicans are known to have died attempting to cross the border. See http://usinfo.state.gov/wh/ Archive/2004.

36. Good news about acceptance must be weighed against public opinion polls showing increased U.S. concern over immigration when the economy is weak. For California, data on subsequent generations appear in Hayes-Bautista 1993: 134–41, Burgess and Lowenthal 1993: 265, and McCarthy and Vernez

1997. For a personal account of migrant life in the United States, see Hart 1997; also see Gutiérrez 1996.

37. On the cycle, see Jaime Martínez, "Migración y soberanía," *La Jornada*, April 3, 1997.

38. Martin 1997: 96. On projections, see Weintraub 1990: 192.

39. See Rosenfeld and Tienda (1997), who see probable net benefit to the U.S. economy; also on net benefit, see Muller and Espenshade 1985. Mexicans tend to see the United States rather than Mexico as the major beneficiary of migration, and the Mexican government wants recognition of the contribution of Mexican migrants to the U.S. economy (Weintraub et al. 1998: 456–63).

40. A review of fifteen studies of the fiscal impact finds a net negative impact of immigration, though there is great variation in methods and findings (including whether the focus is on all immigrant groups, just Mexicans, just unauthorized migrants, etc.) as well as important exceptions. Most studies now find immigrants using more in services than they pay in taxes, particularly at the state level; some find they are now at least as likely as citizens to use public services. See Baker, Cushing, and Haynes 1997: 145–72. The *Mexico–United States Binational Migration Study 1998* includes several studies that find such negative impacts alongside positive ones. Also on economic and social effects, see McCarthy and Vernez 1997.

41. See Maciel and Herrera-Sobek 1998 on culture; on crime, see Wolf 1988. Some negative effects are unintended and not the fault of migration or migrant culture. For example, when Castañeda (1993) writes of the "de-democratization" of California, he refers to the political impact of a growing population unable — as noncitizens — to vote or participate politically, creating massive political inequality.

42. Pastor and Castañeda 1988: 355–62.

43. On the Black perception of job competition, see Burgess and Lowenthal 1993: 269, though they come out on the side of those who find the perception unfounded. A RAND study of immigration in California, however, finds that the population most negatively affected by competition with Mexican migrants was African-Americans, though the overall impact remained relatively minor. See McCarthy and Vernez 1997.

44. See de la Garza and DeSipio 1998: 408–16. Mexican-Americans were initially split on Proposition 187. They wound up voting heavily against it because they perceived that the promoters played on anti-Mexican sentiment. Their initial split shows that they did not simply follow the Mexican government's position. Mexico cannot always count on Mexican-American support to offset its weakened negotiating power in bilateral relations. Some other U.S. ethnic groups have shown greater ability to mobilize for or against the government of the ancestral homeland.

45. Clinton backed a bill requiring deportation of anyone illegally using public services, even those as minimal as English classes. Before subsequent legislation remedied some pernicious effects, the bill facilitated the deportation of some who had lived in the United States for years. Also troubling were proposals to give the INS near immunity from charges of abuses (only the Supreme Court could enjoin the INS from continuing illegal practices). In the face of horrifying

accounts of migrants getting beaten, this immunity struck some observers as more typical of Mexican rather than U.S. governmental contempt for the rule of law and accountability. The campaigning president also proudly emphasized that his Army Corps of Engineers was busy constructing more steel fence on the border. Clinton went against public opinion to provide a massive rescue loan for Mexico, but that was also more of a one-shot (or occasional) issue compared with migration. Moreover, he deemed it (like NAFTA) vital for key U.S. economic interests.

46. See, for example, Durand and Massey 1992: 22.

47. www.uscis.gov/graphhics/shared/aboutus/statistics/2003Yearbook.pdf.

48. The INS reports a jump in the number of "illegal aliens" it expelled from the United States, from 42,471 in 1993 to 172,312 in 1998, and attributes its success in part to a budget that jumped from $1.5 billion to $4 billion in the same period. Of course, history teaches that many migrants caught and expelled reappear, along with new migrants (Suárez-Orozco 1998).

49. See Castañeda 1993, including a call for emulating those European countries that allow migrants to vote in their host countries' elections.

50. Díaz-Briquets and Weintraub 1991 (vol. 2) conclude that while no good alternative short of major economic development in Mexico will greatly reduce migration, reducing bilateral income differentials has an effect. The same would hold for increased employment and decreased population growth in Mexico. Arroyo, de León Arias, and Valenzuela (1991: 74) suggest greater credit, savings, and development policy for regional hubs within Mexico. But Smith 2000: 121 notes that U.S. and Mexican demographics suggest a major migration over the next thirty years. President Fox sees mutual opportunity in this. On the U.S. public's rejection of harsh steps, see Espenshade and Belanger 1997.

51. An example here is Bank of America, which has focused on selling banking services to unauthorized migrants in particular (checking accounts, wire transfer capability, etc.). Bank of America has also been at the forefront of efforts to get the U.S. government to accept the "consular identification card" (*matricula consular*), issued by Mexican authorities, as valid proof of identity in the United States.

52. www.world-tourism.org; http://datatur.sectur.gob.mx.

53. http://datatur.sectur.gob.mx.

54. Needler (1995: 113) puts the Mexican share of U.S. tourist income at one-fourth.

55. See Rochlin 1997: 14 on "sex tourism." Mexican laws on prostitution are restrictive but not strictly enforced.

56. By 1987, 100 percent of rooms in the luxury "Gran Turismo" category and 71 percent of rooms at or above the five-star ranking were linked to foreign chains. In 1991, the largest five hotel chains in Mexico included those linked to Holiday Inn (at number one), Sheraton, and Best Western. Clancy 2001: 141.

57. These sites might rely on abundant semiskilled and unskilled labor, especially because it is cheaper to create jobs in smaller resorts. See Hiernaux and Rodríguez Woog 1991. The government's case for development of large sites is that they have a bigger net impact and can be monitored more easily.

58. Or some Mexicans may understandably resent tourists who seem un-

interested in Mexican reality, though it seems harsh to fault a tourist whose abiding aim is fun and relaxation.

59. Images of Mexican dependence are exaggerated in that many being counted as U.S. tourists to Mexico — by 2002 estimates, about 31 percent — are actually Mexicans returning to visit family or favorite destinations. http://datatur.sectur.gob.mx.

60. For additional sources on trade and NAFTA, not directly cited below, see Baer and Weintraub 1994, Blank and Haar 1998, Hoebing, Weintraub, and Baer 1996, Mayer 1998, Grinspun and Cameron 1993, and Orme 1996.

61. von Bertrab 1997: xiii.

62. Ibid.: 39.

63. Ibid.: xiv.

64. One of the issues that would have galvanized even PRI opposition was high on the U.S. wish list: privatization of the state-owned oil industry. Mexican negotiators successfully resisted pressure for transfer of assets to the private sector. Yet they opened the door to U.S. participation by allowing subcontracting to foreign companies and committing to an eventual privatization of subsidiary industries, like petrochemicals.

65. For discussion of legislative politics in Mexico and the United States, see Pastor and Fernández de Castro 1998.

66. NAFTA covers not only manufacturing but also agriculture and services, especially financial services, transportation, and telecommunications.

67. While only 41 percent of U.S. exports to Mexico were tariff free from the first day of NAFTA, nearly 80 percent of Mexican exports to the United States faced no tariff at this time. An additional 20 percent of Mexican tariff reductions would be made five years into the agreement (that is, in 1999), and almost 40 percent would wait ten years. The goal of moving Mexicans into more productive and efficient sectors of the economy will take time. By delaying implementation, both sides hoped to limit the possibility of political unrest.

68. There are separate committees and subcommittees for transportation, financial services, telecommunications, phytosanitary measures, and so on; working groups deal with matters involving rules of origin, standards, and competition.

69. The latter gave foreign companies some assurance that they would retain control over the technology involved in direct investment in Mexico. The regulatory reforms simply reduced the costs associated with investment.

70. In contrast to the previous law, which limited foreign investment to 49 percent in many sectors unless expressly authorized, approval of majority ownership for most foreign investments has become automatic and not subject to review. Review is still required for acquisition of Mexican companies worth more than $25 million; in 2004 the threshold increases to $150 million.

71. Other strategic activities include the postal service, currency minting, and operation of ports and airports. For other types of services foreign investment was limited to 49 percent of stock until January 1, 2001. Then, foreign investors may own up to 51 percent of services, including development banks, credit unions, retail gasoline, television (except cable), and domestic land transportation of passengers. In 2004 these areas will open to 100 percent foreign capital.

72. www.cbo.gov; Jamar and Young 1999: 27–28.

73. In 1980, before Mexico's economic crisis, Mexico exported $12.5 billion to the United States and imported $15.1 billion. By 1993, the last pre-NAFTA year, exports to the United States had increased to $43.1 billion and imports to $46.5 billion. After four full years of NAFTA, exports to the United States had risen to $103.1 billion and imports to $93.1 billion. Levy and Székely 1987: 204; Banco de Información Económica, data available on-line at dgcnesyp.inegi .gob.mx. Recent figures are taken from the Congressional Budget Office's report on "NAFTA at Ten" (available at www.cbo.gov), but are broadly consistent with most estimates.

74. Hornbeck 2004: 2. However, critics legitimately complain that crediting overall "trade volume" to NAFTA overlooks many important sources of increasing (or decreasing) trade, such as world market conditions. And no matter what governments decide, companies make their own cost calculations, which may lead them to relocate despite the absence of a trading agreement or not to relocate despite its existence.

75. For example, according to the U.S. Trade Commission, 60 percent of Mexican exports to the United States in 2001 were machinery and vehicles, mostly produced in cooperation with foreign companies. See www.usembassy -mexico.gov/eNAFTA_figures.htm.

76. www.imf.org.

77. After an initial increase in dependence on the United States for imports (up to 74 percent in 1998), U.S. imports have fallen back to their historic level. The most significant new source of imports for Mexico is China, which went from less than 1 percent of imports in 1993 to over 5 percent of imports in 2003. Under NAFTA rules, Canada also became a more popular market, but increased to only 1.7 percent of Mexican exports and 2.2 percent of imports. http://economia-snci.gob.mex.

78. In 1980, Mexico accounted for 3.7 percent of total U.S. imports; by 2001, it supplied 11.8 percent of U.S. imports. Likewise, the share of U.S. exports going to Mexico rose from 4.6 percent in 1986 to 11.8 percent by the end of 2001. www.cbo.gov; Levy and Székely 1987: 204 and Espinosa and Noyola 1997: 27

79. Even imports — which fell for Mexico overall in 1995 — fell significantly less (2.1 percent) for NAFTA partners, compared with 25 percent declines in imports from Japan and the European Union. Weintraub 1997: 31.

80. Santiso 1999: 50.

81. In 1980 $1.1 billion in U.S. foreign direct investment flowed into Mexico; in 1995 — a recession year — $4.3 billion flowed in. By the end of the second quarter of 1996, more than twice that amount had come in. Jamar and Young 1999: 30. www.economia.gob.mx.

82. Ibid.: 30; Banco de Información Económica, data available on-line at dgcnesyp.inegi.gob.mx; SALA 1998: 883.

83. Estimates for annual investment are similar, though there was a slight dip in 2003 in new U.S. investment. www.economia.gob.mx.

84. The Mexican government reached this figure by counting the seven hundred thousand jobs that resulted from new foreign direct investment and one million jobs "connected" to growth in exports.

85. Initial reports claimed that total U.S. jobs connected to exports to Mexico grew almost a million in 1998, up from 350,000 in 1993. (Jamar and Young 1999: 30) However, more recent reports by the Congressional Research Service suggest a net gain of less than 300,000 jobs in ten years. Hornbeck 2004: 4.

86. Until 2000, for example, Mexico's labor costs per person, per hour (a common index of competitiveness) were nearly 50 percent lower than in Chile; since then, costs have been higher in Mexico, and the gap is growing. http://dgcnesyp.inegi .gob.mx.

87. For a summary of these efforts, see Grayson 1998 and von Bertrab 1997.

88. After this debate, in which Perot came across as ill informed and inconsistent, U.S. public opinion began to swing more toward NAFTA.

89. Its efforts in this regard were less successful. The Hispanic community was divided over NAFTA; even Mexican-American Latinos did not overwhelmingly support the initiative. Still, some groups did become part of the diverse pro-NAFTA coalition that lobbied Congress in the days leading up to the final vote.

90. See, for example, Thorup 1991, Cook 1997, and Rosen 1999: 37–40.

91. For example, see the Web sites of the Mexico Solidarity Network (www .mexicosolidarity.org), Global Exchange (www.globalexchange.org), or the popular Ejército Zapatista de Liberación Nacional (EZLN) (www.ezln.org). Global Exchange is not exclusively focused on Mexico (although Mexico is a high priority), and the EZLN does not focus solely on the United States (although the United States is a principal target and many articles on its Web site are translated into English). Each site offers links to related sites. For educational efforts, see also Public Citizen Global Trade Watch (www.citizen.org/pctrade/nafta).

92. Jesús Reyes Heroles, Mexico's ambassador to the United States and the honorary president of the U.S.-Mexican Chamber of Commerce, called it a "key player in enhancing friendship between our two great nations" (see www.usmcoc .org/relo598a.html). The chamber's home page (at www.usmcoc.org) is worth exploring for data on NAFTA as well as for its links to government and business players. In addition, the sites of the Heritage Foundation (www.heritage.org) and the Cato Institute (www.cato.org) are not exclusively focused on Mexico but publish Mexico reports.

93. Compared with the type of integration achieved during the Porfirian period, the previous highlight of U.S.-Mexican economic integration, modern economic integration is more profound. Both ownership and production are integrated today. Splitting off part of the process through expropriation would offer few benefits and substantial costs — indeed, the asset might become worthless.

94. The two governments signed an agreement on water and air quality in 1983, and a decade later the U.S. Environmental Protection Agency and Mexico's social development ministry put together another agreement. (In midcentury agreements had been reached on air quality, sanitation, wildlife, and water rights.) But policy lies largely outside easy government control. Environmental protection requires increased private cooperation, as when nongovernmental organizations in both countries do pro-environment research and lobbying. The environment also brings bilateral tensions. U.S. critics attack lax Mexican policy and especially implementation that falls far short of what bilateral agreements demand. Mexico is portrayed, as in the drug and migration issues, as a source of

trouble (for example, when maquiladoras produce toxic waste that winds up in Texas water or when Tijuana sewage hits California beaches). Illegal aspects appear when environmental laws are violated. The bilateral issue becomes a complicated domestic politics issue in both the United States and Mexico, often pitting environmental against business groups.

U.S.conservatives split over preserving the environment or promoting Mexican business, while U.S. liberals split between the environment and giving a still poor nation the latitude to develop economically. Should bilateral agreements impose the same environmental controls on Mexican as on U.S. industry and agriculture even where such controls did not exist when U.S. enterprises were at earlier development levels, and even though Mexico does not come close to its neighbor in consuming the earth's natural resources? What does it tell us about Mexican development's ties to U.S. influence when U.S. environmental standards force abandonment of pesticides that could hurt U.S. consumers, but the substitutes are pesticides that do greater damage to Mexican workers?

Some Mexicans defend their government against unfair U.S. demands while others rise to echo them and force their government toward more environmentally friendly development. Increasingly, competing forces within Mexico appeal to U.S. allies. Mexico has become more dependent on U.S. judgments. There is also a feeling that matters spin unfairly out of control; as Mexico steps up its efforts in both research and policy, it comes off worse as domestic and bilateral economic development tends to bring environmental damage — or very high costs to avoid it. Political damage comes as the gap between performance and expectations grows. Once again Mexico may try harder to please and yet fall into greater disfavor, both at home and on a large international platform where it desperately seeks legitimacy. Once again the U.S. role is especially critical. For more on Mexico's environmental policies now and historically, including the U.S.-Mexico dimension, see Simonian 1995; for an environmentalist view, see Simon 1997.

95. For overviews of modern Mexico-U.S. bilateral issues, see Bosworth, Collins, and Lustig 1997, Smith 2000, de la Garza and Velasco 1997, Weintraub 1990, Pastor and Castañeda 1988, and Grayson 1984. El Colegio de México annually publishes *México-Estados Unidos* (and the same institution's *Foro Internacional* remains the journal that deals most fully with Mexican foreign policy). Also see the review essay by Mumme (1990).

CHAPTER EIGHT

1. Borjas Benavente 2003: 400.

Selected References

Adler, Ilya. 1993. The Mexican Case: The Media in the 1988 Presidential Election. In *Television, Politics, and the Transition to Democracy in Latin America*. Edited by Thomas E. Skidmore. Washington, D.C.: Woodrow Wilson Center Press; Baltimore, Md.: Johns Hopkins University Press.

Aguayo, Sergio. 1991. Mexico's Definition and Use of "National Security": Toward a New Concept for the 1990s. In *Mexico's External Relations in the 1990's*. Edited by Riordan Roett. Boulder, Colo.: Lynne Rienner Publishers.

————. 1993. The Uses, Misuses, and Challenges of Mexican National Security: 1946–1990. In *Mexico: In Search of Lost Security*. Edited by Bruce M. Bagley and Sergio Aguayo. Coral Gables, Fla.: North-South Center/University of Miami; New Brunswick, N.J.: Transaction Publishers.

————. 1998a. *1968: Los archivos de la violencia*. México City: Grijalbo Reforma.

————. 1998b. *Myths and [Mis] Perceptions: Changing U.S. Elite Visions of Mexico*. La Jolla: Center for U.S.-Mexican Studies, University of California, San Diego; Centro de Estudios Internacionales, El Colegio de México.

Aguilar García, Javier. 2001. *La población trabajadora y sindicalizada en México en el período de la globalización*. Mexico City: Fondo de Cultura Económica.

Alarcón González, Diana. 1994. *Changes in the Distribution of Income in Mexico and Trade Liberalization*. Tijuana, México: El Colegio de la Frontera Norte.

Alatorre, Javier. *Las mujeres en la pobreza*. Mexico City: Centro de Estudios Sociológicos, El Colegio de México.

Alba, Francisco. 1982. *The Population of Mexico: Trends, Issues, and Policies*. Translated by M. Mattingly Urquidi. New Brunswick, N.J.: Transaction Publishers.

Albarrán de Alba, Gerardo. 1997. El PRD, ante su nuevo reto. *Proceso* 1081: 24.

Almond, Gabriel A., Scott C. Flanagan, and Robert J. Mundt, eds. 1973. *Crisis, Choice, and Change: Historical Studies of Political Development*. Boston: Little, Brown.

Almond, Gabriel, and Sidney Verba. 1963. *The Civic Culture: Political Attitudes and Democracy in Five Nations*. Princeton, N.J.: Princeton University Press.

Andreas, Peter. 1998. The Paradox of Integration. In *The Post-NAFTA Political Economy*. Edited by Carol Wise. University Park: Pennsylvania State University.

Anguiano, Arturo. 1997. *Entre el pasado y el futuro: La izquierda en México, 1969–1995*. Mexico City: Universidad Autónoma Metropolitana.

Arroyo, Jesús, Adrián de León, and Basilia Valenzuela. 1991. Patterns of Migration and Regional Development in the State of Jalisco. In *Regional and Sectoral Development in Mexico as Alternatives to Migration*. Edited by Sergio Díaz-Briquets and Sidney Weintraub. Boulder, Colo.: Westview Press

Aspin, Chris. 1992. Is There Life for Mexico after Debt? *El Financiero International Weekly Edition* 2, no. 10.

Baer, M. Delal. 1988. Electoral Trends. In *Prospects for Mexico*. Edited by George W. Grayson. New Brunswick, N.J.: Transaction Publishers.

Baer, M. Delal, and Sidney Weintraub, eds. 1994. *The NAFTA Debate: Grappling with Unconventional Trade Issues*. Boulder, Colo.: Lynne Rienner Publishers.

Baer, Werner. 1986. Growth with Inequality: The Cases of Brazil and Mexico. *Latin American Research Review* 21, no. 2: 197–207.

Bagley, Bruce M., and Sergio Aguayo, eds. 1993. *Mexico: In Search of Security*. Coral Gables, Fla.: North-South Center/University of Miami; New Brunswick, N.J.: Transaction Publishers.

Bailey, David C. 1973. *Viva Cristo Rey!* Austin: University of Texas Press.

Bailey, John, and Sergio Aguayo, eds. 1996. *Strategy and Security in U.S.-Mexican Relations beyond the Cold War*. La Jolla: Center for U.S.-Mexican Studies, University of California, San Diego.

Baker, Susan, Robert Cushing, and Charles Haynes. 1997. Fiscal Impacts of Mexican Migration to the United States. In *At the Crossroads: Mexico and U.S. Immigration Policy*. Edited by Frank Bean et al. Lanham, Md.: Rowman & Littlefield.

Baloyra, Enrique. 1995. Latin America, Cuba, and the United States. In *United States Policy in Latin America: A Decade of Crisis and Challenge*. Edited by John D. Martz. Lincoln: University of Nebraska Press.

Barragán, Pablo Moctezuma. 1997. *Los orígenes del PAN*. Mexico City: Editorial Ehecatl.

Bartell, Ernest, and Leigh A. Payne, eds. 1995. *Business and Democracy in Latin America*. Pittsburgh, Pa.: University of Pittsburgh Press.

Bartolomé, Miguel Alberto. 1996. Indians and Afro-Americans at the End of the Century. In *Changing Structure of Mexico: Political, Social, and Economic Prospects*. Edited by Laura Randall. Armonk, N.Y.: M. E. Sharpe.

Bartra, Roger. 1989. Changes in Political Cuture. In *Mexico's Alternative Political Futures*. Edited by Wayne Cornelius, Judith Gentleman, and Peter Smith. La Jolla: Center for U.S.-Mexican Studies, University of California, San Diego.

Basáñez, Miguel. 1981. *La lucha por la hegemonía en México, 1968–1980.* Mexico City: Siglo XXI.

———. 1991. *El pulso de los sexenios: 20 años de crisis en México.* Second Edition. Mexico City: Siglo XXI.

Bazdresch, Carlos, and Santiago Levy. 1991. Populism and Economic Policy in Mexico, 1970–1982. In *The Macroeconomics of Populism in Latin America.* Edited by Rudiger Dornbusch and Santiago Levy. Chicago: University of Chicago Press.

Bean, Frank, et al. 1998. The Quantification of Migration between Mexico and the United States. In *Mexico–United States Binational Migration Study.* Vol. 1. Mexico City: Mexican Ministry of Foreign Affairs; Washington, D.C.: U.S. Commission on Immigration Reform.

———, et al., eds. 1997. *At the Crossroads: Mexico and U.S. Immigration Policy.* Lanham, Md.: Rowman & Littlefield.

Becker, Marjorie. 1995. *Setting the Virgin on Fire: Lázaro Cárdenas, Michoacán Peasants, and the Redemption of the Mexican Revolution.* Berkeley: University of California Press.

Beltrán, Ulises, and Santiago Portilla. 1986. El proyecto de descentralización del gobierno mexicano (1983–1984). In *Descentralización y democracia en México.* Edited by Blanca Torres. Mexico City: El Colegio de México.

Benjamin, Thomas. 1985. The Leviathan on the Zócalo: Recent Historiography of the Postrevolutionary Mexican State. *Latin American Research Review* 20, no. 3: 195–217.

Bennett, Vivienne. 1995. *The Politics of Water: Urban Protest, Gender, and Power in Monterrey, Mexico.* Pittsburgh, Pa.: University of Pittsburgh Press.

Beristain, Javier. 1996. Mexico City: Toward Its Sustainable Development. In *Changing Structure of Mexico: Political, Social, and Economic Prospects.* Edited by Laura Randall. Armonk, N.Y.: M. E. Sharpe.

Bertrab, Hermann von. 1997. *Negotiating NAFTA: A Mexican Envoy's Account.* Washington, D.C.: Center for Strategic and International Studies.

Blank, Stephen, and Jerry Haar. 1998. *Making NAFTA Work: U.S. Firms and the New North American Business Environment.* Coral Gables, Fla.: North-South Center Press, University of Miami.

Booth, John, and Mitchell Seligson. 1984. The Political Culture of Authoritarianism in Mexico: A Reexamination. *Latin American Research Review* 19, no. 1: 106–24.

Borjas Benavente, Adriana. 2003. *Partido de la Revolución Democrática: Estructura, organización interna y desempeño público (1989–2003).* Vol. 2. Mexico City: Ediciones Gernika.

Bosworth, Barry, Susan Collins, and Nora Lustig, eds. 1997. *Coming Together? Mexico–United States Relations.* Washington, D.C.: Brookings Institution Press.

Brachet de Márquez, Viviane. 1994. *The Dynamics of Domination: State, Class, and Social Reform in Mexico, 1910–1990.* Pittsburgh, Pa.: University of Pittsburgh Press.

Brandenburg, Frank. 1964. *The Making of Modern Mexico.* Englewood Cliffs, N.J.: Prentice Hall.

Bray, David Barton, and Matthew B. Wexler. 1996. Forest Policies in Mexico. In *Changing Structure of Mexico: Political, Social, and Economic Prospects.* Edited by Laura Randall. Armonk, N.Y.: M. E. Sharpe.

Bruhn, Kathleen. 1996. Social Spending and Political Support: The "Lessons" of the National Solidarity Program in Mexico. *Comparative Politics* 28, no. 2: 151–77.

———. 1997. *Taking on Goliath: The Emergence of a New Left Party and the Struggle for Democracy in Mexico.* University Park: Pennsylvania State University Press.

———. 1998. The Partido de la Revolución Democrática: Diverging Approaches to Competition. In *Governing Mexico: Political Parties and Elections.* Edited by Monica Serrano. London: Institute of Latin American Studies, University of London.

———. 1999. The Resurrection of the Mexican Left in the 1997 Elections: Implications for the Party System. In *The Transformation of Mexico's Parties, Campaigns, Elections, and Public Opinion.* Edited by Jorge Domínguez and Alejandro Poire. New York: Routledge Press.

Burgess, Katrina, and Abraham F. Lowenthal. 1993. Challenges from the South: Enhancing California's Mexico Connection. In *The California-Mexico Connection.* Edited by Katrina Burgess and Abraham F. Lowenthal. Stanford, Calif.: Stanford University Press.

Bustamante, Jorge A. 1979. El estudio de la zona fronteriza México-Estados Unidos. *Foro Internacional* 19, no. 1: 471–516.

Bustamante, Jorge A., et al. 1998. Characteristics of Migrants: Mexicans in the United States. In *Mexico–United States Binational Migration Study.* Vol. 1. Mexico City: Mexican Ministry of Foreign Affairs; Washington, D.C.: U.S. Commission on Immigration Reform.

Butler, Edgar W., and Jorge A. Bustamante, eds. 1991. *Sucesión Presidencial: The 1988 Mexican Presidential Election.* Boulder, Colo.: Westview Press.

Cabildo, Miguel. 1996. México maltrata a los migrantes. *Proceso* 1003.

Camacho, Manuel. 1994. *Cambio sin ruptura.* Mexico City: Alianza Editorial.

Camp, Roderic. 1985. The Political Technocrat in Mexico and the Survival of the Political System. *Latin American Research Review* 20, no. 1: 97–118.

———. 1989. *Entrepreneurs and Politics in Twentieth Century Mexico.* New York: Oxford University Press.

———. 1992. *Generals in the Palacio: The Military in Modern Mexico.* New York: Oxford University Press.

———. 1997. *Crossing Swords: Politics and Religion in Mexico.* New York: Oxford University Press.

———. 1999a. *Militarizing Mexico.* Policy Paper on the Americas. Washington, D.C.: Center for Strategic and International Studies.

———. 1999b. *Politics in Mexico: The Decline of Authoritarianism.* Third Edition. New York: Oxford University Press.

———. 2002. *Mexico's Mandarins: Crafting a Power Elite for the Twenty-First Century.* Berkeley: University of California Press.

Camp, Roderic, ed. 1986. *Mexico's Political Stability: The Next Five Years.* Boulder, Colo.: Westview Press.

———. 1996. *Polling for Democracy: Public Opinion and Political Liberalization in Mexico*. Wilmington, Del.: Scholarly Resources.

Carpizo, Jorge. 1996. *El presidencialismo mexicano*. Thirteenth Edition. Mexico City: Siglo XXI.

Carr, Barry. 1985. *Mexican Communism, 1968–1983*: Eurocommunism in the Americas? Research Report Series no. 42. La Jolla: Center for U.S.-Mexican Studies, University of California, San Diego.

———. 1996. *La izquierda mexicana a través del siglo XX*. Mexico City: Ediciones Era.

Castañeda, Jorge. 1985–86. Mexico at the Brink. *Foreign Affairs* 64, no. 2: 287–303.

———. 1993. Mexico and California: The Paradox of Tolerance and Dedemocratization. In *The California-Mexico Connection*. Edited by Katrina Burgess and Abraham F. Lowenthal. Stanford, Calif.: Stanford University Press.

———. 1994. *Sorpresas te da la vida: México 1994*. Mexico City: Editorial Aguilar.

Castro Martínez, Pedro. 1994. México y Canadá: La búsqueda de una nueva relación. *Foro Internacional* 34, no. 4: 592–608.

Cavarozzi, Marcelo. 1994. Mexico's Political Formula, Past and Present. In *The Politics of Economic Restructuring*. Edited by Maria Lorena Cook, Kevin Middlebrook, and Juan Molinar Horcasitas. La Jolla: Center for U.S.-Mexican Studies, University of California, San Diego.

Centeno, Miguel Angel. 1997. *Democracy within Reason: Technocratic Revolution in Mexico*. Second Edition. University Park: Pennsylvania State University Press.

Centro de Estudios Históricos. 1994. *Historia general de México*. Fourth Edition. Mexico City: El Colegio de México.

Chabat, Jorge. 1989. The Making of Mexican Policy toward the United States. In *Foreign Policy in U.S.-Mexican Relations*. Vol. 5. Edited by Rosario Green and Peter H. Smith. Prepared for the Bilateral Commission on the Future of United States–Mexican Relations. La Jolla: Center for U.S.-Mexican Studies, University of California, San Diego.

Clancy, Michael. 2001. Mexican Tourism: Export Growth and Structural Change since 1970. *Latin American Research Review* 36, no. 1: 128–150.

Clavijo, Fernando, and José I. Casar, eds. 1994. *La industria mexicana en el mercado mundial: Elementos para una política industrial*. Lecturas de El Trimestre Económico, no. 80. Mexico City: Fondo de Cultura Económica.

Coatsworth, John, and Carlos Rico, eds. 1989. *Images of Mexico in the United States*. La Jolla: Center for U.S.-Mexico Studies, University of California, San Diego.

Cockcroft, James. 1998. *Mexico's Hope: An Encounter with Politics and History*. New York: Monthly Review Press.

Colin, MacLachlan, and William Beezley. 1998. *El gran pueblo: A History of Greater Mexico*. Englewood Cliffs, N.J.: Prentice Hall.

Collier, Ruth Berins. 1992. *The Contradictory Alliance: State-Labor Relations and Regime Change in Mexico*. Research Series no. 83. Berkeley: International and Area Studies, University of California.

Collier, Ruth Berins, and David Collier. 1991. *Shaping the Political Arena: Critical Junctures, the Labor Movement, and Regime Dynamics in Latin America.* Princeton, N.J.: Princeton University Press.

Conaghan, Catherine M., and James M. Malloy. 1994. *Unsettling Statecraft: Democracy and Neoliberalism in the Central Andes.* Pittsburgh, Pa.: University of Pittsburgh Press.

Connor, Walker, ed. 1985. *Mexican-Americans in Comparative Perspective.* Washington, D.C.: Urban Institute Press.

Contee, Christine. 1989. U.S. Perceptions of United States–Mexican Relations. In *Images of Mexico in the United States.* Edited by John Coatsworth and Carlos Rico. La Jolla: Center for U.S.-Mexican Studies, University of California, San Diego.

Cook, Maria Lorena. 1996. *Organizing Dissent: Unions, the State, and the Democratic Teachers' Movement in Mexico.* University Park: Pennsylvania State University Press.

———. 1997. Cross-border Labor Solidarity: Cooperation between Labor Unions in North America. *Dissent* 44, no. 1: 49.

Cook, Maria Lorena, Kevin Middlebrook, and Juan Molinar Horcasitas, eds. 1994. *The Politics of Economic Restructuring.* La Jolla: Center for U.S.-Mexican Studies, University of California, San Diego.

Cordera Campos, Rolando, and Enrique González Tiburcio. 1991. Crisis and Transition in the Mexican Economy. In *Social Responses to Mexico's Economic Crisis of the 1980s.* Edited by Mercedes González de la Rocha and Agustín Escobar Latapí. La Jolla: Center for U.S.-Mexican Studies, University of California, San Diego.

Córdova, Arnaldo. 1974. *La política de masas del cardenismo.* Mexico City: Ediciones Era.

Cornelius, Wayne A. 1973. Nation Building, Participation, and Distribution: The Politics of Social Reform under Cárdenas. In *Crisis, Choice, and Change: Historical Studies of Political Development.* Edited by Gabriel A. Almond, Scott C. Flanagan, and Robert J. Mundt. Boston: Little, Brown.

———. 1996. *Mexican Politics in Transition: The Breakdown of a One-Party-Dominant Regime.* La Jolla: Center for U.S.-Mexican Studies, University of California, San Diego.

———. 1999. Subnational Politics and Democratization: Tensions between Center and Periphery in the Mexican Political System. In *Subnational Politics and Democratization in Mexico.* La Jolla: Center for U.S.-Mexico Studies, University of California, San Diego.

Cornelius, Wayne, Ann Craig, and Jonathan Fox, eds. 1994. *Transforming State-Society Relations in Mexico: The National Solidarity Strategy.* La Jolla: Center for U.S.-Mexican Studies, University of California, San Diego.

Cornelius, Wayne, Todd Eisenstadt, and Jane Hindley, eds. 1999. *Subnational Politics and Democratization in Mexico.* La Jolla: Center for U.S.-Mexican Studies, University of California, San Diego.

Cornelius, Wayne, and David Myhre, eds. 1998. *The Transformation of Rural Mexico: Reforming the Ejido Sector.* La Jolla: Center for U.S.-Mexican Studies, University of California, San Diego.

Cornelius, Wayne A., Judith Gentleman, and Peter H. Smith, eds. 1989. *Mexico's Alternative Political Futures*. La Jolla: Center for U.S.-Mexican Studies, University of California, San Diego.

Cornelius, Wayne A., Philip Martin, and James Hollifield, eds. 1994. *Controlling Immigration: A Global Perspective*. Stanford, Calif.: Stanford University Press.

Cosío Villegas, Daniel. 1964. *American Extremes*. Translated by Américo Paredes. Austin: University of Texas Press.

———. 1965. *La república restaurada*. Mexico City: Editorial Hermes.

———. 1975. *La sucesión presidencial*. Mexico City: Cuadernos de Joaquín Mortiz.

Covarrubias Velasco, Ana. 1994. La política mexicana hacia Cuba durante el gobierno de Salinas de Gortari. *Foro Internacional* 34, no. 4: 652–82.

Craig, Ann, and Wayne Cornelius. 1989. Political Culture in Mexico: Continuities and Revisionist Interpretations. In *The Civic Culture Revisited*. Edited by Gabriel Almond and Sidney Verba. Newbury Park, Calif.: Sage.

Craig, Richard. 1980. Operation Condor. *Journal of Interamerican Studies and World Affairs* 22, no. 3: 345–64.

Cross, John. 1998. *Informal Politics: Street Vendors and the State in Mexico City*. Stanford, Calif.: Stanford University Press.

Cruz, Angeles. 2000. Con anemia, 30% de los menores de cinco años: encuesta nacional. *La Jornada*. 5 July, 36.

Cuellar, Mireya, and Nestor Martínez. 1994. Profundas inequidades. *La Jornada*. 23 October, 1

Dahl, Robert. 1971. *Polyarchy: Participation and Opposition*. New Haven, Conn.: Yale University Press.

———. 1985. *A Preface to Economic Democracy*. Berkeley: University of California Press.

De la Garza, Rodolfo O., and Louis DeSipio. 1998. Interests Not Passions: Mexican-American Attitudes toward Mexico and Issues Shaping U.S.-Mexico Relations. *International Migration Review* 32, no. 2: 401–22.

De la Garza, Rodolfo O., and Gabriel Székely. 1997. Policy, Politics, and Emigration: Reexamining the Mexican Experience. In *At the Crossroads: Mexico and U.S. Immigration Policy*. Edited by Frank Bean et al. Lanham, Md.: Rowman & Littlefield.

De la Garza, Rodolfo O., and Jesús Velasco, eds. 1997. *Bridging the Border: Transforming Mexico-U.S. Relations*. Lanham, Md.: Rowman & Littlefield.

Del Valle, Angelina. 1995. Reestablecer el estado de derecho. *El Universal,* 29 October.

Del Villar, Samuel. 1986. La narcotización de la cultura en Estados Unidos y su impacto en México. In *México-Estados Unidos, 1985*. Edited by Gabriel Székely. Mexico City: El Colegio de México.

De Swaan, Mony, Paola Martorelli, and Juan Molinar Horcasitas. 1998. Public Financing of Political Parties and Electoral Expenditures in Mexico. In *Governing Mexico: Political Parties and Elections*. Edited by Monica Serrano. London: Institute of Latin American Studies.

Diamond, Larry. 1998. *Political Culture and Democracy in Developing Countries*. Boulder, Colo.: Lynne Rienner Publishers.

Diamond, Larry, Juan Linz, and Seymour Martin Lipset. 1995. Introduction: What Makes for Democracy? In *Politics in Developing Countries: Comparing Experiences with Democracy*. Second Edition. Edited by Larry Diamond, Juan Linz, and Seymour Martin Lipset. Boulder, Colo.: Lynne Rienner Publishers.

Díaz-Briquets, Sergio, and Sidney Weintraub, eds. 1991. *Regional and Sectoral Development in Mexico as Alternatives to Migration*. Boulder, Colo.: Westview Press.

Domingo, Pilar. 1999. Citizenship and Access to Justice in Mexico. *Estudios Mexicanos/Mexican Studies* 15, no. 1: 151–91.

Domínguez, Jorge, ed. 1997. *Technopols: Freeing Politics and Markets in Latin America in the 1990s*. University Park: Pennsylvania State University Press.

Domínguez, Jorge, and James A. McCann. 1996. *Democratizing Mexico: Public Opinion and Electoral Choices*. Baltimore, Md.: Johns Hopkins University Press.

Domínguez, Jorge, and Alejandro Poiré, eds. 1999. *Toward Mexico's Democratization: Parties, Campaigns, Elections, and Public Opinion*. New York: Routledge Press.

Drake, Paul, and Eduardo Silva, eds. 1986. *Elections and Democratization in Latin America, 1980–85*. La Jolla: Center for U.S.-Mexican Studies, University of California, San Diego.

Dresser, Denise. 1991. *Neopopulist Solutions to Neoliberal Problems: Mexico's National Solidarity Program*. La Jolla: Center for U.S.-Mexican Studies, University of California, San Diego.

———. 1993. Exporting Conflict: Transboundary Consequences of Mexican Politics. In *The California-Mexico Connection*. Edited by Katrina Burgess and Abraham F. Lowenthal. Stanford, Calif.: Stanford University Press.

Durand, Jorge, and Douglas S. Massey. 1992. Mexican Migration to the United States: A Critical Review. *Latin American Research Review* 27, no. 2: 3–42.

Elizondo, Carlos. 1995. El estado mexicano después de su reforma. *Política y Gobierno* 2, no. 1: 95–113.

———. 2000. Adiós al estado. In *La UNAM a debate*. Edited by Nelia E. Tello, José Antonio de la Peña, and Carlos Garza. Mexico City: Cal y Arena.

Encarnación, Omar. 2003. *The Myth of Social Capital: Social Capital and Democratic Consolidation in Spain and Brazil*. New York: Palgrave Macmillan.

Erb, Richard D., and Stanley R. Ross, eds. 1981. *United States Relations with Mexico: Context and Content*. Washington, D.C.: American Enterprise Institute for Public Policy Research.

Escobar L., Agustín, et al. 1998. Factors That Influence Migration. In *Mexico-United States Binational Migration Study*. Vol. 1. Mexico City: Mexican Ministry of Foreign Affairs; Washington, D.C.: U.S. Commission on Immigration Reform.

Espenshade, Thomas J., and Maryann Belanger. 1997. U.S. Public Perceptions and Reactions to Mexican Migration. In *At the Crossroads: Mexico and U.S.*

Immigration Policy. Edited by Frank Bean et al. Lanham, Md.: Rowman & Littlefield.

Espinosa, J. Enrique, and Pedro Noyola. 1997. Emerging Patterns in Mexico-U.S. Trade. In *Coming Together? Mexico-U.S. Relations*. Edited by Barry P. Bosworth, Susan M. Collins, and Nora Claudia Lustig. Washington, D.C.: Brookings Institution Press.

Espinoza Valle, Víctor Alejandro. 1998. *Alternancia política y gestión política: El Partido Acción Nacional en el gobierno de Baja California*. Tijuana, México: El Colegio de la Frontera Norte.

Fernández Poncela, Anna M., ed. 1995. *Participación política: Las mujeres en México al final del milenio*. Mexico City: El Colegio de México.

Figueroa Perea, Juan Guillermo. 1996. Three Comments on Population Policies in Mexico from a Reproductive Rights Approach. In *Changing Structure of Mexico: Political, Social, and Economic Prospects*. Edited by Laura Randall. Armonk, N.Y.: M. E. Sharpe.

Foley, Michael N. 1991. Agenda for Mobilization: The Agrarian Question and Popular Mobilization in Contemporary Mexico. *Latin American Research Review* 26, no. 2: 39–74.

Foweraker, Joe. 1993. *Popular Mobilization in Mexico: The Teachers' Movement, 1977–87*. Cambridge: Cambridge University Press.

Foweraker, Joe, and Ann Craig, eds. 1990. *Popular Movements and Political Change in Mexico*. Boulder, Colo.: Lynne Rienner Publishers.

Fowler-Salamini, Heather. 1993. The Boom in Regional Studies of the Mexican Revolution: Where Is It Leading? *Latin American Research Review* 28, no. 2: 175–90.

Fox, Jonathan. 1994. Political Change in Mexico's New Peasant Economy. In *The Politics of Economic Restructuring: State-Society Relations and Regime Change in Mexico*. Edited by Maria Lorena Cook, Kevin Middlebrook, and Juan Molinar Horcasitas. La Jolla: Center for U.S.-Mexican Studies, University of California, San Diego.

———. 1995. Governance and Rural Development in Mexico: State Intervention and Public Accountability. *Journal of Development Studies* 32: 1–30.

Freeman, Gary P., and Frank Bean. 1997. Mexico and U.S. Worldwide Immigration Policy. In *At the Crossroads: Mexico and U.S. Immigration Policy*. Edited by Frank Bean et al. Lanham, Md.: Rowman & Littlefield.

Fuentes, Carlos. 1964. *The Death of Artemio Cruz*. Translated by Sam Hileman. New York: Farrar, Straus and Giroux.

———. 1996. *A New Time for Mexico*. New York: Farrar, Straus and Giroux.

Fuentes-Beraín, Rossana. 1992. Chronicle of a Debt Crisis Not Foretold. *El Financiero International Weekly Edition* 2, no. 10.

Furtak, Robert K. 1978. *El partido de la revolución y la estabilidad política en México*. Mexico City: Universidad Nacional Autónoma de México.

Gallegos, Elena. 2000. Explotó la insurrección priísta en contra del presidente Zedillo. *La Jornada*. 5 July, 3.

García del Castillo, Rodolfo. 1999. *Los municipios en México: Los retos ante el futuro*. Mexico City: Centro de Investigación y Docencia Económica.

Garrido, Luis Javier. 1982. *El Partido de la Revolucion Institucionalizada: La formación del nuevo estado en México (1928–1945)*. Mexico City: Siglo XXI.

———. 1989. The Crisis of Presidencialismo. In *Mexico's Alternative Political Futures*. Edited by Wayne Cornelius, Judith Gentleman, and Peter Smith. La Jolla: Center for U.S.-Mexican Studies, University of California, San Diego.

———. 1993. *La ruptura: La Corriente Democrática del PRI*. Mexico City: Grijalbo.

Garza Elizondo, Humberto. 1994. Los cambios de la política exterior de México: 1989–1994. *Foro Internacional* 34, no. 4: 534–44.

Gelbard, Alene H., and Marion Carter. 1997. Mexican Immigration and the U.S. Population. In *At the Crossroads: Mexico and U.S. Immigration Policy*. Edited by Frank Bean et al. Lanham, Md.: Rowman & Littlefield.

Gentleman, Judith. 1987. Mexico after the Oil Boom. In *Mexican Politics in Transition*. Edited by Judith Gentleman. Boulder, Colo.: Westview Press.

Gereffi, Gary. 1996. Mexico's "Old" and "New" Maquiladora Industries. In *Neoliberalism Revisited*. Edited by Gerardo Otero. Boulder, Colo.: Westview Press.

Gilbert, Alan. 1989. *Housing and Land in Urban Mexico*. Monograph series no. 31. La Jolla: Center for U.S.-Mexican Studies, University of California.

Gilbert, Dennis. 1997. Rewriting History: Salinas, Zedillo, and the 1992 Textbook Controversy. *Mexican Studies/Estudios Mexicanos* 13, no. 2: 271–97.

Gómez Tagle, Silvia. 1990. *Las estadísticas electorales de la reforma política*. Mexico City: El Colegio de México.

González Amador, Roberto. 2000a. .0001% de la población domina la economía. *La Jornada*. 27 May. Available on-line at www.jornada.unam.mx/2000/mayoo/000527/poblacion.html.

———. 2000b. Se elevó la deuda pública por el rescate bancario a 40% del PIB. *La Jornada*. 4 June. Available on-line at www.jornada.unam.mx/2000/junoo/000604/eco1.html.

González Casanova, Pablo. 1970. *Democracy in Mexico*. Translated by Danielle Salti. London: Oxford University Press.

González de la Rocha, Mercedes, and Agustín Escobar Latapí, eds. 1991. *Social Responses to Mexico's Economic Crisis of the 1980s*. La Jolla: Center for U.S.-Mexican Studies, University of California, San Diego.

Graham, Richard, and Peter H. Smith, eds. 1974. *New Approaches to Latin American History*. Austin: University of Texas Press.

Grayson, George W. 1984. *The United States and Mexico: Patterns of Influence*. New York: Praeger Publishers.

———. 1992. *The Church in Contemporary Mexico*. Washington, D.C.: Center for Strategic and International Studies.

———. 1995. *The North American Free Trade Agreement: Regional Community and the New World Order*. Miller Center Series on a New World Order. Vol. 3. New York: University Press of America.

———. 1998. Lobbying by Mexico and Canada. In *The Controversial Pivot: The U.S. Congress and North America*. Edited by Robert Pastor and Rafael Fernández de Castro. Washington, D.C.: Brookings Institution Press.

Green, Rosario. 1977. México: La política exterior del nuevo régimen. *Foro Internacional* 18, no. 1: 1–9.

Green, Rosario, and Peter H. Smith, eds. 1989. *Foreign Policy in U.S.-Mexican Relations.* Vol. 5. Prepared for the Bilateral Commission on the Future of United States–Mexican Relations. La Jolla: Center for U.S.-Mexican Studies, University of California, San Diego.

Greenwood, Michael J., and Marta Tienda. 1998. U.S. Impacts of Mexican Immigration. In *Mexico–United States Binational Migration Study.* Vol. 1. Mexico City: Mexican Ministry of Foreign Affairs; Washington, D.C.: U.S. Commission on Immigration Reform.

Grinspun, Ricardo, and Maxwell Cameron, eds. 1993. *The Political Economy of North American Free Trade.* New York: St. Martin's Press.

Guedea, Virginia. 1996. *Los guadalupes de México: En busca de un gobierno alterno.* Mexico City: Instituto de Investigaciones Históricas de la Universidad Nacional Autónoma de México.

Guillen López, Tonatiuh. 1993. *Baja California 1989–1992: Alternancia política y transición democrática.* Tijuana, México: El Colegio de la Frontera Norte.

Gutiérrez, David. 1996. *Between Two Worlds: Mexican Immigrants in the United States.* Wilmington, Del.: Scholarly Resources.

Gutiérrez Garza, Esthela. 1988. De la relación salarial monopolista a la flexibilidad del trabajo. In *Testimonios de la crisis: La crisis del estado de bienestar.* Edited by Esthela Gutiérrez Garza. Mexico City: Siglo Veintiuno Editores.

Haggard, Stephan. 1990. *Pathways from the Periphery: The Politics of Growth in the Newly Industrializing Countries.* Ithaca, N.Y.: Cornell University Press.

Hale, Charles. 1989. *The Transformation of Liberalism in Late Nineteenth-Century Mexico.* Princeton, N.J.: Princeton University Press.

Hamilton, Nora. 1982. *The Limits of State Autonomy: Post-Revolutionary Mexico.* Princeton, N.J.: Princeton University Press.

Hamnett, Brian. 1999. *A Concise History of Mexico.* Cambridge: Cambridge University Press.

Hansen, Roger D. 1974. *The Politics of Mexican Development.* Second Edition. Baltimore, Md.: Johns Hopkins University Press.

Hart, John Mason. 1997. *Revolutionary Mexico: The Coming and Process of the Mexican Revolution.* Tenth Anniversary Edition. Berkeley: University of California Press.

Harvey, Neil. 1998. *The Chiapas Rebellion : The Struggle for Land and Democracy.* Durham, N.C.: Duke University Press.

Hayes-Bautista, David E. 1993. Mexicans in Southern California. In *The California-Mexico Connection.* Edited by Katrina Burgess and Abraham F. Lowenthal. Stanford, Calif.: Stanford University Press.

Heredia, Blanca. 1996. State-Business Relations in Contemporary Mexico. In *Rebuilding the State: Mexico after Salinas.* Edited by Mónica Serrano and Víctor Bulmer-Thomas. London: Institute of Latin American Studies, University of London.

Hernández, Rogelio. 1994. Inestabilidad política y presidencialismo en México. *Mexican Studies/Estudios Mexicanos* 10, no. 1: 187–216.

Hernández Laos, Enrique, and Jorge Córdoba. 1982. *La distribución del ingreso en México.* Mexico City: Centro de Investigación para la Integración Social.

Hernández Rodríguez, Rogelio. 1998. The Partido Revolucionario Institucional. In *Governing Mexico: Political Parties and Elections.* Edited by Mónica Serrano. London: Institute of Latin American Studies, University of London.

Herzog, Lawrence, ed. 1992. *Changing Boundaries in the Americas.* La Jolla: Center for U.S.-Mexico Studies, University of California, San Diego.

Hiernaux, Daniel, and Manuel Rodríguez Woog. 1991. Tourism and Absorption of the Labor Force in Mexico. In *Regional and Sectoral Development in Mexico as Alternatives to Migration.* Edited by Sergio Díaz-Briquets and Sidney Weintraub. Boulder, Colo.: Westview Press.

Himmelstein, Jerome L. 1990. *To the Right: The Transformation of American Conservatism.* Berkeley: University of California Press.

Hinojosa, Oscar. 1988. Al estilo tómbola. *Proceso 633.*

Hoebing, Joyce, Sidney Weintraub, and M. Delal Baer, eds. 1996. *NAFTA and Sovereignty: Trade-offs for Canada, Mexico, and the United States.* Washington, D.C.: Center for Strategic and International Studies.

Hornbeck, J.F. 2004. "NAFTA at Ten: Lessons from Recent Studies." http:// www.usembassy-mexico.gov/bbf/NAFTAatTen.pdf.

Huntington, Samuel. 1991. *The Third Wave: Democratization in the Late Twentieth Century.* Norman: University of Oklahoma Press.

Inglehart, Ronald, et al. 2004. *Human Beliefs and Values: A Cross Cultural Sourcebook Based on the 1999–2002 Values Surveys.* Mexico City: Siglo XXI Editores.

Inglehart, Ronald, Neil Nevitte, and Miguel Basáñez. 1996. *The North American Trajectory: Cultural, Economic, and Political Ties among the United States, Canada, and Mexico.* New York: Aldine de Gruyter.

Instituto Federal Electoral (IFE). 1991a. *Contienda electoral en las elecciones de diputados federales.* Mexico City: IFE.

———. 1991b. *Relación de los 300 distritos federales electorales.* Mexico City: IFE.

———. 1994. *Elecciones federales 1994.* Mexico City: IFE.

———. 1997. *Elecciones federales 1997.* Mexico City: IFE.

———. 2000. *Cómputos por entidad federativa para diputados por representación proporcional.* Mexico City: IFE. Available on-line at www.ife.org .mx/wwwife/computos.

Instituto Nacional de Estadística, Geografía e Informática (INEGI). 1985. *Anuario Estadístico de los Estados Unidos Mexicanos.* Mexico City: Instituto Nacional de Estadística, Geografía e Informática.

———. 1993. *Resumen general: XI Censo general de población y vivienda, 1990.* Mexico City: INEGI.

———. 1995. *Cuaderno de información oportuna.* Mexico City: INEGI.

Inter-American Development Bank (IDB). 1980. *Economic and Social Progress in Latin America.* Washington, D.C.: IADB.

Izquierdo, Rafael. 1994. *La política hacendaria del desarrollo estabilizador, 1958–1970.* Mexico City: Fondo de Cultura Económica.

Jamar, Christen, and Angelo Young. 1999. NAFTA @ 5. *MB* 5, no. 10: 26–34.

Jauberth, H. Rodrigo, et al. 1992. *The Difficult Triangle: Mexico, Central America, and the United States*. Boulder, Colo.: Westview Press.

Jenkins, Vlad. 1991. Salinas and the New Untouchables. *CEO International Strategies* 4, no. 1: 34–40.

Johnson, Kenneth, and Philip Kelly. 1986. Political Democracy in Latin America. *LASA Forum* 16, no. 4.

Joseph, Gil, and Daniel Nugent, eds. 1994. *Everyday Forms of State Formation: Revolution and the Negotiation of Rule in Modern Mexico*. Durham, N.C.: Duke University Press.

Kandell, Jonathan. 1988. *La Capital: The Biography of Mexico City*. New York: Random House.

Karl, Terry L. 1997. *The Paradox of Plenty: Oil Booms and Petro-States*. Berkeley: University of California Press.

Katz, Friedrich. 1983. *The Secret War in Mexico*. Chicago: University of Chicago Press.

———. 1998. *The Life and Times of Pancho Villa*. Stanford, Calif.: Stanford University Press.

Kaufman, Robert. 1998. The *Politics of Debt in Argentina, Brazil, and Mexico*. Berkeley: Institute of International Studies, University of California.

Klesner, Joseph. 1993. Changing Patterns of Electoral Participation and Electoral Alignment in Mexico. *Mexican Studies/Estudios Mexicanos* 9, no. 2: 187–223.

———. 1994. Realignment or Dealignment? Consequences of Economic Crisis and Restructuring for the Mexican Party System. In *The Politics of Economic Restructuring: State-Society Relations and Regime Change in Mexico*. Edited by Maria Lorena Cook, Kevin Middlebrook, and Juan Molinar Horcasitas. La Jolla: Center for U.S.-Mexican Studies, University of California, San Diego.

———. 1995. The 1994 Mexican Elections: Manifestation of a Divided Society. *Mexican Studies/Estudios Mexicanos* 11, no. 1: 137–49.

Knight, Alan. 1986. *The Mexican Revolution*. 2 vols. New York: Cambridge University Press.

———. 1987. *U.S.-Mexican Relations, 1910–1940: An Interpretation*. La Jolla: Center for U.S.-Mexican Studies, University of California, San Diego.

Krauze, Enrique. 1986. *Por una democracia sin adjetivos*. Mexico City: Joaquín Mortiz-Planeta.

———. 1997. *La presidencia imperial: Ascenso y caída del sistema político mexicano*. Mexico City: Tusquets Editores.

Laichas, Thomas Michael. 1980. Mexico in the U.S. Press: A Quantitative Study, 1972–1978. In *Statistical Abstract of Latin America*. Vol. 20. Edited by James W. Wilkie. Los Angeles: UCLA Latin American Center Publications.

Lajous de Solana, Roberta, and Jesús Velasco Márquez. 1985. Visión de México en la prensa de Estados Unidos: 1984. In *México–Estado Unidos, 1984*. Edited by Manuel García y Griego and Gustavo Vega. Mexico City: El Colegio de México.

Lamicq, Pedro. 1913. *Piedad para el indio*. Mexico City: Revista de Revistas.

Langston, Joy. 1995. Sobrevivir y prosperar: Una búsqueda de las causas de las facciones políticas intrarrégimen en México. *Política y Gobierno* 2, no. 2: 243–77.

Larin, Nicolás. 1968. *La rebelión de los cristeros (1926–1929)*. Translated by Angel C. Tomás. Mexico City: Ediciones Era.

Laso de la Vega, Jorge, ed. 1987. *La Corriente Democrática: Hablan los protagonistas*. Mexico City: Editorial Posada.

Latapí, Pablo. 1996. Los caminos de la eficacia. *Proceso* 1003.

Lawson, Chappell. 2000. Mexico's Unfinished Transition: Democratization and Authoritarian Enclaves in Mexico. *Mexican Studies/Estudios Mexicanos* 16, no. 2 (Summer): 267–287.

———. 2002. *Building the Fourth Estate: Democratization and the Rise of a Free Press in Mexico*. Berkeley: University of California Press.

Levy, Daniel. 1980. *University and Government in Mexico: Autonomy in an Authoritarian System*. New York: Praeger Publishers.

———. 1986a. *Higher Education and the State in Latin America*. Chicago: University of Chicago Press.

———. 1986b. The Implications of Central American Conflicts for Mexican Politics. In *Mexico's Political Stability: The Next Five Years*. Edited by Roderic Camp. Boulder, Colo.: Westview Press.

Levy, Daniel, and Kathleen Bruhn. 1999. Mexico: Sustained Civilian Rule and the Question of Democracy. In *Democracy in Developing Countries: Latin America*. Second Edition. Edited by Larry Diamond, Jonathan Hartlyn, Juan Linz, and Seymour Martin Lipset. Boulder, Colo.: Lynne Rienner Publishers.

Levy, Daniel, and Gabriel Székely. 1987. *Mexico: Paradoxes of Stability and Change*. Second Edition. Boulder, Colo.: Westview Press.

Levy, Santiago. 1994. La pobreza en México. In *La pobreza en México, causas y políticas para combatirla*. Edited by Félix Vélez. Lecturas de El Trimestre Económico, no. 79. Mexico City: Fondo de Cultura Económica.

Lewis, Oscar. 1959. *Five Families: Mexican Case Studies in the Culture of Poverty*. New York: Basic Books.

Lieuwen, Edwin. 1968. *Mexican Militarism: The Political Rise and Fall of the Revolutionary Army, 1910–1940*. Albuquerque: University of New Mexico Press.

Lissakers, Karin. 1991. *Banks, Borrowers, and the Establishment: A Revisionist Account of the International Debt Crisis*. New York: Basic Books.

Loaeza, Soledad. 1994. Political Liberalization and Uncertainty in Mexico. In *The Politics of Economic Restructuring: State-Society Relations and Regime Change in Mexico*. Edited by Maria Lorena Cook, Kevin Middlebrook, and Juan Molinar Horcasitas. La Jolla: Center for U.S.-Mexican Studies, University of California, San Diego.

———. 1999. *Partido Acción Nacional: La larga marcha, 1939–1994, oposición leal y partido de protesta*. Mexico City: Fondo de Cultura Económica.

López, Gustavo. 1998. Coyotes and Alien Smuggling. In *Mexico–United States Binational Migration Study*. Vol. 3. Mexico City: Mexican Ministry of Foreign Affairs; Washington, D.C.: U.S. Commission on Immigration Reform.

López Acuña, Daniel. 1979. Salud, Seguridad Social y Nutrición. In *Mexico, hoy*. Edited by Pablo González Casanova and Enrique Florescano. Mexico City: Siglo XXI.

López y Fuentes, Gregorio. 1996. *El Indio*. Translated by Anita Brenner. New York: Continuum.

Lorey, David. 1999. *The U.S.-Mexican Border in the Twentieth Century*. Wilmington, Del.: Scholarly Resources.

Lowenthal, Abraham F., and Katrina Burgess, eds. 1993. *The California-Mexico Connection*. Stanford, Calif.: Stanford University Press.

Lozano, Fernando. 1998. Las remesas de los migrantes mexicanos en Estados Unidos: Estimaciones para 1995. In *Mexico–United States Binational Migration Study*. Vol. 3. Mexico City: Mexican Ministry of Foreign Affairs; Washington, D.C.: U.S. Commission on Immigration Reform.

Luna, Matilde, and Ricardo Tirado. 1997. *El Consejo Coordinador Empresarial, una radiografía*. Mexico City: Universidad Nacional Autónoma de México.

Lupsha, Peter. 1994. Mexican Narco-Trafficking. *Encuentros* 1, no. 1: 9–11.

Mabire, Bernardo. 1994. El fantasma de la antigua ideología y su resistencia al cambio de la política exterior en el sexenio de Salinas de Gortari. *Foro Internacional* 34, no. 4: 545–71.

Mabry, Donald. 1973. *Mexico's Acción Nacional: A Catholic Alternative to Revolution*. Syracuse, N.Y.: Syracuse University Press.

Macías, Javier. 1991. En 11 estados, CSG entrega más de 800 kms de autopistas de 4 carriles. *El Nacional,* August 10, 1.

Maciel, David R., and María Herrera-Sobek. 1998. "What Goes Around, Comes Around": Political Practice and Cultural Response in the Internationalization of Mexican Labor, 1890–1997. In *Culture across Borders: Mexican Immigration and Popular Culture*. Edited by David Maciel and Maria Herrera-Sobek. Tucson: University of Arizona Press.

MacLachlan, Colin, and William Beezley. 1998. *El gran pueblo: A History of a Greater Mexico*. Englewood Cliffs, N.J.: Prentice Hall.

Mainwaring, Scott, and Timothy Scully. 1995. *Building Democratic Institutions: Party Systems in Latin America*. Stanford, Calif.: Stanford University Press.

Márquez, Enrique. 1995. *Por qué perdió Camacho: Revelaciones del asesor de Manuel Camacho Solís*. Mexico City: Océano.

Martin, Philip. 1996. Mexican-U.S. Migration. In *Changing Structure of Mexico: Political, Social, and Economic Prospects*. Edited by Laura Randall. Armonk, N.Y.: M. E. Sharpe.

———. 1997. Do Mexican Agricultural Policies Stimulate Emigration? In *At the Crossroads: Mexico and U.S. Immigration Policy*. Edited by Frank Bean et al. Lanham, Md.: Rowman & Littlefield.

Martínez, Fabiola. 2000. 20 millones de mexicanos están en la economía formal. *La Jornada*. 21 May. Available on-line at www.jornada.unam.mx/2000/mayoo/000521/pol2.html.

Martínez Verdugo, Arnoldo, ed. 1985. *Historia del Comunismo en México*. Mexico City: Grijalbo.

Maxfield, Sylvia, and Ricardo Anzaldúa Montoya, eds. 1987. *Government and Private Sector in Contemporary Mexico*. La Jolla: Center for U.S.-Mexican Studies, University of California, San Diego.

Mayer, Frederick. 1998. *Interpreting NAFTA: The Science and Art of Political Analysis*. New York: Columbia University Press.

Mayo, Sebastián. 1964. *La educación socialista en México*. Rosario, Argentina: Bear.

McCarthy, Kevin, and Georges Vernez. 1997. *Immigration in a Changing Economy: California's Experience*. Santa Monica, Calif.: RAND.

Mexico–United States. 1998. *Mexico–United States Binational Migration Study*. 3 vols. Mexico City: Mexican Ministry of Foreign Affairs; Washington, D.C.: U.S. Commission on Immigration Reform.

Meyer, Lorenzo. 1977. *Mexico and the United States in the Oil Controversy, 1917–1942*. Austin: University of Texas Press.

———. 1990. The United States and Mexico: The Historical Structure of Their Conflict. *Journal of International Affairs* 43, no. 2: 251–71.

———. 1991. Mexico: The Exception and the Rule. In *Exporting Democracy: The United States and Latin America*. Edited by Abraham Lowenthal. Baltimore, Md.: Johns Hopkins University Press.

Meyer, Michael C., and William L. Sherman. 1995. *The Course of Mexican History*. Fifth Edition. New York: Oxford University Press.

Michels, Robert. 1962. *Political Parties: A Sociological Study of the Oligarchical Tendencies of Modern Democracy*. Translated by Eden Paul and Cedar Paul. New York: Free Press.

Middlebrook, Kevin. 1995. *The Paradox of Revolution: Labor, the State, and Authoritarianism in Mexico*. Baltimore, Md.: Johns Hopkins University Press.

Mizrahi, Yemile. 1994a. *A New Conservative Opposition in Mexico: The Politics of Entrepreneurs in Chihuahua*. Berkeley: University of California Press.

———. 1994b. Rebels without a Cause? The Politics of Entrepreneurs in Chihuahua. *Journal of Latin American Studies* 26, no. 1: 137–58.

———. 1998. The Costs of Electoral Success: The Partido Acción Nacional in Mexico. In *Governing Mexico: Political Parties and Elections*. Edited by Monica Serrano. London: Institute of Latin American Studies, University of London.

———. 2003. *From Martyrdom to Power: The Partido Acción Nacional in Mexico*. Notre Dame: University of Notre Dame Press.

Molinar Horcasitas, Juan. 1991. *El tiempo de la legitimidad: Elecciones, autoritarismo, y democracia en México*. Mexico City: Cal y Arena.

———. 1996. Renegotiating the Rules of the Game: The State and Political Parties. In *Rebuilding the State: Mexico after Salinas*. Edited by Mónica Serrano and Víctor Bulmer-Thomas. London: Institute of Latin American Studies, University of London.

Monsiváis, Carlos. 1987. Las repercusiones sociales y culturales del auge. In *El auge petrolero: De la euforia al desencanto*. Edited by Rolando Cordera and Carlos Tello. Mexico City: Universidad Nacional Autónoma de México.

———. 1996. Will Nationalism Be Bilingual? In *Mass Media and Free Trade: NAFTA and the Cultural Industries*. Edited by Emile McAnany and Kenton Wilkinson. Austin: University of Texas.

Morris, Stephen D. 1995. *Political Reformism in Mexico: An Overview of Contemporary Mexican Politics*. Boulder, Colo.: Lynne Rienner Publishers.

Muller, Thomas, and Thomas Espenshade. 1985. *The Fourth Wave: California's Newest Immigrants.* Washington, D.C.: Urban Institute.

Mumme, Stephen P. 1990. Policy and Prescription in U.S.-Mexico Relations. *Latin American Research Review* 25, no. 3: 177–87.

Murray, Pamela. 1997. Diverse Approaches to Nineteenth-Century Mexican History. *Latin American Research Review* 32, no. 3: 187–92.

Nacional Financiera. 1977. *Statistics on the Mexican Economy.* Mexico City: Nacional Financiera.

———. 1998. *La economía mexicana en cifras 1998.* Mexico City: Nacional Financiera.

Nash, June. 1995. The Reassertion of Indigenous Identity: Mayan Responses to State Intervention in Chiapas. *Latin American Research Review* 30, no. 3: 7–41.

Needler, Martin. 1994. The Consent of the Governed? Coercion, Co-optation, and Compromise in Mexican Politics. *Mexican Studies/Estudios Mexicanos* 10, no. 2: 383–90.

———. 1995. *Mexican Politics: The Containment of Conflict.* Third Edition. Westport, Conn.: Praeger.

Nickson, R. Andrew. 1995. *Local Government in Latin America.* Boulder, Colo.: Lynne Rienner Publishers.

Norris, Pippa. 2002. *Democratic Phoenix: Reinventing Political Activism.* New York: Cambridge University Press.

O'Donnell, Guillermo. 1988. *Bureaucratic Authoritarianism: Argentina, 1966–1973, in Comparative Perspective.* Berkeley: University of California Press.

———. 1994. Delegative Democracy. Journal of Democracy 5, no. 1: 55–69.

Ojeda, Mario. 1976. *Alcances y límites de la política exterior de México.* Mexico City: El Colegio de México.

———. 1977. México ante los Estados Unidos en la coyuntura actual. *Foro Internacional* 18, no. 1: 32–53.

———, ed. 1985. *Las relaciones de México con los países de América Central.* Mexico City: El Colegio de México.

Oppenheimer, Andrés. 1996. *Bordering on Chaos: Guerrillas, Stockbrokers, Politicians, and Mexico's Road to Prosperity.* Boston: Little, Brown.

Organization for Economic Cooperation and Development (OECD). 1995. *Estudios económicos de la OCDE: México 1995.* Paris: OECD.

Orme, William A., Jr. 1996. *Understanding NAFTA: Mexico, Free Trade, and the New North America.* Austin: University of Texas Press.

———, ed. 1997. *A Culture of Collusion: An Inside Look at the Mexican Press.* Coral Gables, Fla.: North-South Center, University of Miami.

Ortega, Fernando. 1988. Una cena en las Lomas de Chapultepec. Como cuates Fidel Castro, Miguel Alemán, Carlos Slim, Madero Bracho, . . . *Proceso* 632: 14–17.

Partido Revolucionario Institucional (PRI). 1990. *El partido en el poder: Seis ensayos.* Mexico City: PRI.

Pastor, Robert, and Jorge Castañeda. 1988. *Limits to Friendship: The United States and Mexico.* New York: Knopf.

Pastor, Robert, and Rafael Fernández de Castro, eds. 1998. *The Controversial*

Pivot: The U.S. Congress and North America. Washington, D.C.: Brookings Institution Press.

Paz, Octavio. 1972. *The Other Mexico: Critique of the Pyramid.* Translated by Lysander Kemp. New York: Grove Press.

———. 1979. *Reflections: Mexico and the United States.* Translated by Rachel Phillips. *New Yorker,* September 17, 136–53.

Pedersen, Mogens. 1990. Electoral Volatility in Western Europe, 1948–1977. In *The West European Party System.* Edited by Peter Mair. Oxford: Oxford University Press.

Pellicer de Brody, Olga. 1972a. Cambios recientes en la política exterior mexicana. *Foro Internacional* 13, no. 2: 139–54.

———. 1972b. *México y la revolución cubana.* Mexico City: El Colegio de México.

Philip, George D. E. 1992. *The Presidency in Mexican Politics.* New York: St. Martin's Press.

Pick, James B., and Edgar W. Butler. 1997. *Mexico Megacity.* Boulder, Colo.: Westview Press.

Prud'homme, Jean-Francois. 1998. The Instituto Federal Electoral (IFE): Building an Impartial Electoral Authority. In *Governing Mexico: Political Parties and Elections.* Edited by Monica Serrano. London: Institute of Latin American Studies, University of London.

———. 1999. State Electoral Conflicts and National Interparty Relations in Mexico, 1988–1994. In *Subnational Politics and Democratization in Mexico.* Edited by Wayne Cornelius, Todd Eisenstadt, and Jane Hindley. La Jolla: Center for U.S.-Mexican Studies, University of California, San Diego.

Przeworski, Adam. 1986. Some Problems in the Study of the Transition to Democracy. In *Transitions from Authoritarian Rule.* Edited by Guillermo O'Donnell, Philippe Schmitter, and Laurence Whitehead. Baltimore, Md.: Johns Hopkins University Press.

Purcell, John F. H., and Susan Kaufman Purcell. 1980. State and Society in Mexico: Must a Stable Polity Be Institutionalized? *World Politics* 32, no. 2: 194–227.

Ramírez de la O, Rogelio. 1996. *The Mexican Peso Crisis: International Perspectives.* Edited by Riordan Roett. Boulder, Colo.: Lynne Rienner Publishers.

Randall, Laura, ed. 1996. *Changing Structure of Mexico: Political, Social, and Economic Prospects.* Armonk, NY: M. E. Sharpe.

Reavis, Dick J. 1990. *Conversations with Moctezuma: Ancient Shadows over Modern Life in Mexico.* New York: Morrow Press.

Reuter, Peter, and David Ronfeldt. 1992. Quest for Integrity: The Mexican-U.S. Drug Issue in the 1980s. *Journal of Interamerican Studies and World Affairs* 34: 89–153.

Reyna, José Luis, and Richard Weinert. 1977. *Authoritarianism in Mexico.* Philadelphia, Pa.: Institute for the Study of Human Issues.

Reyna, José Luis, et al. 1976. *Tres estudios sobre el movimiento obrero en México.* Mexico City: El Colegio de México.

Rico, Carlos. 1989. The Making of U.S. Policy toward Mexico: Should We Expect Coherence? In *Foreign Policy in U.S.-Mexican Relations.* Edited by

Rosario Green and Peter H. Smith. Vol. 5. Prepared for the Bilateral Commission on the Future of United States–Mexican Relations. La Jolla: Center for U.S.-Mexican Studies, University of California, San Diego.
———. 1991. The Postelectoral Conjuncture in Mexico and Mexican-United States Relations. In *Sucesión Presidencial: The 1988 Mexican Presidential Election*. Edited by Edgar W. Butler and Jorge A. Bustamante. Boulder, Colo.: Westview Press.
Riding, Alan. 1985. *Distant Neighbors: Portrait of the Mexicans*. New York: Knopf.
Roberts, Bryan R., and Agustín Escobar. 1997. Mexican Social and Economic Policy and Emigration. In *At the Crossroads: Mexico and U.S. Immigration Policy*. Edited by Frank Bean et al. Lanham, Md.: Rowman & Littlefield.
Rochlin, James. 1997. *Redefining Mexican Security*. Boulder, Colo.: Lynne Rienner Publishers.
Rodríguez, Jaime. 1990. *The Revolutionary Process in Mexico*. Los Angeles: UCLA Latin American Center Publications.
———, ed. 1994. *The Origins of Mexican National Politics, 1808–1847*. Wilmington, Del.: Scholarly Resources.
Rodríguez, Victoria. 1997. *Decentralization in Mexico: From Reforma Municipal to Solidaridad to Nuevo Federalismo*. Boulder, Colo.: Westview Press.
Rodríguez, Victoria, and Peter Ward. 1992. Policy-Making, Politics, and Urban Governance in Chihuahua: The Experience of Recent PANista Governments. *U.S.-Mexican Policy Report* No. 3. Austin: University of Texas.
———. 1994. *Political Change in Baja California: Democracy in the Making?* La Jolla: University of California, San Diego.
———, eds. 1995. *Opposition Government in Mexico*. Albuquerque: University of New Mexico Press.
Roett, Riordan, ed. 1991. *Mexico's External Relations in the 1990's*. Boulder, Colo.: Lynne Rienner Publishers.
———, ed. 1996. *The Mexican Peso Crisis: International Perspectives*. Boulder, Colo.: Lynne Rienner Publishers.
Ronfeldt, David, ed. 1984. *The Modern Mexican Military: A Reassessment*. Monograph Series No. 15. La Jolla: Center for U.S.-Mexican Studies, University of California, San Diego.
Ros, Jaime. 1987. La economía y la política macroeconómica durante el auge petrolero. In *El auge petrolero: De la euforia al desencanto*. Edited by Rolando Cordera and Carlos Tello. Mexico City: Universidad Nacional Autónoma de México.
Rosen, Fred. 1999. The Underside of NAFTA: A Budding Cross-Border Resistance. *NACLA Report on the Americas* 32, no. 4: 37–40.
Rosenau, James N. 1993. Coherent Connection or Commonplace Contiguity?: Theorizing about the California-Mexico Overlap. In *The California-Mexico Connection*. Edited by Katrina Burgess and Abraham F. Lowenthal. Stanford, Calif.: Stanford University Press.
Rosenfeld, Michael J., and Marta Tienda. 1997. Labor Market Implications of Mexican Migration. In *At the Crossroads: Mexico and U.S. Immigration Policy*. Edited by Frank Bean et al. Lanham, Md.: Rowman & Littlefield.

Ross, John. 1971. *The Economic System of Mexico*. Stanford: California Institute of International Studies.

Ross, Stanley, ed. 1966. *Is the Mexican Revolution Dead?* New York: Knopf.

Rubio, Luis. 1994. *A la puerta de la ley: El estado de derecho en México*. Mexico City: Cal y Arena.

Ruiz, Ramón Eduardo. 1998. *On the Rim of Mexico*. Boulder, Colo.: Westview Press.

Russell, Philip. 1994. *Mexico under Salinas*. Austin, Tex.: Mexico Resource Center.

Safford, Frank. 1974. Bases of Political Alignment in Early Republican Spanish America. In *New Approaches to Latin American History*. Edited by Richard Graham and Peter H. Smith. Austin: University of Texas Press.

Saltiel Cohen, Jenny. 1991. *Contienda electoral en las elecciones presidenciales*. Mexico City: Instituto Federal Electoral.

Sanderson, Steven. 1986. *The Transformation of Mexican Agriculture: International Structure and the Politics of Rural Change*. Princeton, N.J.: Princeton University Press.

Santiso, Javier. 1999. Wall Street and the Mexican Crisis: A Temporal Analysis of Emerging Markets. *International Political Science Review* 20, no. 1: 49–50.

Sauer, Franz von. 1974. *The Alienated "Loyal" Opposition: Mexico's Partido Acción Nacional*. Albuquerque: University of New Mexico.

Schmitt, Karl. 1974. *Mexico and the United States 1821–1973*. New York: John Wiley.

Schmitter, Philippe. 1974. Still the Century of Corporatism? In *The New Corporatism: Social-Political Structures in the Iberian World*. Edited by Frederick Pike and Thomas Stritch. Notre Dame, Ind.: Notre Dame University Press.

Schoultz, Lars. 1989. Foundations and Premises of United States Foreign Policy. In *Foreign Policy in U.S.-Mexican Relations*. Edited by Rosario Green and Peter H. Smith. Vol. 5. Prepared for the Bilateral Commission on the Future of United States–Mexican Relations. La Jolla: Center for U.S.-Mexican Studies, University of California, San Diego.

Scott, Robert. 1971. *Mexican Government in Transition*. Second Edition. Urbana: University of Illinois Press.

Secretaría de Gobernación. 1991a. *Tercer informe de gobierno*. Mexico City: Oficina de la Presidencia, Secretaría de Gobernación.

———. 1991b. *Tercer informe de gobierno: Dónde estamos y a dónde vamos, solidaridad y bienestar social*. Mexico City: Secretaría de Gobernación.

———. 1998. *IV Informe de gobierno*. Mexico City: Secretaría de Gobernación.

Secretaría de Hacienda y Crédito Público. 1991. *El nuevo perfil de la economía mexicana*. Mexico City: Secretaría de Hacienda y Crédito Público.

Secretaría de Programación y Presupuesto. 1979. *La población*. Mexico City: Secretaría de Programación y Presupuesto.

Secretaría del Trabajo y Previsión Social. 1979. *Proyecto: Plan nacional de empleo, 1980–1982*. Mexico City: Secretaría del Trabajo y Previsión Social.

Serrano, Mónica. 1995. The Armed Branch of the State: Civil-Military Relations in Mexico. *Journal of Latin American Studies* 27, no. 2: 423–48.

Serrano, Mónica, and Víctor Bulmer-Thomas, eds. 1996. *Rebuilding the State:*

Mexico after Salinas. London: Institute of Latin American Studies, University of London.

Sheahan, John. 1987. *Patterns of Development in Latin America.* Princeton, N.J.: Princeton University Press.

Simon, Joel. 1997. *Endangered Mexico: An Environment on the Edge.* San Francisco, Calif.: Sierra Club.

Simonian, Lane. 1995. *Defending the Land of the Jaguar: A History of Conservation in Mexico.* Austin: University of Texas Press.

Singer, Morris. 1969. *Growth, Equality, and the Mexican Experience.* Austin: University of Texas Press.

Skidmore, Thomas E., ed. 1993. *Television, Politics, and the Transition to Democracy in Latin America.* Washington, D.C.: Woodrow Wilson Center Press; Baltimore, Md.: Johns Hopkins University Press.

Sklair, Leslie. 1993. *Assembling for Development: The Maquila Industry in Mexico and the United States.* La Jolla: University of California, San Diego.

Smith, Clint. 2000. *Inevitable Partnership: Understanding Mexico-U.S. Relations.* Boulder, Colo.: Lynne Rienner Publishers.

Smith, Peter. 1979. *Labyrinths of Power: Political Recruitment in Twentieth-Century Mexico.* Princeton, N.J.: Princeton University Press.

Solís, Leopoldo. 1970. *La realidad económica mexicana: Retrovisión y perspectivas.* Mexico City: Siglo XXI Editores.

Statistical Abstract of Latin America (SALA). 1998. *Statistical Abstract of Latin America.* Edited by James W. Wilkie, coedited by Eduardo Alemán and José Guadalupe Ortega. Los Angeles: UCLA, Latin American Center Publications.

Story, Dale. 1986a. *Industry, the State, and Public Policy in Mexico.* Austin: University of Texas Press.

———. 1986b. *The Mexican Ruling Party: Stability and Authority.* New York: Praeger.

Suárez-Orozco, Marcelo, ed. 1998. *Crossings: Mexican Immigration in Interdisciplinary Perspectives.* Cambridge: Harvard University, David Rockefeller Center for Latin American Studies.

Tannenbaum, Frank. 1950. *The Struggle for Peace and Bread.* New York: Columbia University Press.

Teichman, Judith. 1995. *Privatization and Political Change in Mexico.* Pittsburgh, Pa.: University of Pittsburgh Press.

Tenenbaum, Barbara. 1975. Straightening out Some of the Lumpen in the Development. *Latin American Perspectives* 2, no. 2: 3–16.

Thorup, Cathryn L. 1991. The Politics of Free Trade and the Dynamics of Cross-Border Coalitions in U.S.–Mexican Relations. *Columbia Journal of World Business* 26, no. 2: 12–26.

Tocqueville, Alexis de. 1969. *Democracy in America.* Translated by George Lawrence. New York: Anchor Books.

Toro, María Celia. 1995. *Mexico's "War" on Drugs: Causes and Consequences.* Boulder, Colo.: Lynne Rienner Publishers.

Trejo Delarbre, Raúl. 1979. El movimiento obrero: Situación y perspectivas. In *México, hoy.* Edited by Pablo González Casanova and Enrique Florescano. Mexico City: Siglo XXI.

———. 1996. Medios: Competencia todavía sin reglas claras. *Nexos* 19, no. 217: 23–24.

Turner, Frederick C. 1968. *The Dynamic of Mexican Nationalism*. Chapel Hill: University of North Carolina Press.

Urbina Fuentes, Manuel, and Alfonso Sandoval Arriaga. 1993. Hacia el nuevo milenio: El poblamiento en perspectiva. In *El poblamiento de México*. Vol. 4, *México en el siglo XX*. Mexico City: Secretaría de Gobernación y Consejo Nacional de Población.

Urquidi, Víctor. 1994. The Outlook for Mexican Economic Development in the 1990s. In *The Politics of Economic Restructuring: State-Society Relations and Regime Change in Mexico*. Edited by Maria Lorena Cook, Kevin Middlebrook, and Juan Molinar Horcasitas. La Jolla: Center for U.S.-Mexican Studies, University of California, San Diego.

Vargas Llosa, Mario. 2000. De la dictadura perfecta a una democracia difícil. *Reforma* 2000. 3 July, 11A.

Vaughan, Mary Kay. 1982. *The State, Education, and Social Class in Mexico, 1880–1928*. Dekalb: Northern Illinois University Press.

Vázquez, Josefina Zoraida. 1998. *La intervención norteamericana, 1846–1848*. Mexico City: Secretaría de Relaciones Exteriores.

Vázquez, Josefina Zoraida, and Lorenzo Meyer. 1985. *The United States and Mexico*. Chicago: University of Chicago Press.

Verduzco, Gustavo, and Kurt Unger. 1998. Impacts of Migration in Mexico. In *Mexico–United States Binational Migration Study*. Vol. 1. Mexico City: Mexican Ministry of Foreign Affairs; Washington, D.C.: U.S. Commission on Immigration Reform.

Vernon, Raymond F. 1963. *The Dilemma of Mexico's Development: The Roles of the Private and Public Sectors*. Cambridge: Harvard University Press.

Wager, Stephen, and Donald Schulz. 1995. Civil-Military Relations in Mexico: The Zapatista Revolt and Its Implications. *Journal of Interamerican Studies and World Affairs* 37, no. 1: 1–42.

Ward, Peter M., and Victoria E. Rodríguez, with Enrique Cabrera Mendoza. 1999. New Federalism and State Government in Mexico. *U.S.-Mexican Policy Studies Report* no. 9. Austin: University of Texas.

Weintraub, Sidney. 1990. *A Marriage of Convenience: Relations between Mexico and the United States*. New York: Oxford University Press.

———. 1997. *NAFTA at Three: A Progress Report*. Washington, D.C.: Center for Strategic and International Studies.

Weintraub, Sidney, et al. 1998. Responses to Migration Issues. In *Mexico–United States Binational Migration Study*. Vol. 1. Mexico City: Mexican Ministry of Foreign Affairs; Washington, D.C.: U.S. Commission on Immigration Reform.

Whiting, Van R. 1992. *The Political Economy of Foreign Investment in Mexico: Nationalism, Liberalism, and Constraints on Choice*. Baltimore, Md.: Johns Hopkins University Press.

Williams, Edward J. 1986. The Implications of the Border for Mexican Policy and Mexican–United States Relations. In *Mexico's Political Stability: The Next Five Years*. Edited by Roderic Camp. Boulder, Colo.: Westview Press.

Wise, Carol, ed. 1998. *The Post-NAFTA Political Economy: Mexico and the Western Hemisphere.* University Park: Pennsylvania State University Press.

Wolf, Daniel. 1988. *Undocumented Aliens and Crime: The Case of San Diego County.* San Diego: Center for United States–Mexican Studies, University of California, San Diego.

Womack, John, Jr. 1996. Societies in Transition. *CLAS Newsletter,* no. 8. Boston: David Rockefeller Center for Latin American Studies, Harvard University.

World Bank. 1980. *World Development Report.* Washington, D.C.: World Bank.

———. 2004. *World Development Report 2004.* New York: Oxford University Press.

Zahniser, Steven S., and Michael J. Greenwood. 1998. *Mexico–United States Binational Migration Study.* Vol. 3. Mexico City: Mexican Ministry of Foreign Affairs; Washington, D.C.: U.S. Commission on Immigration Reform.

Zapata, Francisco. 1995. *El sindicalismo mexicano frente a la restructuración.* Mexico City: El Colegio de México.

Zebadúa, Emilio. 1994a. *Banqueros y revolucionarios: La soberanía financiera de México.* Mexico City: El Colegio de México, Fideicomiso Historia de las Américas, and Fondo de Cultura Económica.

———. 1994b. Del Plan Brady al TLC: La lógica de la política exterior mexicana, 1988–1994. *Foro Internacional* 34, no. 4: 626–51.

Zermeño, Sergio. 1993. The Defeat of Society. Modernization and Modernity in the Mexico of North America. *Revista Mexicana de Sociología* 55, no. 2: 273–90.

Ziccardi, Alicia, ed. 1995. *La tarea de gobernar: Gobiernos locales y demandas ciudadanas.* Mexico City: Universidad Nacional Autónoma de México.

WEB SITES MENTIONED

http://www.cbo.gov
www.cddhcu.gob.mx
www.census.gov
www.cia.gov/cia/publications/factbook/
www.conggro.gob.mx
http://datatur.sectur.gob.mx
http://dgcnesyp.inegi.gob.mx
www.economia.gob.mx
http://economia-snci.gob.mx
www.ezln.org
www.ife.org.mx
www.ilo.org
www.imf.org
www.inegi.gob.mx
www.mapleleafweb.com/features/economy/us-canada/sleeping-elephant.html
http://www.mexidata.info/id317.html
www.nationmaster.com
www.parametria.com.mx
www.publicintegrity.org

www.rsf.org
www.semarnat.gob.mx
www.uscis.gov/graphics/shared/aboutus/statistics/2003 Yearbook.pdf
www.usdoj.gov/dea
http://www.usdoj.gov/dea/major/greenair.htm
http://www.usdoj.gov/dea/major/trifecta/index.html
www.usembassy-mexico.gov/eNAFTA_figures.htm
www.usinfo.state.gov/wh/Archive/2004
www.world-tourism.org
www.wsws.org/articles/2003/mar2003/chre-m04_prn.shtml

Index

abortion, 17–18, 282n25
Acapulco, 243, 244
accountability, 126, 173, 274; enhanced presidential, 131–36; growth of civil society and, 70–71; increased, through increased independent groups, 260; judicial reform as key part of, 105; political competition and, 102; of political leaders. xviii, 127–31; privatization and, 174. *See also* corruption
Acosta, Mariclaire, 139
acronyms and abbreviations, ix–x
"adaptive authoritarianism," 7
AFL-CIO, 236, 255
agriculture, 79, 152–53. *See also* peasants
Aguayo, Sergio, 284n41, 308n10
Alemán, Miguel, 49, 64
alemanista approach, 49, 50, 64
Alliance for Progress, 185
America First, 235
Americanization, 30–33, 222
Amnesty International, 139
Andreas, Peter, 315n8
Asian Pacific Economic Community, 208
assassinations, 7–8, 44, 46, 52
assertiveness, 186–87, 310n28; leftist, 188–91
Association for Latin American Integration, 205
asymmetry, 257, 313n41; of tourism, 244–46; of trade, 246, 251, 256

attorney general, 315n14
authoritarianism, 263, 279–80n3; "adaptive," 7; nostalgia for, 179; persistence of, 2, 3, 264, 271, 273; porfirian, 42–44; in unions, 75, 77
Avila Camacho, Manuel, 49, 56, 299n43
Azcárraga Televisa, 117, 118
Aztecs, 36–37

Bank of America, 320n51
Bank of Mexico, 173
banks: nationalization of 50, 84–85, 162; privatization of, 174
Barrio, Francisco, 137
Bartlett, Manuel, 93
Bejarano, René, 118
Belize, 313n46
Beristain, Javier, 283n33
Berlin, Isaiah, 294n3
Bilateral Commission on the Future of United States–Mexican Relations, 284n43
bilateral issues, 210–12, 256–57. *See also* drugs; migration; NAFTA; tourism
Blacks, 25
bracero program, 185, 229
Brady Plan, 169, 305n42
Brozo, 118
Bucareli Agreements, 184
Bush, George H. W., 30, 201, 316n15
Bush, George W., 30, 192, 197, 239
business: democratization and, 85–86;

Compositor: BookMatters, Berkeley
Indexer: Andrew Christenson
Text: 10/13 Sabon
Display: Sabon
Printer and Binder: Sheridan Books, Inc.